No End Save Victory

BOOKS BY David Kaiser

*Economic Diplomacy and the Origins of the
Second World War (1980)*

*Postmortem: New Evidence in the Case of Sacco and
Vanzetti (co-author William Young) (1985)*

*Politics and War: European Conflict from
Philip II to Hitler (1990)*

Epic Season: The 1948 American League Pennant Race (1998)

*American Tragedy: Kennedy, Johnson, and
the Origins of the Vietnam War (2000)*

*The Road to Dallas: The Assassination of
John F. Kennedy (2008)*

No End Save Victory

How FDR
Led the Nation
into War

DAVID KAISER

BASIC BOOKS
A Member of the Perseus Books Group
New York

A CIP catalog record for this book is available from the Library of Congress.
ISBN: 978-0-465-01982-3
ISBN (e-book): 978-0-465-06299-7

10 9 8 7 6 5 4 3 2 1

"War is the realm of uncertainty; three quarters of the factors on which action in war is based are wrapped in a fog of greater or lesser uncertainty. A sensitive and discriminating judgment is called for; a skilled intelligence to scent out the truth."

Carl von Clausewitz, *On War*

"There were giants in the earth in those days."

Genesis 6:4

CONTENTS

INTRODUCTION
A Generation, a Man, a Moment

"This generation," Franklin Roosevelt told the Democratic convention of 1936, "has a rendezvous with destiny." By "this generation" he presumably meant his own. But in words much less often quoted, he elaborated on the nature of the challenge that the country faced, involving not only its own future but the future of the whole civilized world. "In this world of ours in other lands," he said, "there are some people, who, in times past, have lived and fought for freedom, and seem to have grown too weary to carry on the fight. . . . They have yielded their democracy. I believe in my heart that only our success can stir their ancient hope. They begin to know that here in America we are waging a great and successful war. . . . We are fighting to save a great and precious form of government for ourselves and for the world."[1] Four years later, after German victories in Europe that threatened the invasion and defeat of Great Britain, Roosevelt and the nation had to prepare to defend democracy actively by force. Thanks to FDR, the United States from May 1940 until December 1941 declared and prepared to meet an even greater objective: the total defeat of both Germany and its ally Japan. Although much of the nation and the U.S. Army and Navy would have been content simply to defend the western hemisphere, Roosevelt in the second half of 1941 insisted on planning for total victory, in order to make sure that democracy would not only survive, but prevail. His brilliant leadership crowned that effort with success.

Mankind must often revisit history in light of new experiences and new insights. In the last twenty years, a new perspective has allowed us to

understand the nature of the crisis the United States and the industrial-
ized world faced in the 1930s and 1940s, and to appreciate Franklin Roosevelt's extraordinary insight into the role of his own generation in
deciding the fate of the nation and the world for decades to come. The
last two centuries of Western history had been marked roughly every
eighty years by crises that had destroyed an old order and created a new
one. Each crisis had given way to an era of stability, during which a
uniquely favored generation of young people had been born. During
their childhood they had time to think; in their young adulthood, a secure society allowed them to give vent to their feelings. William Strauss
and Neil Howe, the historians who identified the eighty-year cycle, have
characterized each of these successive generations as Prophet generations. To them had fallen the task, first, of undermining and destroying
the political, social, economic, and international order their grandparents and parents had created, and then of leaving something different
behind that would once again endure for decades. Roosevelt, who saw
himself above all as the embodiment of broad historical forces, showed
both in his acceptance speech and on many later occasions that he understood both the nature of this process and the stakes in his own era.
More than once, he explicitly compared his own time to that of the
American Revolution and the Civil War, and his 1936 convention acceptance speech was the first of many occasions on which he assumed the
mission of preserving democracy for the good of the whole world.[2]

The first great crisis of American and Western European life had taken
place roughly from 1774 through 1803 and had turned above all on the
clash between the Enlightenment doctrines of equality and the rights of
man, on the one hand, and traditional authority on the other. That crisis
had radically different results in different nations. In the United States it
gave birth to modern democracy. In Britain, it led to the strengthening of
older institutions such as the monarchy and the Church of England and
to a severe setback for the lot of the common man. In much of continental Europe, it created authoritarian, bureaucratic governments whose citizens enjoyed equality before the law without any direct influence on their
rulers. Slavery in the southern states was, of course, a feature of the new
American republic, but one that the Constitution spoke of as little as possible (and never explicitly), and one that many of the Founders had hoped
would disappear. When slavery first became a controversial national
issue in 1820 on the occasion of the Missouri Compromise, the surviving

Founding Father Thomas Jefferson saw the shape of the future clearly. "I regret that I am now to die in the belief that the useless sacrifice of themselves by the generation of 1776, to acquire self-government and happiness to their country, is to be thrown away by the unwise and unworthy passions of their sons," he wrote. Forty years later his prophecy came true.[3]

The Transcendental generation, the first American generation born under the Constitution (approximately 1792–1821), saw slavery and the future very differently. Southern Transcendentals lauded slavery as a positive good that needed to be expanded, while many northern Transcendentals identified it as a terrible evil that must be excised from the body politic like a cancer. Each rated the success of their cause, slavery or abolition, far more highly than the preservation of the Constitution or the Union. The issue of slavery grew in importance along with their own rise in power and influence. Even as a young man, Abraham Lincoln, the greatest of all Transcendentals, understood his generation's historical role to an almost uncanny degree. He posed the problem in an address to the Springfield, Illinois, Lyceum in 1838, at the age of only twenty-eight, after recapitulating the achievements of the Founding Fathers. New men of ambition, he said, would now inevitably arise. "And, when they do, they will as naturally seek the gratification of their ruling passion, as others have so done before them. The question then, is, can that gratification be found in supporting and maintaining an edifice that has been erected by others? Most certainly it cannot. . . . Towering genius . . . thirsts and burns for distinction; and, if possible, it will have it, whether at the expense of emancipating slaves, or enslaving freemen."

Twenty-three years later it fell to Lincoln to lead the Union in its attempt to preserve itself and to restrict and, later, to abolish slavery. From his first inaugural address onward he cast the struggle as an attempt to show that democratic government could survive against armed insurrection—and in so doing, he made the northern cause the cause of democrats across the Atlantic in Europe, where the elite generally favored their fellow aristocrats, the southerners. The Union victory had tremendous consequences in Europe. Only Italy in 1865 elected a legislature through universal male suffrage, but within two more years Germany did so as well, and Britain had broadened its franchise. France became a republic based on universal male suffrage in 1871. Political democracy was one of the main achievements of the nineteenth-century crisis of the Atlantic World.

Yet it was not the only one. In the United States the years following the Civil War unleashed powerful new economic forces, while political authority and civic spirit declined. The triumphant Republican Party stood not only for emancipation, but also for high tariffs, unregulated national banks, and frenzied railroad development. In the South, the white aristocracy spent the first two postwar decades restoring white supremacy through terror. Big city machines stole millions from the taxpayers, and public services were often disgracefully poor. Extremes of wealth and poverty had never been greater. Serious financial crises occurred at least once in every decade. The political climate reached new heights of anti-intellectualism.

Into this world came a new postwar generation, now known as the Missionary generation, born roughly from 1863 to 1884. Like the Transcendentals on the one hand and the post–Second World War Boom generation on the other, the Missionary generation grew up in rebellion against the world around them. In their case, however, that meant seeking to impose order on chaos, to bring a scientific spirit to public affairs, to provide a more decent life for all, and to restore some vitality to democracy. They wanted new institutions to increase human happiness—institutions based, crucially, on a mixture of science and high moral purpose. In their twenties they, like the Boomers of the 1960s, produced an impressive cadre of young revolutionaries and agitating writers such as Emma Goldman, Upton Sinclair, the Wobblies or International Workers of the World, and Lincoln Steffens. "If bad institutions and bad men can be got rid of only by killing them, then the killing must be done," wrote newspaper editor William Randolph Hearst not long before the assassination of President McKinley. Thousands of educated youth joined the settlement house movement, including such future stalwarts of the Franklin Roosevelt cabinet as Frances Perkins and Harold Ickes. The Missionaries also produced the first generation of black Americans unreservedly committed to racial equality, led by Harvard graduate W. E. B. Du Bois, and the shock troops of the women's suffrage movement. But as they reached their forties in the first decade of the twentieth century, many found a new home in the reform movements of the Progressive era.

Republican Theodore Roosevelt and Democrat Woodrow Wilson belonged to an earlier generation. Both had childhood memories of the Civil War, and both favored a more conciliatory approach to politics than younger Missionaries. They were, however, the great inspiration to the progressives of the younger generation, and the first modern Presidents to embrace the idea that the government must work actively to moderate extremes of wealth, improve the lives of average citizens, and curb the excesses of the free market. They also introduced another aspect of the Missionary spirit, activism in foreign affairs. That led Roosevelt to imperialism in the Caribbean—also justified by the need to bring order out of chaos, partly by enforcing the contracts on which some governments had defaulted—and Wilson to his active defense of neutral rights and attempts to promote peace in the early stages of the Great War in Europe. When the German Empire trampled on Wilson's principles by declaring unrestricted submarine warfare early in 1917, the President joined the war. He did so to make the world safe for democracy—and eventually, to try to extend the rule of law to international affairs through the new League of Nations. All of this aroused intense opposition in certain circles. Missionaries like the historian Charles Beard and domestic progressive politicians like Senators George Norris of Nebraska, Hiram Johnson of California, and William Borah of Idaho regarded imperialism as a betrayal of ideals of justice and militarism as a threat to American democracy. And indeed, their opposition to the war, along with bitter Republican partisanship, led in 1920 to the final rejection of the Versailles Treaty and the end of Wilson's dreams. A decade of reaction followed.

This was the world into which Franklin Roosevelt was born in January 1882, the only child of a wealthy Hudson Valley aristocrat, James Roosevelt, and his much younger second wife, Sarah Delano. The apple of his parents' eye, he had a truly idyllic childhood, traveling frequently to Europe, vacationing at Campobello in Canada, and all the while surrounded by devoted relatives from two famous families, horses, ship models, and the Hudson Valley countryside. Roosevelt witnessed the death of a cousin by fire when he was only two years old, watched his parents sit out a violent Atlantic storm that nearly sank their ship a year later, and learned the art of maintaining a sunny disposition in the face of almost any circumstances. His father was a prominent New York Democrat, and in 1887, on a family visit to Washington, Franklin, age five, met President Grover Cleveland in the White House. In the next decade, as a teenager, he watched his distant cousin Theodore Roosevelt ascend through the political ranks, first as Assistant Secretary of the Navy, then Governor of New York, Vice President, and after the assassination of William McKinley, as the youngest President in the history of the United States. Like another child of a famous American family, Henry Adams, the young Franklin, one might think, would not have been the least surprised had the family gardener remarked to him at an early age, "You'll be thinkin' you'll be President, too!"[4]

Yet the idyllic childhood came to an abrupt end at the age of fourteen in 1896, when his parents put him under the care of the Reverend Endicott Peabody, the famous headmaster of the Groton School west of Boston. Although parental affection had kept him in Hyde Park for two years beyond Groton's normal entrance age of twelve, the Spartan environment, which housed boys in doorless cubicles and kept them busy from morning until night to discourage nasty sexual habits, must have been a rude shock. Young Franklin quickly ingratiated himself with his teachers, and his letters home betrayed no sign of unhappiness. Such an experience was not uncommon among his contemporaries. The late nineteenth century was the dawn of the great age of American education, one that lasted about one hundred years. General, as opposed to classical, education taught the Missionary generation to think for themselves and stand up for their own opinions, but the prevailing ethos also held that young men and women needed hard work and discipline well into their twenties. At Groton another cleric on the faculty tried to inspire the students with ideals of public service. Graduating in 1900, Franklin went on to Harvard, where he took a relaxed attitude toward his studies and poured his energy into the *Harvard Crimson*, of which he became the editor.

Young Franklin also knew that he needed a woman in his life, and he, an only child, dreamed of a large family. As a Harvard undergraduate of twenty he evidently proposed to a beautiful girl from a prominent local family, Alice Sohier, and shared his wish for at least six children. She decided not to marry him, she told a friend many years later, because "I did not wish to be a cow." Not long after, he met his distant cousin Eleanor, then only eighteen, an orphan whose childhood had been as wretched as Franklin's had been idyllic, and who was now the niece of the President of the United States. Although Eleanor was very nervous, not pretty, and lacking in self-confidence, Franklin seems to have been genuinely attracted to her. Two years later they were engaged, and in 1905 they were married in the White House. Like so many young people of their era, they knew how husbands and wives ought to feel and act toward one another, and their voluminous correspondence shows that they tried to do so. Yet their ideas and feelings about life, duty, love, and sex were so different that trouble was eventually bound to result. Eleanor did in fact bear Franklin the six children that he wanted, one of whom died in infancy, but when the last of them was born, in 1916, she evidently told Franklin that that part of their life was over. Typically, he does not seem to have put up a struggle, but his affair with Eleanor's social secretary, Lucy Mercer—probably the great love of his life—began quite shortly thereafter.[5]

Eleanor's Uncle Theodore, meanwhile, had emerged as the model for the career Franklin had in mind. He was now tall, handsome, and gregarious—a political natural. After law school and a brief and not very engaged career as a New York lawyer, he entered politics for the first time as a state legislator from his native Dutchess County in 1910. After his fellow Democrat Woodrow Wilson was elected in 1912, he managed to secure the position that had made his cousin a national figure, Assistant Secretary of the Navy. Secretary of the Navy Josephus Daniels, a North Carolina newspaper editor, cared little about the Navy, and Roosevelt exercised enormous influence throughout the tumultuous years of the First World War. When the United States entered the war in 1917, Roosevelt wanted to enlist because he did not believe that any man of his age could become President if he had *not* gone to the front, but Daniels and President Wilson persuaded him to stay in Washington. By 1920 he had become sufficiently prominent to secure the Democratic nomination as Vice President at the age of thirty-eight—a full three years earlier than his famous cousin. However, he and his running mate, Governor James Cox of Ohio, suffered a staggering defeat in the backlash against Wilson, the war, and the whole Progressive era.

In 1921, when vacationing at Campobello island just north of Maine, Roosevelt contracted polio and permanently lost the use of his legs. He bore his ordeal cheerfully despite inner despair and resolved not to let it interfere with his plans. His political comeback began in 1924, when he nominated New York Governor Alfred E. Smith for the presidency at the Democratic Convention in Madison Square Garden. Four years later Smith won that nomination, and Roosevelt accepted his invitation to try to succeed him as governor. So strong was the anti-Catholic bigotry against Smith, as well as the feeling that he simply was not presidential timber, that he lost even his own state of New York in the landslide for Republican Herbert Hoover. In a remarkable turn of events, however, FDR won narrowly and became the new governor of the Empire State, and thus one of the leading Democratic politicians in the country.

New and unforeseen circumstances now transformed Roosevelt's career. Those circumstances, too, had generational roots.

Now well into middle age, the businessmen and financiers of the Missionary generation were enjoying almost unprecedented prosperity during the 1920s, and like the Boomers of the first decade of the twenty-first century, they had come to accept it as their due. They now dominated the Republican Party, while the Democrats during the 1920s were fatally split on what would now be called "social issues"—Prohibition and the growing power of the Ku Klux Klan. Wilson had created the Federal Reserve in 1913 to try to make rampant speculation impossible, and despite a severe postwar recession in 1920–1921 there had been no financial panic since. In the 1920s there was also a tremendous boom in real estate, which came to a smashing halt in 1928. Fueled by rules allowing buyers to put down just 10 percent of the value of their stock as margin and by inflows of capital from Europe, the stock market continued rising at extraordinary rates. In October 1929, Wall Street, too, came crashing down, and for more than three years the market refused to revive. Incomes fell, surpluses glutted both agricultural and industrial markets, and by 1932 unemployment was nearing 25 percent of the workforce. These events—the fruits of his own generation's unrestrained greed—made Franklin Roosevelt President in 1933 and gave him a unique opportunity to transform the foundations of American life. During the next four years he made full use of it.

Roosevelt had been no economic revolutionary before 1933. He shared the progressive belief in the use of science and planning to conserve soil, build healthier cities, and design better communities. He believed in lower tariffs—long an orthodox Democratic Party position—and in the public ownership of electric power. He supported some emergency measures to fight the depression as Governor, particularly on behalf of farmers (of which he liked to point out he was one), but he did nothing dramatic to alienate the business interests that were nearly as strong in the Democratic Party as in the Republican. After the 1930 elections returned him to office with a huge majority of 725,000 votes and nearly gave the Democrats control of Congress, he and his lieutenant, Louis Howe, embarked upon a determined campaign for his party's presidential nomination, cultivating party leaders in the agrarian South and West. In 1932 he faced determined opposition from House Speaker John Nance Garner of Texas and from his former patron, Alfred E. Smith. After three inconclusive ballots in which Roosevelt secured a clear majority but lacked the necessary two-thirds vote for nomination, Garner, prodded by William Randolph Hearst, switched to Roosevelt in return for the vice presidency, a decision Garner regretted for the rest of his life.[6]

Thus began the climax of the most extraordinary political career in American history. Roosevelt in November 1932 defeated Hoover with 57 percent of the popular vote and 472 electoral votes to 59. Hoover carried five of six New England states, Pennsylvania, and Delaware. The Democratic Party and its allies had 318 seats in the House to 117 for the Republicans, and ruled the Senate 59–36.

Faced with an equally serious crisis in 1861, Lincoln in his inaugural address had defined the nation's problems in strictly legal and political terms. Secession, he had argued, would destroy democratic government if allowed to prevail, and the elected federal government must assert its powers. Roosevelt on the other hand discussed the crisis the nation faced in his first inaugural address in blunt moral terms. After famously declaring that "the only thing we have to fear is fear itself," and summarizing the country's drastic economic state, he identified the moral sources of the nation's crisis. "Our distress comes from no failure of substance," he said. "Plenty is at our doorstep, but a generous use of it languishes in the very sight of the supply. Primarily this is because rulers of the exchange of mankind's goods have failed through their own stubbornness and their own incompetence, have admitted their failure, and have abdicated. Practices of the unscrupulous money changers stand indicted in the court of public opinion, rejected by the hearts and minds of men . . . The money changers have fled from their high seats in the temple of our civilization. We may now restore that temple to the ancient truths. The measure of the restoration lies in the extent to which we apply social values more noble than mere monetary profit. . . . Happiness lies not in the mere possession of money; it lies in the joy of achievement, in the thrill of creative effort. The joy and moral stimulation of work no longer must be forgotten in the mad chase of evanescent profits." Roosevelt's emphasis on values as the source of civilization and his view of daily life as an almost sacred enterprise were highly characteristic of his generation. The new President then listed the essence of his own agenda: "to put people to work," to raise the value of farm products, to stop a plague of foreclosures, and to put strict limits on speculation "with other people's money." Within a year, progress on all those fronts was well underway.[7]

As the economy improved over the next four years, the Democratic majorities in Congress increased still further in both 1934 and 1936, when Roosevelt was famously reelected against Governor Alf Landon of Kansas with more than 60 percent of the popular vote and an electoral vote margin of 523 to 8. The Republican Party in 1936 turned the election into a referendum on American values, arguing that the New Deal was a European-style dictatorship that would destroy traditional American initiative, and Roosevelt met that challenge head on. Although unemployment remained high in 1936 and a number of major New Deal laws had been nullified by a hostile Supreme Court, Roosevelt had successfully defined and implemented a dramatically new philosophy of American government involving a substantially increased federal role in the economy. He had also cast himself bluntly as the defender of the common man and woman against entrenched industrial and financial interests. "They hate me," he declared famously in a campaign speech in 1936, "and I welcome their hatred."

In his second inaugural, with unemployment cut in half from just over 20 percent to a still devastating 10 percent, Roosevelt built on the same themes. Four years before, a frightened citizenry "dedicated ourselves to the fulfillment of a vision—to speed the time when there would be for all the people that security and peace essential to the pursuit of happiness." The American people, he said, had recognized "the need to find through government the instrument of our united purpose to solve for the individual the ever-rising problems of a complex civilization." Without the aid of government, "we had been unable to create those moral controls over the services of science which are necessary to make science a useful servant instead of a ruthless master of mankind." In so doing, Americans "were writing a new chapter in our book of self-government."[8]

Although Roosevelt in these and so many other speeches cast the New Deal as a new stage in the history of American democracy, his work obviously had a critical international dimension as well. Within another four years the task of extending moral controls over science would broaden again, this time to encompass the whole world. During the last twenty years the old order had collapsed all over the civilized world, giving way successively to Communism in Russia, Fascism in Italy, a militaristic authoritarian state in Japan, and National Socialism in Germany, which had taken power under Hitler just five weeks before FDR's inaugural in 1933. France and Britain, which had undertaken few reforms in response to the Depression, seemed to be declining. New ideas would rule the future, and although Roosevelt was far too radical for most well-to-do Americans and not nearly radical enough for many others, he had clearly put forth a genuine alternative to the dictatorships of the Left and Right. He built upon this idea when the world ideological struggle became a world war in the two years after 1939, and decided to do everything he could to make his own ideals prevail.

The details of the specific measures embodied in the New Deal and their effects lie outside the scope of this book, but their impact does not. Relief measures, public works, and agricultural programs literally saved millions of Americans from despair or worse. His most lasting legacies were the regulation of financial markets, the most important aspects of which lasted until the late 1990s, and the establishment of a Social Security system. He benefited not only from the progressive philosophy of government but from the depth of the crisis. Although business interests argued almost from the beginning that New Deal measures were inhibiting rather than promoting recovery, very few people could argue, especially in 1933–1936, that the situation did not require drastic measures, and the financial markets themselves had suffered heavily enough to accept restrictions that they have now (as of 2013) overthrown.

Kenneth S. Davis, who wrote a five-volume biography of Roosevelt, concluded that FDR saw himself above all as the instrument of broader historical forces. Roosevelt knew that both the nation and the Western world stood at a turning point, and that he might shape the course of history for many years to come. He surrounded himself with other men, and a few women, of drive, intellect, and ambition, and he allowed them to exercise considerable freedom and initiative in achieving the broader objectives he laid down. Members of all Prophet generations grow up with great confidence in their own opinions, and the New Deal enabled certain of Roosevelt's contemporaries and some of the next-younger Lost generation to put their ideas into practice on an unprecedented scale.[9]

Henry Wallace, the Secretary of Agriculture, implemented the New Deal's farm policy, which raised prices from catastrophically low levels by restricting acreage and slaughtering newly born livestock by the millions. Harold Ickes, the blunt, cantankerous Secretary of the Interior, led the New Deal's fight for public power and built roads and bridges as head of the Public Works Administration. Harry Hopkins, who like Ickes had begun life as a social worker, put unemployed workers ranging from laborers to writers to work for the Works Progress Administration, frequently competing with Ickes for the same projects. Frances Perkins, the first woman in the cabinet, oversaw the extension of collective bargaining rights to unions under the Wagner Act. Eleanor Roosevelt rapidly emerged as a key political figure in her own right, maintaining cordial relations with extreme left-wing groups and speaking out courageously for the cause of civil rights. Mrs. Roosevelt, wrote W. E. B. Du Bois, the founder of the National Association for the Advancement of Colored People (NAACP), "consorts with Negroes and Communists and says so." The cast of characters in Washington changed significantly in 1940–1941, but Roosevelt's leadership techniques did not. Then, too, he gave critical responsibilities to men of experience and very strong views, and allowed them to plan and advocate drastic courses of action both publicly and privately.[10]

The Missionary generation combined a strong sense of moral purpose with the knowledge that they were living in one of the most transformative periods in human history. No generation has lived through more profound changes in their adult lives than those born from about 1863 to 1883. The economic and industrial innovations that touched their lives included the telephone, the advent of electricity as the most important source of power, the industrial assembly line, the automobile, the skyscraper, the airplane, motion pictures, the radio, and nuclear fission. Henry L. Stimson, a New Yorker destined to become Hoover's Secretary of State and FDR's Secretary of War, was fifteen when the first modern suspension bridge was finished between Brooklyn and Manhattan, and lived to see dozens of others, including the George Washington, San Francisco Bay, and Golden Gate bridges, completed as well. New technologies also built dams and reservoirs of unprecedented size. Every one of these innovations increased human capabilities, knit the country and the world closer together, and allowed for organization and human enterprise on a much larger scale—either for evil or for good.

These innovations also held enormous military implications, from the dreadnought battleship invented in the 1900s to tanks, bomber and fighter aircraft, machine guns and semiautomatic rifles, and effective submarines. Woodrow Wilson, who had been born in 1856 and remembered the Civil War and its aftermath, concluded during the First World War that these changes demanded that warfare be rendered obsolete. The Missionary generation that followed was more concerned to put them to good use, and the Second World War became their supreme test. Having founded history's largest enterprises and created markets of unprecedented size, they proved more than willing to create a far larger army, navy, and air force than Americans had ever dreamed of, and to build terrible new weapons. Exactly how Roosevelt and his contemporaries prepared not merely for war, but for victory, in the eighteen months after the fall of France in 1940 is the story of this book. In so doing, they created the world in which we have all spent our lives.

Having dealt with the threatened collapse of the U.S. economy and society in 1933, Roosevelt in 1940–1941 had to face an even more critical situation abroad. The world crisis that became progressively worse during Roosevelt's second term stemmed from political crises and new regimes in other major nations—regimes determined to overturn regional and world order. The First World War had introduced totalitarianism to Europe, first in the Soviet Union and then in Mussolini's Italy. In Germany, the Weimar Republic, hampered from the beginning by the legacy of the First World War, had failed to survive the combination of the Great Depression, the death of its two most effective statesmen, President Friedrich Ebert and Foreign Minister Gustav Stresemann, and the rise of Hitler and the Nazi Party, who seized power in 1933. Although Japan retained its constitution and the semblance of a parliamentary regime, the Japanese Army and Navy seized effective control of policy after 1931, partly by assassinating politicians who refused to defer to them. Germany and Japan denounced and withdrew from disarmament agreements during the 1930s and proclaimed their need for more territory to solve their economic problems.

The rise of expansionist powers posed particular challenges to the opinions, traditions, and military strength of the United States. Woodrow Wilson's controversial decision to enter the First World War had failed to secure the just peace of which he had dreamed, and the American people also remained bitter over their allies' failure to pay their war debts. In one sense Wilson's ideas remained very much alive during the 1920s and early 1930s: an overwhelming majority of Americans believed that the world should be ruled by law, insisted that their own government respect its obligations, and expected other governments to do the same. But when the Senate rejected the League of Nations in 1920, the United States gave up any idea of imposing these views on the rest of the world by force, or of once again raising huge armies to fight overseas. Its military establishment shrank accordingly.

Although the U.S. Navy still ranked with the British as one of the two largest in the world, the U.S. Army in the interwar period barely exceeded 100,000 men, the same size to which the German Army was limited by the Versailles Treaty. Little was done to develop air power in either the Army or the Navy. Appropriations for the War and Navy departments remained low, and Roosevelt's cabinet appointments to those departments were among his weakest. In 1935, as the European situation worsened, Congress passed, and Roosevelt signed, a sweeping Neutrality Act banning American ships from travel to war zones or warring nations from borrowing money in the United States—a clear attempt to make sure that the events of 1914–1917 would never be repeated and draw the United States into another foreign war.

Many Americans preferred to regard the serious threats that developed on both sides of the world in the late 1930s as regional rather than global. By the late 1930s Japan was at war in China and Hitler had rapidly rearmed and blackmailed Europe into allowing him to annex Austria and most of Czechoslovakia. More important, both Hitler and the Japanese leadership openly proclaimed a right to vast economic hinterlands from which other powers would largely be excluded—Hitler's in Eastern Europe, and Japan's in China and the Southwest Pacific region. In the western hemisphere, the Roosevelt administration had been pursuing an opposite course, renouncing intervention in the affairs of Latin American states, and the U.S. government also favored the free worldwide movement of trade. But most Americans counted on other powers—particularly the British and French—to hold off new threats to the European order. When the European war broke out in September 1939, polls showed most Americans confident of an Anglo-French victory over Germany in what they expected to be another long war.

The three extraordinary months of April, May, and June 1940 destroyed the political, military, and strategic foundations of the world order upon which the United States had relied. In April, the Germans seized Denmark and Norway, using their air force—the envy of the world—to neutralize British sea power. On May 10 they attacked Belgium, Holland, and France. The new strategy of *Blitzkrieg*—a combination of massed tank formations and tactical air support—broke through the French Army, drove the British from the continent, and in June secured an armistice with a compliant French government that allowed the Germans to occupy the whole French coast. Japan immediately took advantage of the German conquest of Holland and France to put pressure on those nations' colonies in the Far East. The whole world now expected a German invasion of Britain by the end of the summer, and most observers—including the President of the United States—gave it an excellent chance of success. The consequences for the United States would be almost incalculable.

Simply put, the United States in the spring of 1940 faced the prospect of a nearly overwhelming worldwide coalition that it would have to fight on its own. Its Navy had been designed to fight the Japanese in the Pacific—a task for which it was now barely adequate at best—while the British handled any threats in the Atlantic. Should Britain fall, the German and Italian navies would be able to add British and French warships to their forces, easily take control of the whole Atlantic, and land forces in the western hemisphere. Germany had already neutralized the Soviet Union by concluding the Nazi-Soviet Pact in 1939, and Germany and Japan now had a common interest in the defeat of the European powers.

In addition, the Germans in Norway had shown how they could use air power to expand their zone of control, and if Britain fell the same tactics might easily allow the Germans to reach the western hemisphere. They might move into the Azores and the Canaries in the Atlantic, march through the friendly dictatorships of Spain and Portugal and into French North Africa, and cross the narrow 1,500-mile ocean between Dakar in West Africa and Brazil. Alternatively they might leapfrog across the North Atlantic, first to Iceland, then to Greenland, and then to Newfoundland, from which their planes could reach the United States. The Japanese at any moment might decide to enter the war against the United States by attacking the Philippine Islands. This was the scenario for which Washington had to prepare on an emergency basis in the spring and summer of 1940, and indeed, the possibility of a British defeat continued to preoccupy American planners all through 1941. Initially American military leaders hoped to avoid war in the Pacific, but in September 1940 a world war became a near-certainty when Germany, Italy, and Japan signed the Tripartite Pact, pledging in effect to go to war with the United States should it declare war on any of them. Having avoided an economic collapse in the early 1930s and laid the foundation for a new kind of society, the Roosevelt administration now faced an imminent threat to the security of the United States.

Roosevelt typically responded not only by defining the problem for the American people but also by choosing new men to deal with it. In June 1940 he replaced his secretaries of War and of the Navy with two prominent Republicans. Henry L. Stimson, who had served as Hoover's Secretary of State, took over the War Department, while Frank Knox, a newspaper publisher who had been the Republican vice presidential candidate in 1936, became Secretary of the Navy. Roosevelt knew very well not only that both men took the threat to the United States very seriously, but that Stimson in particular favored immediate mobilization, including a draft, and the soonest possible American entry into the war. The uniformed chiefs of the Army and Navy, General George Marshall and Admiral Harold Stark, had their own very definite ideas about the strategic situation and did not hesitate to share them with the President and each other. All four of these men belonged to the Missionary generation, and indeed, all four had served in uniform during the First World War. For the next eighteen months they and their own key subordinates focused not only on preparing for war, but on trying to determine when, under what circumstances, and with what objectives the United States should enter the conflict. Meanwhile, another contemporary, Secretary of State Cordell Hull, made clear publicly and privately that the war pitted two philosophies of life against one another, that it was bound to come to the United States, and that the United States could not afford to wait until it did so.

The mobilization of the country's resources now became the Roosevelt administration's most critical task. To accomplish it, Roosevelt in 1940–1941 used the same techniques he had developed to fight the Depression. He created a series of new agencies—the National Defense Advisory Commission (NDAC) in the spring of 1940, the Office of Production Management (OPM) in the winter of 1940–1941, and the Supply Priorities and Allocations Board (SPAB) in the summer of 1941—to set production targets, acquire raw materials, let out contracts, and estimate the immediate and potential requirements of various levels of national effort. Representatives of industry and labor led by William Knudsen of General Motors and Sidney Hillman of the Amalgamated Clothing Workers and New Deal officials staffed these agencies. They immediately enlisted both industry and labor in the much larger enterprise that was just beginning. Meanwhile, the civil rights movement took advantage of the crisis to push for full-scale participation by Negro Americans, as they were then called, in the war and the industrial mobilization that went with it. And although some business and labor leaders tried to guard their autonomy or even opposed the war effort, the administration gradually broke their resistance down. The scale of the necessary effort was utterly unprecedented. In the weeks after the fall of France, the United States decided to increase its Army tenfold and double the size of its Navy within five years. Ultimately the Army was increased more than fiftyfold.[11]

The critical question that emerged by early 1941 involved the scope of the war to come. Would the United States confine itself to a war to defend the western hemisphere after the fall of the British Isles, or would it embark together with available allies on an all-out worldwide effort to defeat the Axis? Because no one could know how the war would turn out, the answers to these questions are far more complicated than many have tended to believe.

At no time, to begin with, did Roosevelt commit himself to do everything possible to ensure Britain's survival—largely because there was so little that the United States *could* do. Well into 1941, he and most of his principal subordinates anticipated a possible British defeat and were preparing to face its consequences. Roosevelt justified his initial moves in the Atlantic—the September 1940 gift of fifty destroyers to Britain in exchange for bases in British possessions in the western hemisphere, and the occupation of Iceland in June 1941—as extensions of the U.S. defense perimeter into the Atlantic, and this was the truth.

When, however, in June 1941 Germany attacked the Soviet Union and Japan escalated the war in the Far East, Roosevelt evidently decided not only that the United States had to enter the war at a relatively early date, but that it should seek the complete defeat of all its enemies. Within a month, he authorized planning for an all-out effort, and in August, in his first meeting with British Prime Minister Winston Churchill, he committed the United States to the destruction of Nazi rule. Roosevelt might have preferred that war begin in the Atlantic, but because the United States had broken Japanese diplomatic codes, he knew both that Japan was preparing further expansion southward in the second half of 1941 and that Japan would join Germany in war against the United States in any case. As it turned out, Japanese expansionism became the trigger for the world war. Thanks to Roosevelt's foresight and that of his leading subordinates, they had a remarkably good idea, within days after Pearl Harbor, of when that war would be brought to a successful climax.

Franklin Roosevelt was both a devoted sailor and a naval enthusiast, and for the whole of these crucial nineteen months he remained at the mercy of world events every bit as much as a sailing ship depends on the vagaries of the weather. The shape of the war to come and its ultimate outcome depended on many strategic decisions in Berlin, Tokyo, London, and Moscow, and on the performance of various armies and navies already at war. The British won the Battle of Britain in the summer of 1940 on their own, largely because they were already outproducing the Germans in fighter aircraft. Had Hitler listened to his own naval commanders and moved aggressively into the Atlantic instead of turning his eyes eastward at the end of 1940, the history of the twentieth century might have been very different indeed. The Japanese in mid-1941 decided to attack British, Dutch, and American possessions in the Far East on their own initiative, not because of anything the United States had done. The Soviet Union, to the surprise of most observers, managed to halt and eventually defeat the German attack, thereby making the Allied victory possible. Roosevelt and his administration could not, and did not, make any of these things happen, but their wisdom, energy, and leadership enabled the United States and the world to take full advantage of their good fortune when they did.

Roosevelt and his contemporaries in the Missionary generation had chosen a lifelong goal of bringing order out of chaos and laying a foundation for sustained human progress. To do so they had to exercise authority—and Roosevelt's maintenance of the American peoples' confidence in the authority of their government in the midst of depression and world war was his greatest achievement. He and his contemporaries combined energy, self-confidence, ambitious new visions of the future, and above all, a capacity for dramatic action and organization to an extent that no other generation has been able to match. They needed those qualities more than ever in the spring of 1940, when the American democratic experiment and the security of the nation itself suddenly were threatened by a global coalition of hostile powers that might have within a few more months threatened the shores of the United States. At that moment, Roosevelt's 1936 vision of a democratic United States alone in a world of nations that had abandoned or lost their freedom seemed on the verge of coming true. Fortunately, the President had begun to envision this possibility and his government had begun to plan for it nearly three years earlier.

CHAPTER 1

Civilization Under Threat, May 1940

THE WORLDWIDE EVENTS OF APRIL AND MAY 1940 PARALLELED THE domestic crisis that had struck the United States on the eve of Franklin Roosevelt's first inauguration in 1933. At that earlier moment, three years of inadequate efforts had failed to halt the decline in the economy since the stock market crash of October 1929. Then, in February 1933, a series of bank failures threatened to destroy the basis of the American economy itself. Roosevelt managed to restore confidence in the economy by declaring a bank holiday, during which Congress rushed through the Glass-Steagall Act insuring bank deposits and banning commercial banks from investment banking.

Similarly, by the spring of 1940, the international order in both Europe and Asia had been coming apart for ten years. In the Far East, Japan had seized Manchuria in 1931 and embarked upon a gigantic war with China in 1937. They had also renounced their naval arms agreements with the United States and Britain and embarked upon a new naval building program. In Europe, Italian dictator Benito Mussolini had defied the League of Nations and conquered Ethiopia in 1935, while Adolf Hitler had denounced the armaments limitations of the Versailles Treaty that Germany had signed in 1919. Hitler had remilitarized the Rhineland in 1936, occupied and annexed Austria in March 1938, and intimidated the Western powers into handing him frontier districts of Czechoslovakia at Munich in September of that year. In March 1939 Hitler had occupied the rest of what is now the Czech Republic and provoked a new crisis with Poland. That finally persuaded the British and French governments to take a firm stand against further Nazi aggression, and war seemed likely throughout the summer of 1939. In late August Hitler dropped another bombshell, concluding a Nonaggression Pact with the Soviet Union that doomed plans for an Anglo-French-Soviet alliance.

When Hitler attacked Poland on September 1, 1939, Britain and France declared war on Germany. Poland fell within a month, occupied by German troops from the west and Soviet forces from the east. Then followed the winter of the "Phony War." French and German troops faced one another across their common border without firing a shot, both sides eschewed the bombing of enemy territory, and Belgium and Holland remained neutral. On the eastern front, the Soviet Union attacked Finland, initially encountering heavy resistance but ultimately moving its frontier significantly westward in the spring of 1940.

These events, we now know, were merely the opening skirmishes in a titanic struggle to determine which nations would rule the world during the second half of the twentieth century. Nazi Germany, Imperial Japan, and even Fascist Italy each dreamed of creating a great new empire that would make them at least the equal of the British Empire and the United States, while destroying the Soviet Union. More specifically, Hitler was determined to create a huge, autarkic land empire centered on the Ukraine in Eastern Europe, settle it with Germans and other "Aryans," and reduce the local population to slavery. Japan wanted to make China a vassal state and extend its influence over Southeast Asia and the Southwest Pacific, particularly if Germany prevailed over the French, British, and Dutch in Europe. Italy wanted a great empire in the Mediterranean and across the Adriatic. Public opinion polls showed the overwhelming majority of the American people opposed to participation in the war, and both hopeful and confident of an Allied victory. But the events of April, May, and June of 1940 entirely transformed the world situation, threatening to leave the United States alone against a coalition of hostile, expansionist states.

"GERMANS OCCUPY DENMARK, ATTACK OSLO," screamed the first of many consecutive eight-column headlines in the *New York Times* on April 9, 1940. The neutral nations of the Scandinavian Peninsula were a key economic target in the European war because Germany depended on high-grade Swedish iron ore. During much of the year that ore came to Germany through the Baltic Sea, but when the Baltic froze during the winter it went by rail to the port of Narvik in northern Norway and thence down the Norwegian coast, whose waters were warmed by the Gulf Stream. During the first week of April the British Navy had begun mining Norwegian territorial waters to force freighters bound for Germany into the open sea, where they would be vulnerable to the British blockade. The British were also planning landings at key points along the Norwegian coast. Hitler had now stolen a march on the Allies. Using a mixture of warships, merchant ships, and aircraft, the Germans in a single day managed to get troops to Oslo, Bergen, Trondheim, and Narvik right under the noses of Royal Navy ships covering the mining operation, much to the disgust of Franklin Roosevelt, who had counted on the British Fleet to keep the Germans bottled up.

Although the Germans suffered heavy naval losses when British warships reached Narvik, they were well-established in the key positions, and the British took a week to get ground forces on their way to Trondheim and Narvik. Those around Trondheim found themselves forced to evacuate by May 2–3 in the face of German air power which the Royal Air Force (RAF) could not match. The Narvik campaign went much better for the British and French but was eventually overtaken by events farther south in May and June.

The Norway campaign shocked senior American observers because it suggested that sea power could not contain the Germans. Representative Carl Vinson of Georgia, Chairman of the House Naval Affairs Committee, told Chief of Naval Operations Harold Stark on May 4 that the events in Norway had convinced him and presumably the American people that "the defense of this country, and its interests in the western hemisphere, depends on being strong on the sea, under the sea and in the air over the sea." The public was indeed becoming more doubtful and concerned about the war. By the first week in May only 55 percent of those polled expected the Allies to win the war, down from 81 percent just five weeks earlier.[1]

The Norwegian fiasco brought down the British government. Prime Minister Neville Chamberlain's popularity ratings had remained very high all through the winter, but more and more members of his own Conservative Party had lost confidence in him, and the failure to hold most of Norway despite Britain's overwhelming superiority at sea doomed him. Forty of his own Conservative Party abstained in a no-confidence motion on May 9, and Chamberlain knew he would have to quit. The

Labor and Liberal opposition now insisted on an all-party National Government and refused to serve with him. The most logical possible successors were Lord Halifax, the Foreign Secretary who had loyally carried out Chamberlain's appeasement policy before the war, and First Lord of the Admiralty Winston Churchill, who had opposed it. At a climactic meeting with King George VI, Halifax took himself out of the running on the grounds that a modern Prime Minister had to sit in the House of Commons, not the House of Lords. Churchill took office on May 11, but the *New York Times* had to bury that news below the fold.

On May 10, with the Norway campaign still in progress, the Germans had invaded neutral Belgium and Holland while launching a tank attack at Sedan, near the Franco-Belgian border, designed to outflank the French Maginot line to the south. Light French defenses could not stand up to tanks and dive-bombers, and the Germans had crossed the Meuse River and had begun their drive to the channel coast by May 13. By May 15 Churchill was telling Ambassador Joseph P. Kennedy that he thought France was probably beaten. German spearheads reached the English Channel by May 21, isolating the British Expeditionary Force (BEF), and the King of the Belgians surrendered his army a week later. In the last days of May the British desperately evacuated hundreds of thousands of men from Dunkirk but left their heavy equipment behind. Britain was obviously threatened with invasion, and the international position of the United States trembled as badly as its economic system had in the late winter of 1933. The country was almost completely unprepared to face the worst-case scenario that was rapidly emerging.[2]

In the two decades after the First World War the American people and even the U.S. Army had given up the idea of any large-scale participation in land wars across the seas. To preserve their security in an increasingly uncertain world, they essentially trusted two navies, their own and the British. Most of the American Fleet was based in the Pacific at San Diego with an eye on a possible war with Japan, and the United States effectively depended on the British Fleet to safeguard the Atlantic. Already the American position in the Pacific had been weakened because the British, since the formation of the Axis alliance between Germany and Italy in the spring of 1939, had given up the idea of sending a large naval force to Singapore in the event of war in the Far East. Now, however, the collapse of France and the threatened invasion of Britain—universally expected by the end of the summer—left the United States in a potentially cata-strophic situation.

Although in response to the Japanese exit from the 1922 treaty sys-tem, the United States had finally begun modernizing its fleet in 1935, progress had been slow. Should Britain and France make peace with Ger-many yet retain control of their navies—a most optimistic prospect—the United States, with 15 battleships, 6 aircraft carriers, 18 heavy cruisers, and 19 light cruisers, might easily face the combined fleets of Germany, Italy, and Japan, which at that moment totaled 19 battleships, 6 aircraft carriers, 26 heavy cruisers, and 44 light cruisers. But in the more likely worst case that the British and French fleets fell into Axis hands, the total enemy fleets might include 41 battleships, 14 aircraft carriers, 43 heavy cruisers, and 97 light cruisers—between two or three times the strength of the United States. Such Axis naval superiority could not only threaten the United States' overseas possessions but also allow the Axis to land troops virtually anywhere in the Pacific or the western hemisphere. Nor was this all. Germany's air strength, the key weapon in the conquest of Norway, the Low Countries, and France, dwarfed the United States Army Air Corps and was indeed thought to be much larger than it really was. Should they dispose of Britain, the Germans could easily move aircraft to Iceland, then to Greenland, and then to Newfoundland, putting them within range of the northeastern United States. The woefully unequipped U.S. Army had a strength of less than 200,000 men, tiny by European standards, and was backed only by an even less-prepared national guard. Not since the British had landed their forces on Long Island in 1776 had the United States faced such a potentially critical situation.

The danger aroused a great deal of press and public comment. As early as May 11, the day after the German attack on Holland, Belgium, and France, Chicago newspaper editor Frank Knox, who had been the Re-publican vice presidential candidate in 1936, announced that these events "struck the hour of decision for the United States," warned of a combined German-Japanese attack, and called for a much larger fleet. On May 13 even the isolationist, antiadministration *Chicago Tribune* argued that the United States should occupy Greenland at once to keep the Germans from making it a "stepping-stone" to the western hemisphere. On May 18, just a week after the German attack on France, the respected *Christian Science Monitor* spoke openly of the possibility of an Allied defeat and the need to organize the defense of the western hemisphere. On the

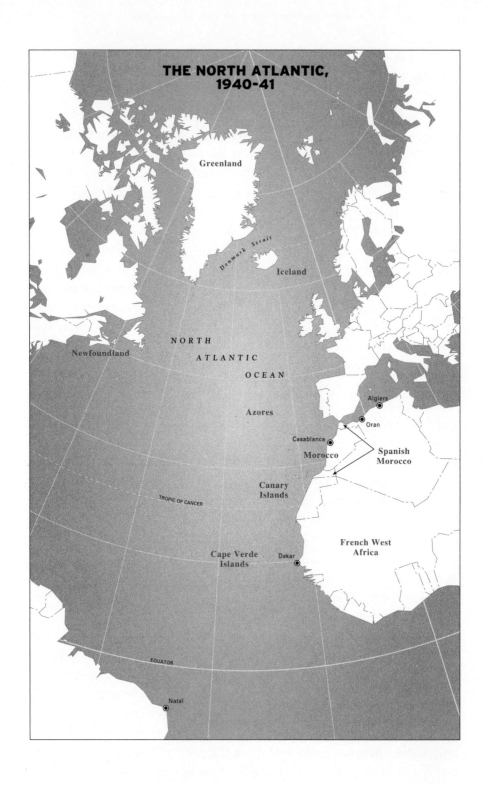

THE NORTH ATLANTIC,
1940-41

Greenland

Denmark Strait

Iceland

Newfoundland

NORTH

ATLANTIC

OCEAN

Algiers

Oran

Azores

Casablanca

Morocco

Spanish
Morocco

Canary
Islands

TROPIC OF CANCER

French West
Africa

Cape Verde
Islands

Dakar

EQUATOR

Natal

same day a Gallup poll reported that a bare majority of Americans now expected the United States to become involved in the war, a major shift from just a few months earlier. In a radio address on May 27, as the Germans were encircling the British at Dunkirk, former President Herbert Hoover demanded that the United States prepare the defense of the western hemisphere. On June 19, with the surrender of France imminent, Hoover's one-time Secretary of State, New York lawyer Henry L. Stimson, gave a radio address arguing that the United States had to institute universal military training, and warning that we might have to shelter the British Fleet if German air attacks drove it out of its home bases. Clearly this largely unexpected emergency required drastic measures. And as it happened, both President Roosevelt and his military planners had been preparing to face it for about three years.[3]

From the time of Roosevelt's presidential election campaign in 1932 until 1937, he had focused almost entirely on domestic affairs, taking advantage of the Depression to promote and implement a truly revolutionary new view of the government's role in the economy. In foreign affairs, meanwhile, he had been not merely cautious, but entirely conventional. Although his domestic policies aroused both passionate support and violent opposition, his foreign policy was about as mainstream and noncontroversial as it could be in the face of the worsening world situation.

Whether or not his foreign policy reflected his own views, it certainly embodied those of the majority of his countrymen. Thus Roosevelt in 1932 made sure of the eventual endorsement of the powerful Hearst newspaper chain by publicly renouncing any intention to join the League of Nations. In a speech in February of that year, he avowed that he had campaigned for entry into the League in 1920, but rejected membership now on the grounds that the League "has not developed through these years along the course contemplated by its founder. . . . What the world needs most today is a national policy, which will make us an example of national honor to other nations. . . . No honorable nation may break a treaty in spirit any more than they may break it in letter." Virtually all Americans shared these views. Proud of their observance of law at home, the American people at least since Wilson had agreed that law should rule the nations of the world as well. That did not, however, mean, as Roosevelt well understood, that they favored American participation in attempts to *enforce* international law against those who defied it, and most did not. Americans believed that world problems arose because other nations pursued evil ends with wicked means, including armed force, and that things would improve only when they, like the United States, began to respect their obligations. Thus, before taking office in March 1933, FDR met with outgoing Secretary of State Henry L. Stimson and agreed to continue Stimson's Nonrecognition Doctrine in the Far East, refusing to assent formally to Japan's establishment of Manchukuo, while disclaiming any efforts to force Japan to change its behavior. Roosevelt's Secretary of State, former Senator Cordell Hull of Tennessee, held strictly to these views as well, and Roosevelt himself echoed them consistently until the fateful late summer of 1937.[4]

In the western hemisphere the new administration practiced what it preached. The United States had intervened frequently and repeatedly around the Caribbean since the presidency of Theodore Roosevelt, but his younger cousin proclaimed "the policy of the good neighbor" in his inaugural address, and later that year, Secretary Hull declared that no nation had the right to intervene in the affairs of another. Two long-standing American military interventions in Haiti and Nicaragua came to an end in 1934, and the United States even accepted the nationalization of American oil properties by the government of Mexico. That policy would pay big dividends in 1940–1941, when real threats to the western hemisphere suddenly arose.

When trouble began to arise in the Old World in 1935, Roosevelt went along with the overwhelming desire of his countrymen to stay out of it. With war beginning between Italy and Ethiopia, Congress passed a strict Neutrality Act prohibiting arms sales on any basis to nations at war and banning American ships from war zones. Roosevelt signed it with only a brief protest about its inflexibility. The United States embargoed arms to both the Italians and Ethiopians in 1936 and to both belligerents in the Spanish Civil War that broke out a year later, including the democratically elected government that was trying to fight off the Fascist General Franco and the regular Army. "The primary purpose of the United States of America," Roosevelt said on November 11, 1935, "is to avoid being drawn into war. . . . If we as a nation, by our good example, can contribute to the peaceful well-being of the fellowship of nations, our course through the years will not have been in vain." "I hate war," he declared during his 1936 reelection campaign, and he continued to oppose any involvement in Europe's increasingly dangerous quarrels. During the next year, however, Roosevelt drastically revised both his rhetoric and his approach to world affairs in response to renewed war in the Far East.[5]

Full-scale open warfare between Japan and China broke out in 1937. Having consolidated their position in Manchuria, the Japanese Kwantung Army had begun taking advantage of unrest in North China to move troops farther south. The Nationalist Government of Chiang Kai-shek, which had been preoccupied with subduing the Communist Party in the early 1930s and had in fact driven it into the interior of North China at Yan'an by 1935, had done little to resist the Japanese. In September 1936 the Communists managed to kidnap Chiang in Sian and extorted a promise from him to cooperate in fighting against the Japanese. When on July 7, 1937, a clash erupted between Japanese and Chinese troops at the Marco Polo Bridge near Beijing, both sides decided to escalate the conflict. The Japanese government, following the lead of the Kwantung Army and the Army General Staff, sent five divisions into North China. Chiang Kai-shek, meanwhile, refused to acknowledge a settlement that local commanders had arranged and declared that Japan would not be allowed to control any further territory. Fighting also broke out in Shanghai, where Japan and the Western powers maintained small garrisons of troops. During the late summer the better-equipped and more disciplined Japanese won a series of quick victories in North China, taking Beijing and a number of other cities. Chiang then opened a new front around Shanghai, where a major campaign began in August. Although this huge and bloody conflict had not yet reached its climax, it had certainly attracted the attention of the entire world.

The Far Eastern war confronted Roosevelt at a difficult moment. No sooner had he been inaugurated for his second term on January 20 than he had stunned the country—including his own huge majorities in Congress—by proposing legislation giving him the right to appoint an additional Supreme Court justice every time a sitting justice failed to retire at the age of seventy. The bill, which would have given him six immediate appointments, correctly struck Congress and much of the country as an attempt to pack the court. Heretofore accusations that Roosevelt aspired to a dictatorship parallel to those of Mussolini, Stalin, and Hitler had generally been limited to Republicans; now they resonated among the broader public. After months of bitter debate—during which the Supreme Court also staged a retreat by upholding several significant pieces of New Deal legislation, and one justice chose to resign—the Senate on July 19 killed the bill by the humiliating vote of 70 to 20. That signaled the end of Roosevelt's dominance over Congress, and as it turned out, he did not score a single major legislative victory for the rest of the 1937 session. Then, in the second half of that year, four years of recovery gave way to a very severe recession, opening up the administration to a new barrage of criticism from its opponents on the right. But meanwhile, Roosevelt edged toward both a rhetorical and an active response to the Far Eastern crisis, showing the same techniques that he would employ when things became much more serious three years later.

The Japanese declined to declare war against China, consistently referring to the conflict as the "China Incident," but the conflict was obviously the most serious step yet toward international anarchy. The outlines of a possible world war, moreover, had already been drawn in 1936, when Japan, Italy, and Germany had concluded the Anti-Comintern Pact, officially a measure designed to oppose Communism worldwide but actually an informal understanding based on hostility to the Soviet Union. Moscow in 1935–1936 had begun supporting Popular Fronts of leftist and liberal parties in Western countries, and Soviet Foreign Minister Maxim Litvinov had become the leading advocate of a worldwide alliance against both Germany and Japan. Leading Japanese had already begun talking of establishing a Monroe Doctrine of their own in East Asia, and Germany was already establishing an economic sphere of influence in Eastern Europe while Hitler trumpeted the Soviet threat. Hitler had denounced the disarmament clauses of the Versailles Treaty in 1934–1935, and both Britain and France were now rearming in response.

Despite the enormous distances separating the United States and the Far East, Americans and their government after 1919 had more of an emotional and even legal stake in events there than in Europe, where they had definitely sworn off any involvement in political quarrels in 1920 when they rejected the Versailles Treaty. At the Washington Conference in 1921–1922 the United States had helped negotiate treaties attempting to set up a new order in the Far East. The Four Power Treaty among Japan, Britain, the United States, and France committed all parties to consult in response to any threats to their possessions in the Far East, including Hong Kong and Malaya for the British, Indochina for the French, Formosa for the Japanese, and the Philippines for the United States. In the Nine-Power Treaty a larger group of powers had affirmed the "sovereignty, the independence, and the territorial and administrative integrity of China," in principle renouncing the kinds of spheres of influence many of them had established before 1914. Most importantly, the Five Power Naval Treaty between Great Britain, the United States, Japan, France, and Italy fixed the ratios of their capital ships—that is, battleships—at 5-5-3 among the British, the Americans, and the Japanese, while the British and Americans pledged not to fortify Singapore or the Philippines. Because of the great distances from Britain and the United States to the Far East and because their navies also had to patrol the Atlantic, these ratios were expected to make it impossible for any one of the three powers to prevail in a Far Eastern war. Similar ratios had been extended to cruisers as well at the London Conference of 1930.

In 1931, when the Japanese seized Manchuria, Secretary of State Stimson had taken these treaties sufficiently seriously to try to organize some kind of joint action against the Japanese, but failed to do so thanks to both opposition in the British government and the lack of interest shown by President Hoover. When the League of Nations refused to bless Japan's action, the Japanese withdrew from it. Then in 1934, younger Japanese naval officers—who had literally terrorized leading politicians by assassinating several of them—successfully insisted on allowing the naval treaties to lapse in 1936 and seeking parity with the United States. On the other side of the Pacific, the U.S. Navy regarded Japan—known officially for war planning purposes as "Orange"—as by far its most likely antagonist in a war, all the more so since Japan was now increasing its Navy at an unknown rate and disregarding its international obligations.

The Roosevelt administration's initial response to the outbreak of the Sino-Japanese war in 1937 called for respect for international law. Only days after the Marco Polo Bridge incident, Secretary Hull released a statement advocating "adjustment of problems in international relations by processes of peaceful negotiation and agreement" and "faithful observance of international agreements." Significantly, however, Roosevelt—following, in effect, the lead of the Japanese government—declined to declare the Sino-Japanese conflict a war, and thereby failed to invoke the provisions of the Neutrality Act that would have forbidden any sales of arms to China and banned U.S. ships from carrying goods to the belligerents. Meanwhile, the Chief of Naval Operations (CNO), Admiral William Leahy, took a more militant view. "If it were possible to obtain an equitable agreement with Great Britain to share the effort and the expense," he wrote in his diary on August 24, "this appears to be a wonderful opportunity to force Japan to observe Treaty agreements, and to depart from the mainland of Asia, which would insure Western trade supremacy in the Orient for another century. The cost of accomplishing this purpose at a later date will be enormously increased, and it does still appear inevitable that a major war between the Occident and the Orient must be faced at some time either now or in the future."[6]

Although Roosevelt had done nothing to move the United States deeper into world affairs during his first five years in office, he was no neophyte in international affairs. He had been an active, and indeed eager, advocate of American involvement in the First World War as Assistant Secretary of the Navy. Interestingly enough, he had evidently blamed that conflict on German aggression from the beginning—a verdict that a consensus of historians now endorses as well—and in a private letter, he had expressed the hope in September 1914 that the conflict would end with the meeting of French and Russian armies in Berlin. In 1915–1917 he had been among the most vigorous proponents in the Wilson administration of intervention in the war, far in advance of his boss, Navy Secretary Josephus Daniels, who like Woodrow Wilson was almost a pacifist.

When Wilson took the United States into the war in April 1917 in response to German unrestricted submarine warfare, Roosevelt took a leading part in the mobilization of the Navy and in planning its role in the conflict, and he traveled to Europe in the middle of 1918 to coordinate naval matters with European allies. In October of that year he helped supervise the negotiations for the Armistice from Washington and insisted on the complete surrender of the German Fleet. He would have preferred that the war continue until Germany had been completely defeated rather than grant the Germans an armistice in November 1918. Unlike so many Americans, he never seems to have had any second thoughts about the decision to go to war, and as the Democratic vice presidential candidate in the doomed campaign of 1920 he had argued loyally for the acceptance of the Versailles Treaty and entry into the League of Nations. He had never accepted the idea that the First World War might lead to eternal peace, and as a navalist of long standing, he was concerned with Japan's plans and how they might be thwarted.[7]

In the fall of 1937 he decided on a daring initiative. In Chicago on October 5, three months after the war in China had broken out, Roosevelt dramatically enunciated a new but characteristically vague policy that clearly marked a break with the past and ignited a huge controversy

over America's role in the world for the first time since the rejection of
the Versailles Treaty.

The world situation, Roosevelt now told his countrymen, demanded
their attention. The hopes for peace embodied in the Kellogg-Briand Pact
of 1926, in which virtually all the nations of the world had renounced
war as an instrument of policy, had vanished in the face of a "reign of terror and international lawlessness" that had begun a few years ago. At stake,
he claimed, was nothing less than the civilization that it had taken centuries to establish. "The landmarks and traditions which have marked
the progress of civilization toward a condition of law, order and justice
are being wiped away," he declared. "Without a declaration of war and
without warning or justification of any kind, civilians, including vast
numbers of women and children, are being ruthlessly murdered with
bombs from the air. In times of so-called peace, ships are being attacked
and sunk by submarines without cause or notice. Nations are fomenting
and taking sides in civil warfare in nations that have never done them
any harm. Nations claiming freedom for themselves deny it to others. Innocent peoples, innocent nations, are being cruelly sacrificed to a greed
for power and supremacy which is devoid of all sense of justice and humane considerations."

Roosevelt then stated the principle that would govern his policies for
the next four years: that these events directly threatened the western
hemisphere and the United States. "If those things come to pass in other
parts of the world, let no one imagine that America will escape, that
America may expect mercy, that this western hemisphere will not be attacked and that it will continue tranquilly and peacefully to carry on the
ethics and the arts of civilization." And thus, something had to be done:
"The peace-loving nations must make a concerted effort in opposition to
those violations of treaties and those ignoring of humane instincts which
today are creating a state of international anarchy and instability from
which there is no escape through mere isolation or neutrality. Those who
cherish their freedom and recognize and respect the equal right of their
neighbors to be free and live in peace, must work together for the triumph of law and moral principles in order that peace, justice and confidence may prevail in the world."

"Surely," he said later, "the ninety per cent [of the world's population]
who want to live in peace under law and in accordance with moral standards that have received almost universal acceptance through the centuries,

can and must find some way to make their will prevail." But how? No one ever chose his words more carefully than Roosevelt, and in this case he selected his key word with calculated ambiguity. An epidemic of world lawlessness was spreading, he said, and when epidemics of physical diseases broke out, "the community approves the plan and joins in a quarantine of the patients in order to protect the health of the community against the spread of the disease. . . . War is a contagion, whether it be declared or undeclared. It can engulf states and peoples remote from the original scene of hostilities. . . . The will for peace on the part of peace-loving nations must express itself to the end that nations that may be tempted to violate their agreements and the rights of others will desist from such a course. There must be positive endeavors to preserve peace."[8]

In this momentous speech Roosevelt had characteristically laid out the dilemma and the danger facing the world, stressed the necessity of some response, but failed to provide any real specifics. Admiral Leahy believed that "such a policy, if carried out, will almost certainly bring about a war with Japan, declared or undeclared," but Roosevelt had not laid out any definite course of action. When queried the next day in a press conference, he declared the subject "off the record" and proceeded to give a striking example of one of his most frequent and infuriating tactics. Determined not to reveal any meaningful information about either his plans or even his thoughts, he took refuge in a long series of denials and non sequiturs whose flavor cannot be captured in a paraphrase. Because he would employ this technique so frequently during the next four years, this press conference deserves to be quoted in full.[9]

> Q. Returning to that speech of yesterday, in view of its extreme importance, I think it would be very valuable if you would answer a few questions or else talk for background.
>
> THE PRESIDENT: I think on that I can only talk really completely off the record. I don't want to say anything for background.
>
> Q. I had two major things in mind. One was what you had in mind with reference to quarantining—what type of measure. Secondly, how would you reconcile the policy you outlined yesterday with the policy of neutrality laid down by the Act of Congress?

THE PRESIDENT: Read the last line I had in the speech. That gives it about as well as anything else. (Looking through *New York Herald Tribune* of October 6.)

Q. I don't believe that paper carried it. (Laughter)

THE PRESIDENT: Here it is: "Therefore America actively engages in the search for peace."

Q. But you also said that the peace-loving nations can and must find a way to make their wills prevail.

THE PRESIDENT: Yes?

Q. And you were speaking, as I interpreted it, you were speaking of something more than moral indignation. That is preparing the way for collaborative—

THE PRESIDENT: Yes?

Q. Is anything contemplated? Have you moved?

THE PRESIDENT: No; just the speech itself.

Q. Yes, but how do you reconcile that? Do you accept the fact that that is a repudiation of the neutrality—

THE PRESIDENT: Not for a minute. It may be an expansion.

Q. Is that for use?

THE PRESIDENT: All off the record.

Q. Doesn't that mean economic sanctions anyway?

THE PRESIDENT: No, not necessarily. Look, "sanctions" is a terrible word to use. They are out of the window.

Q. Right. Let's not call it that. Let's call it concert of action on the part of peace-loving nations. Is that going to be brought into play?

THE PRESIDENT: I don't know that I can give you spot news because the lead is in the last line, "America actively engages in the search for peace." I can't tell you what the methods will be. We are looking for some way to peace; and by no means is it necessary that that way be contrary to the exercise of neutrality.

Q. Is there a likelihood that there will be a conference of the peace-loving nations?

THE PRESIDENT: No; conferences are out of the window. You never get anywhere with a conference.

Q. Foreign papers put it as an attitude without a program.

THE PRESIDENT: That was the *London Times*.

Q. Would you say that that is not quite it, that you are looking toward a program as well as having an attitude?

THE PRESIDENT: It is an attitude, and it does not outline a program; but it says we are looking for a program.

Q. Wouldn't it be almost inevitable, if any program is reached, that our present Neutrality Act will have to be overhauled?

THE PRESIDENT: Not necessarily. That is the interesting thing.

Q. That is very interesting.

Q. You say there isn't any conflict between what you outline and the Neutrality Act. They seem to be on opposite poles to me and your assertion does not enlighten me.

THE PRESIDENT: Put your thinking-cap on, Ernest [Lindley].

Q. I have been for some years. They seem to be at opposite poles. How can you be neutral if you are going to align yourself with one group of nations?

THE PRESIDENT: What do you mean, "aligning"? You mean a treaty?

Q. Not necessarily. I meant action on the part of peace-loving nations.

THE PRESIDENT: There are a lot of methods in the world that have never been tried yet.

Q. But, at any rate, that is not an indication of neutral attitude—"quarantine the aggressors" and "other nations of the world."

THE PRESIDENT: I can't give you any clue to it. You will have to invent one. I haven't got one.

Q. Did you notice that Senator Borah praised the speech?

Q. This is no longer neutrality.

THE PRESIDENT: On the contrary, it might be a stronger neutrality.

Q. I mean as related to— (interrupted)

Q. This is all off the record?

THE PRESIDENT: Yes, this is all off the record.

Exchanges like this occurred often during FDR's presidency, both in press conferences and in meetings with his leading subordinates. Such tactics were an important part of Roosevelt's personality and must, indeed, have dated from his childhood. He had learned at an early age that he must please his devoted parents, even when, for instance, they jerked him out of his idyllic childhood and dispatched him to the cold and Spartan environment of Groton Academy. This dilemma, familiar to so many children, had led him to adopt an almost invariably cheerful demeanor and to say, to the extent possible, what the situation seemed to require. Having chosen a wife whose tastes, habits, and needs differed so radically from his own, he faced the same dilemma in his marriage and, for a long time, handled it in a similar way. This was, of course, excellent preparation for a career in politics, a profession in which the frank expression of one's feelings can often be disastrous. Roosevelt's own particular solution to this problem—one that he often employed in his personal life as well, and which we shall repeatedly encounter during the tense months of 1940 and 1941—was to enunciate clear and striking principles, but to string together miscellaneous words and phrases without expressing any clear meaning when asked what in practice they might mean.

Both hostile contemporaries and latter-day historians have seized on exchanges like this press conference to paint FDR as a buffoon or an intellectual lightweight, but nothing could be further from the truth. In this case as in many others, he showed in the next few months that he had a very clear idea of what he wanted to achieve, but he could not share it with the American people or the rest of the world until he had brought it closer to fruition. Roosevelt hoped to arrange an Anglo-American naval confrontation with the Japanese that would force them to stop the war in China. When the British refused to cooperate, he began to think that the United States might well have to face the threat of international lawlessness alone.

The quarantine speech immediately ignited a storm of controversy. Internationalists, as they were called, praised it while calling for more specific action, while isolationists attacked it as evidence of further perfidy on Roosevelt's part. The President continued to resist all attempts to get him to clarify his thoughts publicly. To his cabinet he admitted that action against Japan might include a naval blockade but insisted that it might "bring Japan to terms without war"—a fantasy which he may or may not have believed. In November a conference called by the League of Nations failed when the Japanese refused to attend, and in December the conflict became even more violent, as the Japanese, having taken Shanghai, also occupied Chiang Kai-shek's capital of Nanking, killing tens of thousands of civilians. And on December 13, a Japanese air raid sank the U.S. gunboat *Panay*, killing three sailors and wounding many others, after it had helped evacuate American civilians from Nanking. Although the Japanese apologized later in the month, these new developments, along with some overtures about naval cooperation from the British, moved Roosevelt to propose steps that might actually have led to war with Japan in 1938.[10]

When undertaking sensitive matters, Roosevelt frequently liked to move outside established channels. In October 1937 he began discussing the most sweeping diplomatic initiative of his administration, not with Secretary Hull, but with Hull's subordinate, Undersecretary of State Sumner Welles. He contemplated an Armistice Day appeal to the nations of the world to reverse course, reaffirm the principles of international law upon which peace depended, halt their armaments programs, and work for a more prosperous and stable world. According to Welles, even if he could not bring about such an agreement, he hoped to rally world opinion on behalf of peace and resistance to aggression just as he had outlined in the quarantine speech. Several unnamed advisers urged against it, however, and Roosevelt decided to hold off for a couple of months. Meanwhile, he investigated the possibility of Anglo-American naval action against Japan.[11]

Franklin Roosevelt had an unusual mind. Although he was not a systematic thinker or in any way a theoretician, he had an encyclopedic knowledge of subjects in which he had become deeply interested, including stamp collecting, ship models, rare books, and the naval forces of the United States, over which he had exercised substantial responsibility from 1913 to 1920. In the latter stages of the First World War, President Wilson had decided that the United States should have the world's largest Navy so as to be able to enforce its beneficent principles on more selfish states, including Britain, and had authorized the construction of forty-eight battleships, one for every state. The Harding administration had abandoned those plans and accepted parity with the British in the Washington Conference in 1922, but Roosevelt still regarded the Navy as the key to American security. He had, indeed, in 1935 started an ambitious program to modernize (although not to increase) the fifteen battleships that the naval treaties allowed the United States to possess, and in 1936 the Navy ordered two new battleships scheduled for completion in 1941 and 1942.

Roosevelt often showed his particular affection for the Navy, and his cabinet members enjoyed referring to it as his branch of the service. Now, in an episode that very few historians have noticed—he was willing to begin planning its use. A possible war with Japan had been the main mission of the American Fleet since the United States had acquired the Philippines, and Japan, an island nation, was almost uniquely vulnerable to naval pressure. At the Brussels Conference that met in November 1937 to discuss the situation, Roosevelt, true to his quarantine speech, refused any discussion of economic sanctions against Japan. But when British Foreign Secretary Anthony Eden in mid-December indicated to the United States that London would welcome a joint Anglo-American naval demonstration against Japan, Roosevelt saw a chance to use their navies to impose their will on an aggressor nation. The Navy, in fact, was going to provide the "quarantine" which Roosevelt had suggested in Chicago in October.[12]

Meeting with the British Ambassador on December 17, Roosevelt alluded to secret conversations between a British Naval attaché and an American Navy Captain in 1915–1917, when he had been Assistant Secretary of the Navy, and suggested sending an American officer to London now. He then made a series of sweeping proposals that astonished the Ambassador, Sir Ronald Lindsay, but which had evidently been carefully thought out. When the Japanese committed a new outrage in the Far East (he was evidently thinking of the bombing of British and American ships that had just taken place), the two nations should establish a cruiser blockade—a "quarantine"—from the Aleutians to Hawaii, thence north of the Philippines and terminating at the British possession of Hong Kong. Cruisers would man the line, while the United States held its battleships in reserve and the British dispatched a small number of theirs to Singapore. Roosevelt insisted that Japan could be blockaded without war and cited the precedent of the United States' "quasi war" with France in 1798. Somewhat to Lindsay's astonishment, Roosevelt expressed confidence that the American public would support such action. Neither Roosevelt nor Hull, who was present, made any record of this talk for State Department archives. Despite his own doubts about the plan—especially the idea that it would not mean war—Lindsay recommended accepting the President's suggestion and the British government announced that it would receive an American officer in London. Roosevelt and Leahy responded at once, dispatching Captain Royal Ingersoll, the Chief of the Navy's War Plans Division, the intellectual nerve center of the U.S. Navy.[13]

Arriving in London on December 31, Ingersoll on the very next day met with Foreign Secretary Eden, a strong proponent of Anglo-American cooperation, who wanted to know exactly why Ingersoll had come and how much discussion had taken place between Roosevelt, Hull, and the Ambassador. Ingersoll's mission was so sensitive that Leahy in his own diary had given an official version of it—to discuss technical requirements of the London Naval Treaty of 1936—but now Ingersoll replied simply that the President had asked Leahy "to send me to London to obtain naval information on which to plan and to base decisions, if necessary, as to future action." Eden referred him to Lord Chatfield, the First Sea Lord, and a series of intense discussions took place at the Admiralty from January 3 through January 15. The British Fleet was every bit as oriented toward Japan as the American, and Chatfield and Ingersoll tentatively agreed that in the event of either war or a confrontation with Japan designed to end the Sino-Japanese War, the British Fleet would deploy at Singapore and the U.S. Fleet at Pearl Harbor and establish a distant blockade—a "quarantine," in Ingersoll's word—of the Japanese home islands. The discussions covered operations details, including the use of codes and ciphers. Ingersoll made clear that the United States would first have to declare a national emergency, but both sides seemed quite serious about forcing a confrontation on the Japanese. Unfortunately, the political basis for joint action was collapsing.[14]

Roosevelt's behavior during the fall and early winter of 1937–1938 suggests that he already anticipated a resumption of the Anglo-American alliance to meet aggression in the Far East and, conceivably, in Europe. British Foreign Secretary Anthony Eden, the dynamic young rising star of the British cabinet, shared that view, but Prime Minister Neville Chamberlain, who had taken office earlier in 1937, did not. He distrusted the United States and hoped above all to avoid a future European war by settling outstanding disputes with both Italy and then Germany, a pursuit in which he was already actively engaged. On January 11, while talks about some joint Anglo-American naval action were still in progress, Chamberlain wrote confidentially that he had little confidence in American willingness to act, but that in any event he did not want to send the British Fleet to the Far East at the present time.[15]

On the very next day, Roosevelt dropped another private bombshell in a message he passed to the British through Sumner Welles. Echoing the language of the quarantine speech, he spoke of the threatening collapse of civilization, the great and increasing burden of armaments expenditures, and the horrible new methods of war. To meet the threat he proposed to call an international conference in Washington, to be attended by lesser, neutral nations that might propose steps to alleviate the situation including perhaps the revision of certain postwar treaties. Chamberlain immediately overruled Lindsay and the Foreign Office (Eden was in Europe at the time) and wrote Roosevelt refusing to endorse the scheme on the grounds that it would undercut his dealings with the Germans and Italians. When Eden returned to London and learned of the exchange he asked the Prime Minister to reconsider, but Chamberlain refused. Eden then decided to leave the cabinet as soon as possible—he could not do so based on an exchange of which neither the public nor even the cabinet was aware—and did so in the following month. During the next three years Japan advanced steadily into China, occupying one major population center after another and driving Chiang Kai-shek's regime deep into the interior at Chungking in a conflict of extraordinary scope and brutality.[16]

If international initiatives designed to avert further war or halt aggression did not bear fruit, the United States had to prepare to fight a world war of uncertain dimensions on its own. In a message to Congress on January 28, 1938, Roosevelt described the world situation in terms similar to those of the quarantine speech and asked for some modest new steps to deal with it. His requests included about $20 million in new authorizations for equipment for the Army (but no increase in its very modest size), the completion of an already planned expansion of the Navy up to the existing treaty limits (which the United States had fallen behind), and the laying down of three new battleships designed to meet the threat of new Japanese battleships. Once again using the legal and moral language so characteristic of his generation, he insisted that the threat of lawlessness could easily reach the Americas. "It is necessary for all of us to realize that the unfortunate world conditions of today have resulted too often in the discarding of those principles and treaties which underlie international law and order; and in the entrance of many new factors into the actual conduct of war. Adequate defense means that for the protection not only of our coasts but also of our communities far removed from the coast, we must keep any potential enemy many hundred miles away from our continental limits," he declared.[17]

The focus of international attention in 1938 shifted to Europe, where Hitler annexed Austria in March and immediately began threatening Czechoslovakia, claiming that the Prague government was persecuting its German minority. The Nazis immediately tried to force the Jewish population of Austria to emigrate, and Roosevelt did what he could to allow more of them to come to America within the framework of the rigid quota system that had been established by law in 1924. He was indeed the only world leader to make a serious effort to find a home for Jewish refugees in Europe during the late 1930s, although he had only very limited success. The danger of war grew throughout the summer, and by September it seemed quite likely that a German attack on Czechoslovakia might mean war with France and Great Britain as well. On September 19, after Britain and France had asked Czechoslovakia to surrender its German-inhabited territory to Hitler, Roosevelt had another remarkable conversation with Ambassador Sir Ronald Lindsay in Washington. This conversation, to which previous accounts have failed to do justice, gave an excellent indication of his views of the world scene.[18]

After swearing Lindsay to secrecy, Roosevelt indicated that he regarded war as nearly certain. Even if the Czechs agreed to the demands on them—which he did not think they would do—Hitler was bound to make further demands against Denmark, Poland, or Rumania. If war came now he did not believe that Britain, France, *and the Soviet Union* (then allied with France) could defeat Germany and Italy. Should war come, then, he suggested that Britain and France refrain from declaring it and simply blockade Germany. Neutrals, he felt, would have to cooperate, and if the allies could choose a less provocative blockade instead of a full-scale war, the United States could observe it as well based on presidential authority. He also speculated that Japan might join Germany and attack Hong Kong or Indochina in the Far East, but he did not expect that to happen at once. After emphasizing that the revelation of this conversation might lead to his impeachment, he speculated that only a German invasion of Britain could move American opinion to endorse the dispatch of a new army across the seas.[19]

Roosevelt was both surprised and relieved that war did not break out. The Czechs accepted the Anglo-French proposals, only to have Hitler make new and humiliating demands when Chamberlain met him for a second time at Bad Godesberg. The British cabinet refused to accept them, and war seemed imminent. Roosevelt himself on September 27 appealed to Hitler not to attack Czechoslovakia, and on September 30 Hitler accepted an invitation from Mussolini to discuss the situation with

Chamberlain and French Premier Daladier at Munich. There he secured most of what he had asked for.

The outcome of the Munich crisis led to a new phase in American policy and strategy, one that lasted at least until the middle of 1941. Hitler had in fact been bluffing the British and French in 1938. He knew that he was not ready to fight them, and during that summer he told his generals, who feared war, that the French and the British were bound to give in without a fight. He won that gamble partly by convincing London and Paris that he was already substantially superior to them militarily, especially in the air. This was not true, but it was what American military observers also felt. Only a month after Munich, U.S. Ambassador Joseph P. Kennedy struck a blow for Chamberlain and appeasement in a public speech, arguing that dictatorships and democracies could "advantageously bend their energies toward solving their remaining common problems and attempt to re-establish good relations on a world basis." That was not, however, the President's view. Roosevelt continued to expect war in Europe and possibly in the Far East as well—and he evidently thought it highly possible, if not probable, that the Western powers would lose. Under his direction, the United States now began preparing and planning for war—*not* a war in which they would assist France and Britain in Europe, but a war in which they might have to defend the western hemisphere against the combined forces of Germany, Italy, and Japan without any major allies at all.[20]

The war preparations that Roosevelt set in motion early in 1939 continued right up until Pearl Harbor, and consistently proceeded on three parallel fronts. First, Roosevelt had to define the kind of conflict the United States might face, and Army and Navy planners had to begin writing plans for various contingencies. Secondly, the military and naval forces of the United States—relatively strong at sea, but much weaker in the air and nearly nonexistent on the ground—had to be vastly increased so as to carry out the new missions that the planners had identified. And last, Roosevelt himself had to convince the American people and their other elected representatives that war might indeed be necessary, certainly to defend the western hemisphere and possibly to do much more. Diplomatic preparation might also become important, but the administration from the beginning planned to fight Germany, Italy, and Japan alone. Roosevelt's initial attempt to inspire the American people to meet the world crisis in the fall of 1937 had not been very successful, and his

second, in the spring and summer of 1939, fared even worse. But the
groundwork he and the Army and Navy leadership laid during 1939 on
the planning and production fronts paid significant dividends when the
situation obviously became critical in May of 1940.

Never in its history has the government of the United States had to
cope with the enormous range of world military and naval threats that
faced it from 1938 until 1945, and it undertook the task with a bureaucratic
structure that in retrospect seems at first glance to be hopelessly inadequate. The Department of Defense did not yet exist; the secretaries of War
and of the Navy were in charge of the nation's two military arms, and the
Air Corps was part of the War Department. The secretaries of War and of
the Navy, Harry Woodring and Charles Edison, were undoubtedly the
least well-known and least effective of all the members of the great Roosevelt cabinet, reflecting the administration's domestic priorities. Their departments resided in "temporary" quarters constructed on the Mall to
accommodate their expansion during the First World War. Their senior
military officers were the Chief of Staff of the Army, who in 1938 was General Maylon Craig, and the Chief of Naval Operations, Admiral Leahy,
who generally deferred to the commander of the U.S. Fleet in operational
matters and had less authority than his counterpart today. The Navy was
one of the world's largest; the Army was extraordinarily small, with a regular complement in 1938 of about 120,000 men. Yet the intellectual caliber
of senior officers was extremely high. The typical Army and Navy career
officer had received a thorough general education and wrote a highly com-
petent brand of English. Senior naval officers often had spent several years
teaching at the Naval War College in Newport, Rhode Island—a tradition
which unfortunately lapsed after the Second World War. Beginning in
1938, a very few of these men had the responsibility of estimating the
threats to the United States, drawing up the plans to meet them, and
deciding how many men, weapons, and ammunition would be necessary
to carry those plans out.

The Army and Navy were separate independent services and the
Navy, the richer of the two, jealously guarded its independence, but one
small, critical institution—the Joint Board—oversaw the development
of War Plans. That Board in November 1938 had just six permanent
members and a secretary. The former included the Army Chief of Staff
and Chief of Naval Operations, their immediate deputies, and the re-
spective heads of the two services' War Plans divisions, General George

V. Strong and Captain Robert L. Ghormley, who had replaced Captain Ingersoll earlier in the year. Ghormley and Strong in turn were the heads of the Joint Planning Committee, to whom the task of writing the nation's overall war plans was delegated. Today the formation of war plans involves literally hundreds of military officers and civilians in numerous different commands. It was surely the tiny size of the group charged with dealing with the greatest world crisis in history that enabled it to reach decisions quickly and within the framework of an overall strategic conception. The Joint Planning Committee wrote Joint Army and Navy plans, specifying the campaigns to be undertaken. After they were approved by the service secretaries and the President, the War Plans divisions of the Army and Navy wrote separate plans for their services, and subordinate commands then wrote their own plans to carry them out.

This spare bureaucratic structure also served Franklin Roosevelt's needs very well. Actively interested in military and especially naval affairs himself, he frequently met privately with both the CNO and the Chief of Staff, and often with subordinate officers, including some from the War Plans divisions, as well. He alone remained the supreme strategic authority, and he could generally trust his senior officers' discretion. On July 5, 1939, he issued an executive order that the Joint Board "and other service elements" could report to him directly rather than through the War and Navy departments, and we shall see that many of the most important military plans of the years 1940–1941 were undertaken at the direct behest of the President—usually without any formal written record of what exactly he had asked them to do. So it was in November 1938 when, in the wake of the Munich agreement, the Joint Board ordered up an entirely new war plan to meet a frightening contingency. Roosevelt met frequently with his service chiefs that month, and no one else would have had the authority to kick off such a sweeping reevaluation of American strategy.[21]

Until 1938, war plans had focused on individual countries, each designated by a color—Red for Britain, Orange for Japan, Black for Germany, and so on. The government of the United States in the first third of the twentieth century did not yet reflexively divide the world into friends and enemies, and the military planners simply assumed that literally any nation might at some point be drawn into a conflict with the United States. The Navy always focused primarily on Plan Orange, involving a campaign against Japan in the western Pacific, but both services spent a surprising amount of time on Plan Red, involving a possible war with Britain fought in the North Atlantic and in Canada, and both services wrote plans for interventions in Mexico, Cuba, and elsewhere in the Caribbean. Because the United States had always distrusted foreign alliances and did not now belong to a single one, most plans said little or nothing about cooperation with any allied powers. Now, however, the world situation was changing, and in the midst of a flurry of meetings on the world situation after Munich, FDR apparently directed Army Chief of Staff General Craig and CNO Admiral Leahy to get to work.[22]

Roosevelt laid out a frightening picture of the world situation in a cabinet meeting on October 14, 1938. Britain and France, he argued, gave in at Munich because they would have been helpless before the German Air Force, whose size virtually everyone was now enormously overestimating. The situation was not about to improve, he said, and Germany might easily dominate Europe all the way to the Black Sea, move into the Middle East, and strangle the British Empire. In the Far East, "Japan is supreme in the air and on the water and that brings in question the status of Hong Kong, Australia, the Dutch East Indies and French holdings." The Germans also might easily foment a Franco-style revolution in South America. The United States, he said, desperately needed to increase aircraft production so as not to be bullied by Hitler as the French and British had been.[23]

It could hardly have been a coincidence that on November 9, 1938, the Joint Board instructed the Joint Planning Committee to undertake "exploratory studies and estimates" of possible U.S. courses of action in the event that Germany and/or Italy attempted to violate the Monroe Doctrine by establishing a presence in the western hemisphere, while Japan simultaneously tried to extend its influence over the Philippines. The committee was instructed to assume that Germany, Italy, and Japan would act in support of one another, while "democratic nations will remain neutral as long as their possessions in the western hemisphere are unmolested." Worried by the apparent weakness and accommodating spirit of the British and the French, the United States was planning to fight on its own. Essentially, the Roosevelt administration was planning for life in a world in which one great power might dominate each continent: Germany in Europe, Japan in East Asia, and the United States in the western hemisphere.[24]

The Joint Planning Committee submitted a rather prescient preliminary statement on April 21, 1939. Germany and Italy, they speculated,
might easily promote a Fascist revolution in one of several Latin American countries and subsequently establish sea and air bases and introduce
troops there. German influence was already significant in Brazil, Argentina, Chile, and Peru. The Axis powers' close relations with Fascist Spain
and Portugal might also allow them to seize the Azores, Canaries, or
Cape Verde Islands. In the Pacific they rightly suspected Japan of wanting to eliminate British, Dutch, and U.S. influence, in the latter case even
from Hawaii and Alaska. Japan might easily attack the Philippines if the
U.S. Fleet were occupied in the Atlantic. "If the U.S. Fleet is in the Pacific," they wrote prophetically, "a probable Japanese measure would be
attempts to damage Major Fleet Units without warning, or possibly attempts to block the Fleet in Pearl Harbor. Japan would plan the inauguration of these initial measures without warning, and with as little
preliminary indication as possible." A long analysis of a possible war
with Japan indicated that America's current Navy was almost surely inadequate to advance to the western Pacific, especially if forces were also
needed in Europe, and would be only barely adequate to defend Hawaii
and Alaska. Interestingly enough, the study ruled out the invasion of
Japan as impractical, since it would require the stationing of huge numbers of troops on the Asian mainland. Meanwhile, the United States would
also need parity with the smaller German and Italian navies to deal with
their threats to communications in the Atlantic. The paper said nothing
about forming alliances to deal with these threats.[25]

On May 12, 1939—by which time the possibility of a European war
over Poland had become very real—the Joint Board received a draft directive calling for the preparation of four plans, known as Rainbow plans
to distinguish them from the earlier, single-country "color" plans. All
four were to assume initially that the United States would be fighting
alone against Germany, Italy, and Japan, although the planners were instructed to consider the possibility that other nations might be involved
on the side of the United States. Rainbow 1 would provide merely for the
defense of the western hemisphere to 10° south, that is, around the northern boundary of Bolivia. Rainbow 2, bowing to the Navy's priorities,
added the mission of securing control of the western Pacific as well.
Rainbow 3 would anticipate projecting power even farther south and
into the eastern Atlantic, and Rainbow 4 would assume the cooperation

of Britain and France and call for the projection of American power into Africa and/or Europe to secure "the decisive defeat of Germany, or Italy, or both." The Joint Board approved this directive on June 15.[26]

During the next two weeks, senior army and navy planners secured an important revision in the directive, inserting a new Rainbow 2 into the sequence, and asking that the joint war plans be prepared in numerical order. Rainbow 2, unlike the existing concepts for the previous first three Rainbows, assumed that the United States would be fighting alongside Britain, France, and possibly even the Soviet Union, but that the American effort would be almost totally focused in the Pacific—evidently the preferred option of the U.S. Navy. Work on Rainbow 1 proceeded rapidly, and it was completed in late July and approved by the Joint Board on August 10. Confined totally to the defense of the western hemisphere down to 10° south, it foresaw the dispatch of 30,000 troops to Oahu and 4,000 to Alaska. While the Army would try to hold Subic Bay in the Philippines against the Japanese, the Navy would establish its defense line in the Pacific at longitude 160° west, only a couple of hundred miles west of Hawaii. In the Atlantic, troops would land in various Caribbean regions and, critically, in Northeast Brazil, which had key significance because it lay only 1,900 miles from West Africa. An Atlantic Fleet based in Guantánamo in Cuba and in Puerto Rico would attempt to interdict all communications between Germany and Italy and the Americas. The plan's distinctly limited objective was "to bring to bear on the enemy such military and economic pressure as will enable the United States to impose terms favorable to itself in the eventual peace settlement."

Although the United States did not want to be drawn into an alliance with Britain, a later annex anticipated asking the British for bases in Trinidad, Bermuda, Jamaica, Barbados, and British Honduras, in addition to bases in six Central and South American countries. The War and Navy departments forwarded the plan on August 14, and Roosevelt added his approval exactly two months later. Rainbow 2, calling for the United States to make its major effort against Japan while Britain and France held down the Axis in Europe, was not completed until May 1940, by which time it was being rendered obsolete by dramatic events.[27]

President Roosevelt, meanwhile, had personally ordered the redeployment of some naval forces to meet the Atlantic contingencies foretold by these plans. In early September 1938, with war in Europe threatening, he ordered the formation of an Atlantic squadron including seven light cruisers and seven new destroyers to stop potential Axis raids on the Caribbean, and three heavy cruisers to show the flag in Latin America. In December he asked Admiral Leahy and Admiral James Richardson, the commander of the U.S. Fleet, to put several of the most important support units of the Navy on a war footing. In February 1939 the Navy actually ran an exercise based on the contingency of a pro-Nazi revolt in Brazil which requested help from Germany, and concluded that such operations would require more bases in the Caribbean. In April of that year, the President added the carrier *Ranger* and four heavy cruisers to the Atlantic squadron. And on April 24, he broached the idea of declaring a neutrality zone west of an unspecified meridian of longitude in the Atlantic and sinking any Axis ships that crossed over it in the event of war. This was only one of several instances in which Roosevelt planned a move years in advance. The United States would in fact secure bases from the British in 1940 and implement the neutrality zone in 1941.[28]

Rainbow 1—until the late spring of 1940 the only available war plan to meet the increasingly threatening world situation—was based on the existing military and naval forces of the United States, but Roosevelt and the services knew that they might well prove inadequate. Lacking any plans to send armies outside the western hemisphere, they made no plans during 1939 for any major expansion of the Army, but the Navy and the nascent Air Corps were a different story.

Four years had now passed since the Japanese had denounced the Naval Treaties of 1922 and 1930 in 1935, and the Japanese were now suspected of building three battleships of at least 46,000 tons, nearly a third larger than the treaty limit of 35,000 tons. The Vinson-Trammell Act of 1938, named after Representative Carl Vinson of Georgia of the House Naval Affairs Committee and Senator Park Trammell of Florida, had authorized a 20 percent increase in warship tonnage across the board, but most of it had not been funded. The United States in 1938 had announced plans for two 45,000-ton-battleships, but their construction had not yet begun. In the summer of 1939 the Navy's War Plans Division recommended two more for fiscal 1941 (that is, July 1940 to June 1941), in addition to a new aircraft carrier and more cruisers and destroyers. Not until after war broke out in September, however, did the Naval Planners seriously address the gigantic problem of carrying out the tasks assigned in Rainbow 1, that is, the single-handed defense of the western hemisphere against Germany, Italy, and Japan.[29]

Air power was the great wild card of military planning in the 1920s and 1930s. In 1921 the Italian general Guido Douhet had published *The Command of the Air*, arguing that air power, through the bombing of cities and industrial centers, would decide the outcome of future wars. Douhet's impact differed from country to country, but one of his most avid disciples was the U.S. Army Air Corps general Billy Mitchell, who created a sensation in 1921 when he managed to stage a bombing raid against the captured German battleship *Ostfriesland* and proved that aerial bombardment could sink a capital ship. Although the test, significantly, was not entirely realistic—the *Ostfriesland* was not only unmanned, but at anchor, during the attack—Mitchell had convinced at least his fellow air enthusiasts that bombers might usurp the role of the U.S. Navy and dominate the sea. Mitchell's outspoken advocacy led to his court-martial and the termination of his career, but a cadre of Air Corps officers continued to push the idea of making a long-range bomber force a key weapon in the American arsenal. During the 1930s they managed to let contracts for the development of a large bomber with a range of at least 2,000 miles. The winner was Boeing's B-17, destined to become the most famous American aircraft of the Second World War. Its enthusiasts justified its 2,000-mile range as necessary to reach Alaska and Hawaii, and claimed that it would keep hostile naval forces away from American coasts in any future war. The B-17 made a number of impressive test flights in 1937–1938, flying from the United States to Buenos Aires with just one stop to refuel and intercepting both American and foreign ships far out at sea, but the War Department, strapped for cash and skeptical about long-range bombing, refused to put it into mass production. By 1938 the Army Air Corps had only thirteen of them.[30]

The war that did *not* occur in Europe in September and October 1938 transformed the situation. Although it is now clear that the combined air strength of Britain and France was roughly equal to that of Germany, and that all of those powers were relying largely on older, inferior types of fighters and bombers, the fear of the Luftwaffe did much to convince the British and French to agree to German demands rather than call Hitler's bluff over Czechoslovakia. Western observers such as the famous American aviator Charles Lindbergh had vastly overestimated German air strength. By the end of the Munich Crisis, Lindbergh, who had talked to leading aviation figures in all three major European nations, believed that Germany had 6,000 modern aircraft ready—an overestimate of 100 percent—and that it was now producing 2,000 new aircraft a month, four times as many as France and more than twice as many as Britain. The American Ambassador to France, William Bullitt—a Roosevelt confidante—shared these views and imparted them to FDR in a private letter at the height of the Munich Crisis on September 28, 1938. He also passed on a request from the French Air Ministry regarding the possibility of securing aircraft, engines, and machine tools in the United States should war break out. Bullitt made the same points in a personal meeting with Roosevelt while visiting Washington on October 13, and the two further discussed the matter at Hyde Park on the following weekend.[31]

On November 14 Roosevelt met with Treasury Secretary Henry Morgenthau and a subordinate; high civilian and military officials from the War Department, including Chief of Staff General Craig, his deputy General Marshall, and General "Hap" Arnold of the Air Corps; one Navy representative; and Secretary of Commerce and WPA Administrator Harry Hopkins to discuss the European situation in general and the air situation in particular. The President customarily forbade subordinates from writing up his comments in such meetings, but on this occasion Morgenthau's deputy made a very full record. Drawing on contemporary estimates, Roosevelt said that France had 600 military aircraft of all types, Britain 1,500–2,200, Italy 2,000 first line planes, and Germany between 5,000 and 8,000 of the best type. The "recrudescence of German power" at Munich—implicitly a result of this imbalance—"had completely reoriented our own international relations; for the first time since the Holy Alliance in 1818 the United States now faced the possibility of an attack on the Atlantic side in both the Northern and Southern hemispheres," he continued. The situation demanded a huge air force, "so that we do not need to have a huge army to follow that air force," which would be "undesirable and politically out of the question." Evidently expecting Germany to defeat Britain and France, FDR added that in the next war, unlike in 1917, the United States would not have thirteen months in which to prepare forces. Nor was this all. "I am not sure now I am proud of what I wrote to Hitler in urging that he sit down around the table and make peace," he said. "That may have saved many, many lives now, but that may ultimately result in the loss of many times that number of lives later. . . . Had we had this summer 5000 planes and the capacity to produce 10000 per year, *even though I might have had to ask Congress for authority to sell or lend them to the countries in Europe,* Hitler would not have dared to take the stand he did."[32] Once again, FDR had predicted a key move—making American military equipment freely available to European powers—about two years before he put it into effect.

Laying out his goals in typically sweeping fashion and combining diplomatic, military, and domestic goals, Roosevelt said he would ask for a standing force of 20,000 military aircraft with annual productive capacity of 24,000, while expecting Congress to cut the request in half. He wanted both to be able to provide military aircraft to the British and French to put them in a stronger position for the next crisis and to create a strong deterrent force to keep potential enemies out of the Americas. Roosevelt wanted to divide the production between existing commercial aircraft firms and seven new plants to be built by the WPA, a project that would help the United States emerge from the recession. Five of those plants would be held in reserve for a future contingency. For the first time, he was talking specifically about using the same kind of huge, government-funded projects that the New Deal had set up to fight unemployment to deal with the world crisis. Roosevelt now faced the problem that bedeviled his administration from then right up until Pearl Harbor: how to create the enormous productive capacity that a war with the Axis would require in time to fight, even though Congress and the American people hoped to remain at peace.

Curiously enough, Roosevelt's plans met with some opposition in the War Department itself. Most of the generals, including Marshall and Arnold, were far more interested in building up a balanced Air Corps— including not only planes but the men necessary to fly and maintain them—than in increasing aircraft production by orders of magnitude. In subsequent weeks Roosevelt used press leaks to provoke some discussion of the need for a vastly increased Air Corps, but when he made a formal request to Congress on January 13, 1939, he followed the lead of the War Department and asked for just 3,000 new aircraft. Meanwhile, bypassing Secretary of War Woodring, he gave his Dutchess County neighbor and confidante Henry Morgenthau Jr., the Treasury Secretary, the right to conclude contracts for aircraft sales to Britain and France. From the middle of 1938 until the outbreak of war the British ordered 250 bombers and 650 training planes. The program began slowly, but it fostered increases in the capacity to produce aircraft and engines and was the germ of what became Lend-Lease exactly two years later.[33]

It did not take long for Roosevelt to share the broad outlines of his concerns and plans with the public. In a January 2, 1939, message to Congress asking for an additional half billion dollars for defense, $210 million to be spent in fiscal 1940, he stated that the United States would not, as in 1917, have an entire year to get ready should a new war break out, but disclaimed any thought of becoming involved once again in a European war. In his State of the Union address the very next day, he both returned to his theme of international lawlessness and drew a sharp contrast between the democracies of the New World and the dictatorships elsewhere—a line based on a difference of values. "Storms from abroad," he said, "directly challenge three institutions indispensable to Americans, now as always. The first is religion. It is the source of the other two—democracy and international good faith. . . . There comes a time in the affairs of men when they must prepare to defend, not their homes alone, but the tenets of faith and humanity on which their churches, their governments and their very civilization are founded. The defense of religion, of democracy and of good faith among nations is all the same fight. To save one we must now make up our minds to save all." He took comfort that the western hemisphere lived "under a common ideal of democratic government, . . . but the world has grown so small and weapons of attack so swift that no nation can be safe in its will to peace so long as any other powerful nation refuses to settle its grievances at the council table." The President was already warning Americans that they would have to defend their values and their way of life by force of arms.[34]

Americans generally shared most of these views. Very few Americans sympathized with the institutions or aims of Germany, Italy, or Japan in 1939, and virtually all Americans recognized the need to defend the western hemisphere against potential threats. Gallup polls, which had just become a regular feature of American political life, showed overwhelming dislike of Germany, sympathy for China in the Far East, and support for a stronger army, navy, and air force. Americans' attitudes toward a possible war, however, were far more complex. More than 60 percent of Americans consistently favored doing everything short of war to help the British and French beat the Germans if war broke out. But even though 62 percent believed that a victorious Germany would probably start a war with the United States after beating the British and French, only 17 percent favored sending the Army and Navy overseas to help them in the spring of 1939. Majorities also favored making a referendum mandatory before the United States entered a new war. In short, although fully aware that the totalitarian states posed a military threat, the majority of the American people, like their military planners and the President of the United States, seemed content to wait to meet it at the frontiers of the western hemisphere.[35]

This view was reaffirmed in controversies over neutrality in the first half of 1939. With war in Europe once again looking likely after the eruption of a new crisis over Poland in March, the administration sought changes in the Neutrality Act to allow it to sell arms to belligerents, and thereby spur American production. In March and in May, Democratic leaders in the Senate and House introduced bills to allow wartime purchases of arms by belligerents. Both bills would have continued to give the President the authority to declare war zones and ban American ships and passengers from traveling to them. Gallup polls showed 57 percent of respondents in support of arms sales, although 69 percent opposed lending money to finance them.[36]

Roosevelt's political capital, however, had sunk to a new low. Most Americans expected him not to run for a third term and a substantial majority told pollsters that they would not vote for him if he did. Several months of congressional deliberation ended in an embarrassing defeat. Although the House passed a bill on June 30 after Roosevelt had argued that it might spell the difference between victory and defeat for the British and French, the Senate Foreign Relations Committee absolutely refused to budge. Significantly, all through the debates in both houses, both sides focused on the issue of whether changes in the law would make U.S. involvement in a new war more or less likely, without emphasizing any American stake in any particular outcome. Both Congress and the public were more willing to take economic action against Japan in response to Tokyo's continuing attempts to subdue China, however, and on July 29, 1939, Roosevelt, responding to bipartisan pressure, announced that the United States would terminate its commercial treaty with Japan on January 26, 1940.[37]

On September 1, Germany—emboldened by the Nazi-Soviet Pact that Ribbentrop and Molotov had signed a week earlier—invaded Poland, and on September 3 Britain and France declared war on Germany. Addressing the United States in a brief fireside chat that evening, Roosevelt reaffirmed his devotion to peace and his determination to keep war away from the western hemisphere. On September 5 he officially proclaimed

American neutrality, and then, on September 8, he issued a proclamation that "a national emergency exists in connection with and to the extent necessary for the proper observance, safeguarding, and enforcing of the neutrality of the United States and the strengthening of our national defense within the limits of peacetime authorizations." He also summoned Congress for a special session to take up neutrality legislation once more.[38]

That was not all. It took less than two weeks for Roosevelt to begin to implement his idea of keeping belligerent ships—especially those of the Axis—out of the western Atlantic. During the first half of September the President and the administration made known that forty destroyers from the First World War were being recommissioned to take part in a "neutrality patrol," and Roosevelt in a September 15 press conference said that the patrol would extend as far east as "necessary." In fact he had ordered the Atlantic squadron to report on the movement of all belligerent ships out to two hundred miles. In late September he queried CNO Admiral Stark about patrolling the whole area west of longitude 60° west, from between Nova Scotia and Newfoundland down to British Guiana, two hundred miles east of Bermuda. Although Stark immediately protested that the Navy lacked the necessary ships and planes, Roosevelt insisted on its doing what it could, and by October American ships were reporting on the movement of belligerent ships and thereby helping British and French warships to intercept a number of Axis vessels. The Navy was clearly going to be the President's preferred personal instrument of strategy, designed to quarantine as much of the western hemisphere as possible and help the Anglo-French blockade of Germany by making reports.[39]

Roosevelt's address to Congress on the neutrality question on September 22, 1939, was the longest and most intricate speech he had yet made on issues of foreign policy. After reviewing his most important statements on the world crisis since early 1938, he called for a return to the observance of long-standing international law, thus allowing the United States once again to trade with the belligerents. Only once before, he pointed out, during the Napoleonic Wars, had the United States abandoned such policies with the Embargo and Nonintercourse Acts, and these had ruined American commerce and eventually led to a war that culminated in the invasion of North America and the burning of Washington, DC. Current laws, he noted, would allow the shipments of raw materials to belligerents, and the production of war material in the United States would benefit our industry and—a critical point—strengthen our own defenses as well. He specifically offered to restrict or ban travel by Americans or American ships into war zones and loans to belligerents. And while frequently reiterating his and his countrymen's devotion to peace, he closed with a warning of a long and difficult period ahead, and once again defined the stakes in world-historical terms. "Darker periods may lie ahead," he said, thanks to "the forces which assault the foundations of civilization," and the United States had more than a "selfish interest" in the war. "Destiny first made us, with our sister nations on this Hemisphere, joint heirs of European culture," he said. "Fate seems now to compel us to assume the task of helping to maintain in the Western world a citadel wherein that civilization may be kept alive"—an echo of his 1936 convention acceptance speech. "In a period when it is sometimes said that free discussion is no longer compatible with national safety, may you by your deeds show the world that we of the United States are one people, of one mind, one spirit, one clear resolution, walking before God in the light of the living."[40]

Although amendments to allow for "cash-and-carry" sales of arms to belligerents eventually passed both houses in late October and early November by votes of 63–30 in the Senate and 243–181 in the House, the debate was long and difficult, with the administration's supporters once again insisting over and over that they regarded this change as the best way of keeping the United States out of war. The President himself, in a radio address on October 26, insisted very accurately that "no person in any responsible place in the national administration in Washington, or in any State Government, or in any city Government, or in any county Government, has ever suggested in any shape, manner or form the remotest possibility of sending the boys of American mothers to fight on the battlefields of Europe. That is why I label that argument a shameless and dishonest fake." None of the war plans under active preparation in Washington now foresaw the dispatch of any Americans beyond the frontiers of the western hemisphere.[41]

The war now underway was a European, not a world war, largely because of the extraordinary diplomatic coup that had preceded it, the Nazi-Soviet Pact. Stalin had become an ally of Hitler's, collaborated in the occupation and destruction of the Polish state during September 1939, and secured Hitler's permission to attack Finland (which he did in December), occupy the Baltic states, and secure the Rumanian province of Bessarabia. In return he provided food and oil that enabled Hitler to prepare new offensives in the West. The Nazi-Soviet Pact had led to the collapse of talks for a German-Italian-Japanese alliance against France, Britain, and the Soviet Union, and indeed, Italy at the last moment had decided not to join the European war. Across the Atlantic the war had transformed the political situation in the United States. Before September 1, substantial majorities had told the Gallup pollsters that they did not expect FDR to seek a third term and that they would vote against him if he did. By November 5, 1939, 57 percent of respondents thought FDR would run for a third term, 56 percent expected him to win it, and other polls showed Roosevelt leading Thomas E. Dewey of New York, the leading Republican prospect, in trial heats.[42]

Roosevelt, however, remained almost powerless to affect the course of events in Europe. He explained to Assistant Secretary of State Sumner Welles in early January that he feared either that Hitler would win the war and immediately pose a danger to the United States, or that the Allies would win after a long, disastrous, drawn-out struggle, and he dispatched Welles to visit the major European capitals to investigate the chances of peace. Others were even less optimistic. Cordell Hull had predicted the defeat of France and Britain on September 2, 1939, and his view was shared by Joseph P. Kennedy, whom Roosevelt had sent to London as Ambassador in 1938. The American people disagreed. On March 31, 1940, a Gallup poll announced that 84 percent of respondents expected the British and French to win. A month earlier, 77 percent had rejected American entry into the war even to save the British and French from defeat. Substantial majorities not only favored increases in the Army and Navy but expressed willingness to pay higher taxes to make them possible. They were prepared if necessary to fight Germany and Japan, but they had no intention of resuming the role the United States had played in the First World War. The only way the United States seemed likely to become involved in the war was if the British and French were defeated.[43]

On April 1, 1940, the Pacific Fleet left its base in San Diego for six weeks of maneuvers around Hawaii. Press reports explained that the Navy was exploring the problem of establishing a defense perimeter from the Aleutians to Hawaii. This reflected the existing war plan for a conflict against Germany, Italy, and Japan. By the time the fleet exercise was finished in mid-May, it seemed that exactly that situation was indeed coming to pass. Germany had occupied Holland and Belgium and was winning the battle of France. Within a few more weeks the British had evacuated the continent and appeared to face an imminent invasion. The Japanese had begun planning new advances of their own. The contingency that Roosevelt had asked military and naval planners to provide for in 1938—a war against the Axis, fought without European allies—might come to pass within a few more months. President Roosevelt directed that the fleet remain at Pearl Harbor.[44]

At least from 1937 onward, Roosevelt had seen the aggressor nations of Japan, Germany, and Italy as threats to Western civilization. He had tried and failed to secure British help in checking the Japanese at a relatively low cost, but after Munich, he clearly had begun preparing for an Axis victory in Europe and ordering his subordinates to do the same. Now the worst was happening. The time had come to begin implementing the plans laid during the last two years, to arm in order to meet frightening new contingencies, and to lay the political basis for war.

CHAPTER 2

Arms and Politics, May–August 1940

THE NAZI TRIUMPHS IN EUROPE, CULMINATING IN HITLER'S ARMISTICE
with a new French government on June 22, ushered in a summer of frantic activity in the United States. Nearly every informed observer, including Franklin Roosevelt, expected a successful German invasion of Great
Britain before the fall. New Japanese aggression in the Pacific and Axis
moves into the western hemisphere might immediately follow. Roosevelt,
meanwhile, had to respond to a series of impassioned pleas for help from
Winston Churchill, who wanted him to enter the conflict at once, even
though the United States had very little help to offer. The men and machines necessary for the defense of the western hemisphere had to be
assembled as soon as possible. And at the very same time, FDR faced
perhaps the most critical decision of his presidency: whether or not to
seek an unprecedented third term in office.

The threat of an Axis victory in Europe and Japanese aggression in
Asia created an overwhelming consensus in the United States for a massive arms program. During the late spring and early summer of 1940, Congress acceded to Roosevelt's request for a vastly expanded air force, passed
a law that nearly doubled the size of the Navy during the next six years or
so, and even instituted an unprecedented peacetime draft. While almost
no Americans called for immediate intervention to try to save Great Britain, nearly all agreed on the need to prepare for hemispheric defense.

Broadening his political base to help cope with the world crisis,
Roosevelt helped split the Republican Party by appointing two leading

Republicans, former Secretary of State Henry L. Stimson and 1936 vice presidential candidate Frank Knox, to head the War and Navy departments. He was gratified in June when the Republican Party chose Wendell Willkie, who also supported vigorous rearmament and aid to Britain, as its presidential candidate, rather than an isolationist. In July, after squeezing every ounce of drama out of the situation that he could, he accepted his party's nomination for the third term. And in the next month he decided to give Churchill fifty destroyers, which the Prime Minister claimed he had to have to meet the German threat—but only after securing a chain of U.S. bases in British possessions in the western Atlantic and Caribbean regions that would give the United States a more advanced defense line if, as so many expected, the British were to fall.

Forced to prepare for the immediate defense of the western hemisphere against vastly larger forces than had hitherto been imagined, the government of the United States needed significantly to expand the Navy, and Air Force, and the Army, make new war plans, and begin a drastic expansion of war production with major implications for the civilian economy. The nation lacked the wherewithal to do much to affect the course of events in France, but the President, his military planners, and the press reacted with lightning speed. The great national emergency that FDR had foretold was now at hand.

On May 16, Roosevelt asked Congress for an immediate appropriation of an additional $898 million for the Army and Navy, an increase of 50 percent from what he had asked for in January and a sum equal to about one-eighth of the entire federal budget. Implicitly acknowledging the possibility of an imminent Axis victory in Europe, the President discussed possible air attacks on the United States and the rest of the western hemisphere from bases in Greenland, the Azores, Bermuda, the West Indies, and the Cape Verde Islands, only 1,500 miles from Brazil. Once established in Brazil, he noted, an unnamed hostile power would be only one or two stops away from the Panama Canal. Stressing the possible threat from the air, he called in particular for an Air Force of 50,000 planes and for productive capacity to build 50,000 planes annually—figures far in excess of anything even contemplated by the Air Corps at that time. The massive proposal shows that Roosevelt anticipated an all-out struggle with hostile powers even then, and that he was determined to take advantage of American industrial might to play a decisive role in it.[1]

Former Secretary of State Henry L. Stimson immediately wrote FDR conveying his "most hearty sympathy and approval" for the message to Congress and adding that he was "much gratified to see what appears to be the evidence of a truly united national feeling springing up all over the country." "That kind of a note helps to keep a fellow going," FDR replied on May 28, but the President was less sanguine about American opinion. "When I read Lindbergh's speech," he said, "I felt that it could not have been better put if it had been written by Goebbels himself." Aviator Charles A. Lindbergh on May 19 had argued that the only danger to America came from its own "quarreling and meddling" with affairs abroad and called for an end to "this hysterical chatter of calamity and invasion." "What a pity that this youngster has completely abandoned his belief in our form of government and has accepted Nazi methods because apparently they are efficient," Roosevelt wrote. The President spoke more bluntly to Treasury Secretary Morgenthau the next day. "If I should die tomorrow," he said, "I want you to know this. I am absolutely convinced that Lindbergh is a Nazi."[2]

Testifying before a Senate Appropriations subcommittee on May 30, Army Chief of Staff General Marshall called for the immediate expansion of the Army to its authorized peacetime strength of 200,000 men and anticipated that 400,000 might be needed "before we finish with this business of preparing for emergencies short of full mobilization." Following a suggestion from Treasury Secretary Morgenthau, who was for the time being the most important cabinet member on issues relating to preparedness, Roosevelt had directed that Marshall, not his civilian superiors in the War Department, handle the testimony because Republicans and antiadministration Democrats trusted his judgment. The General was about to show that the President, the Congress, and the American people could always expect a blunt statement of his opinion of what the situation called for.[3]

Two years older than the President, Marshall had grown up in Uniontown, Pennsylvania, in the southwest corner of that newly industrial state. His father, a successful producer of coke, had lost most of his money in land speculation when Marshall was nine—a typical casualty of the unstable economy of the Gilded Age—and his region was rocked in the 1880s and 1890s by coal miners' strikes, all of them successfully repressed by the mine owners with the help of hired deputies and militia. Young George Marshall's favorite school subject was history, and he dreamed of being a soldier. Coming from a Democratic family in a Republican district and state, he had little hope of an appointment to West Point, and went instead to the Virginia Military Institute (VMI) in 1897. There he was introduced to the drama of the Civil War from the Virginian point of view, and endured a discipline even harsher than what Franklin Roosevelt encountered at Groton at the same time. The Superintendent, a one-time Confederate general named Shipp, wanted his school to guide his cadets "to habits of obedience, self-denial, and self restraint; to respect for lawful authority, and to that self-respect which the consciousness of duty well done carries with it." Marshall rose to become First Captain, the cadet leader of his class, and his college years coincided with the United States' entry onto the world stage as an imperial power in the Spanish-American War and the subsequent Philippine insurrection. The war in Cuba revealed the Army he intended to enter to be woefully unorganized and incapable of rapidly assembling the supplies and equipment needed even for a "splendid little war."[4]

So small was the Army even in the wake of this war that upon his graduation from VMI in 1901, Marshall managed to secure permission to take an examination for a commission only with the help of well-connected friends who got him an introduction to President McKinley. For most of the first thirty-eight years of his career, the Army was an extraordinarily small organization that made up for its lack of resources with intense intellectual preparation designed to train leaders to handle any contingency. The Command and General Staff College at Leavenworth, Kansas, where Marshall studied in 1906–1908 and taught from 1908 to 1910, sought to "make junior officers go through a process in which they alone must make decisions or make recommendations on which decisions could be based" by studying military history and literally refighting on paper the major campaigns of the Civil War.

Marshall served as a high-ranking staff officer in the First World War, learning firsthand about the intricacies of modern warfare and the problems of dealing with allies. From 1928 to 1932 he was the head of the Infantry School at Fort Benning, where an astonishing number of the major commanders of the Second World War came under his influence. Not until 1936, however, did he become a Brigadier General. Within three years he had become Deputy Chief of Staff and then, on September

1, 1939—the day Hitler attacked Poland—the Chief of Staff and senior officer in the U.S. Army.[5]

Now, less than eight months later, Marshall used his leadership skills and intellectual training to find a way through the world crisis. Unlike their children and grandchildren, leaders from Marshall and FDR's Missionary generation (born 1863–1883) did not ask their subordinates for widely differing options from which to choose or forge a compromise. They expected those who worked for them to say exactly what they thought needed to be done, and that is what they did. On May 22, Marshall helped Major Matthew Ridgway, the Latin American specialist in the Army War Plans Division, draft a two-page memo, "National Strategic Decisions," to take to the White House the next day. Ridgway, a Marshall favorite, had been promoted exactly once since serving with Marshall as a captain in China in the mid-1920s. This was the typical fate of the professional Army officers of the interwar period, including others such as Dwight Eisenhower and Omar Bradley, who had the most limited opportunities for either command or promotion and evidently spent a great deal of their free time reading and reflecting on their profession. Marshall had kept his own list of promising officers, many of whom, led by Eisenhower, he jumped in rank when the war came. During the fifteen years after 1940, Ridgway became the commander of an airborne division and corps, Supreme Commander in the Far East in 1951, NATO Commander, and Army Chief of Staff.

Marshall and Ridgway's memo began by listing four immediately possible contingencies: a Nazi-inspired revolution in Brazil, trouble in Mexico, Japanese attacks on U.S. interests in the Far East, and "decisive allied defeat, followed by German aggression in the Western Hemisphere. . . . There should be an immediate decision," it continued bluntly, "as to what major military operations we must be prepared to conduct." Lacking forces for either the Far East or Europe, the United States for at least a year would have to content itself with "offensive-defensive operations in defense of the Western Hemisphere and of our own vital interests," to include "possible protective occupation of European possessions in Western Hemisphere" and the defense of U.S. Pacific territory "east of the 180th Meridian," that is, *not* to include the Philippines. "Intelligent, practical planning, and later successful action," the memo concluded forthrightly, "require an early decision regarding these matters: 1st—As to what we are *not* going to do, 2d—As to what we *must prepare* to do." At the White House that very afternoon with FDR and his naval counter-part Admiral Stark and in a talk with Undersecretary of State Sumner Welles the next morning, Marshall found them all "in general agree-ment," convinced that the United States had to avoid involvement with Japan, and focused on South America, to which they planned to dispatch several cruisers with Marines aboard to react if necessary to revolutions in certain capitals.[6]

Naval planners were thinking along similar lines, already anticipat-ing the probable defeat of France, the possible entry into the war of both Italy and Spain, and, most catastrophically, the possible loss of the Brit-ish Navy to the Germans. The mathematics of these contingencies were terrifying. Of the fifteen U.S. battleships, only three of the oldest type were now stationed in the Atlantic. Germany had already laid down two modern battleships, the *Tirpitz* and the *Bismarck*, and had four smaller battleships superior to any American ship in the Atlantic already at sea. Italy had two modern battleships afloat and two under construction, as well as four older types more than a match for the heaviest American cruisers. To these now had to be added three up-to-date French battle-ships and two more nearly as formidable—and, potentially, twelve more British battleships, three British battle cruisers, and five new British battleships under construction. The United States, as columnists in the press were now arguing, would need a whole new Navy to cope with this threat if both Britain and France fell, and it would take years to build.

To forestall the impending catastrophe, naval planners even con-templated immediate U.S. entry into the war, but that possibility was not followed up. The Navy also wanted to start planning the occupation of European and British possessions in the western hemisphere. But in a portent of things to come, the Navy War Plans Division successfully objected to any major movement of ships from the Pacific Fleet, now in Hawaii, into the Atlantic. Officially Captain R. K. Turner of that division opposed this move because he thought the fleet was exerting a stabilizing influence in the Pacific and restraining the Japanese, who could easily be tempted by the fall of the Netherlands and France and the possible fall of Britain to move into their possessions in Southeast Asia. Beyond that, the Navy did not want to abandon its decades-old mission of executing War Plan Orange against the Japanese until forced to do so by a British collapse.[7]

On May 31, 1940, while British troops were evacuating Dunkirk, the Joint Planning Committee submitted a new war plan, Rainbow 4, to the Joint Board, based on the worst-case scenarios that had now come so close to life. "Even the destruction of the British and French Fleets," the Committee wrote, "will afford Germany and Italy naval freedom of action in the Atlantic. The surrender of the main British and French naval units will eventually afford Germany and Italy naval equality or superiority with respect to the United States fleet." They estimated that the Axis would need at least six months to prepare captured fleets for participation in operations. In order to occupy the positions specified by the new war plan in time, the United States would have to mobilize and activate the National Guard as soon as the British and French fleets surrendered. Only then, apparently, would the bulk of the U.S. Fleet move to the Atlantic.

The plan assumed that Germany and Italy, after defeating Britain and France as well as Belgium and Holland, would immediately announce their intention to occupy the colonial possessions of all those powers, and would indeed at an early date secure Iceland in the Atlantic; Senegal, Gambia, French Guinea, and Sierra Leone in West Africa; and Syria, Lebanon, Palestine, and Egypt in the eastern Mediterranean. They did not assume that Japan would immediately join the war and, indeed, called for every effort to adjust diplomatic differences with Japan, but did not make any plans to defend anything west of Alaska and Hawaii and assumed the Japanese might seize the Philippines. They assumed that Canada would declare its independence, occupy Newfoundland and Labrador (in 1940 still British possessions), and fight in alliance with the United States. They hoped that U.S. mobilization, "particularly in naval, air and mechanized forces," would eventually allow the United States to undertake operations in the western Pacific, the eastern Atlantic, and even in West Africa, allowing the United States "to impose terms favorable to itself in the eventual peace settlement," but not, evidently, to secure the complete defeat of the Axis powers.

Following the outline of Ridgway's memorandum, the plan specified nine joint tasks, beginning with the seizure of British, French, Dutch, and Danish possessions in the western hemisphere, from Greenland to the Caribbean, as well as several of their Pacific island groups. Other tasks included garrisons around the Panama Canal; stationing the major portion of the U.S. Fleet in the Caribbean to control the western Atlantic;

occupying northeastern Brazil; defending communications between the
West Coast and Oahu; denying the Axis and Japan bases in western
South America; and intervening as necessary to remove Axis forces or
pro-Axis governments in any of the major governments in Latin America. Overseas tasks were deferred until more forces were available. The
Joint Board approved the plan exactly a week later on June 7, and Roosevelt himself approved it two months later, in August. It remained the
most current approved Rainbow plan for many months. No plan to try to
save the British Isles was ever commissioned or approved by the Joint
Board.[8]

Roosevelt, meanwhile, was attacking another critical problem, war
production. A War Industries Board had handled the far more limited
industrial mobilization required by the First World War, and everyone
recognized that something similar would be needed now. Roosevelt had
made a false start in this direction in August 1939, when world war, as
opposed to European war, seemed a fairly likely prospect, by establishing
a War Resources Board chaired by Edward Stettinius, the Chairman of
the Board of U.S. Steel. The Board became controversial after the President reportedly told it that the nation might well be at war by the middle
of the winter, however, and dissolved itself after making a few recommendations in October. Evidently burned by this experience, Roosevelt
on May 13 told Morgenthau, Secretary of War Woodring, and others that
the nation did not need any new machinery to promote preparedness,
but General Marshall, who never hesitated to speak his mind, dissented
strongly. Stating a deeply held managerial principle among the Missionary generation, Marshall insisted that preparedness could go forward
only if one person were in charge. With Morgenthau in his corner he evidently persuaded Roosevelt that he was right—but as it turned out, Roosevelt left himself in charge of the new machinery.[9]

On Sunday evening, May 26, Roosevelt addressed the nation in a
fireside chat. As usual, he surveyed the problem before the nation, described the measures being taken to meet it, confidently forecast success,
and put the matter into the broadest possible historical context. Many
Americans, he said, had persuaded themselves for reasons ranging from
false confidence to blind partisanship that the European war was of no
concern, but now found themselves in a panic. "I did not share those illusions," he continued. "I do not share these fears." He reviewed what his
administration had already done to improve the national defense, but

argued that modern war obviously required both more and better weapons and defined a large government role to secure them. "The Government of the United States," he said, "stands ready to advance the necessary money to help provide for the enlargement of factories, the establishment of new plants, the employment of thousands of necessary workers, the development of new sources of supply for the hundreds of raw materials required, the development of quick mass transportation of supplies. . . . We are calling on men now engaged in private industry to help us in carrying out this program, and you will hear more of this in detail in the next few days." Yet he insisted that the national emergency would mean no increase in working hours or decrease in wages or collective bargaining rights for America's workers. He also warned against "fifth columnists"—internal subversives who might try to use strikes or sabotage to slow production down. He concluded with another attempt to put the news of the day into a world-historical context. "For more than three centuries we Americans have been building on this continent a free society, a society in which the promise of the human spirit may find fulfillment. . . . It is this that we must continue to build—this that we must continue to defend. It is the task of our generation, yours and mine. But we build and defend not for our generation alone. We defend the foundations laid down by our fathers. We build a life for generations yet unborn. We defend and we build a way of life, not for America alone, but for all mankind." Led by Roosevelt, the Missionary generation was now pursuing its dream of action on behalf of moral values on a world scale.[10]

On May 28, Roosevelt announced the new membership of the Advisory Commission to the Council of National Defense. The Council, which dated from the First World War, was an informal body of six cabinet members. The Advisory Commission, which quickly became known as the Defense Commission, was the first of three different bodies, all composed largely of the same personnel, that successively oversaw war production for the next eighteen months, until a fourth body, the War Production Board, took over after Pearl Harbor. The Defense Commission included William S. Knudsen, the Chairman of the Board of the automotive giant General Motors, responsible for industrial production; Edward Stettinius, the thirty-nine-year-old boy wonder chairman of U.S. Steel, for industrial raw materials; Sidney Hillman, the head of the Amalgamated Clothing Workers' Union, for labor affairs; economist Leon Henderson, to watch over prices; Chester Davis, a former head of the

Agricultural Adjustment Administration, to assess and help fulfill requirements for agriculture; political scientist Harriet Elliott, for consumer interests; and railroad man Ralph Budd, for transportation. A month later the Commission added Donald Nelson of Sears, Roebuck as Coordinator of National Defense Purchases. Following another First World War precedent, the members of the Defense Commission—several of them very wealthy—served for a dollar a year plus per diem or, as in Knudsen's case, for nothing at all. They received the authority to hire a large staff and soon secured space in a new building that had been designed to house the Social Security Administration. Knudsen, who as Chairman of the Board of GM knew as much as anyone about the requirements of sustained, large-scale production, made an immediate and vital contribution by telling the War Department on June 11 that he had to know how many munitions the nation needed and when it had to have them.

Roosevelt decreed that the Defense Commission would report directly to him, not to the Advisory Council, but he refused to designate a single member as chairman because he wanted to retain ultimate decision-making power for himself. The reason, in all probability, was that only he could make some of the most critical decisions regarding the scope and objectives of the U.S. war effort—and even he was not ready to make them.[11]

Publicly the President remained calm, reassuring, and as usual, very much in tune with the electorate. In mid-May, 80 to 93 percent of respondents to Gallup polls agreed that the United States should increase the size of its clearly inadequate armed forces, opposed declaring war on Germany, and favored war to keep the Axis out of range of the Panama Canal. During the second half of May, 79 percent thought FDR had done a good job of handling the war crisis in Europe and 57 percent said they would vote for him for a third term. Privately, however, the President expressed doubts, faced pressures, and contemplated contingencies of which the public was unaware.

As early as May 15, Prime Minister Churchill, with whom FDR had established direct contact back in September when Churchill became First Lord of the Admiralty, cabled Roosevelt anticipating the French defeat and pleading desperately both for aid and for possible American entry into the war. He foresaw air and paratroop attacks on the British Isles and promised that Britain would if necessary fight on alone even if, as he expected, Mussolini entered the war on Hitler's side. "But I trust you realize, Mr. President," he continued, "that the voice and force of the United States may count for nothing if they are withheld too long"—Britain might succumb to "a completely Nazified Europe." He asked Roosevelt to proclaim nonbelligerency (the status then claimed by Mussolini) and to provide forty to fifty "of your older destroyers," new types of aircraft, ammunition, and steel. Five days later he warned that while he would never surrender the British Fleet, another government might come in and do so. Roosevelt, however, did not think that any of this was likely to have a decisive effect, and he also had to deal with the legalities of the situation and the attitudes of the War Department. Congress had now required that the War and Navy departments certify any surplus equipment sold to a foreign power as unnecessary to the United States, and General Marshall, who took his legal responsibilities very seriously, did not believe in particular that the United States had any new aircraft to spare. Roosevelt immediately explained this problem to Churchill, but by June 7 he had found a way to get some surplus rifles and ammunition to the British, by declaring them surplus, selling them to private manufacturers, and allowing their resale.[12]

The President took another public step forward on June 10 in a commencement address at the University of Virginia. Addressing some of the young people who might be called on to fight, he for the first time explicitly compared the current crisis to the other critical moments in American history. As in the time of the Revolution and the "War Between the States," he said, "today the young men and the young women of America ask themselves with earnestness and with deep concern this same question: 'What is to become of the country we know?' . . . They ask, not only what the future holds for this Republic, but what the future holds for all peoples and all nations that have been living under democratic forms of Government—under the free institutions of a free people. Overwhelmingly we, as a nation—and this applies to all the other American nations—are convinced that military and naval victory for the gods of force and hate would endanger the institutions of democracy in the western world, and that equally, therefore, the whole of our sympathies lies with those nations that are giving their life blood in combat against these forces." He concluded with a violent attack on Mussolini's decision, announced that very day, to enter the war, and with a pledge to "extend to the opponents of force the material resources of this nation."[13]

Secret exchanges with Churchill and French Premier Paul Reynaud now raised the issue of whether the United States might help France, Britain, or both of them carry on the war outside of Europe. In a series of telegrams on June 12–14, Churchill and Roosevelt agreed that it was essential to keep the fleet of the collapsing French out of German hands, and Roosevelt specifically referred to the possibility of the British and French fleets carrying on the struggle from North Africa and the Americas, as Churchill had already promised to do, if necessary, in a magnificent speech to the House of Commons on June 4. On June 15 Churchill pleaded again that the United States enter the war, claiming that this might save France. Roosevelt refused, however, to publish his message to Reynaud advocating further resistance or to intervene directly in the conflict. Yet he took the possibility sufficiently seriously to set informal military planning in motion for it.[14]

In the midst of these exchanges, on June 13, Roosevelt received the intelligence chiefs of the Army and Navy in his office and asked them to evaluate a situation that might arise during the fall and winter of 1940: that Britain and the British Empire would remain intact; that France would be occupied while the French government continued to resist from its colonies in North Africa; that the United States would have joined the war, albeit with naval and air forces only, and would be shipping material to Britain and Morocco; and that the British, French, and U.S. navies would still control the Atlantic, the Persian Gulf, and "a precarious hold" on the western Mediterranean. The Soviet Union and Japan, he assumed, would remain neutral. The intelligence chiefs passed the request on to their War Plans divisions, and Colonel Clark and Captain Moore now drafted a reply that they presented to Marshall and Stark on June 26, four days after France had signed an armistice with Germany. The President, they concluded, had been much too optimistic. They did not believe that the British, faced with German bases in the Low Countries, France, Denmark, and Norway, would be able to successfully defend the British Isles against a determined attack from the German Air Force, which they mistakenly believed to be far superior to the British, nor did they think that the French government and Army would be able to hold North Africa, lacking any sources of supply. They also doubted that Japan and the Soviet Union would stay out of the war. Their most devastating conclusions, however, concerned a possible American role.

"Participation in the war, with the naval and air forces of the United States, to prevent the defeat of France and Great Britain," they wrote, "cannot be sufficiently timely." The United States had to keep most of its effective destroyers with the fleet; the older ones (which Churchill had already asked for) lacked antiaircraft guns and antisubmarine listening devices. The United States could not spare aircraft to send to Europe since its trained personnel were now trying to form new units. Immediate entry of the United States would, they believed, quickly leave it as the lone belligerent against the totalitarian powers, and the United States should avoid war until it was more adequately prepared. U.S. entry into the war would also unleash German subversive activities in Latin America, and might easily bring in the Japanese as well.[15]

General Marshall and Admiral Stark put together their own appreciation, "Basis for Immediate Decisions Concerning the National Defense," by Friday, June 22, and talked it over with the President when he returned from one of his monthly weekends in Hyde Park on Monday, June 24. They agreed in principle that the "major part" of the U.S. Fleet would move to the Atlantic if Germany secured the French Fleet. Marshall and Stark definitely recommended against any further shipments of arms to Britain on the grounds that they would weaken the United States without helping the British, and opposed any new British orders for equipment from the United States. "In general, yes," FDR replied, but added that the Army and Navy should continue to assess what equipment might be provided and that commercial orders "would be accepted as long as materiel could be employed to block Germany and 'without seriously retarding' Army and Navy procurement." The President also agreed to plan for the U.S. occupation of British, French, and Dutch possessions in the western hemisphere, and approved possible agreements to occupy strategic positions in Latin America. Marshall and Stark also called for an immediate selective service act, followed by complete naval and military mobilization, but FDR changed "complete" to "progressive" and favored only one year of post–high school service, either in the Army or Navy, or in war production, or in the Civilian Concentration Corps. The American leadership was preparing the implementation of Rainbow 4, rather than any serious attempt to save the British. This decision, as Roosevelt realized himself, paralleled a decision that Churchill made in the latter stages of the Battle of France to withhold most of the RAF to try to save the British Isles from invasion, rather than commit it to a losing battle on the continent.[16]

While Washington prepared for hemispheric defense, the sense of crisis in the United States had tragic effects on another aspect of foreign policy, the U.S. attitude toward refugees. Hitler's conquest of Western Europe increased the potential refugee flow by orders of magnitude, including Jews, anti-Nazi Germans who had long since fled their homeland, and leftists of all kinds. Roosevelt in October 1939 had written a memo himself warning of the flood of Jewish and Christian refugees that would issue from Europe when the war was over. But the American response suffered not only from the strict U.S. immigration policies, but from the belief that German "fifth columnists" or spies had played a key role in the fall of Norway, Belgium, and France. Communists, who had indeed worked to undermine the Allied war effort since the Nazi-Soviet Pact, were particularly suspect, but even Jewish refugees, many thought, could be blackmailed into helping the German government by threatening relatives still at home. Although Roosevelt administration opinion split on these questions, those opposed on principle to taking in more refugees—led by Breckinridge Long, a Democratic politician from Missouri who had served as Ambassador to Italy and was now an Assistant Secretary of State—prevailed. Long insisted in telegrams to missions in Europe on the strictest possible conditions for visas to the United States, and the number of refugees entering the country fell during the next eighteen months. Roosevelt, who had shown so much sympathy for refugees before the war began, did nothing to reverse the policy, and he referred frequently in his speeches to the dangers of domestic fifth columnists as well.[17]

No naval planner kept a closer track of the naval balance of power than Franklin Roosevelt, who received a monthly tally of the strength of the world's fleets from the Navy Department. Faced with the possibility of the fall of France and Britain, the administration in June and July pushed through perhaps the single most dramatic expansion of U.S. military power in the country's history—one that ultimately changed the course of the Second World War.

Since the summer of 1939 the planners in the Navy's War Plans Division had been reassessing the Navy's future needs and had finally decided to build a Navy not only qualitatively better but also numerically

larger than that specified by the 1922 and 1930 naval arms control treaties. Back in October 1939, a Navy planner had noted that to maintain
the 5–3 ratio against the Japanese while at the same time equaling existing German and Italian programs—a minimum requirement to meet the
tasks already outlined in Rainbow 1—would require the construction of
an additional 1.348 million tons of warships, costing $4.3 billion—nearly
a doubling of the current tonnage of 1.557 million tons. But when Admiral Stark had appeared before the Senate Naval Affairs Committee on
April 15, 1940, he asked for only a 25 percent increase. Roosevelt himself,
in a moment of characteristic opacity on May 14, described a "two-ocean
Navy" as "an entirely outmoded conception of naval defense" in a press
conference. Still, the program that the administration was shepherding
through Congress in May and June expanded the U.S. battleship fleet
from fifteen to twenty-six over the next four years.[18]

Suddenly, on June 12—with France collapsing and Britain under
attack—the Chairmen of the House and Senate Naval Affairs Committees, Carl Vinson of Georgia and David Walsh of Massachusetts, introduced another huge expansion at the administration's request, to include
3 additional aircraft carriers, 12 new cruisers, 41 destroyers, and 28 submarines. On June 17 the Navy's General Board weighed in, demanding
the immediate introduction of the program they had discussed in the
previous fall. Setting a maximum objective of the defense of one ocean
and offensive action in the other against a victorious coalition of Germany, Italy, and Japan, they asked for totals of 32 battleships, 15 aircraft
carriers, 87 cruisers, and 373 destroyers—roughly a doubling of currently
projected strength.[19]

On July 1, the General Board of the Navy wrote the new Secretary of
the Navy, Frank Knox, that "the emergency now faced is one of worldwide dimensions which menaces every foreign policy of the United States,
our national interest and welfare and, possibly even, our political concepts and form of government. . . . Naturally the Navy is not at present
ready to meet an emergency of the worldwide dimensions indicated
above." Within less than two weeks, on the eve of the Republican Party's
national convention, a bill based on the General Board's proposals passed
the House almost unanimously. The Senate Committee took up the bill
in the first week of July, hearing only two witnesses, and the full Senate
passed it, again with almost no debate, by July 11. By that time the total
cost of the new Navy, which was projected to be completed by 1946–1947,

was estimated at $10 billion, well in excess of the entire original projected federal budget for fiscal 1941.[20]

The rapid passage of this extraordinary measure, virtually without dissent, confirms once again that nearly all Americans and their representatives believed in doing whatever was necessary to defend the western hemisphere. They were indeed preparing to live in a world of superstates similar to that forecast years later by Orwell in *1984*, with the Germans and Italians supreme in Europe, the Japanese in Asia, and the United States in the western hemisphere. Although both parties were bitterly divided over possible involvement in the war in Europe, almost no one questioned the need for a Navy large enough to keep all hostile forces from U.S. shores. Yet the new ships would not be ready for three years and more. One potential catastrophe was at least postponed when France and Germany reached an armistice agreement on June 22. Although the Germans occupied the northern 60 percent of French territory, including the entire Atlantic coastline, they allowed the French government to continue to function in southern France and in North Africa and made no attempt to secure the French Fleet, now mostly in ports on both sides of the Mediterranean. That was not enough to satisfy Churchill, who had pleaded with the French government to send its heavy ships overseas and now demanded that it do so. When the new Vichy government refused, Churchill on July 3 ordered a naval attack on French ships at Mers-El-Kebir, near Oran, killing over a thousand French sailors and putting one French battleship and two smaller craft out of action.

While one disaster followed the next in Europe, another critical American question remained to be resolved: the political future of Franklin D. Roosevelt. The greatest international crisis since the Napoleonic Wars coincided with the possibility that a sitting President might for the first time be nominated for a third term in office. That possibility had dominated political news coverage throughout the spring.

Although no President had ever served more than eight years, several had unsuccessfully challenged the two-term tradition established by Washington and Jefferson. Ulysses S. Grant had nearly been nominated yet again by the Republican Party in 1880 after a four-year retirement, and Theodore Roosevelt had formed his own party in 1912 after losing a bitter renomination fight to his successor William Howard Taft. Woodrow Wilson, ill and delusional, had dreamed of a third term early in 1920, but the idea had gone nowhere. The idea that FDR might try again had emerged seriously during 1939, pushed mainly by New Dealers who feared that the party would nominate a conservative Democrat such as Vice President John Nance Garner or Postmaster General Jim Farley in 1940 if he did not run. One such, Secretary of the Interior and Public Works Administrator Harold Ickes, made this case in *Look* magazine early in June 1939. Roosevelt immediately declined comment on the article, but he thanked Ickes for it privately later that month, suggesting that the fear of his candidacy would keep "reactionary Democrats who hate my guts" in line for the next year.[21] No left-wing administration figure seemed to command enough support to win the nomination. Ickes, the "Old Curmudgeon," was a lifelong Republican and temperamentally unsuited to running for office; Harry Hopkins, the WPA Administrator, was both seriously ill and tremendously controversial; and Henry Wallace, the Secretary of Agriculture, was something of a visionary whose rhetorical flights disturbed many Americans. After Ickes's article appeared many liberal Democrats began talking up the idea of a third term, but the polls showed the country solidly opposed to it— until the war in Europe broke out and brought about a dramatic change in its opinion.

Roosevelt himself did nothing to clarify the situation during the first half of 1940. In early February he reportedly told a senior Democrat that he was "tired" and did not intend to run again unless Germany overran Great Britain and "headed in our direction." Meanwhile, both Garner and Farley announced their candidacies. State conventions, not primaries, chose most delegates in those distant days, and the Roosevelt forces successfully prevented a number of delegations from endorsing one of the other candidates. Ickes, working with an ambitious young New Deal Congressman named Lyndon Johnson, helped keep the Texas delegation uncommitted in late April. The Republican Party, meanwhile, was split between moderate eastern internationalists on the one hand, and rabidly anti–New Deal midwesterners on the other. The Republican Convention was scheduled to meet in Philadelphia on June 24, and the Democratic Convention in Chicago about four weeks later.[22]

Many months later, one of Roosevelt's closest confidantes said that the fall of Norway had convinced him that he must run again. In mid-May, he decided to strike an opening blow by bringing two of the most prominent Republicans in the country into his cabinet in charge of the war effort. The choices—which he purposely delayed announcing until the eve of the Republican Convention—were sensational in themselves, and one of them was one of the most important appointments that Roosevelt ever made.[23]

Born in 1874, Frank Knox had served as one of Teddy Roosevelt's Rough Riders in 1898 and returned to the colors during the First World War. Meanwhile, he had had a distinguished career as a newspaper publisher in Michigan, New Hampshire, Boston (where he had run the local Hearst newspapers) and, beginning in 1931, at the *Chicago Daily News*. In 1935 he had discovered an unexpected talent as a Republican fundraiser, and by October of that year he was being prominently mentioned as a Republican presidential possibility. He won the second spot on the national ticket in 1936 behind Alf Landon, and ran a far more rabidly anti–New Deal campaign than Landon did. The new Social Security Act, he said, would put "half the working people of America under federal control." The New Deal, Knox said in one speech, had held back recovery "by assaulting business men, by regimenting production, by competing with private business, by squandering public money, by increasing taxes, by terrorizing investment, by inciting industrial strife; in other words, by a so-called New Deal." Landon and Knox went down to the worst electoral defeat in modern U.S. history, but two years later Knox returned to the charge with an anti–New Deal polemic, "*We Planned It That Way*," explicitly warning that Roosevelt seemed bent on becoming a dictator along the lines of Hitler, Mussolini, and Stalin. "Without fully recognizing it," he wrote, "Mr. Roosevelt has taken us far along the path of Socialism. That path leads straight into Communism, Nazism, Fascism, or whatever 'ism' the fancy of the moment dictates it be called."[24]

Yet Knox fervently supported a strong U.S. Navy, and in September 1937 he had praised FDR's quarantine speech. Amazingly, Knox and Roosevelt had evidently established a relationship of some mutual confidence. Knox visited the White House sometime in the late fall of 1939, and Roosevelt, in the course of a discussion of the world crisis, astonished Knox by offering him the position of Secretary of the Navy in order to secure bipartisan support for his foreign policy. Knox promised to think it over, and on December 15 he wrote Roosevelt appreciating his willingness to overlook so many of the things he had said about him but declining, for the moment, to accept. The country and the Republican

Party, Knox wrote, did not yet feel enough of a sense of crisis to accept his crossing of party lines—although he felt that he could do so if Roosevelt would also appoint a Republican as Secretary of War! The President replied in the same spirit on December 29, agreeing that the country was not sufficiently concerned, but adding that for that very reason, "I fear that to put two Republicans in charge of the armed forces might be misunderstood in both parties!" Should a more serious situation develop, however, "it would be necessary to put aside in large part strictly old fashioned party government, and the people would understand such a situation."[25]

Knox came to Washington again on May 14, 1940, and spent the night with Chicago native Harold Ickes. Although Knox remained a staunch Republican, he now saw a third term for FDR as inevitable and feared that Germany would win in Europe and move into South America. Ickes, meanwhile, was so disturbed by Harry Woodring's continued presence as Secretary of War that on Friday, May 17, he told FDR he thought the whole cabinet should offer their resignations to allow the President to get rid of him. When Roosevelt promised to take care of the matter, Ickes—who had been losing ground within the administration—offered to take the job himself. Roosevelt instead suggested Mayor Fiorello La Guardia of New York, and said he planned to give Knox the Navy Department. The idea of La Guardia at the War Department disturbed leading New York Democrats, but FDR already had another ace up his sleeve. Weeks earlier, on April 29, Treasury Secretary Morgenthau had brought up the War Department situation with Roosevelt as well, and endorsed either La Guardia or Ickes. "They are both good suggestions," said FDR, but added, "I have another suggestion. Stimson." "WHAT??" said Morgenthau. "Yeah. He's a New Dealer and a very good executive. I knew you would be surprised," said the President. Morgenthau, who knew very well that Stimson was *not* a New Dealer, was amazed.[26]

Born in 1867 to a well-to-do New York professional family, Henry L. Stimson already counted among the greatest unelected public servants in American history, such as Albert Gallatin, John Hay, Dean Acheson, George C. Marshall (who was about to become his principal subordinate), and Colin Powell. Educated at Phillips Andover Academy, Yale, and Harvard Law School, he had grown up, like so many of his contemporaries from the Missionary generation, somewhat disgusted by the materialism of his elders, and eager to find more important tests of his worth such as trekking through the western wilderness or, possibly, war in a good cause. At New Haven he had found the love of his life, a local girl named Mabel White, but it had taken five years for him to overcome his father's opposition to the match and marry her. In this as in so many other respects, the outward similarity of his background with that of the somewhat younger Franklin Roosevelt masked enormous differences of personality and outlook. Roosevelt, also the product of a leading private school and an Ivy League undergraduate and legal education, was debonair, often lazy in his youth, and had made a rather brilliant marriage to the niece of his distant cousin, the President of the United States, which was blessed with five children. Stimson was more willful, focused, and dedicated from youth onward, married for love, but, apparently because of a youthful case of mumps, never had any children at all. He took everything he did very seriously and kept a thorough diary, earning the everlasting thanks of several generations of future historians.

Stimson had embarked on a career as a New York lawyer, both in private practice and then, in the second administration of Theodore Roosevelt, in the U.S. Attorney's office. Active in politics, he shared the progressive spirit of the time and addressed himself to the issue of the organization and control of an increasingly anarchic industrial society. He shared TR's belief that the federal government had to provide countervailing power to rein in financial and economic trusts. While New Dealers like Harold Ickes, Harry Hopkins, and Secretary of Labor Frances Perkins did their apprenticeship as social workers among the working class before moving into politics, Stimson did his prosecuting sugar monopolies under the antitrust laws. Stimson made one unsuccessful try for public office, running as the Republican candidate for Governor of New York in 1910. Although he was an ally of ex-President Roosevelt in the emerging struggle for the soul of the Republican Party, President Taft in May 1911 suddenly elevated him to the position of Secretary of War. He remained faithful to Taft during the 1912 campaign and returned to private practice after Wilson's election. When the World War broke out in 1914 he, like FDR, became a vocal advocate of preparedness and even of universal military training. He also became convinced, months before American entry into the war, that it pitted the autocracy of the German Emperor William II against governments founded upon the rights of man. He secured a commission after the United States entered the war in

1917. A year later he was commanding an artillery battalion in France at the age of forty-two, but he was sent home for training duty months before the end of the war. After the war he resumed his private law practice.

Stimson returned to public life in 1927, undertaking a mission to Nicaragua, then in the throes of revolution, on behalf of President Coolidge. A year later Coolidge made him the Governor-General of the Philippines, a U.S. possession since 1898. Stimson saw himself as a benevolent imperialist and tried to strengthen the elected legislature and improve the economy. He served from 1929 to 1933 as Herbert Hoover's Secretary of State, and in 1931, he emerged as the first determined American opponent of overseas aggression after the Japanese Kwantung Army had taken control of Manchuria and dragged the Tokyo government along in its wake. Stimson thought that the Japanese government could be induced to rein in the Army under pressure from world opinion, and he associated the U.S. government with League of Nations resolutions calling for Japanese withdrawal. He knew that the United States in general, and President Hoover in particular, merely wanted to keep the United States "an abiding place for law and a sanctuary for civilization" in the face of an act of international lawlessness, but when the crisis worsened he suggested economic sanctions against Japan to Hoover. The President absolutely rejected anything that would increase the chances of war, and eventually Stimson had to content himself with the doctrine of "Nonrecognition" of conquests achieved by force.

Stimson had of course known his fellow New York politician Franklin Roosevelt for many years, and he wrote him regarding various domestic matters during the 1930s, expressing some sympathy with the overall aims of the New Deal while disagreeing with many of its specific measures. He became more and more concerned with the state of the world after 1935 and by 1937 was a determined opponent of neutrality legislation. Not surprisingly, he also reacted strongly to the outbreak of the Sino-Japanese War in 1937, and late in that year he had written Roosevelt pleading for strong action on behalf of the Chinese, who now stood for freedom in the world crisis and who "had an historic faith in us which they had given to no other people." In 1938 two former missionaries in China, Frank and Harry Price, formed the Committee for Nonparticipation in Japanese Aggression, which sought to stop critical U.S. trade with Japan on the grounds that it was making the war possible. In December

1938 Stimson became the Committee's honorary chairman. In 1939 the Committee tried and failed to get provision for economic sanctions against aggressors passed as part of a revised neutrality law.[27]

After the European war broke out, Stimson strongly supported the repeal of the Neutrality Act and assistance to the British and French in a nationwide radio address on October 5, 1939. "The aim of the Allies should be not to crush Germany indiscriminately," he said, "but to oust the Nazi system as recreant to and destructive of the Caucasian civilization of Europe." Five months later, on March 13, 1940, he lunched with Roosevelt at the White House and discussed the world situation. On April 29, Stimson attended a New York lunch with about fifteen distinguished New Yorkers to meet with William Allen White, the seventy-one-year-old Kansas editor of the *Emporia Gazette*, a liberal Republican who also believed the future of civilization depended on the defeat of Germany and who had just organized the Committee to Defend America by Aiding the Allies. The group, nearly all Republicans, agreed that they would try to ensure that the Republican platform would allow for that policy. On May 11, White wrote that an Allied defeat would force the United States into the war: "The world cannot exist half slave and half free." By mid-May both Stimson and Frank Knox were deeply involved in private efforts to set up military training camps for young men, efforts led by Stimson associate (and Roosevelt's college classmate) Grenville Clark of New York.[28]

Not until late June, on the very eve of the Republican National Convention, did the President finally announce the appointment of Stimson and Knox to the War and Navy departments. A devoted and concerned alumnus, Stimson had spent the first half of June 1940 at the commencements of Andover and Yale. On June 17, he gave an address at New Haven that was carried live across the country by NBC radio. The nationwide radio address was a key feature of American public life in the 1930s and 1940s, partly because leading figures of the Missionary generation were expected to hold strong and individual views on questions of public interest and to share them with the public. Attentive Americans could hear a continual stream of politicians, cabinet members, and business and labor leaders giving their opinions on issues of the day in the evening and, often, read the full text of their remarks in their newspaper the next day—a custom without parallel in today's United States. Stimson's was one of the more significant of 1940.

Broadcasting the views of his ally William Allen White, Stimson took advantage of his status as an elder statesman to say things that no presidential candidate would have dared to utter. The nation, he said, faced "probably the greatest crisis of its history," threatening not only itself but also the continuing existence of freedom and self-government. Ever since the end of the Dark Ages, he said, "a struggle has been going on to build up an international civilization based upon law and justice instead of force. . . . Today there has suddenly come a reversal of all those principles, both international and domestic, on the part of a group of powerful governments." Paraphrasing Lincoln and echoing White, Stimson declared, "The world at large . . . cannot endure permanently half slave and half free." The victory of the Fascist powers would mean the end of freedom throughout the world—a position that implied that the mere defense of the western hemisphere would not save the United States. Should German air power force the British Fleet away from the British Isles, he said, the United States should open its ports to the British Fleet, allowing our own to continue "holding the Pacific for us against the manifest dangers which may face us there." Were the British Fleet to fall into German hands, the United States would be immediately open to air attack from hostile air bases. To save itself, the United States had no choice but give Britain all the help it could. Last, going well beyond Roosevelt once again, he called for an immediate "system of universal compulsory training and service" to prepare for war. "In these ways and with the old American spirit of courage and leadership behind them," he concluded, "I believe we should find our people ready to take their proper part in this threatened world and to carry through to victory, freedom, and reconstruction."[29]

Returning to New York the next morning, Stimson took a call from President Roosevelt informing him that Knox was taking over the Navy Department and asking that he become Secretary of War, providing a stabilizing influence "in whom both the army and the public would have confidence." After consulting two close friends and his wife, Stimson called back in the evening and asked if his radio address would be embarrassing. Roosevelt replied that he had read it, liked it, and knew Stimson favored a draft. Less than a month before, in his May 28 press conference, Roosevelt had disclaimed any interest in a draft, but now he "gave [Stimson] to understand that he was in sympathy with it." Stimson accepted on the spot. While the President rejected immediate entry into the war, he nonetheless liked the idea of having a Secretary of War who favored exactly that course of action—the role he had played twenty-five years earlier as Assistant Secretary of the Navy. And having advocated the objective of the destruction of Hitler's regime, Stimson would inevitably push for the maximum possible armament of the United States.[30]

The appointments to the cabinet, Roosevelt said in a statement on June 20, "are in line with the overwhelming sentiment of the nation for national solidarity in a time of world crisis and in behalf of our national defense—and nothing else." Reaction to them disappointed these hopes and showed that the European catastrophe had done nothing to alter the views of isolationists in both parties. Meeting in Philadelphia on the eve of the Republican Convention, the Republican National Committee unanimously adopted a stinging resolution before the sun had set on the appointments. "Having entered the Cabinet," it said, "these men are no longer qualified to speak as Republicans or for the Republican organization. Since Colonel Knox and Colonel Stimson have long desired to intervene in the affairs of Europe and the Democratic party has become the war party, we may accept that issue at face value." In the Senate, Democratic isolationists such as Bennett Clark of Missouri and David Walsh of Massachusetts, the Chairman of the Naval Affairs Committee, immediately attacked the appointments as a step toward war. Stimson himself received at least 100 telegrams, most of them intensely hostile. "You have done your best to disrupt the Republican Party Benedict Arnold riding a Trojan horse and leading a fifth column couldn't have done more If your action results in a Democratic victory in the coming election it will be the worst calamity the country ever suffered," read one. Stimson was eventually confirmed on July 9, after the Republican Convention, by a vote of 56–29. The "No" votes included nearly every prominent isolationist, including Senators Walsh, Burton K. Wheeler of Montana, Clark, and Gillette of Iowa among the Democrats, and failed presidential candidates Robert Taft of Ohio and Arthur Vandenberg of Michigan, Gerald Nye of North Dakota, and Hiram Johnson of California among the Republicans. Twelve out of twenty-two Republicans voting voted no. Only two Senators actually spoke in favor of Stimson in the debate. Knox was confirmed by a more comfortable 66–16 vote the next day.[31]

The votes against Stimson reflected a Republican Party split that was both regional and ideological. From its birth in 1854 until the early twentieth century the Republicans had been solidly based in the American Midwest, and especially in Ohio, the home of five of their nine Presidents. The two New York Republicans who reached the White House, Chester Arthur and Theodore Roosevelt, did so via the vice presidency, as had Calvin Coolidge from Massachusetts. Yet during the first half of the twentieth century Republicans had followed a course quite similar to that traveled by Democrats half a century later: they had become dominant within the eastern establishment, including universities, banks, and the press. Both eastern and midwestern Republicans, of course, had come to hate the name of Roosevelt, but the hatred was far more violent in the heartland. The struggle for the nomination in 1940 was the latest in a long series of battles between the party's two wings for its control, struggles that only came to an end in 1980 when Ronald Reagan won the nomination and election and the venerable genus Republicanus liberalis began moving rapidly toward extinction.

The discussion of possible Republican candidates in 1940 had focused on three names. Thomas Dewey of New York led the field. Young and photogenic, Dewey had made a big name for himself as New York District Attorney from 1937 onward thanks to some sensational prosecutions of organized crime figures such as Lucky Luciano. He had narrowly failed in 1938 to defeat longtime Governor Herbert Lehman in New York, but that had not dimmed his luster. His chief opponents were two rock-ribbed midwestern conservative Senators, Arthur Vandenberg of Michigan and Robert Taft, son of the late President, of Ohio. Dewey clearly stood out as the moderate candidate among the three, but by April, in an effort to broaden his party appeal, he had begun criticizing the Roosevelt administration for its foreign policy. On June 21, on the eve of the convention, Dewey violently attacked FDR's domestic policies and argued that the appointments of Stimson and Knox showed that he wanted to drag the country into the war. While endorsing a Navy strong enough to defend both oceans and a stronger Army and Air Force, Dewey totally rejected participation in the European conflict.[32]

American presidential politics in 1940 are almost unrecognizable to twenty-first-century Americans. Primaries, invented only thirty years earlier, elected only a very small number of delegates; state party conventions chose the rest. Large numbers of delegates arrived at conventions without any firm commitment to any candidate, or pledged to a local favorite who had thrown his hat into the ring to secure bargaining power at the convention. Meanwhile, an odd mixture of press lords, businessmen, local bosses, and longtime party activists brought their own ideas to conventions and occasionally exerted critical influence. The idea of objectivity had not yet taken over the media, and newspaper and magazine publishers, as well as columnists such as Drew Pearson and Robert Allen, authors of the *Washington Merry-Go-Round*, thought of themselves as major political players who worked hard for their preferred candidates. FDR in 1932 could not have been nominated without the support of William Randolph Hearst. In 1940, Henry Luce of *Time*, his subordinate Russell Davenport of *Fortune*, Ogden and Helen Reid of the *New York Herald Tribune*, newspaper chain owner Roy Howard, and William Allen White played critical roles in drumming up support for a virtual unknown, utilities lawyer and executive Wendell Willkie.

An Indiana native, Willkie had lived in New York since 1930. A tall, husky, youthful forty-eight years of age, he had actually been a Democrat until the late 1930s and had relatively moderate domestic views for a Republican. His energy and charisma had made him a frequent guest on radio programs and a popular public speaker. His handlers initially planned to eschew any overt campaigning for him while simply getting his name mentioned widely enough to make him the second choice of enough delegates to win him the nomination should a deadlock develop. They were outflanked, however, by Owen Root, a New York lawyer and scion of another distinguished Republican family, who formed a network of Willkie Clubs in the spring of 1940 and secured endorsements from a number of prominent Republican politicians and editors. Meanwhile foreign developments worked powerfully to his advantage. Like President Roosevelt and the majority of Americans, Willkie favored much greater preparedness and aid to the embattled democracies. That more than anything made him the choice of men like Luce, Ogden Reid, and William Allen White, who rejected the isolationism of Taft, Vandenberg, and Dewey.[33]

By the time the convention opened on Monday, June 24—two days after the Franco-German armistice—Willkie clearly had the momentum in the press and his three rivals were exhausting themselves in unsuccessful attempts to work out a deal between two of them. Former President Hoover, who addressed the convention on Tuesday, further confused the issue by trying to start a draft movement on his own behalf. Now an extreme isolationist, Hoover privately tried to sell himself as the candidate who could best deal with a Hitler-dominated Europe after the European war was over. His speech to the convention, however, showed how difficult the extreme case was becoming to make: He argued that the U.S. Navy would be more than able to defend against any threat from the Atlantic even if Britain fell, in flat contradiction to obvious facts.

The platform's foreign policy plank, adopted on Thursday, took an isolationist position but left a little wiggle room, favoring "the extension of aid to all people fighting for liberty or whose liberty is threatened as long as such aid is not in violation of international law or inconsistent with the requirements of our national defense." That wording was taken almost verbatim from a full-page ad that had run in various major newspapers under the names of various leading isolationists led by Republican Congressman Hamilton Fish of New York. The ad had been written by a German agent, the publisher George Sylvester Viereck, who was in close touch with Hans Thomsen, the Chargé d'Affaires of the German Embassy in Washington. Thomsen had also arranged to bring fifty isolationist Congressmen to the Philadelphia Convention. The German Embassy knew what was at stake.[34]

Helped by a blizzard of telegrams to delegates arranged by his powerful New York supporters, Willkie seized the momentum during nominations on Tuesday night, when his own nomination triggered a gigantic demonstration. The next night, he was nominated on the fifth ballot. Showing greater aptitude for his new trade, he agreed to progressive isolationist Charles McNary of Oregon as his vice presidential candidate, breaking a promise to Governor Raymond Baldwin of Connecticut. Roosevelt told the cabinet that the Republicans had nominated their strongest candidate.

The Democratic Convention would not meet in Chicago for another month, and enormously sensitive issues needed to be faced in the meantime, led by the question of a military draft. American opposition to once again sending young men to fight overseas was nearly as general as support for a strong Navy. This time Roosevelt let others take the lead. On June 20–21, Democratic Senator Burke of Nebraska and Republican Representative James Wadsworth of New York introduced a bill to require the registration of all men eighteen to sixty-five, making those twenty-one to forty-five subject to military training and the rest available for home defense. Roosevelt made no comment on the proposal, but the

Senate Military Affairs Committee opened hearings on July 3, and several distinguished witnesses, including Harvard President James Bryant Conant and General John J. Pershing, the Commander of the U.S. Expeditionary Force in the First World War, testified in favor of it. Prodded by Stimson, who had now been confirmed as Secretary of War, Roosevelt in his message to Congress asking for $5 billion in additional naval and military appropriations on July 10 noted approvingly that "the Congress is now considering the enactment of a system of selective training for developing the necessary man power to operate this materiel and man power to fill army noncombat needs." Marshall endorsed a draft in testimony on July 12, and the next day the War Department gave *Life* a statement calling "some form of compulsory selective service and training as essential to our system of national defense, and pressingly necessary in the present international situation." On July 12, Roosevelt announced plans to mobilize 50,000 National Guardsmen, including four full divisions.[35]

William Knudsen of the Advisory Council of National Defense had helped bring the War Department's interest in a draft to a head. His June 11 demand for an estimate of munitions requirements had forced Marshall and his subordinates to decide how big an army they needed. Within forty-eight hours, Colonel James Burns, an assistant to the Assistant Secretary of War, had put his own ideas on paper, calling for a combat strength of 1 million men by October 1, 1941; 2 million by January 1, 1942; and 4 million just three months later. Now, however, for the first time, the problem of reconciling short-term emergency needs and long-term goals came into focus. Knudsen and his men explained that the 4 million man target would require massive expansion of the production of iron, steel, and machine tools—production that would have to take place initially at the expense of the immediate production of weapons. Marshall was deeply concerned that the United States could not even afford to wait until October 1, 1941, to have 1 million men under arms, and FDR did not want to ask Congress for too much money for the Army. The 4 million target was temporarily abandoned to reach the 2 million figure—estimated as the requirement of hemispheric defense—as soon as possible. Even this figure, however, obviously required selective service at once. Marshall on July 17 made the War Department's thinking public and affirmed the need for 2 million men to defend the western hemisphere.[36]

Both Marshall and Stimson believed deeply in the duty of every citizen to help defend the United States, and both were equally strict with themselves. Speaking to the Veterans of Foreign Wars on June 19, Marshall did not waste a single minute sharing experiences of the First World War or thanking the audience for their service. "In talking to veterans I feel free to go straight to the point in discussing the problems of national defense," he said. "Today the United States faces perhaps the most critical period in its history." A month later, on July 18, Marshall wrote a rare note to Roosevelt. Stimson, he explained, had flown home to his Highhold estate on Long Island for the previous weekend, but because he had taken Mrs. Stimson with him he had refused a military aircraft and flown by commercial plane. The Secretary of War, Marshall wrote, "is seventy two years of age," and his burden, "particularly during the next two months, will be tremendous." He asked Roosevelt to tell Stimson to make free use of military planes for the trip, and added that the Secretary would never bring the matter up himself. Three months later Stimson returned the favor, ordering a very tired Marshall to spend the weekend at Charlotte, North Carolina, "for the purpose of making a report upon the comparative skill and valor of the football teams of Davidson and Virginia Military Institute," Marshall's alma mater.[37]

Roosevelt simultaneously took a covert but critical step toward possible American participation in the war. On July 12, he met with Admiral Stark, who evidently informed him that the British had suggested that the United States send a high-ranking officer to London to discuss possible wartime naval cooperation on June 20—the same procedure that Roosevelt claimed to have arranged in 1915, and used once again in late 1937 when he sent Captain Ingersoll to talk about possible action against Japan. They settled on Rear Admiral Robert Ghormley, and Ghormley had an extraordinary conversation with the President and Stark on July 25. Roosevelt laid out three possibilities with which the United States had to reckon. If Germany defeated Britain and secured the British and French fleets, the United States would have to anticipate European intervention in Latin America and Japanese advances in the Pacific within a year. Alternatively, Roosevelt once again speculated that the British government might have to abandon the British Isles but would carry on the fight with its fleet from Canada. Lastly, if Britain held out and retained command of the Atlantic, the British might develop superior air power and train and equip troops for a possible return to the continent. Either the second or third alternative would require massive assistance from the United States, and Ghormley had the mission of discussing exactly how the two nations might work together in war. Roosevelt insisted that Ghormley's talks had to remain a complete secret. Ghormley was eventually designated "Special Naval Observer" and sailed for Britain, accompanied by generals Strong of the Army and Emmons of the Army Air Force, on August 8. Emmons and Strong remained for about a month; Ghormley remained for the better part of 1941.[38]

On July 15, the Democratic National Convention opened in Chicago. "Franklin Roosevelt," wrote Drew Pearson and Robert Allen on July 11, 1940, "will go down in history as the greatest keeper of a secret in American politics." He had drawn out the question of his possible renomination so long and so skillfully that even his closest intimates doubted his intentions with less than a month to go to the convention. Marguerite "Missy" Lehand had been FDR's secretary since 1921. She was far more of a confidante and constant companion than Eleanor Roosevelt, and is thought by many to have been the President's lover as well. She often passed information between her boss and leading subordinates, and on July 3, she astonished Treasury Secretary Morgenthau by asking him if he thought FDR was indeed going to run. "Why are you asking me?" he began, but concluded that he thought the answer was yes. Pearson and Allen were convinced that FDR would run on the eve of the convention, arguing that Willkie was too strong a candidate for the President to turn the Democratic Party's chances over to anyone else. FDR had made no statement, however, when the convention opened.[39]

Roosevelt had decided to run largely because he thought the country needed him, but he allowed the convention to proceed in such a way as to convince the Democratic Party that it needed him as well. He sent Harry Hopkins, his Secretary of Commerce—who had spent most of the last year deathly ill, and still was not fully recovered—to manage his campaign in Chicago, and gave him a message to be read to the convention stating that all his friends knew that he had no wish to become a candidate but not refusing to accept the nomination if offered. National Chairman Jim Farley, however, had not given up on his candidacy, and for two days Roosevelt supporters such as Harold Ickes (who was hoping to become Vice President himself) were terrified that inaction might allow the strong anti–New Deal forces to gain the initiative. The Platform Committee, meanwhile, produced a foreign policy plank worthy of the Republicans or the German Embassy. "We will not participate in foreign wars," it read, "and we will not send our Army, naval or air forces to fight in foreign lands outside of the Americas, except in case of attack. . . . We pledge to extend to [liberty-loving] peoples all the material aid at our command, consistent with law and not inconsistent with the interests of our own national self-defense." The phrase "except in case of attack" had been inserted at the express request of the President, who had found the original language much too restrictive but had feared the consequences of asking for its removal.[40]

On Wednesday, July 17, Convention Chairman Senator Alben Barkley managed to read FDR's noncommittal message in such a way as to set off a demonstration in his favor, and he was indeed nominated that evening. The next day Roosevelt shocked the convention by making Henry Wallace, one of the most committed New Dealers in his cabinet, his vice-presidential choice, leaving the more conservative Democrats completely out in the cold. Wallace, the Secretary of Agriculture who had administered some of the New Deal's most controversial measures, was repeatedly booed during the nominating process, but the convention approved the choice by a comfortable margin. So determined was Roosevelt to make the election a referendum on the New Deal rather than on himself personally that he prepared a statement declining the nomination during the vice-presidential fight, one he intended to submit if Speaker Bankhead of Alabama, the conservative alternative to Wallace, had won the nomination from Wallace. As usual, however, both calculation and idealism contributed to the choice. Roosevelt in November would surely carry the South and the West, while Willkie could count on at least some inroads in the Northeast. The farm belt would be crucial, and the Secretary of Agriculture was a well-known and generally popular figure there.[41]

In the midst of the convention, on July 16, Knox and Stimson met with FDR in Washington, and Stimson brought up a rumor that the Democrats now in Chicago would block compulsory selective service, "the foundation stone upon which his policy of national defense rested." FDR assured him that he had taken steps to prevent this. On the evening of July 19, Roosevelt, who had broken precedent eight years earlier by accepting his first nomination in person, accepted his third in a radio broadcast from Washington. The address did not always show him at his best. Only the constant pressure of the world situation, he claimed, had made it impossible for him to take himself out of the race before the convention—and, he claimed, the convention had disregarded his wishes after he had made them known. Then, however, he combined his acceptance of their choice with his first public endorsement of the pending draft bill, which General Marshall had publicly called for in the midst of the convention two days earlier. "The fact which dominates our world," he said, "is the fact of armed aggression, the fact of successful armed aggression, aimed at the form of Government, the kind of society that we in the United States have chosen and established for ourselves. . . . In the face of that public danger all those who can be of service to the Republic have no choice but to offer themselves for service in those capacities for which they may be fitted. Those, my friends, are the reasons why I have had to admit to myself, and now to state to you, that my conscience will not let me turn my back upon a call to service."[42]

The congressional debate over the draft, however, showed that conscription remained a third rail in American politics. When the bill reached the Senate floor on July 26, it ignited a storm of opposition, led by Vandenberg, who insisted on trying a volunteer system first, and liberal Democrat Burton K. Wheeler of Montana, one of the most dedicated of isolationists, who denied that the United States faced an emergency, claimed that the Democratic convention would never have approved such a plank, and threatened any Democrat who voted for it with impending defeat. Several old progressive stalwarts including the venerable George Norris of Nebraska, the father of the Tennessee Valley Authority, and Hiram Johnson of California, regarded a peacetime draft as the first step toward a dictatorship in the United States. The public favored the draft by nearly 2–1, but older isolationists would not be moved. They reportedly hoped to kill the bill by filibustering it until Congress had to adjourn for the campaign. By August 1, Stimson was complaining to his diary that Selective Service had stalled partly because Germany had not yet invaded Britain and partly because FDR had refused to fight for it. The Secretary of War publicly thought the unthinkable in order to secure passage. Testifying before the House Military Affairs Committee on July 31, he said that the United States "must take into account the possibility that Britain may be conquered within 30 days and her fleet come under enemy control. . . . There is a very grave danger of attack on the United States if England falls." Knox weighed in with a radio address on August 4, arguing that only a draft could keep the war from the western hemisphere.[43]

In early August, Senator Maloney of Connecticut unveiled an amendment that would have postponed any actual inductions until January 1, pending an attempt to persuade 400,000 men to enlist voluntarily by shortening enlistments from three years to one and raising the pay of privates from twenty-one dollars a month to thirty dollars. Not until August 23, after Roosevelt had attacked it and Willkie had endorsed a draft, did the amendment fail. The final bill passed the Senate two days later, along with an amendment allowing the government to seize plants if necessary for war production. Yet the final version imposed important limits on the new forces and reaffirmed that it was designed for nothing more than the defense of American territory and the western hemisphere. Only those twenty-one to thirty years of age, not eighteen to forty-five as originally envisioned by the War Department, became subject to the draft; their term of service would expire after only one year; and draftees could not be sent outside the western hemisphere, except for the defense of distant U.S. territories. Roosevelt signed the bill on September 16, and Marshall gave a nationwide radio address on the same day, stressing how much more serious the situation was than in 1917. "The next six months include the possibility of being the most critical period in the history of this nation," he said.[44]

The U.S. rearmament program was calculated to increase its ground and air forces by nearly a factor of ten during the next eighteen months or so, yet by world standards it remained comparatively small. The War Department now planned to have nine Army divisions ready by the middle of 1941, with twenty-seven projected as the eventual total. The British Empire was planning for fifty-five, while the Germans already had more than a hundred. The new Navy would eventually be the world's largest, but it would not be at sea for three to six years. The expansion of aircraft production was going to proceed quite slowly. General Marshall in particular was a highly logical thinker who matched military plans to declared political objectives, and those were now confined to the defense of the western hemisphere—a task for which the new plans were barely adequate at best. Yet this was clearly the limit of what the Congress and the country would accept in the summer of 1940. When in late October Army subordinates suggested doubling the projected number of bombers for 1942, Marshall replied characteristically that "he did not know why we should suddenly propose a new program which is vast in scope unless some foreign situation requires it." He did not see how "a deluge of

President Roosevelt signs the Selective Service Act, September 16, 1940. Looking on, from left, are Secretary of War Henry L. Stimson; Congressman Andrew J. May; General George C. Marshall; and Senator Morris Sheppard. (Courtesy of the Franklin D. Roosevelt Presidential Library and Museum.)

bombers could be sent into the Western Hemisphere," and, he might have added, the American public was not interested in fighting outside it.[45]

Meanwhile, Britain was holding out against a sustained German bombing campaign while Churchill pleaded for immediate help from the United States. The American response to Churchill's requests illustrated American priorities nearly as clearly as the controversy about the draft and the war plans approved by the Joint Board.

Churchill had of course begun badgering Roosevelt for increased material aid from the moment he took office in May 1940, and in June had essentially begun to argue that only such aid could save Britain from invasion and collapse. Roosevelt immediately let Morgenthau (who had already negotiated aircraft contracts with the British) and the War and

Navy departments know that he wanted to help both France and Britain, but formidable obstacles immediately emerged. The United States was woefully short of equipment itself, and more important, one of the congressional authorizations for rearmament had specified that no U.S. war material could be sold or given away unless the War or Navy Department certified that the transfer was in the interests of American national defense. Marshall in particular took this responsibility very seriously, and thus he explained patiently to his superiors, including the President himself, that the British could not have most of the P-38 and B-17 aircraft or French-made .75 artillery pieces that they urgently wanted because the Air Corps and Army had to have them for training purposes, and possibly for war.[46]

Churchill renewed his desperate plea for at least 35 destroyers on June 15, reporting that the British had only 68 destroyers in service compared to 433 in 1918 and stressing the danger of invasion. William Allen White of the Committee to Defend America by Aiding the Allies met with Roosevelt on June 29 and discussed the destroyer issue, but the President refused to commit himself. The committee opened a public relations campaign to give Britain destroyers during July, culminating in a six-column ad in major newspapers on July 30. The British also got this message into the American press through columnists like Joseph Alsop and Drew Pearson, but Roosevelt on July 3 told Ickes that he did not think he could certify that the destroyers were not necessary to the defense of the United States. Another new interventionist organization, the Century Group, a body of establishment New Yorkers, including publisher Henry Luce, also took up the call for destroyers. Newly minted Secretary of the Navy Frank Knox also favored giving them to the British, but FDR on July 22 wrote him that legislation would be required and that he did not think Congress would pass it. Churchill renewed his suit on July 31, asking for 50–60 destroyers and reporting 4 sunk and 7 damaged in the last few days.[47]

While Stimson pushed the draft along, Frank Knox now found the formula that allowed a deal with the British to proceed. Rainbow 4 called for the American occupation of British, French, and Dutch possessions in the western hemisphere at the outset of hostilities with the Axis, and Secretary of State Hull had just secured the agreement of the American republics to such a move at a conference in Havana. During the Century Group meetings in New York, Henry Luce of *Time-Life* had mentioned the possibility of trading the destroyers Churchill wanted for bases in British possessions in the Caribbean, and he raised the same possibility both with FDR and with Knox on a trip to Washington at the end of July. On Friday, August 2, Ickes called Knox to push for a destroyer deal, and Knox suggested that the United States might receive bases in British possessions immediately in return. Stimson, he said, also favored the deal, and he promised to bring it up in the regular cabinet meeting that afternoon.[48]

At the cabinet meeting, Hull reported on the Havana Conference of American republics and predicted that several South American countries would go over to Hitler if Britain fell. Pro-Nazi groups were already trying to overthrow the governments of Uruguay, Argentina, and Chile, and President Vargas of Brazil was talking about a more pro-German policy should Britain fall. Knox then proposed the destroyer deal, which met with general approval, provided that Churchill would once again promise to send the British Fleet to the western hemisphere if Britain fell. The acquisition of bases in British territory, which was already part of American war plans, would allow the administration honestly to claim that the deal would strengthen U.S. defenses. Much of the cabinet thought legislation was still necessary, but doubted that Congress would give it to candidate FDR. The President planned to talk to interventionist Republican William Allen White to see if he could persuade Willkie to have Republicans, including Willkie's running mate Senator McNary, introduce the legislation. The story of how the cabinet came to adopt the proposal takes on a new meaning in light of William Allen White's statement that Roosevelt had actually discussed a destroyers-for-bases deal with him in a meeting in late June. FDR had evidently had the idea all along, but waited, as he so often did, for someone else to suggest it.[49]

The trade of destroyers for bases, then, was not a public relations device to justify an unpopular move to the American public, but rather a logical step based on current U.S. war plans and the ever-present possibility that Britain might fall and force the United States immediately to defend the western hemisphere. In a press conference on Friday, August 16, Roosevelt announced for the first time that he was seeking bases from the British and added that the United States would discuss the defense of the western hemisphere with Canada.

The next day Roosevelt and Stimson drove to the northernmost regions of upstate New York to inspect U.S. troops and to have dinner with

Canadian Prime Minister Mackenzie King and discuss the common defense of North America. Roosevelt briefed King thoroughly on the destroyers deal, pledged himself to the defense of Canada against any attack from Europe, and asked for a base in Nova Scotia as well as the one Churchill was promising him in Newfoundland. On the next day the two men announced that the United States and Canada were setting up a Joint Board to coordinate their defense—a remarkable step, given that Canada was already in the war alongside Great Britain. That board began preparing a plan for the joint defense of North America in the event that Britain fell. Meanwhile, officers from the War Department, led by Major Matthew Ridgway of War Plans, undertook a long series of staff conversations with virtually every Latin American nation to provide for military cooperation in the event of an Axis attack on the western hemisphere. All the governments, armies, and navies of the Americas were taking this threat very seriously indeed.[50]

It took another month, until September 3, to consummate the destroyers-for-bases deal. Candidate Willkie, approached by William Allen White, indicated his general support but refused to make a statement in advance or come out in support of legislation that had not yet been introduced. On August 13 Roosevelt cabled Churchill that it "may be possible" to furnish at least fifty destroyers and a few aircraft, in return for an assurance that the British Fleet would "not be turned over to the Germans or sunk" but would be sent to other parts of the Empire should Britain fall, and that Britain either sell or lease for ninety-nine years bases in seven British possessions in the western hemisphere in an arc from Newfoundland to Trinidad. On August 17 Willkie, accepting the Republican nomination in his home town of Elwood, Indiana, supported selective service and affirmed that the fall of Great Britain would be a calamity for the United States because Germany would then dominate the Atlantic. In a conference of Hull, Stimson, Knox, and Sumner Welles on August 21, someone suggested easing political difficulties by transferring the destroyers to Canada instead of Great Britain, but the upright Stimson promptly quashed the idea, one "that . . . would simply add a discreditable subterfuge to the situation." Later that day Admiral Stark certified that the deal would be a net gain for the defense of the United States. That, combined with an opinion from Attorney General Robert Jackson, allowed Roosevelt to proceed without Congress.[51]

On September 2, just a few days before the traditional kick-off of the presidential campaign on Labor Day, Roosevelt dedicated the Great Smokey Mountains National Park in North Carolina and once again trumpeted the threat to American values. "We have come to realize the greatest attack that has ever been launched against freedom of the individual is nearer the Americas than ever before. . . . If the spirit of God is not in us, and if we will not prepare to give all that we have and all that we are to preserve Christian civilization in our land, we shall go to destruction." On the train back to Washington, Roosevelt held a press conference and released the exchange of notes between the British and American governments consummating the destroyers-for-bases deal. He compared it at length to the Louisiana Purchase, pointing out that Thomas Jefferson had made that deal without a formal treaty or two-thirds vote in the Senate and that he had made it for the purposes of national defense, to remove Napoleon's influence from the western hemisphere. The agreement gave the United States base rights in Newfoundland, and in the islands of Bermuda, the Bahamas, Jamaica, St. Lucia, Trinidad, and Antigua, and in British Guiana. The next day, candidate Willkie protested that the deal had been arrived at without consulting Congress but predicted that the country would approve it.[52]

The destroyer deal was not the only move toward Anglo-American cooperation taking place that summer. While Churchill and Roosevelt bargained over its details, Rear Admiral Ghormley, late of the War Plans Division, was secretly discussing possible wartime cooperation in London. But the Roosevelt administration did not make the destroyer deal because it was now committed to Britain's survival at all costs. The air Battle of Britain had now passed its peak, and by mid-September it seemed more and more likely that no German invasion of Britain was imminent. Yet both the President and his military leaders still rated Britain's chances for survival as quite low. The situation that they faced had some parallels with the U.S. dilemma during the first year after it entered the First World War, when the French and the British had pleaded for an immediate infusion of American manpower into their own armies to deal with an expected German offensive in the spring of 1918. Wilson, supported by his commander General Pershing, had refused to amalgamate U.S. troops into foreign units, insisting that they be used to form a separate U.S. Army that would fight for American objectives. Marshall, who had served under Pershing during that year, had made hemispheric defense

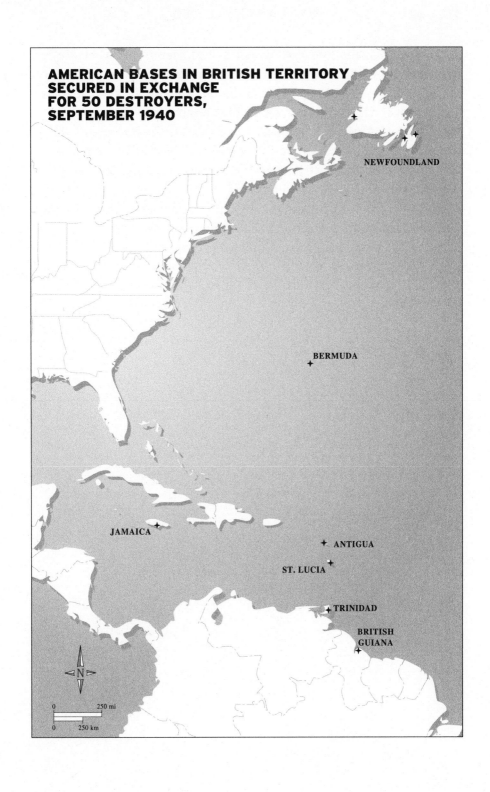

AMERICAN BASES IN BRITISH TERRITORY
SECURED IN EXCHANGE
FOR 50 DESTROYERS,
SEPTEMBER 1940

NEWFOUNDLAND

BERMUDA

JAMAICA

ANTIGUA

ST. LUCIA

TRINIDAD

BRITISH
GUIANA

0   250 mi
0   250 km

his first priority, and Roosevelt clearly agreed. Hemispheric defense represented not only the limit of what the American people would support but also the limit of what American military forces might be capable of. The destroyer deal could contribute only marginally to Britain's survival, but it allowed American authorities to accelerate the implementation of American plans for hemispheric defense. The new bases—upon which work began almost immediately—bought insurance against the at least equally likely possibility of Britain's defeat. The Roosevelt administration was preparing for war, but not for any immediate intervention in Europe. Meanwhile, the administration had to define the needs of American production, and assure its own continuance in office at home.

CHAPTER 3

The Growing Threat of World War, June–September 1940

FROM MOSCOW TO WASHINGTON, LONDON TO TOKYO, AND BERLIN TO Rome, leaders in the major world capitals reassessed their positions in light of the French defeat during the summer of 1940, negotiating for new alliances and moving closer to world war. In Washington, planning began for a surge in production to allow the United States to defend the western hemisphere. Roosevelt's new National Defense Advisory Commission (NDAC), or Defense Commission, as it was usually called, laid plans for industrial expansion, while legislation authorized the letting of weapons contracts to private industry on relatively generous terms. A number of New Deal institutions already gave the government a direct role in the national economy, and the administration now began to use them to quicken the rearmament program. The Defense Commission made rapid progress, but the question of how big a war the United States had to fight remained unclear, making it impossible to plan for any contingency beyond hemispheric defense.

Meanwhile, the defeat of the French, Belgians, and Dutch and the threatened invasion of Britain, which so alarmed Washington, had set off a chain reaction around the world. Adolf Hitler initially attempted to coerce the British into making peace with German bombs while preparing for a possible invasion of the British Isles. Those tactics did not succeed, however, and in September Hitler became alarmed by the Roosevelt-Churchill destroyer deal, a harbinger of an Anglo-American alliance. Rather than focus on eliminating the British threat, he began to think about moving as soon as possible against his real target, the Soviet Union, instead.

On the other side of the globe, the German victories in Europe encouraged the Japanese government to pursue further expansion in cooperation with the Germans. By the end of the summer they had signaled their intention to move south, forcing the British to close the Burma Road from British Burma to Chiang Kai-shek's stronghold in the interior of China and successfully demanding that the Vichy French government allow Japanese troops into Indochina. These moves led leading figures in Washington, including Stimson, Morgenthau, and Interior Secretary Harold Ickes, to push Roosevelt to embargo key raw materials, including oil, bound for the Japanese. But Roosevelt, the Navy, and the State Department refused, fearing that such a move would provoke an immediate Japanese attack in the Far East, which the United States was unprepared to meet.

In late September, the conclusion of the Tripartite Pact between Germany, Italy, and Japan made world war a near-certainty. The three expansionist powers effectively promised to go to war with the United States should it become involved in a conflict with any of them either in Europe or in Asia. Once again Roosevelt's more bellicose cabinet members, led by Stimson and Knox, wanted a forceful response, but at exactly the same moment, a War Department paper laid out the actual military situation of the United States in chilling detail. Largely because of a shortage of ammunition, the United States would be entirely unable to undertake major military operations for at least a year. Roosevelt, who well understood the practical requirements of war, knew that he needed time. For many months to come, the United States would remain a hostage to the fortune of other nations fighting across the seas, without resources to affect events and without any way of knowing when, and under what circumstances, it might participate in the spreading war.

When Roosevelt created the Defense Commission in May 1940, making all its members report directly to himself, he saw it as his personal mechanism for arming the United States. Not until December 1941 was he finally convinced that he had to centralize authority under one subordinate. Yet the problem that the Defense Commission faced in the second half of 1940 was one of ultimate ends as well as adequate means. Whatever happened in Europe, Roosevelt—as his call for 50,000 aircraft in May 1940 showed—wanted to prepare for conflict on an unprecedented scale, but the laws now making their way through the Congress foresaw nothing more than a bare-bones defense of the western hemisphere, combined with the construction, over the next six years, of the world's largest Navy. How much production the nation would require would depend, obviously, on exactly how big a war it had to fight. Congressional authorizations in the second half of 1940 were initially limited to the new two-ocean Navy; equipment for a 2-million-man Army; *productive capacity* sufficient to allow a possible 4-million-man Army to function; and 18,000 new aircraft.[1]

The Defense Commission had to arrange for the production of the weapons America needed, but widespread disagreement persisted about how much that would be. In one of their first meetings on July 3, the commissioners agreed to assume that "the emergency," as they referred to the situation facing the nation, would last about four years, but they differed widely on what it would entail. As Commissioner Donald Nelson explained after the war, the key argument divided men like himself, Leon Henderson, Treasury Secretary Morgenthau, and Stimson, who believed that the United States would soon be fighting all over the world, and those like William Knudsen, Edward Stettinius, and Commerce Secretary Jesse Jones who focused on the western hemisphere and may even have believed that the European war might come to an end without U.S. intervention. Meanwhile, much of American industry, powerfully represented on the Commission by members like Knudsen of General Motors and Stettinius of U.S. Steel, wanted the minimum possible disruption of the civilian economy and the maximum possible profit, while labor wanted to conserve its gains in wages and hours amid increasing employment. With GDP destined to increase from $101 billion in 1940 to $126 billion in 1941, $162 billion in 1942, and $198 billion in 1943, the stakes were obviously enormous. So was the necessary productive effort.[2]

The United States faced the production challenge with an odd mixture of strengths and weaknesses. The United States in those distant days was an unequalled industrial giant and controlled a huge percentage of the world's energy resources. It made more than twice as much pig iron and steel as its nearest competitor and pumped six times as much petroleum, but faced major shortages of various nonferrous metals; rubber, whose principal source of supply in Southeast Asia would be cut off the moment war with Japan broke out; and aluminum, whose production would have to double to meet the needs of the war. The nation's ship-building capacity was roughly adequate to construct the huge new Navy that had just been approved, but neither its airplane nor arms industry was remotely adequate to the demands of modern war. The necessary expansion of plant capacity would strain every interconnected feature of the complex civilian economy, including labor and housing markets, transportation, and construction. Meanwhile, the civilian economy was trying to satisfy consumer demand, already fueled by a year of relatively rapid economic expansion. Planning the economy—a largely unrealized dream of New Dealers during the 1930s—had now become a necessity.[3]

Donald Nelson, who eventually emerged as the leader of the American productive effort after Pearl Harbor, became a key planner at the end of June 1940. The Defense Commission had immediately asked for the right to approve Army and Navy contracts in order to resolve conflicts over scarce resources, and in June, Roosevelt himself had appointed a committee composed of economist Leon Henderson, labor leader Sidney Hillman, and raw materials coordinator Edward Stettinius to study that issue. On June 28 the committee made Nelson responsible for "elimination of competition and overlapping among the several established procurement agencies."[4]

Nelson had come to Washington to work on the NDAC in May 1940 on the recommendation of his boss, General Robert Wood, the chairman of the retailing giant Sears, Roebuck, who ironically emerged during the next six months as one of the country's leading isolationists. His choice was fortuitous. Nelson had spent the 1930s as Vice President in Charge of Merchandising before rising to head of the company's executive committee in 1939. He was that relative rarity among businessmen, a Democrat, and had in fact worked briefly for the National Recovery Administration before its demise. Merchandising dealt with far more than marketing: it involved Nelson deeply in numerous sectors of the American consumer economy because he had to make sure that hundreds of enterprises would provide the products Sears wanted to sell when they needed them on their shelves and in their catalogue warehouses. That had taught him how to adjust to seasonal rhythms in the production of various commodities, and how to find idle capacity that might be put to use. As Coordinator of Purchases for the Defense Commission, he began performing the same tasks he had done for Sears on behalf of the American military establishment. Nelson found Roosevelt far in advance of most of his commissioners in anticipating a worldwide war, while they remained focused on the defense of the western hemisphere. Not until October 11, however, did the Board secure presidential authority to incorporate civilian needs into Nelson's priorities scheme, and not until December did it get full authority to exercise this power.[5]

William Knudsen, who with Sidney Hillman was the cochairman of the Advisory Council, understood the demands of mass production as well as any man in America. "I have been in shops all of 40 years," Knudsen told a House committee in January 1941, "shipbuilding, railroad locomotives, bicycles"—and now, automobiles. After emigrating from Denmark to the United States at the age of twenty in 1900, apparently without a great deal of formal education, he had gone to work in shipyards and railroad yards before catching on with Henry Ford, the most innovative industrialist of the Missionary generation, for whom Knudsen set up assembly lines. He had then moved to General Motors, eventually rising by 1940 to the top of the corporate hierarchy. Such career paths were not unknown in the first half of the twentieth century, when industrial executives were expected to have substantial practical experience. The enormous job he was now undertaking involved the construction of new factories and new tools with which to make the parts that would be turned into finished tanks and aircraft, all of which would take months before products began to roll off assembly lines. Here, as in so many other fields, the Missionary generation was now putting its civilian experience to use to prepare for war.[6]

Knudsen immediately met with FDR upon assuming his job and continued to meet with him at increasingly more frequent intervals during the next eighteen months—ten times during the remainder of 1940 and twenty-three more during 1941. The expansion of the aircraft industry, the President's top priority, became Knudsen's own. On June 4 he told General Arnold of the Air Corps that he planned to meet FDR's goal of 50,000 aircraft within two and a half years. Work could not, however, proceed until legislation specified a key provision of new contracts. During the First World War, steel and other industries had expanded so rapidly that they found themselves forced after the war to destroy and dismantle some of their new plants. They were determined not to take losses on such plants again. In late May, Congress had taken up a bill to impose a 10 percent surcharge on most taxes and to limit excess profits in an attempt to raise more than $600 million a year in additional revenue while raising the ceiling on the national debt by $30 billion. That bill, which took all summer to pass, became the vehicle for hashing out complicated issues of financing production and mobilizing a capitalist economy for national defense.[7]

In an attempt to protect themselves against the costs of surplus capacity, industrialists demanded contracts that would allow firms to collect 20 percent of the cost of any new plants every year for five years. That struck Treasury Secretary Morgenthau's staff of New Dealers as overly generous, and in September, they attempted to insist on a corollary that would allow the government to take possession of or sell such plants when the war was over in recognition of the government's having in effect paid for them. On September 4, Knudsen and three other Commission members all told a Senate committee that this provision would dry up private investment in new plant capacity and demanded its removal. Stimson also sided with the industrialists. "The whole thing," he confided in his diary in typically sweeping terms, "is a great clash between two theories and interests. If you are going to try to go to war, or to prepare for war, in a capitalist country, you have got to let business make money out of the process or business won't work, and there are a great many people in Congress who think that they can tax business out of all proportion and still have business men work diligently and quickly. That is not human nature." Although the Treasury did not drop its opposition, an amended bill giving industry what it wanted eventually passed during the first week of October, and Roosevelt signed it. By that time Knudsen and Stimson had become seriously alarmed by the delay.[8]

Whatever its critics thought, the New Deal was designed to save rather than destroy the capitalist system, but New Dealers from Roosevelt on down also believed that the private sector simply could not meet all the nation's needs and that the federal government had to fill the gaps it left behind. So it was with respect to war finance, and Congress and the President turned to another domestic agency, the Reconstruction Finance Corporation (RFC), to build plants and acquire needed raw materials, as well. Herbert Hoover had founded the RFC in 1932 to supply the capital industry could not get from banks, and Roosevelt had greatly expanded it. Its chairman, wealthy Texan construction magnate Jesse Jones, had grown in power during the 1930s and was now Secretary of Commerce as well.

In June 1940 Congress passed a law allowing the RFC to create defense subsidiaries, and it quickly created the Defense Plant Corporation, the Metals Reserve Corporation, the Rubber Reserve Company, and the Defense Supplies Corporation. During the second half of 1940, the Defense Plant Corporation put up the money for new aircraft plants in Nebraska, Kansas, Oklahoma, and Texas, far away from potentially vulnerable coastlines. The NDAC arranged for the letting of $9 billion worth of contracts by the end of 1940, more than $5.4 billion of them privately financed. Direct military construction accounted for $1.6 billion, $3.7 billion went to expand industry, and the rest was for housing, agricultural projects, roads, and miscellaneous construction. That was nearly 10 percent of GDP and far more than had ever been spent domestically under the New Deal.

Aircraft production was the biggest goal, reflecting the President's own views. The Commission on September 9, 1940, laid down a target of 33,467 aircraft by April 1, 1942, including 14,375 for the British. Three months later, new plans called for 82,890 planes (of which fewer than three thousand already existed) by July 30, 1943: 42,000 for the Army, 11,000 for the Navy, 26,000 for the British, and a few thousand for other foreign countries. Knudsen put his engineering skills to work on the problem of aircraft production and came up with a striking innovation by October. Finding that the dies—the metal tools used to shape parts—for aircraft production were currently being made by hand, he suggested to Stimson that the auto manufacturers be contracted to mass-produce them, as they already did for automobiles, and that they cut back on the production of new car models, if necessary, to make this happen. Stimson was delighted, although the full implementation of this plan turned out to be more difficult than he had hoped.[9]

The letting of enormous contracts in the midst of an ongoing social and economic revolution raised many issues of economic justice and labor policy. Knudsen wanted to get his own auto industry into the business of building airplanes for the government, but the Ford Motor Company was under indictment for its refusal to recognize the United Auto Workers union in defiance of the National Labor Relations Board. General Motors and Chrysler had recognized the union after the sit-down strikes of 1937, but Ford was holding out, making frequent use of hired thugs. Sidney Hillman wanted to bar such noncompliant firms from receiving government contracts, but Knudsen successfully insisted on a case-by-case review, and Ford got significant airplane contracts by the end of the year. Nelson and Hillman also pushed for more contracts for smaller firms that could continue the flow of production while the larger ones were attending to other needs, but Knudsen preferred dealing with industrial giants like his own General Motors.[10]

Raw materials posed a bigger problem. Although current stocks of tin, rubber, and even high-octane gasoline would clearly run out almost immediately should war break out, estimates of potential requirements were very difficult to make. Jesse Jones of the RFC, whose new subsidiaries had the responsibility for building up stockpiles, was evidently among the skeptics regarding the likelihood of a huge war. Stettinius's raw materials division of the Defense Commission established ambitious targets for raw materials such as chromium (a key alloy for steel products), manganese, mica, quinine (vital for potential operations in the tropics), silk, tin, and tungsten. Commission members spoke optimistically about raw materials acquisitions during the fall, but by the end of the year the actual stockpiles were generally between 10 percent and 30 percent of what had been specified as required.

The situation was even worse with respect to key materials that would have to be produced industrially, including steel, aluminum, aviation gas, and synthetic rubber. Although some of these industries had increased capacity after the European war broke out to meet anticipated Anglo-French needs, they cut back after the fall of France on the assumption that the war was almost over. During the second half of 1940, nothing was done to increase stockpiles of aviation gasoline. Aluminum production capacity did increase, especially after Knudsen and Stettinius convinced Congress to allow the Tennessee Valley Authority to provide more electric power to ALCOA—another instance of a New Deal program enlisted in the war effort. But synthetic rubber production hardly got off the ground. The Defense Commission discovered that the six companies that could make it planned a capacity of 10,000 tons per year for early 1941, and convinced them to adopt a new target ten times larger to be completed within 18 months at a cost of $50 million. When, however, the RFC got control of the program, it quickly cut the 100,000-ton target twice, first to 40,000 tons and then, in March 1941, to 10,000. Yet everyone knew that the United States would lose virtually all access to natural rubber the minute a war with Japan began.[11]

In their efforts to make the United States a military power second to none within two to three years, men like Knudsen, Jones, Stimson, and their younger colleagues like Hillman and Nelson were drawing on the

Missionary generation's extraordinary ability to move the present into the future. Henry Ford had created the assembly line nearly forty years earlier; Morgenthau's Treasury Department had redesigned the financial structure of the United States; and Jesse Jones's RFC had financed dozens of large domestic projects. Since the latter stages of the twentieth century, the U.S. economy has focused at least as much on destruction as creation, and a new fetish for free markets has made planning on behalf of the national interest virtually impossible. The new expansion of industry that began in the summer of 1940 also occurred without environmental impact studies, and took advantage of much larger open spaces around metropolitan areas in a country whose total population was only about half of what it is today. The Missionaries (to use Strauss and Howe's name for them) now combined their belief in national purpose with their organizational skill to prove that a democracy could mobilize as effectively as a totalitarian state.

The rapid awakening of the sleeping American industrial giant immediately had repercussions in foreign capitals. Both Germany and Japan reached key decisions during the summer and early fall of 1940—some of them fortunate for the United States, but others vastly increasing the chance of a two-front war. The United States' key military and political moves in the summer and fall of 1940, including the new aircraft program, the two-ocean Navy, the draft, and even the destroyer deal with Britain, were designed for the moment to prepare for the defense of the western hemisphere. Yet those moves convinced both Adolf Hitler and the Japanese government in Tokyo that the United States posed a long-term threat to their expansionist plans. The chain reaction set off by the fall of Belgium, Holland, and France reverberated around the globe, leading in September to a new alliance among the Axis and a reconsideration of the strategic problems facing the United States.

The Second World War in Europe took the course that it did because Adolf Hitler's primary goals lay in the East, not in the West. He had hoped that Britain and France would stand aside when he attacked Poland, but when they did not, he decided to try to defeat France as quickly as possible. After France actually collapsed, he confidently expected the British to make peace, thus allowing him to attack the Soviet Union and create a huge land empire centered on Ukraine. Like Roosevelt, Hitler envisioned a subsequent long-term, worldwide struggle among empires, relying mainly on huge navies and air forces. In January 1939, while U.S. naval planners were estimating the requirements of a war with Germany, Italy, and Japan, Hitler approved the Z-Plan for the German Navy, calling for 10 new battleships, 3 battle cruisers, 5 heavy cruisers, 30 light cruisers, 8 aircraft carriers, 249 U-boats, and 70 destroyers, more than half of this force to be ready by about 1943 and the rest five years later. Hitler initially gave this program the highest priority, but work on new battleships had to be halted when war broke out in September. Hitler in early July 1940 promised that the program would resume as soon as England made peace.[12]

The British cabinet did in fact discuss the possibility of peace in the last week of May, but Churchill prevailed on his colleagues to reject it, at least for the time being.[13] As expected by Churchill, Roosevelt, and virtually the entire world, Hitler and his generals immediately began planning to attack Britain, first from the air and then, if conditions allowed, possibly with a ground invasion as well. But Hitler was never fully committed to the invasion, which remained militarily doubtful in any case. Even had the German Luftwaffe obtained air superiority, the German Navy, which had suffered heavy losses in the Norway campaign, was almost certainly too small to convoy a large force across the channel and support it once it got there.

The battle for air supremacy over southern England that began on August 13 captured the world's imagination, not least because of the famous short-wave radio broadcasts from London by Edward R. Murrow of CBS. But the Germans had to improvise their campaign using forces that had largely been designed and trained for other purposes, and it took place on a far smaller scale than the later campaigns the Allies waged against the Germans in 1943–1945. The British, meanwhile, had revolutionized their air defenses with the critical invention of radar, and had expanded their aircraft industry in the years immediately before the war. Although neither side seems to have realized this, their monthly production of combat aircraft—about 1,500 a month—was superior overall to the Germans' and 50 percent superior in the key area of fighters. Facing a deadline of about ten weeks within which the invasion of Britain would have to take place before bad weather set in, the Germans found it impossible to find an effective strategy. By September 14 Hitler was expressing skepticism about Sea Lion—the code name for the invasion of Britain. On September 17 he postponed the landing "until further notice," and on

October 12 he rescheduled it for the following spring. Although Hitler was still planning on a relatively short war, he now knew it was going to last well into 1941, and he was already mulling over the possibility of attacking the Soviet Union even before Britain had made peace. Meanwhile the destroyer deal had made the United States a factor in his calculations as well.[14]

Roosevelt's prodemocracy, antitotalitarian statements at Charlottesville on June 6 and in his acceptance speech on July 19 evidently convinced Hitler that he must reckon with American support for Britain. Although Hitler, as his naval Z-Plan showed, envisioned eventual conflict with the United States in the mid- to late 1940s, he saw no means of striking it directly yet, nor was he as yet interested in an offensive in the Atlantic of the kind Roosevelt, Marshall, and Stark feared so much. The American problem as he saw it related to Britain, which was counting on the United States and the Soviet Union for eventual help. He was already thinking about eliminating the Soviet threat, and on July 31 he remarked that with Russia disposed of, Japan would be free to occupy the United States in the Pacific. His fears became much more acute by mid-August after the Roosevelt-Churchill destroyers-for-bases deal and the defense agreement between the U.S. and Canadian governments became known. The idea of enlisting the Japanese against the United States now became the basis for another diplomatic revolution ultimately at least as significant as the Nazi-Soviet Pact.[15]

At least since the early 1930s, Japanese statesmen and military and naval leaders had become increasingly determined to replace the old international order in the Far East, as embodied in the Nine-Power Treaty and the Washington naval agreements of 1922, with a new order, now frequently referred to as the Greater East Asia Co-Prosperity Sphere. Japan would assume the responsibility for establishing and keeping order in the region while the influence of colonial powers either declined or disappeared. Their costly and brutal attempt to turn China into a vassal state—now nearly three years old—was only the second step in this process, after the creation of Manchukuo. The Japanese understood very well how events in Europe might affect their plans, and during 1939 they had had long negotiations with the Germans for some sort of alliance against the Soviet Union, Britain, and France. These talks had collapsed when Hitler signed the Non-Aggression Pact with the Soviets instead.

The European events of the late spring of 1940 had entirely transformed the situation. The fall of Holland and France and the threatened collapse of Britain, which had aroused so much concern in Washington over the fate of those countries' possessions in the western hemisphere, had left far more important territories at the mercy of the Japanese. France and Holland could not protect French Indochina (now Vietnam, Cambodia, and Laos) or the Dutch East Indies (now Indonesia), and British possessions such as Hong Kong, Singapore, and rubber-rich Malaya were potentially vulnerable as well. Equally important, the new U.S. plans for a two-ocean Navy posed a long-term threat to Japanese projects and thus encouraged Tokyo to act at once.[16]

Although in theory Japan remained a parliamentary democracy with a civilian government, government by political parties had effectively come to an end on May 15, 1932, when naval officers assassinated Prime Minister Inukai. Subsequent Prime Ministers had been bureaucrats or senior officers selected by a small group around the Emperor and approved by the Army and Navy, and the military leadership had increasingly taken control of strategy and foreign policy. On July 3, 1940, key Army officials approved an "Outline of the Main Principles for Coping with the Changing World Situation." It argued that Japan had to take advantage of the current situation to create a self-sufficient economic sphere centering on Japan, Manchuria, and China "and stretching from the Indian Ocean to the South Seas north of Australia and New Zealand." Now was the time to act, with Britain losing the war in Europe and the United States only beginning to rearm, and the Army wanted to be ready by the end of August to take advantage of Britain's collapse and move immediately into Hong Kong and Singapore. When naval leaders saw these plans they were delighted that the Army was now interested in a "southward advance," which would guarantee the Navy a much larger role than the alternative of a war with the Soviets, but they insisted that Japan would have to accept the probability of war with the United States as well. In July the Japanese took the first steps toward the realization of this program, demanding that the French Vichy government allow Japanese troops into northern Indochina to police its border with China.[17]

To secure their prospective position in Asia the Japanese also had to reach a new agreement with Germany. Berlin had already informed Tokyo that it was not interested in the fate of the Dutch East Indies, but the Japanese wanted a more explicit German endorsement of their plans for the Far East, not least because, like the Americans, they feared Germany's potential naval power should the Germans capture the British Fleet. In June and July the Yonai cabinet, in its last month in office, decided on negotiations designed to strengthen its ties with the Axis on the basis of a mutual recognition of interests that would leave the Japanese free to expand southward at their pleasure. The government believed that such an agreement could deter the United States from interfering with its plans. In June Foreign Minister Arita refused a U.S. suggestion for an exchange of notes pledging not to change the status of European possessions in Asia except by peaceful means, and on June 29 Arita publicly declared that the destiny of those possessions "is a matter for grave concern to Japan in view of her mission and responsibility as the stabilizing force in East Asia." To establish world peace, he said, "peoples who are closely related with each other geographically, racially, culturally and economically should first form a sphere of their own for co-existence and co-prosperity and establish peace and order within that sphere, and at the same time secure a relationship of common existence with other spheres." Governments aiding Chiang Kai-shek, he argued, stood in the way of peace in the Far East.[18]

A new cabinet of Prime Minister Konoye, War Minister Tojo, and Foreign Minister Matsuoka—who had always favored the alliance with Germany—took over in July and pursued the same course. They also hoped to bring the Soviet Union into the alliance, channeling its expansionist energies southward into the British Empire, in order to defuse the danger of war on the Manchurian border. On July 24, Matsuoka gave a remarkable interview to an American correspondent, echoing FDR's view of the world situation as a battle between political systems and ways of life. "In the battle between democracy and totalitarianism the latter adversary will without question win and will control the world. The era of democracy is finished and the democratic system bankrupt. There is not room in the world for two different systems or for two different economies. The one must yield to the other and totalitarianism will achieve universal control." The governments of Germany, Great Britain, Japan, and the United States were all declaring a worldwide ideological war. On August 1 the new Japanese government issued a long public statement leaving no doubt that it expected to play a critical role in the reconstruction of the world political order now underway. It promised to strengthen its economy, military, and naval forces and to create a "new order for

Greater East Asia," based on, but not limited to, Japan, Manchukuo, and China. Within days sources in Tokyo confirmed that the Greater East Asia Co-Prosperity Sphere would include Indochina and the Dutch East Indies and that they foresaw a world composed of European, Soviet, Pan-American, and Asian superstates, with Germany and Japan dominating the first and last of those.[19]

Since December 1938, the U.S. State Department had consistently refused to accept Japanese pronouncements and plans for a "new order" in Asia. "The American government," it had informed Tokyo with Roosevelt's approval in that month, "cannot accept the implication that enjoyment of equality of opportunity [in China] is to be contingent upon its admission of the validity of the conception of Japanese authorities of a 'new order' and a 'new situation' in East Asia. . . . The Government and people of the United States cannot assent to the termination of the provisions of treaties to which this Government is party or of rights and obligations thereunder by the arbitrary action of any other country." In the summer of 1940 Stimson's accession as Secretary of War added a new and more aggressive element to U.S. policy in the Far East. Stimson had tried and failed to organize international opposition to Japan's seizure of Manchuria as Hoover's Secretary of State. Ever since 1937 he had been closely associated with the Committee for Non-Participation in Japanese Aggression, whose head, Roger S. Greene, had long been agitating for an embargo on trade with Japan, especially of exports of strategic materials and petroleum, without which the Japanese could only carry on the war in China with the greatest difficulty. In May and June of 1940 Greene had successfully lobbied to put a clause giving the President the right to embargo strategic materials into the National Defense Act, a success about which he kept Stimson fully informed.[20]

Within a month of the passage of the Act, in late July 1940, an alliance of three powerful cabinet members—Treasury Secretary Morgenthau, who had the primary responsibility for enforcing the Act; Interior Secretary Ickes, who was interested in the oil situation; and Stimson— was advocating an embargo on key materials to Japan. On the other side stood Secretary of State Hull and Undersecretary Sumner Welles, who believed that such a measure would be too provocative and would lead to a Japanese attack on their nearest oil source, the Dutch East Indies, and perhaps on U.S. possessions as well. Washington authorities were well aware of Japanese intentions because Naval Intelligence had broken certain Japanese diplomatic codes. For security reasons, specific Japanese cables rarely circulated in print, but senior cabinet members, including the President, were often briefed about them, and one translated intercept was left in the White House in mid-July. Summarizing an exchange between the Foreign Minister and the Japanese Minister in Budapest, it discussed the necessity for southward expansion and speculated about the proper moment to enter the war.[21]

When Knox, Stimson, and Morgenthau all had dinner at the British Embassy on July 18, Stimson criticized the British for agreeing to close the Burma Road for three months to give the Japanese a chance to work out peace with China and noted that a new law would allow the United States to impose an embargo. The British Ambassador Lord Lothian replied that Japan might attack French and Dutch possessions in response, but he also assured Stimson that the British would be able to destroy the oil fields in the Dutch East Indies before the Japanese got there. The next day Stimson made one of his first visits to the White House and found Knox and Sumner Welles with Roosevelt. Their talk turned to oil and its influence on the war, and Stimson reported the previous evening's conversation and pushed for the embargo again. He believed that Japan in 1919 had been forced out of its occupation of the Russian Far East quite easily by threats of U.S. economic pressure, and that an oil embargo would have the same effect. Stimson kept the pressure on all week, and on Thursday, July 25, Morgenthau used the new legislation to get a directive from FDR creating an export licensing system for scrap iron, steel, and all petroleum products. At the regular Friday afternoon cabinet meeting the next day, Sumner Welles protested angrily on behalf of Secretary Hull, now in Havana, that a full embargo would mean war with Japan, and after a lengthy discussion, the embargo was limited to high-grade aviation fuel. Typically, Roosevelt had allowed two determined cabinet members, Stimson and Morgenthau, to take the initiative, only to back away somewhat when others weighed in.[22]

Undeterred, the Japanese on August 30 reached a new agreement with the French authorities in Indochina allowing them to move troops into the northern part of that country and to make full use of its transportation facilities. That in turn led to American cabinet decisions to lend $25 million to China and to embargo scrap iron exports to any nation outside the western hemisphere except Great Britain, which the administration announced on September 25 and 26. The State and Navy departments continued, however, to oppose an oil embargo. Their estimate of its consequences—shared by the President—was correct. The Japanese Navy had already decided that Japan would have to respond to a full U.S. embargo with an attack on the Dutch East Indies and war. As the summer wore on, Drew Pearson and Robert Allen repeatedly reported high-level speculation that the Japanese would move south against British, Dutch, and French possessions immediately if Britain were defeated.[23]

The Japanese Navy's decision to accept the possibility of war with Britain and the United States led it to drop its opposition to an alliance with Germany and Italy, and Foreign Minister Matsuoka thought that better relations with Germany, Italy, and the USSR might make the Americans back off. The Japanese remained confident into September that Germany was on the point of defeating Great Britain. The Germans, meanwhile, led by Foreign Minister Joachim von Ribbentrop—a diplomatic amateur who had risen through the Nazi Party to secure his post—labored under parallel misconceptions. A pact pledging Japan to enter a war against the United States if Washington entered the European war, they thought, would frighten the Americans and isolate the British and make them more amenable to a compromise peace. The Anglo-American destroyers-for-bases deal alarmed both Berlin and Tokyo and increased their interest in an agreement. In late August Ribbentrop dispatched a special envoy to Tokyo, and the talks were concluded within three weeks of his arrival on September 7. Although the talks took place mainly in Tokyo, the signature of the pact between Germany, Italy, and Japan took place in Berlin on September 27. The key passages of the pact—published in full—read as follows:

ARTICLE 1. Japan recognizes and respects the leadership of Germany and Italy in the establishment of a new order in Europe.

ARTICLE 2. Germany and Italy recognize and respect the leadership of Japan in the establishment of a new order in Greater East Asia.

ARTICLE 3. Japan, Germany, and Italy agree to cooperate in their efforts on aforesaid lines. They further undertake to assist one another with all political, economic and military means if one of the Contracting Powers is attacked by a Power at present not involved in the European War or in the Japanese-Chinese conflict.

A secret exchange of notes specified that the three parties would have to agree that events had brought Article 3 into play. Foreign Minister Matsuoka, the prime Japanese mover in the talks, explained to imperial Privy Council that he expected the pact to end U.S. support to Chiang Kai-shek and thus to force a settlement of the "China Incident" on Japanese terms. The Japanese do not seem to have realized, as the Germans already knew, that Britain's defeat was no longer imminent and that Germany would not invade England at least until the spring. Just three days later, Japanese troops entered into northern Indochina in fulfillment of an agreement reached with the Vichy government in the preceding week. In August the Tokyo government had drawn up sweeping economic demands on the Dutch East Indies.[24]

Article 3 of the pact, which could hardly have been clearer had it identified the United States by name, instantly aroused the attention of the American public. "JAPAN JOINS AXIS ALLIANCE SEEN AIMED AT U.S.," screamed the eight-column headline in the *New York Times.* In the long run, the pact ensured that the conflict in Europe would become a true world war. In the short run, however, it did exercise something of a restraining influence on Washington, for the simple reason that the United States lacked the resources even to fight on one front, much less two.[25]

While Berlin, Rome, and Tokyo negotiated their alliance, U.S. and British officers were exploring the possibilities of military cooperation in London. Their talks revealed widely differing views of the situation and probable future course of the war. Anticipating the possibility that the British and U.S. navies might be fighting together in the western hemisphere after an invasion of the British Isles, Stark and presumably Roosevelt had sent enough staff to discuss numerous technical questions involving equipment, communications, and tactics with the British. But the British, whose suggestion had led to Ghormley's mission to London, had been intensely preparing for the talks since June and had developed different ideas by the time Ghormley arrived. They expressed great confidence about the current strategic situation and their plans for winning the war, which did not require the active participation of the United States.

In two initial meetings in late August, British officers expressed confidence that they could defeat a German invasion, even though they were at present suffering heavily from bombing attacks both on the homeland and on their shipping. They thought that France would not actively join the Axis, but acknowledged that the Germans could compel Portugal and Spain to cooperate in the war, either take the British base at Gibraltar or render it unusable, and move into North Africa, Dakar, and possibly even "the Atlantic Islands," the Cape Verdes, Canaries, and Azores. Such moves would face the United States with tremendous problems even if Britain continued fighting. Dakar, at the tip of West Africa— which a combined British and Free French force tried and failed to capture in September—was only 1,800 miles from Brazil, and its capture by the Germans would probably trigger the U.S. occupation of the northeastern coast of that country.[26]

Introducing the Americans to the strategy that Churchill stuck to until late 1943, the British indicated that they counted on economic pressure and a strategic bombing campaign to win the war. When Ghormley asked if they agreed that land forces would eventually be necessary for victory, they replied that while the British Army would deliver the coup de grâce, "a serious weakening in the morale and fighting efficiency of the German machine, if not a complete breakdown . . . would make the task of the Army much more easy." They desperately needed more destroyers—a problem which the negotiations between Churchill and Roosevelt were doing something to solve. When Ghormley asked whether they had made any plans in case the Germans successfully invaded the British Isles, they replied in the negative. When Ghormley mentioned a recent spike in sinkings of ships by German U-boats, the British replied that they thought only temporary factors were responsible. That estimate turned out to be much too optimistic. British shipping losses to German U-boats and surface raiders, which had averaged about 200,000 tons a month during the first five months of 1940, eventually averaged 428,000 tons a month during the last seven months of the year and increased another 20 percent during the first six months of 1941—an unsustainable rate of losses that caused enormous concern in Washington.[27]

When Ghormley, speaking unofficially as always, asked if the British were relying on "the continued economic industrial support of the United States, and whether they counted upon the eventual active cooperation of the United States," the British confirmed that they counted on the former but not, they insisted, on the latter. Ghormley did not believe them. "I think that everybody in Great Britain expects the United States to enter the war within a few days after the election, in case the President is reelected," he wrote Admiral Stark on October 11. Should the United States enter the war in Europe, the British expected the U.S. Navy to keep the Axis out of the western Atlantic, and to provide aircraft and destroyers to help guard the convoy routes all the way to the United Kingdom, where they would come under British operational control. They also anticipated that the U.S. Marine Corps might seize key bases in the Atlantic.[28]

In late September, the conclusion of the Tripartite Pact forced the U.S. and British governments to reconsider the Far Eastern situation as well. While focusing on developments in Europe during May and June, Washington had already decided on a new naval strategy in the Far East, one designed to deter Japanese aggression without running undue risks. First, Roosevelt himself ordered the fleet to remain at Pearl Harbor in Hawaii after the completion of maneuvers in mid-May. When Fleet Commander Admiral James "Joe" Richardson protested the move on the grounds that the fleet could be more effectively prepared for war at its San Diego base, Admiral Stark replied on May 27 that the administration wanted to scare the Japanese away from a move into the Dutch East Indies, which Washington feared might accompany an Italian declaration of war on the Allies. Nothing happened when Italy declared war on June 10, but Roosevelt refused to allow the fleet to return. The State Department, led in this case by the Chief of the Far Eastern Division Stanley Hornbeck, thought the fleet's deterrent effect was important, and Roosevelt had apparently decided that it might as well stay in Hawaii at least until the invasion or surrender of Britain triggered an unmistakable threat in the Atlantic. During the first half of June, the Japanese also settled a border dispute involving Manchuria with the Soviets, and rumors of various Japanese actions, including the possible sabotage of the Panama Canal, sufficiently alarmed Washington authorities so as to have an alert ordered for Hawaii on June 17. Two days later Stark ordered the fleet to sail toward Panama for two days in order to discover whether such a movement would trigger sabotage in the canal. The alert was terminated about a month later.[29]

In mid-September, U.S. Ambassador Joseph Grew clearly stated the State Department's rationale for keeping the fleet at Pearl Harbor, as well as the essential principles that would ultimately lead the United States into the war. The "avowed purpose" of Germany and Japan, he cabled, was "the imposition of their will upon conquered peoples by the force of arms," and "American interests in the Pacific are definitely threatened by [Japan's] policy of southward expansion, which is a thrust at the British Empire in the east." To support the British Empire the United States had to try to preserve the status quo in the Far East, and a show of force might suffice to do so. But Grew also warned that while the recent limited sanctions on Japan could be justified by the domestic needs of the United States, an oil embargo would probably provoke violent retaliation because of "the uncalculating 'do or die' temper of the army and navy." Secretary of State Hull echoed Grew's line in a conversation with British Ambassador Lothian after the signature of the Tripartite Pact. "The special desire of this Government," he said, "is to see Great Britain succeed in the war and that its acts and utterances with respect to the Pacific area would be more or less affected as to time and extent by the question of what course would, on the part of this Government, most effectively and legitimately aid Great Britain in winning the war."[30]

Debate persisted at the highest levels, however, over the wisdom of even this policy. Admiral Richardson, who had taken command of the U.S. Fleet on January 16, 1940, at the age of sixty-one, had the strength of character and confidence in his own opinion characteristic of his generation. He had come to know Franklin Roosevelt well during two years as a senior naval staffer in Washington, and he resented the President's continual interference in naval affairs, his disinclination to take responsibility for unpleasant decisions, and what he regarded as the President's untrustworthiness. More importantly, Richardson did not believe his forces were strong enough to carry out the current War Plan Orange, which foresaw an advance into the Central Pacific and the establishment of a base in the Marshall Islands, more than two thousand miles west of Hawaii. After the fall of France, Richardson became desperately alarmed that the United States was drifting toward a war for which the fleet was unprepared, and he protested the order to remain at Pearl Harbor, whose facilities were then quite inferior to San Diego's, because of the enormous logistical, personnel, and training problems that the move initially involved. When Richardson visited Washington in July, Roosevelt assured him that he had no intention of sending the fleet into the western Pacific, but Secretary Knox shocked him when he visited the fleet in Hawaii in early September and told the flag officers present that he expected the United States to be in the war by March 15, 1941.[31]

Discussing the Far Eastern situation after the conclusion of the Tripartite Pact, the Americans and the British found themselves far apart. The British were counting on the United States far more for help against Japan than against Germany. During most of the 1920s and 1930s, the British had planned to deal with any threat to Singapore and Malaya by sending a large naval force to Singapore. But in the spring of 1939, Hitler and Mussolini had concluded their "pact of steel," apparently ensuring that Britain would have to fight Italy as well if a European war broke out. The ships previously designated for Singapore would now have to remain in the Mediterranean. Now, in talks with Ghormley, the British proposed that the U.S. Navy could fill the gap in their defenses by stationing a substantial fleet at Singapore if war with Japan broke out. On October 4 they asked Ghormley if the United States might be willing to send some capital ships to the Far East, that is, either to the Philippines or to Singapore. At the same time, Churchill decided to ratchet up the tension in the Far East himself.[32]

Having survived the Battle of Britain, the British in early October announced that they would reopen the Burma Road into China—Chiang Kai-shek's only remaining supply line—on October 17. Encouraged by the American aviation fuel embargo and some strong statements from Hull, Churchill actually took this step in the hope that a confrontation in the Far East might bring the United States into the war. Washington evidently believed that a possibly imminent war in the Far East required some kind of U.S. action. The President initially ordered one of his scarcest assets—a full Army division—to reinforce Hawaii, but Marshall and Stimson quickly talked him out of it while promising to try to send an antiaircraft regiment instead. Stimson repeated that the United States needed to take some forceful action in order to bring the Japanese to heel, just as he thought the Wilson administration had managed to do in 1918–1920 over the Japanese occupation of the Russian Far East. His fellow Republican Frank Knox wanted to send some U.S. warships to the Far East, and had Stark invite Richardson, then in California, for another visit to Washington to talk the proposal over. The idea, said to be favored by certain admirals, leaked into the press, with the additional argument that the new Atlantic bases would allow the United States to pursue a more forward policy in the Pacific.[33]

On October 5, Richardson and Stark saw Secretary Knox, who said that the President had been discussing the possible repercussions of the

British plan to reopen the Burma Road on October 17. If the Japanese took "drastic action," Knox said, the President was thinking about establishing naval patrols of light forces along two lines, from Hawaii to the Philippines and from Samoa to the Dutch East Indies, to blockade Japanese commerce. Such a plan—similar in concept to the action Roosevelt undertook in the western Atlantic in the second half of 1941—would not necessarily have meant war. To Knox's intense displeasure, Richardson replied that such a plan was impossible, that it would inevitably mean war, and that many of the ships involved would be lost. On October 8 Richardson saw the President, who expressed some interest merely in sending one division of light cruisers on a visit to the Philippines. After another argument over keeping the fleet in Honolulu, Roosevelt told Richardson that he could move the battleships back to San Diego "if I can be given a good statement which will convince the American people and the Japanese Government that in bringing the battleships to the west coast we are not stepping backward." That was not the kind of challenge that Richardson was inclined to accept. Richardson also demanded, in effect, an immediate, "marked" increase in the personnel of the fleet. When it became clear that Roosevelt would not agree—largely, Richardson thought, because of the forthcoming election—the Admiral took a deep breath.

"Mr. President," he said, "I feel that I must tell you that the senior officers of the Navy do not have the trust and confidence in the civilian leadership of this country that is essential for the successful prosecution of a war in the Pacific." "Joe," the President replied, "you just don't understand that this is an election year and there are certain things that can't be done until the election is over." Richardson's views, however, undoubtedly helped influence Roosevelt's resistance to Stimson's, Morgenthau's and Ickes's calls for tough economic sanctions against Japan that might make war more likely. The Navy Department's War Plans Division rushed a draft of a new Rainbow 3 to completion by October 17, presumably on the assumption that Japan might attack Britain when Britain reopened the Burma Road into China, and Stark sent it to Ghormley in London. It assumed that the U.S., British, and Dutch forces in the Far East would undertake a joint defense of "Malaysia"—defined to include not only the Malay Peninsula and Singapore but also the Dutch East Indies—and the Philippines, while attempting to raid and blockade Japanese commerce. Although the final version of the plan foresaw plenty

CNO Admiral Harold Stark (left), Secretary of the Navy Frank Knox, and fleet commander Admiral James Richardson in Knox's office, October 5, 1940. The highest-ranking officers routinely wore civilian clothes to work right up until Pearl Harbor. (Courtesy of the Naval Historical Center.)

of simultaneous threats in the Atlantic and even in the Caribbean, it assumed that the bulk of the U.S. Fleet would remain in the Pacific.[34]

Stimson was more than ready to move toward war and complained in his diary that Knox and Stark were standing in the way of "bold, affirmative action." The Tripartite Pact had struck him as "pretty useful, I think, in waking up our people. . . . Clamors are being made for an alliance with Great Britain already," and now he believed that the world stood at a historic turning point. On October 12, Stimson, after apologizing for "butting into matters which are not my business," wrote to the President to suggest that the entire U.S. Pacific Fleet sail to Singapore, as the British were suggesting in London. Combined with an embargo on oil, he argued, such a move would rapidly reduce Japan to "comparative impotency," and if the Japanese should attack, the United States would be

acting politically and militarily from a very strong position. A few days
later Knox wrote FDR that he had convinced Stimson that a much smaller
diversion would be sufficient, and Richardson had prepared a primarily
defensive war plan for a possible Anglo-American war with Japan that
would send just four cruisers and one carrier to the Philippines while
reinforcing various defensive positions in the Pacific. In the end just two
cruisers made a visit to the Far East.[35]

Stimson's bellicosity also ran up against the hard facts of U.S. capa-
bilities. Marshall and his staff now made clear that the United States sim-
ply could not fight a war with anyone for about eighteen months. In late
September Marshall's staff prepared a critical paper, "The Problem of
Production of Munitions in Relation to the Ability of the United States to
Cope with Its Defense Problems in the Present World Situation," which
Stimson on October 2 circulated to Knox, Morgenthau, and the Presi-
dent after the Joint Board had approved it.

Despite the Tripartite Pact, the paper did not expect Germany and
Italy to engage in open hostilities against the United States until they had
inflicted "a major reverse" on Britain and assured themselves of Soviet
neutrality. The Board had presciently concluded that Britain was not
about to be invaded or succumb to air attack, but they feared that Spain
and Portugal might fall under Axis control, that the possible losses of
Gibraltar and Dakar could force the United States to occupy northeastern Brazil to stop ferrying from Dakar to Natal, and that the Axis might
garrison the Canaries and Azores. Even in the worst case of a British defeat in six months, it would take another six months at least for the Germans and Italians to use the British Fleet, thus forcing the United States
into the war in October 1941. The Germans might also manage to install
some pro-German governments in South America, forcing the United
States to react, or undertake large-scale surface raids in the western Atlantic during the next year. If the British Fleet was destroyed or surrendered, the United States would have three months to "securely occupy all
Atlantic outpost positions from Bahia in Brazil northward to include
Greenland." The Joint Board evidently had no plans whatever to try to
intervene militarily to save Britain from a German invasion, and Roosevelt had not asked for any. Japan, the paper continued, might move into
the Dutch East Indies, the Philippines, or Guam within the next few
months, especially if the United States imposed further sanctions, facing
the United States with "a major effort in the Far East . . . for which we are
not now prepared and will not be prepared for several years to come."

Having surveyed what the United States might have to face, the paper turned to what U.S. forces could do. Necessary operations to protect the western hemisphere could require an Army of 1.4 million and a fully manned Navy, but the munitions for such forces were nowhere near available. United States forces now lacked enough munitions to combine training with *any* sustained combat. On September 30, 1941, the United States would be able to put only 150,000 men in the field. The situation would improve dramatically over the following six months, and by March 31, 1942, the Army might be able to supply its projected 1.4 million men, provided that "we sequester all foreign [British] munitions production in the US." Production for the Army was lagging far behind schedule. Airplane production over the next eighteen months looked far more promising, and a recent agreement between Morgenthau and the British provided for 12,884 planes for the Army, 6,208 for the Navy, and 14,375 for the British by April 1, 1942. The biggest single bottleneck remained machine tools, whose production had to be doubled. The Board recommended that British orders be better integrated with the United States' own needs—a gentle restatement of the Army's long-standing demand that the British receive much less. The United States, in short, desperately needed eighteen months even to be ready to defend the western hemisphere, much less to fight a naval war in the Pacific at the same time. This conclusion remained in the forefront of FDR's mind well into the next year.[36]

Foreign policy took second place in the presidential election campaign that fall because Roosevelt and Willkie both argued for aid to Britain while staying out of the war, but the administration still professed sweeping goals. On October 26, Secretary of State Hull gave the administration's most comprehensive foreign policy statement of the entire fall in a public address. Because Hull was never an intimate of Roosevelt's and played little role in the development of the alliance with Britain, his role in the administration has often been given short shrift, but he did a great deal to define the United States' approach to the world crisis and emerged during 1941 as a major advocate of war. Born in 1871, Hull was the only senior member of the administration to leave behind a thorough autobiography, and his life encapsulated many critical elements of the experience of the Missionary generation.[37]

Hull grew up in the mountain country of northeast Tennessee, one of the border areas torn apart by the chaos of the Civil War. The era's lawlessness touched his own family: His father survived a shot through the head from a Yankee irregular warrior from Kentucky, and eventually tracked the man down and killed him. Living in remote wilderness, Hull's father gradually prospered as a farmer and lumberman, and he and his wife initially home-schooled their sons, of whom Cordell was the third of five, and sent them to any available school when they were about fourteen. Sixty years later Hull vividly remembered winning a school debate by arguing that Washington had done more for America by defending it than Columbus had by discovering it. That convinced his father that Cordell must get the best education that he possibly could, and he sent him to a different and better school, whose teacher he remembered as one of the great inspirations of his life. Hull studied algebra, geometry, trigonometry, surveying, English, rhetoric, Latin, Greek, and German, all before he turned sixteen. The teacher's brother was a congressman who obviously helped inspire Hull's interest in politics. By 1888, when Hull turned seventeen, he was speaking in the reelection campaign of Grover Cleveland. A year earlier he had begun reading law in an office.

At the age of nineteen, when Stimson and Roosevelt were respectively studying at Harvard and Yale, Hull became the chairman of his Democratic County Executive Committee and attended the state convention that nominated a candidate for Governor. After one year at the Cumberland Law School in Lebanon, Tennessee, he passed the bar. He read everything he could find by, and about, Thomas Jefferson, whose principles of equality became the doctrine of his political faith. In 1892 he won election to the state legislature only a month after his twenty-first birthday. Such meteoric careers in law and politics have obviously long been impossible in the United States of the twentieth and twenty-first centuries, although they do occur in newer fields such as computer science. In 1898 Hull volunteered for the Spanish-American War, arriving in Cuba after the fighting had stopped and trying to uproot established, corrupt methods of administration. Returning to his law practice, he became a judge, dispensing severe justice even to relatively minor offenders. In 1906 he became a Democratic congressman. "Like many others," he wrote later, "I carefully studied government from the Acaean League and the Athenian democracy down to the present." It would not be easy today to find an ambitious young man or woman determined on a political career who could say the same.[38]

In Washington, Hull found a titanic struggle building between an older generation in thrall to wealth and privilege and a growing body of his own contemporaries favoring drastic reforms. He immediately decided to address himself to national questions as well as to the needs of his own district and emerged as a leading proponent of a federal income tax and of lower tariffs. The only congressman of the entire Boom generation who arrived in Washington with comparably great ambitions, it is fair to say, was Newt Gingrich of Georgia, and his efforts too met with considerable success. More of Hull's favorite projects became law during the first Wilson administration, and in 1917 he fully supported Wilson's decision to go to war in the face of Germany's lawless reign of terror on the high seas, and later, Wilson's plans for the League of Nations.

Swept out of office in the Republican landslide of 1920, Hull became chairman of the Democratic National Committee. In January 1924, Hull called the Teapot Dome scandal, in which federal oil lands had been given to private interests in return for bribes, "the greatest political scandal of this or any other generation. . . . The Republican reactionary leaders construed the huge majority of 1920 as a license to use the Government for their now selfish and party ends." Like so many of his contemporaries, he viewed history as a great moral drama revolving around issues of law, justice, and equality. He repeatedly tried but failed to prevent the social issues of Prohibition and the Ku Klux Klan from dividing the Democratic Party. Elected to the Senate in 1930, he surveyed the sorry state of the nation. "We cannot deny the view that there has been a sort of decay of our ancient ideals of liberty and democracy," he said. "The Democrat party should conduct a great crusade for a new birth and revival of the ideas, ideals, doctrines and spirit which underlie popular government." Franklin Roosevelt, who appointed him Secretary of State, fulfilled these hopes.[39]

In his first six years as Secretary of State, Hull focused on the Good Neighbor policy toward Latin America and further attempts to lower tariffs and barriers to international trade. But by the fall of 1940 he, like Roosevelt, was convinced that the world was fighting over the future of democracy and all the principles he held dear. In his speech on October 24, he reviewed the entire history of the previous decade, stressing the United States' devotion to peace and international law, its cultivation of better relations with its American neighbors, and its new rearmament program. "The United States, together with most other nations, has stood firmly for the basic principles underlying civilized international relations—peace, law, justice, treaty observance, non-intervention, peaceful settlement of disputes, and fair dealing," he said. "The advocacy of these principles has won for us the friendship of all nations, except those which, vaguely describing themselves as the 'have-nots' and claiming a superior right to rule over other peoples, are today on the march with great armies, air fleets and navies to take by force what they say they need or want. By deed and by utterance, the would-be conquerors have made it abundantly clear that they are engaged upon a relentless attempt to transform the civilized world as we have known it into a world in which mankind will be reduced again to the degradation of a master-and-slave relationship among nations and among individuals, maintained by brute force." Giving supplies to nations that, "while defending themselves against barbaric attack, are checking the spread of violence and are thus reducing the danger to us" was part of "the inalienable right of self-defense." Within months Hull would go further and argue even to Axis diplomats that self-defense did not require the United States to stand by passively until it was attacked.[40]

The presidential election campaign was now well underway, and both candidates, while advocating greater preparedness and support for Britain, were disclaiming any intention of entering the war. Yet the administration's internal deliberations make clear that political problems were a relatively minor factor in Roosevelt's calculations. The United States was almost powerless to affect the immediate course of events. Clearly it had no idea of sending its own land, sea, or air forces to save the British Isles from invasion. Its most immediate threat remained a German advance into the Atlantic and the western hemisphere in the wake of a successful invasion of Britain within six months or so. Japan was making no secret of its plans for a southward advance, which could easily include an attack on the Philippines or even Hawaii and involve the United States in the Pacific as well. The Tripartite Pact vastly increased the possibility that the United States would have to fight both Germany and Japan. Yet the Joint Board had just informed the President that the western hemisphere could not be secured against attack for at least another eighteen months. Roosevelt now faced the immediate problem of securing his own reelection and a Democratic Congress, but even if he succeeded, his greatest need would still be time.

CHAPTER 4

Reelection and Reassessment, October 1940–January 1941

THE PRESIDENTIAL CAMPAIGN OF 1940 WAS ONE OF THE MOST DRAMATIC in American history, rivaling those of 1860, 1896, and 1960 both in excitement and in significance. Roosevelt in 1940 had clearly established himself as one of the most significant Presidents of all time, acquiring both a passionate following among the American people and a host of extraordinarily bitter enemies from one extreme of the political spectrum to the other. Now he was the first President actually on the ballot of a major party ticket for a third term. The world had entered an era of dictatorship, and Roosevelt had already endured repeated accusations of both dictatorial intentions and dictatorial conduct. Anger against him was strongest among well-to-do Americans who had long regarded him as a dangerous Bolshevik and a traitor to his class. Elements of the eastern establishment had secured Willkie's nomination and now were working equally hard for his election, all the more so since Willkie, as well as Roosevelt, shared their interventionist views.[1]

Willkie, a man of considerable intelligence, energy, and achievement, decided to make the preservation of democracy the essence of his platform—but the threat to democracy on which he focused was not the rise of totalitarianism overseas, but the possible election of Franklin Roosevelt to a third term at home. After delaying his acceptance of the Republican nomination until August 17, he told a huge crowd in his home town of Elwood, Indiana, "We are here today to represent a sacred cause—the preservation of American democracy. . . . Party lines are down.

Nothing could make that clearer than the nomination by the Republicans of a liberal Democrat who changed his party affiliation because he found democracy in the Republican party and not in the New Deal party." He endorsed both a military draft and aid to Britain, citing the danger of the British Fleet falling into German hands, but he also accused Roosevelt of inflammatory attacks on foreign powers that threatened to involve the United States in hostilities. Paradoxically, he argued that the New Deal could not lead America to victory over Hitler because of its false principles. "We are not asked to make more for ourselves," he said. "We are asked to divide among ourselves that which we already have. . . . We are told that capital hates labor and labor hates capital. . . . I stand for a new companionship in an industrial society."[2]

Yet the paradox of Willkie's campaign emerged almost at once: Despite his warnings about Roosevelt, he endorsed much of what the New Deal had done, including the regulation of free enterprise, wages and hours laws, collective bargaining, social security, and unemployment insurance. New Deal taxes, he said, had inhibited opportunity and "diverted the money of the rich from productive enterprises to government bonds," leaving 8 million Americans still out of work and 6 million on some form of relief. (Republicans commonly lumped together those employed by the Public Works Administration (PWA), Works Progress Administration (WPA), and other New Deal agencies with those simply receiving public assistance.) The New Deal course, he said, would lead to a defeat like the French defeat, and to "economic disintegration and dictatorship."[3]

Willkie campaigned continually and frantically from Labor Day into early November, narrowing the focus of his campaign as he did so. By the time he spoke in Syracuse, New York, on October 14, he had essentially reduced his pitch to two points. First, "the third term candidate," as he called him, was betraying a fundamental principle of American democracy by putting himself forward as the one "indispensable man." Second, the New Deal had failed economically. The third term, he suggested, was a kind of coup d'état perpetrated not by traditional Democrats like Jefferson, Jackson, and Jim Farley, but by "the New Deal of Hopkins, Ickes, Corcoran and Wallace, which has captured the Democratic Party." In pursuit of power, he said, the "third term candidate" had expanded the government payroll, weakened the civil service, and forced men in the WPA "to contribute to New Deal campaign funds" and sign pledges to vote for New Deal candidates. Should the American people reelect FDR "because of some fine speeches about humanity," he said on another occasion, "you will be serving under an American totalitarian government before the long third term is finished." He also blamed New Deal economics for inadequate preparation for war. "No Administration in the history of America," he said, "has ever understood less about the problems and necessities of production."[4]

Roosevelt in his acceptance speech back in July had actually announced that he would be too busy overseeing defense preparations to campaign and that he had to stay within easy distance of Washington, although he reserved the right to correct misstatements of fact. He scheduled several supposedly "nonpolitical" speeches during September, beginning with an address to the Teamsters Union on the eleventh that made clear he was going to make the election a referendum on the New Deal and cast Willkie's support for its major reforms as a sham. Referring to labor's enormous gains during his two administrations—which had seen the Teamster membership rise from 70,000 to 500,000—he referred to the opposition that "comes only too often from those who regularly for three years and eight months block labor's welfare, and then for four months loudly proclaim that they are labor's true friends," and promised expanded unemployment benefits and old-age pensions.[5]

Receiving an honorary degree at the University of Pennsylvania on September 20, Roosevelt spoke of the "conflict between the point of view of Alexander Hamilton, sincerely believing in the superiority of Government by a small group of public-spirited and usually wealthy citizens, and, on the other hand, the point of view of Thomas Jefferson, an advocate of Government by representatives chosen by all the people." Jefferson understood, he said in a clever if tacit riposte to Willkie, that government by the rich would lead inevitably to the end of free elections. "No dictator in history has ever dared to run the gauntlet of a really free election," he said. "I would rather trust the aggregate judgment of all the people in a factory—the president, all the vice presidents, the board of directors, the managers, the foremen, plus all the laborers—rather than the judgment of the few who may have financial control at the time."[6]

On Columbus Day, October 12, Roosevelt made the most explicit foreign policy statements of the campaign. Addressing not only the United States but all the nations of the Americas, he reiterated his determination to defend the hemisphere, including "the right to the peaceful use of the Atlantic and Pacific Oceans. That has been our traditional policy."

Germany, Italy, and Japan had just signed the Tripartite Pact, pledging to go to war with any power that became involved in war in either Europe or the Pacific against them, and Roosevelt responded. "No combination of dictator countries of Europe and Asia will halt us in the path we see ahead for ourselves and for democracy. No combination of dictator countries of Europe and Asia will stop the help we are giving to almost the last free people now fighting to hold them at bay." Roosevelt consistently led Willkie in Gallup polls in September and October, but his refusal openly to campaign was alarming his supporters in the latter month. On October 16, Ickes told FDR's assistant General Edwin "Pa" Watson that the President was going to lose the election if he didn't start making genuine political speeches, and Watson arranged for him to lunch with Roosevelt the next day. FDR promised a series of speeches along the East Coast, beginning on October 19.[7]

Ickes's concerns were quite understandable. Although the Gallup poll consistently showed Roosevelt with a lead, some others did not—and the President was doing very poorly indeed among opinion leaders. The U.S. press in the 1930s was overwhelmingly Republican. Not once had FDR enjoyed the support of a majority of the nation's newspapers: Hoover had led him by 52–41 percent in 1932, with 9 percent undecided, and Landon, astonishingly, had done even better in 1936, with a lead of 57–36 percent among papers that gave an endorsement. Willkie had even more press support, with 64 percent of a very large sample of papers supporting him and only 22 percent of them endorsing FDR. One after another, even interventionist eastern papers adopted Willkie's arguments against the third term and New Deal economic policies. "We give our support to Mr. Willkie primarily for these reasons," wrote the *New York Times*, which had backed FDR in 1936, on September 19: "Because we believe that he is better equipped than Mr. Roosevelt to provide this country with an adequate national defense; because we believe he is a practical liberal who understands the need of increased production; because we believe that the fiscal policies of Mr. Roosevelt have failed disastrously; because we believe that at a time when the traditional safeguards of democracy are falling everywhere it is particularly important to honor and preserve the American tradition against vesting the enormous powers of the Presidency in the hands of any man for three consecutive terms of office."[8]

On the very next day the *Washington Post* agreed that Willkie would have a better chance of ramping up U.S. production effectively. Saving its last blast for November 3, the conservative *Los Angeles Times* echoed Willkie's warnings that a third term would mean dictatorship for the United States. William Randolph Hearst's huge newspaper chain joined the chorus of opposition to FDR, as did Roy Howard's. Columnists were slightly more favorable. Roosevelt enjoyed the enthusiastic support of the enormously popular daily column, *The Washington Merry-Go-Round*, written by Drew Pearson and Robert Allen, and also of Dorothy Thompson, the leading female columnist of her era. "The President can be a very great man in times of emergency," she wrote on October 9. "He was a great man in 1933, and he has been a great man since the overwhelming crisis in June. . . . While others talked of unity, the President moved swiftly to make unity real." The Olympian columnist Walter Lippmann, however, preferred to remain above the fray and preach the need for national unity no matter which candidate won.[9]

Among the small minority of newspapers supporting the President, in addition to those of the customarily Democratic South, were the urban black press of the North. The *New York Amsterdam News* analyzed the question from a specifically Negro viewpoint. Although it criticized the President for failing to oppose segregation in the armed forces or to work harder to pass an antilynching bill, it saw "no choice except to support the President. It requires no wise man to understand the advantages that have come to the Negro through President Roosevelt's social legislation. . . . The WPA, NYA, PWA and CCC have opened up new vistas for the Negro." The *Chicago Defender* reached the same conclusion, but its endorsement took a broader point of view and made no reference to Negroes at all. "President Roosevelt has placed himself squarely on the side of the people's interests, against those of the 'money changers in the temple.' No administration in our history has done more than the New Deal to achieve economic and social democracy. Roosevelt's defeat would be a victory not only for the dictators of Europe but also for the financial moguls of U.S.A." The leading Negro intellectual of the Missionary generation and cofounder of the NAACP, seventy-two-year-old W. E. B. Du Bois, argued similarly in the *New York Amsterdam News*. Although skeptical that the war would bring any benefit to Negroes anywhere and critical of FDR for his failure to do much about Jim Crow, he stated in early August that he favored the third term because Roosevelt had squarely faced the problem of the condition of the bottom one-third of the nation, something that Willkie would never do.[10]

The Negro vote was now large enough in many northern industrial states to tip the balance in a potentially close election, and both parties did what they could to secure it. Some months after the election, Walter White, the Secretary of the NAACP—by far the leading Negro organization in the country—told Harold Ickes, who ranked with Eleanor Roosevelt as one of the most pro–civil rights members of the administration, that Willkie had invited him to "name his price" for an endorsement of the Republicans, but White had declined and taken no position on the election. The Republicans had better luck with the most famous black man in America, heavyweight champion Joe Louis, who went on a speaking tour for Willkie during the last week of the campaign.[11]

The President's campaign faced another huge challenge. No one could be surprised by Big Business's opposition to FDR, but the President also faced a critical defection from the ranks of organized labor.

The second Roosevelt administration had seen the ranks of organized labor more than double, from 3.4 million to more than 7 million members, thanks largely to the Wagner Act of 1935 and the National Labor Relations Board that it had established. The majority of the growth had taken place within the new Congress of Industrial Organizations, or CIO, founded in 1935 by United Mine Workers leader John L. Lewis, which had mounted successful organizing drives in the factories of U.S. Steel and victorious sit-down strikes in two of the three major auto companies, General Motors and Chrysler. Lewis had quickly split with William Green's American Federation of Labor (AFL), with whom the CIO became involved in hundreds of jurisdictional disputes, some of them violent. By 1940 the AFL had 4.2 million members and the CIO 3.5 million. A commanding, charismatic figure who answered to no one but himself, Lewis, now sixty years old, the greatest labor leader of the Missionary generation, inevitably clashed with FDR, who wanted to cast the government as a neutral arbitrator between business and organized labor. The coming of war in Europe introduced another explosive element into their relationship.

Like so many of the leftist members of the Missionary generation who had lived through the First World War—men like the civil rights leader W. E. B. Du Bois, the historian Charles A. Beard, Progressive Senator Hiram Johnson, and socialist Norman Thomas—Lewis still regarded war as a tool of capitalists of no benefit to the working man. In addition, the CIO had drawn on the Communist Party of the United States

(CPUSA) for many of its most active organizers, and Lewis tolerated Communists at the highest levels of the union, including his general counsel Lee Pressman, who had once belonged to the same Washington, DC, Communist cell as Alger Hiss. From 1936 until August of 1939 the Communist Party had consistently supported rearmament and resistance to German, Italian, and Japanese aggression. After the signature of the Nazi-Soviet Pact in late August of that year the CPUSA immediately changed its line and opposed preparedness in general and aid to Britain in particular. Although further events in 1941 eventually proved beyond any doubt that Lewis himself was not a Communist, he shared his CPUSA allies' view of the world conflict in 1940. "War has always been the device of the political despairing and intellectually sterile statesmen," Lewis said in a Labor Day 1939 address after war had broken out. "It provides employment in the gun factories and begets enormous profits for those already rich. It kills off the vigorous males who, if permitted to live, might question the financial and political exploitation of the race. . . . Labor in America wants no war nor any part of war."[12]

Different stories circulated as to why Lewis in 1940 decided eventually to oppose Roosevelt's reelection. Labor Secretary Frances Perkins claimed to have heard from FDR himself that Lewis had visited the White House in January of that year and argued that only his presence on the ticket could bring the third term home. Roosevelt had already begun cultivating other CIO union leaders such as Phillip Murray of the Steelworkers and Sidney Hillman of the Amalgamated Clothing Workers, and Hillman's appointment as the labor representative on the Defense Commission was another blow to Lewis's prestige. During the first half of the year Lewis had publicly opposed the third term and supported liberal isolationist Burton Wheeler of Montana for the Democratic nomination while trying simultaneously to secure the Republican nomination for Herbert Hoover. The nomination of Willkie, who held foreign policy views similar to Roosevelt's, gave Lewis a chance to reverse course, but he did not take it.[13]

On October 26, the campaign organization Democrats for Willkie paid $45,000 to allow Lewis to address the entire nation on all three major radio networks. He did not disappoint. While claiming to represent about 10 million Americans, he announced that he was speaking only as a citizen. He opposed Roosevelt's reelection, he said, because the President wanted war. Then, after several paragraphs echoing Willkie about the impending dictatorship that the third term would bring about, he accused Roosevelt and the Democrats of betraying organized labor during the previous three years. Willkie's election, he said, was "imperative," and if labor disregarded his opinion and reelected FDR, he promised to step down as its Chairman of the CIO at its forthcoming November convention. Lewis had effectively forced the working men and women of America to choose between the President and himself—and in the end, they did.[14]

More was at stake, of course, than the presidency. In 1938 Democratic strength in the House had fallen from 333 to 262 and in the Senate from 75 to 69. A loss of 45 more House seats, which did not seem impossible, would give the Republican Party control. During 1940 there had been seven special elections for members of the House of Representatives, and the Republicans had gained an average of 6 percent of the vote in each of them. They gained the same 6 percent for Congress when rock-ribbed Republican Maine voted early, as it customarily did, on September 13, meanwhile giving Willkie a large majority. The press speculated freely about a possible Republican takeover of the House regardless of the Presidential outcome, and Democratic incumbents were handicapped by the need to remain in Washington well into October after the Republicans refused to adjourn, claiming that the administration needed to be closely watched. The House and Senate continued to meet even though a quorum of half the membership was often lacking. Democratic House candidates were also strapped for campaign cash, which the Democratic National Committee, itself at a disadvantage against the Republicans, was hoarding for the presidential campaign.

Into the breach stepped Sam Rayburn of Texas, who had just become Speaker of the House after the sudden death of William Bankhead of Alabama. Warning FDR that a Republican Congress would destroy him as they had destroyed Woodrow Wilson in 1919–1920, he secured the appointment of his young protégé Congressman Lyndon Johnson of Texas as an informal assistant to the Congressional Campaign Committee on October 14. Within five days, Johnson and Rayburn had secured $45,000 in contributions from wealthy Texans—more than four times as much as the Democratic National Committee had provided. During the next three weeks, the energetic young Johnson—he was then thirty-three—became a one-man national campaign coordinator, sending out a questionnaire asking candidates what assistance they might require, arranging for speakers, securing favors from federal agencies and legislative deals, and scrambling for more and more money, often working around the strict laws then prevailing against corporate contributions. Johnson, Rayburn, and Roosevelt met at the White House on October 27, in the midst of the President's own campaign tour, and Johnson said that eighty-two incumbent Democrats were in tight races in which even $1,000 might make the difference. Roosevelt recommended that the National Committee provide Johnson with $50,000 to distribute, and when it was not forthcoming, the ambitious Congressman did his best to raise it himself.[15]

Meanwhile, from October 23 until Sunday, November 3, Roosevelt made speeches in Philadelphia, on the radio for a forum staged by the hostile *New York Herald Tribune*, in Madison Square Garden in New York, in Boston, in Buffalo, and in Cleveland. Reminding his audience in Philadelphia that he had promised to correct misstatements of fact, Roosevelt referred specifically to Willkie's accusations that he had promoted the appeasement of the dictators, that Social Security funds would never be paid out, and that his reelection would end American democracy within four years. He accused his enemies of "certain techniques of propaganda, created and developed in dictator countries . . . the very simple technique of repeating and repeating and repeating falsehoods, with the idea that by constant repetition and reiteration, with no contradiction, the misstatements will finally come to be believed. . . . The overwhelming majority of Americans will not be scared by this blitzkrieg of verbal incendiary bombs. They are now calmly aware that, once more, 'The only thing we have to fear is fear itself.'" He denied, quite honestly, the accusation that he had made secret agreements with foreign governments pledging participation in a "foreign war." But then he turned to the domestic record that remained the foundation of his campaign, reminding the voters of Republican opposition to relief, collective bargaining, minimum wages, and maximum hours. "In the month of August of this year over four hundred thousand were added to the payrolls," he boasted. "And last month, September, another five hundred thousand workers went to work in our industries.[16]

A shifting team of staffers led by former New York judge Samuel I. Rosenman had written Roosevelt's speeches since the 1932 campaign, always in close consultation with the President. So strong was his influence that when playwright Robert E. Sherwood joined the team in the fall of

1940, he told Rosenman and Harry Hopkins, his two collaborators, that all Roosevelt's speeches used such a similar style that he thought they must have been written by the President himself. For the speech to the *Herald Tribune* forum, the President flung down the gauntlet in the face of both Hitler and the Japanese, claiming the mixed ancestry of the American people as a strength rather than a weakness. "As to the humorless theory—that we are 'hybrid and undynamic—mongrel and corrupt,' and that, therefore, we can have no common tradition—let them look at most gatherings of Americans and study the common purpose that animates those gatherings. . . . It is the very mingling of races dedicated to common ideals which creates and recreates our vitality. . . . The bold and the adventurous men, of many racial origins, were united in their determination to build a system which guaranteed freedom—for themselves and for all future generations. They built a system in which Government and people are one."[17]

Roosevelt built on the same themes in the remaining speeches while adding other attacks on the Republicans. In Boston he cited the growth of the Navy and Air Corps during his administration and the recent acquisition of new bases in the Atlantic, and noted that a majority of Republicans had voted against naval expansion in 1938 and for *fewer* aircraft in 1939. The draft had now gone into operation, and he assured the mothers of America not only that their boys would be properly housed, trained, and equipped, but that "I have said this before, but I shall say it again and again and again: Your boys are not going to be sent into any foreign wars. They are going into training to form a force so strong that, by its very existence, it will keep the threat of war far away from our shores." He reviewed what the New Deal had done for agriculture, always in the teeth of Republican opposition, and concluded, "In our own American community we have sought to submerge all the old hatreds, all the old fears, of the old world. We are Anglo-Saxon and Latin, we are Irish and Teuton and Jewish and Scandinavian and Slav—we are American. We belong to many races and colors and creeds—we are American."[18]

In Brooklyn, on November 1, he warned the nation of the alliance between Communists and Fascists that seemed to be wreaking havoc abroad and opposing his election at home. "Something evil is happening in this country when a full page advertisement against this administration, paid for by Republican supporters, appears—where, of all places?—in the *Daily Worker*, the newspaper of the Communist Party. Something evil is happening in this country when vast quantities of Republican campaign literature are distributed by organizations that make no secret of their admiration for the dictatorship form of government." Then he returned to domestic issues. "The President's only supporters," a prominent Philadelphia Republican had said, "are paupers, those who earn less than $1,200 a year and aren't worth that, and the Roosevelt family." Those "paupers," Roosevelt said, "are only the common men and women who have helped build this country, who have made it great, and who would defend it with their lives if the need arose. The demand for social and economic justice comes from those who receive less than $1,200 a year, but not from them alone. For I believe that when Americans cross this dividing line of $100 a month, they do not lose their devotion to social and economic justice."[19]

At Cleveland on November 2, Roosevelt—not for the first or the last time—linked rearmament to the building of a new America and called on the American people to face a turning point in history. "This Nation which is arming itself for defense has also the intelligence to save its human resources by giving them that confidence which comes from useful work. This Nation which is creating a great navy has also found the strength to build houses and begin to clear the slums of its cities and its countryside. This Nation which has become the industrial leader of the world has the humanity to know that the people of a free land need not suffer the disease of poverty and the dread of not being wanted. It is the destiny of this American generation to point the road to the future for all the world to see." Meanwhile, in one promise he did not keep, he said the third term would be his last.[20]

On election eve, he concluded his campaign with another paean to democracy in a radio address from Hyde Park. "Democracy is not just a word, to be shouted at political rallies and then put back into the dictionary after election day. The service of democracy must be something much more than mere lip-service. The service of democracy is the birthright of every citizen, the white and the colored; the Protestant, the Catholic, the Jew; the sons and daughters of every country in the world, who make up the people of this land. Democracy is every man and woman who loves freedom and serves the cause of freedom." At a moment when racial dictatorships already dominated much of Europe and Asia, these were no empty words. By all accounts, Roosevelt shared with most of his listeners a simple Christian faith, and he ended his talk with a prayer.[21]

Polling was still in its infancy, but Gallup, the most reliable pollster, showed the race tightened all the way to 52–48 for Roosevelt in its last trial heat, conducted in the last days of October. The same poll showed FDR ahead in 30 states and Willkie in 18, including New York and Pennsylvania, which would have left FDR a victor with 350 electoral votes. The pro–New Deal *Washington Merry-Go-Round* made a similar prediction. *Time* magazine, which did not endorse a candidate but made its Willkie sympathies amply clear, expected a close result, and many Republicans speculated that Willkie might win the Electoral College but lose the popular vote thanks to Roosevelt's large majorities in the solid South. The President himself, who could estimate with the best of them, sat down with pencil and paper during the last days of the campaign and concluded that he would win with 340 electoral votes.[22]

On November 5, 1940, 50 million American voters overwhelmingly reelected Franklin Roosevelt to a third term in office. He won nearly 55 percent of the popular vote and carried 38 of 48 states with 449 electoral votes to Willkie's 82. Willkie could add only Indiana, Michigan, and six farm belt states to Landon's bastions in Maine and Vermont. Nor was this all. The Republicans gained only three Senate seats, leaving the Democrats with 65 out of 96, and Lyndon Johnson's frantic effort allowed the Democrats actually to gain five seats in the House, leaving them with 267 to 162 for the Republicans. Pearson and Allen's *Washington Merry-Go-Round* detailed Johnson's last-minute exploits in a most laudatory column about the "rangy, 32-year old [sic], black-haired, handsome Texan" on November 16. Noting that he had brought $71 million in New Deal money to his district in just three years, they predicted great things for him. "Roosevelt has a fatherly affection for young Johnson, frequently consults him on political affairs, and is quietly grooming him for a high party post," the column said. "That's Lyndon Johnson," they quoted an anonymous friend. "If he tells you he can be elected President of the United States—don't bet against him."[23]

The vote was a rebuke to most of the nation's leading newspapers, nearly all the country's leading businessmen, and John L. Lewis, who promptly carried out his pledge to resign as head of the CIO. Seldom if ever have poorer Americans triumphed over the rich to the extent that they did in the election of 1940, when an October Gallup poll had shown 53 percent of property owners favoring Willkie over Roosevelt. The President carried every major metropolitan area, including many in which he was not favored by a single newspaper.

The common man obviously appreciated Roosevelt's response to the Depression, yet since 1938 the polls had suggested that he would never have been elected again but for the war in Europe. The people trusted him to handle the world crisis, and now he set about preparing to do so. The task had just increased enormously in difficulty. The signature of the Tripartite Pact among Germany, Italy, and Japan in late September had made a one-front war almost impossible, and new studies had shown exactly how unprepared the United States was. To meet the enormous short-, medium- and long-term dangers it faced, the United States had to move forward on many fronts. The President now had to decide how to combine prudence and preparedness in a rapidly evolving world situation.

Three major strategic options emerged after the election in November 1940. The President might, as the War Department wanted, focus on preparing the defense of the western hemisphere at the expense of aid to Britain. Alternatively he could continue assigning at least half of U.S. war production to the British in an attempt to keep them alive. Most radically of all, he might actually prepare to enter the European war almost at once in an attempt to save Britain from the invasion that was almost universally expected to take place in the spring—the course of action advocated by the Chief of Naval Operations, Admiral Stark. As it turned out, he chose the second option, partly because it provided the best means of increasing U.S. war production still further and partly because the United States simply was not yet ready to participate in the war.

During November, Roosevelt confirmed that he still wanted to provide whatever material assistance he could to help prolong the British war effort. Although Stimson had made it publicly clear even before his appointment that he wanted the United States fighting on Britain's side as soon as possible, he now shared General Marshall's view that the rearmament of the United States had to take priority over aid to Britain. Roosevelt did not, and he had left Treasury Secretary Morgenthau in charge of negotiations with the British purchasing mission in Washington during the fall of 1940. The British knew by October of that year that they had survived the immediate crisis in the air and that no German invasion was imminent, but they still believed German aircraft production to be more than twice what it actually was and were counting on the United

States to make up the difference. And to equip their projected army of 55 divisions by the end of 1941, the British would need to draw heavily on U.S. steel capacity of 50 million tons a year, compared to 18.5 million tons in Britain and 42 million tons now at the disposal of the Germans in Europe.[24]

British officials, indeed, were designing larger programs for U.S. industry than the Americans had for themselves. As of October 28 the British had placed $1.6 billion of orders and were trying to place $3.2 billion more, including $237 million for plant expansion. They had ordered 11,000 aircraft and 27,000 aircraft engines, and now wanted to order that many over again. They now hoped to receive 27,000 aircraft by the middle of 1942, even though Defense Commission leader William Knudsen's latest aircraft production plans called for a total of only 16,500 during the whole year of 1942. They also wanted 1 million Enfield rifles and 10,000 artillery pieces for their army to help equip ten new divisions. On that very day, Churchill weighed in with a desperate message for FDR pleading for the acceleration of these planned deliveries. He noted that the Vichy government of France seemed ready to go into a full alliance with Hitler, with disastrous consequences for North America, while the Germans and Italians were now threatening the British position in Egypt. "Having placed all the facts before you," he concluded, "I feel confident that everything humanly possible will be done. The world cause is in your hands." Churchill had not threatened Roosevelt with imminent British defeat, but behind his words lay the possibility that a new string of reverses might bring to power a government willing to make peace with Hitler. Morgenthau discussed Churchill's requests with the President on that same day.[25]

Two years earlier, on November 14, 1938, Roosevelt had talked about the need for a huge number of aircraft, "even though I might have had to ask Congress for authority to sell or lend them to the countries in Europe." The planes allocated to the British still served a dual purpose, all the more so since Britain might fall to invasion long before most of them could be delivered: They could help British morale and the British war effort, while expanding U.S. productive capacity for any future contingencies. During the week following the election, Roosevelt insisted through Morgenthau, over the violent objections of generals Marshall and Arnold, that the British would receive half of future production of B-17 heavy bombers and of B-25 and B-26 medium bombers. Marshall protested futilely that the United States needed these planes to train enough pilots to defend the western hemisphere. On Friday, November 8, Roosevelt confirmed the 50–50 arrangement in a press conference before his afternoon cabinet meeting and endorsed the new British order of a total of 12,000 additional planes, as they had requested. Yet as he noted at the cabinet meeting later that day, another problem had arisen: the British were running out of cash to pay for those orders. He speculated that after they had spent their remaining $2.5 billion, the United States could lease them material that was "loanable, returnable, and insurable"—an idea that would mature during the next seven weeks.[26]

The President made two key personnel moves during November and early December. Roosevelt notoriously disliked firing anyone, but two obvious recalcitrants within his own administration now had to go. Joseph P. Kennedy, the wealthy financier and industrialist whom Roosevelt had sent to Britain as Ambassador in 1938, had never had the slightest faith in Britain's ability to survive the war with Germany and had suggested after the Munich crisis that the United States had to learn to get along with dictatorships as well as democracies. He had spent 1940 in London alone, having sent his large family home, furious at being left out of the Lend-Lease negotiations and Ghormley's staff talks with the British. In October the President had called him home for consultation and persuaded him to endorse him in a nationwide radio broadcast on the eve of the election. On December 1, he and Roosevelt agreed that he would resign. Roosevelt had also decided to relieve Admiral Richardson but did not do so until January. Meanwhile, Donald Nelson of the Defense Commission, who had been placed in charge of purchasing and later of priorities, had become convinced by the time of the election that the Commission did not have enough authority to balance the needs of rearmament on the one hand and the civilian economy on the other. He was also homesick, and a few days after the election, he wrote the President to tell him that he had decided to go home to Sears Roebuck in Chicago.[27]

Roosevelt called him in and announced that he would have to stay. Before Nelson could reply, the President spent twenty minutes discussing the state of the world, the reasons that he had decided to run for a third term, and the weak defenses he had observed along the Canadian coast. Nelson interrupted to repeat that he wanted to go home, but FDR rhapsodized about yachting, discussed the decision to recognize the Soviet

Union, and even referred to the possibility of a German-Soviet war. Suddenly an hour was up and an aide announced that Secretary Hull had arrived to see the President. "Don," Roosevelt said, "I have decided that I very much want you to stay"—and Nelson agreed to do so. Nelson came to learn that this was a standard Roosevelt technique. The President, as subsequent events would show, had identified Nelson as the man he needed to organize production for all-out war.

Meanwhile, Admiral Stark set to work to move the United States into the European war at once. On Wednesday, November 6, the Admiral expressed his deep satisfaction at the outcome of the election in a letter to President Roosevelt. General Marshall typically saw no need to write a similar note. Stark, however—who had believed since September 1939 that it was only a matter of time until the United States became involved in the war—regarded the election as a critical milestone and wanted to make the British belief, as reported by Admiral Ghormley from London, that Roosevelt's reelection would bring the United States into the war come true. Stark, his staff, and other leading officers in the Navy Department were already hard at work on a new general estimate of the world situation to submit to Secretary Knox and the President. He completed a draft by November 4 and a finished version exactly one week after the election, on November 12. It is commonly known as the Plan Dog memorandum.[28]

The Army General Staff in 1940–1941 produced a stream of tightly argued, succinct strategic appreciations, presumably under the influence of its chief, General George Marshall. Admiral Harold "Betty" Stark on the other hand loved to ramble, both in his long private letters to commanders overseas and in his strategic appreciations such as the Plan Dog memorandum. The memorandum, however, argued clearly that the United States had to do whatever it could—including entering the war—to save Great Britain. The problem, Stark stated in his opening paragraph, was simple: "If Britain wins decisively against Germany we could win everywhere; but that if she loses, the problem confronting us would be very great; and, while we might not <u>lose everywhere,</u> we might possibly not <u>win anywhere.</u>" Continuing, he ranked U.S. objectives as, first, the defense of the United States, and second, "the prevention of the disruption of the British Empire." Although his third objective was the "diminution of the offensive military power of Japan," he doubted "that it would be in our interest to reduce Japan to the status of an inferior military and economic power." The fall of Britain, on the other hand, would sooner or later bring the Axis into the western hemisphere. "The present situation of the British Empire," he wrote, "is not encouraging. I believe it easily possible, lacking active American military assistance, for that empire to lose this war and eventually be disrupted. It is my opinion that the British are over-optimistic as to their chance for ultimate success." Even if Britain held out, he continued, she lacked the resources to win the war by bringing about the defeat of Nazi Germany.[29]

Stark believed the British needed U.S. help not only to save their home islands but to avoid the loss of either Egypt or Gibraltar to the Axis, which would make Germany far more difficult to beat. He was apparently willing to gamble that the Japanese would be content to seek economic control over the Dutch East Indies rather than risk war with Britain and the United States. If Japan did attack, Stark clearly preferred a very limited, defensive strategy against the Japanese, and as the paper went on, it seemed clear that Stark hoped to avoid war in the Pacific at all. That would allow the United States to both defend the western hemisphere and provide naval assistance to Britain along the lines Ghormley had discussed in London: protecting the western Atlantic against surface raiders and submarines; providing escorts, minesweepers and "flying boat" (seaplane) reconnaissance around Britain itself; and possibly seizing the Azores and the Cape Verde Islands. Going further, Stark became the very first American planner to suggest that the United States would have to send large air and land forces "to Europe or Africa, or both," and to participate in a decisive land offensive in order to win the war.

Although acknowledging that the American people seemed strongly to want to remain at peace, Stark argued that the United States had to decide where it wanted to fight. After reviewing and rejecting option A, hemispheric defense; B, an offensive against Japan, which some of his own senior officers seemed to favor; and C, a very doubtful war on both fronts, Stark proposed Plan D (Dog), "an eventual strong offensive in the Atlantic as an ally of the British," combined with a defensive posture in the Pacific. The United States would send "strong naval light forces and aircraft" to Britain and the Mediterranean and might capture not only Atlantic islands, but bases in Africa or even Europe. "At the conclusion of that war," he wrote, "even if Britain should finally collapse, we might still find ourselves possessed of bases in Africa suitable for assisting in the defense of South America. . . . The chances for success are in our favor, particularly if we insist upon full equality in the political and military direction of the war." Plan D (Dog) would make it very difficult to defend against Japanese aggression, and he therefore favored an attempt to remain at peace with Japan. He did not propose immediately moving the fleet into the Atlantic, but merely the "redistribution of our naval forces as the situation demanded" when war became imminent. He concluded with a recommendation for new joint plans to meet various contingencies—the only approved plan at this time was still Rainbow 4 for hemispheric defense—and recommended staff talks with the British. Stark evidently favored almost immediate American entry into the war. So did Knox, his civilian chief, who had warned the commanders of the Pacific Fleet to be prepared to be in the war by March 15 when he visited Hawaii in September 1940.[30]

The two critical issues of new war plans and more aid for Britain came to a head between mid-November and mid-December. On November 22 Stark informed Marshall that the President had read the Plan Dog memorandum and had asked for a joint estimate of the world situation. Stark initially carried Marshall along with him, and the Joint Board on December 10 turned an almost verbatim copy of Stark's Plan Dog memo into a draft memorandum by the Secretaries of War and of the Navy. The War Department, meanwhile, reiterated its vehement opposition to war in the western Pacific and proved more skeptical about war in the Atlantic. The War Plans Division wrote Marshall on November 13 that the United States lacked the power to secure Stark's three objectives of hemispheric security, assuring the survival of the British, and weakening Japanese power. It suggested instead defining U.S. objectives as (a) territorial integrity of the United States; (b) aid to the United Kingdom short of war; (c) no military commitments in the Far East; and (d) "Preparation for an eventual unlimited war in the Atlantic to support Great Britain. . . . The President should be advised," WPD continued, "that there are no land possessions now controlled by Great Britain from which the United States can launch a successful attack against any objective vital to Germany." Nor did it seem possible to undertake land operations "via Western or North Africa through Portugal and Spain," because of logistical difficulties and the presence of German forces.[31]

Marshall on November 29 and December 2 definitely rejected the Navy Department's Rainbow 3 plan for action against the Japanese in the Pacific, arguing that such a diversion was exactly what the Germans wanted, and opposing any American attempts to defend "Malaysia," that is, Malaya and the Dutch East Indies. Instead he argued for a new Rainbow 5 (which had not yet been written) to provide for the transfer of the fleet to the Atlantic when an offensive against the Axis began. The War Department was still focused closer to home and had in fact formed two small task forces to occupy the French Caribbean islands of Guadeloupe and Martinique, where the French had two warships docked, if the Vichy government went over to the Axis. The President also remained cautious about war in the Pacific, but in a cabinet meeting on November 29 he announced plans to give China $100 million in economic and military aid.[32]

On December 10 the Joint Board took note that staff talks with the British had been approved at the highest level. The situation in the Atlantic, meanwhile, looked more and more critical. At a high-level meeting in Secretary Hull's office on December 13, Stark told the State, War, and Navy leadership that the British would not be able to hold out for six more months if their shipping losses continued at the present rate. Not only were the British suffering very heavy losses from U-boats, but the Germans were beginning to send surface warships into the Atlantic as commerce raiders as well. Although those ships—initially the pocket battleship *Scheer* and the cruiser *Hipper*—were under orders to avoid any convoy escorted by a British battleship, the *Scheer* had already done substantial damage since November. On December 16, Stimson, effectively acting as Prime Minister with Roosevelt out of town, met with Marshall, Stark, and Knox to discuss what should be done to ensure British survival and to strengthen the extremely weak British and U.S. defenses in the Far East, which Stimson was evidently unwilling to abandon. They decided to ask the British to strengthen Singapore and let some U.S. pursuit planes go to China; that the Army should send some of its most modern pursuit planes and antiaircraft guns to the Philippines; that U.S. "labor and other industrial problems . . . be coordinated and solved on the basis of a national emergency requiring an immediate maximum effort for the security of this country"; and that some way had to be found to allow the Navy to help convoy supplies to Britain. Sounding what was to become a familiar refrain, Stimson suggested that it would be impossible to expand production sufficiently "until we got into war ourselves." Stimson's recommendations could go no further, however, until the President returned from a Caribbean cruise.[33]

Franklin Roosevelt believed in working hard and playing hard. To judge from the senior figures in his administration, the Missionary generation in general appreciated the importance of relaxation and exercise. Stimson, now seventy-three, played paddle tennis and had a massage nearly every day. Marshall and his wife canoed on the Potomac River whenever they could. Roosevelt's crippled legs still allowed him to swim in the White House pool. He also made several trips a year to the resort he had built for polio victims at Warm Springs, Georgia. Most importantly of all, Roosevelt visited his home in Hyde Park about twice a month, thirteen times between May and December of 1940. The domestic arrangements at his permanent home were as complex as the relationships among his cabinet members. His mother, Sarah Delano Roosevelt, now eighty-six, ruled the roost at Hyde Park, which had expanded to fill the needs of three extremely independent adults. As Drew Pearson and Robert Allen explained to their readership in *The Washington Merry-Go-Round* in August, both the President and First Lady now had their own cottages on the grounds. "Though Mrs. Roosevelt has a room in the main house, she seldom uses it," they wrote discreetly, "spending all her time in the Val Kill cottage. This gives her more independence than would be possible under the roof of her mother-in-law, who has a matriarchal tendency toward governing all around her. At Val Kill she is free to receive friends whom the elder Mrs. Roosevelt regards as 'queer.'" But Roosevelt also loved the sea, and took at least one cruise every year. Seeing no reason to be diverted by a threatening world war, he left Washington for Miami on December 2 and spent two weeks in the Caribbean.[34]

Although it issued no statement, the White House allowed correspondents to speculate that the President intended to inspect the sites of some of our new bases in British possessions during his December cruise. His ship, the cruiser USS *Tuscaloosa*, did stop at Jamaica, St. Lucia, and Antigua, and met the British Governor of the Bahamas the Duke of Windsor, formerly King Edward VIII. He also stopped at French-controlled Martinique, which military planners in the War Department on the Mall were currently planning to occupy at a moment's notice. His only companions were a few of his personal military aides and Harry Hopkins, formerly Secretary of Commerce, who was about to step into the role which in future eras would be played by the President's National Security Adviser.

Harry Hopkins was now fifty years old—a milestone which only months earlier he had not been expected to reach. Born in Iowa, he had graduated from Grinnell College in 1912, witnessed the tumultuous Republican Convention of that year in Chicago, and embarked on a career as a social worker in New York City. Nearly twenty years later he had joined Roosevelt's gubernatorial administration, working in a new emergency relief agency, and FDR brought him to Washington in 1933, where he became the relief administrator and then, late in 1933, the head of the new Civil Works Administration, soon to be renamed the Works Progress Administration, or WPA. While the Public Works Administration under Harold Ickes (with whom Hopkins constantly feuded) concentrated on large projects like dams and bridges, Hopkins searched for new ways to put Americans of all kinds back to work, including the federal writers' project (which wrote travel guides for every state in the union) and the highly controversial federal theater group. He became a symbol of the New Deal and a main target of conservative abuse. In 1937 he had had part of his stomach removed as treatment for cancer, and his health never fully recovered. During 1938 he apparently dreamed seriously of succeeding Roosevelt as President. His most enduring legacy was a remark attributed to him—one he violently denied having made—to the effect that the New Deal's strategy was to "tax and tax, spend and spend, and elect and elect."

In December 1938 Roosevelt appointed Hopkins Secretary of Commerce, but his health deteriorated once again during the next year, and when he entered the Mayo Clinic in the fall he was evidently told that he did not have long to live. Roosevelt personally made sure that he returned to Washington and entered the care of Navy doctors, and although he had to spend about eight months at home, he had emerged with at least some renewed energy in mid-1940 and had managed Roosevelt's campaign at the Chicago convention. Hopkins's wife had died in 1938, and in 1940 Roosevelt spontaneously invited him to spend the night at the White House. He lived there until 1943. He still suffered from a severe digestive disorder that made it very difficult for him to absorb food.[35]

Roosevelt, Hopkins, and their few companions—apparently all male—spent the two weeks fishing, playing poker, sunning themselves, and watching movies in the evening. Roosevelt boasted proudly after his return that he did not read any of the working papers he had brought with him, but he did receive one of his longest messages yet from

Churchill. Largely drafted in the British Embassy in Washington, it confirmed what Stark had already been telling the President: that Britain, without American help of several critical kinds, was very likely to lose the war within a year.

Dated December 7, Churchill's telegram followed the line his generals and admirals had been taking with Ghormley in London quite closely but acknowledged that the situation at sea had become desperate. He did not ask for a U.S. expeditionary force and still held out hope that blockade and bombing could eventually defeat Germany, but he clearly implied that defeat was imminent if the German submarine threat could not be met. Recent losses were equal to the worst months of the First World War, and at the current rate British imports were running more than 10 percent below the minimum necessary to sustain the war effort. Churchill was also very worried about the impact of two excellent new German battleships, the *Bismarck* and the *Tirpitz*, and he feared that Germany might draw the Vichy French government directly into the war at any moment and thus occupy North and much of West Africa. He also expressed concerns about the Far East.

In order to meet this critical situation, Churchill asked, first, that the United States in effect abandon its neutrality acts and start sending its own ships across the Atlantic, and that U.S. warships escort them all the way. He had begun his message by arguing that the results of the election showed that the American people regarded British survival as a vital interest, and now he speculated that even U.S. convoys would not necessarily draw Hitler into war against the United States. Failing that, he wanted either a further transfer of warships to Britain along the lines of the destroyer deal or an American assumption of responsibility for controlling "the American side of the Atlantic" to keep the Axis away from the new U.S. bases. He also wanted FDR to try to persuade the Republic of Ireland, which was maintaining a strict neutrality, to allow British and U.S. warships to use its ports. Continuing, he asked for a massive crash shipbuilding program in the United States to replace lost merchant ships and for yet another 2,000 U.S. aircraft in the coming year, most of them heavy bombers, "the weapon on which above all others we depend to shatter the foundations of German military power." He also recommended the expansion of U.S. capacity to produce "small arms, artillery, and tanks." And lastly, he pointed out that Britain would shortly run out of dollars with which to pay for more equipment, without saying exactly what he wanted the United States to do about it. The question of financing new supplies for Britain was perhaps the most politically sensitive of all in the United States, because the British in 1933 had defaulted on the payment of their First World War debt. That as much as anything lay behind the Neutrality Acts and the Johnson Act, which barred new loans to any defaulting debtor of the United States.[36]

Roosevelt evidently shared Churchill's message with Hopkins aboard the *Tuscaloosa* and eventually told Hopkins at least part of what he intended to do. He arrived back in Washington on December 16 with plans to move forward on at least two of Churchill's three most important proposals. On December 17 he had Treasury Secretary Morgenthau to lunch. Morgenthau found him in a very good humor, "very quiet and self-possessed, and very proud of the fact that he didn't look at a single report that he had taken with him from Washington." After some preliminaries, Roosevelt got to the heart of the matter. "I have been thinking very hard on this trip about what we should do for England, and it seems to me that the thing to do is to get away from a dollar sign," he said. After increasing "our productivity," the United States could give the British "the guns and ships" they needed and receive return payment in kind at the end of the war. This was not a completely new idea. In a striking example of his astonishing foresight, FDR had discussed it in the wake of the Munich crisis back in November 1938. Morgenthau immediately called it "the best idea yet," and Roosevelt said he wanted to suggest his plan to Congress on the assumption that Congress would suggest simply giving the British what they needed instead. That proved overoptimistic. Roosevelt then spent two hours with his Attorney General Robert Jackson, and then met with the press to introduce the idea to the public at length.[37]

There was no doubt, said the President, that "a very overwhelming number of Americans" thought that the success of the British was the best possible immediate defense of the United States—an echo of Stark's memorandum. We needed, he said, to increase our productive capacity, and orders from the British "are therefore a tremendous asset to American national defense . . . selfishly, from the American point of view." Rather than repeal the Neutrality or Johnson Acts, he suggested, the United States might "take over" British orders and lend, sell, or lease the material to the British. The United States might also give them away. "I have been at it now three or four weeks, exploring other methods of continuing the building up of our productive facilities and continuing automatically the flow of munitions to Great Britain," he said. "I will just put it this way, not as an exclusive alternative method, but as one of several other possible methods that might be devised toward that end." Then he introduced his famous analogy of lending a neighbor a garden hose to put out a fire next door. Taking questions, Roosevelt equivocated as to whether American ships might carry the goods to Britain or even whether the Neutrality Act might be repealed. He insisted that this would not take America closer to war and acknowledged that the project would require new legislation. And he carefully limited America's aims to the *defense* of the United Kingdom in order to strengthen the *defense* of the United States, without in any way committing the United States to the *defeat* of Germany.[38]

Roosevelt had unveiled what became Lend-Lease as a means of expanding U.S. war production still further while helping Britain defend itself successfully. He had taken another significant step in this direction a month earlier, calling in late November for 143 new destroyers by 1943, instead of the 100 previously scheduled. Yet these steps could do little or nothing to help the British during the next critical six months, in which a German invasion was expected, and the question of direct American intervention remained open. Roosevelt on his return had also received an original report from the U.S. naval mission in London warning that the British could bear the present rate of sinkings for only six months longer, and in the first cabinet meeting after his return on December 19, he discussed the British shipping crisis but proposed nothing more than trying to build a vast fleet of ships in the western hemisphere, a response to Churchill's second demand. Stimson replied that instead of filling a leaky bathtub, "we ought to forcibly stop the German submarines by our intervention." He also wanted "to go to Congress and get the abominable neutrality legislation that we are now shackled with repealed." Roosevelt, Stimson confided in his diary, was not ready to go as far as he or Knox and intervene, but he speculated that the President might be moving in that direction.[39]

In this Stimson was to be disappointed—not for the first time nor for the last. Rather than moving to intervene, Roosevelt in December focused on other problems relating to war production, the long-term key to whatever role the United States might play. The machinery he had set up late in the spring was proving inadequate to overcome certain bottlenecks in aircraft production. Behind them lay broader issues: the provision of adequate raw materials and machine tools, and the necessary curtailment of civilian production.

Steel man Edward Stettinius headed the division of raw materials at the Defense Commission, and during the summer he had begun acquiring stockpiles based on the needs of existing armaments programs—yet another example of the difficulty of preparing for a possible world war before the United States had committed itself to anything more than the defense of the western hemisphere. In late October, he informed his fellow commissioners that aluminum supplies appeared to be more than adequate, but labor commissioner Sidney Hillman immediately suggested that much more might eventually be necessary. Simultaneously, General Arnold of the Air Corps was reporting to General Marshall that airplane production was behind schedule because of a shortage of aluminum forgings and casings. The situation was further complicated by the insistence of the two largest aircraft manufacturers, Douglas and Lockheed, that they could continue to expand the production of civilian airliners while meeting the War Department's demands. They initially persuaded the Defense Commission to allow them to go ahead, but Stimson and his deputy, Robert Patterson, managed to go to FDR himself and get the decision reversed late in November, after Stimson had specifically attacked the President of Douglas Aircraft in a press conference. Two weeks later, in early December, Marshall found the situation was unchanged when he saw idle capacity at an aircraft plant himself. Checking, he informed William Knudsen, the Defense Commission's chief of industrial production, that the Army had received only six planes during November, compared to ninety-four originally planned. Knudsen reacted quickly.[40]

When serious problems threatened in those distant days, leaders in business, government, labor, and even academia did not wait for anyone's approval before sharing their opinions with the public. On December 13, with Roosevelt in the midst of his long cruise, Knudsen sounded an alarm in an address to the National Association of Manufacturers on the demands of rearmament. "Who can say," he quoted the President, "with assurance, that we shall not need for our defense every possible resource that exists or may be developed in our country?" He listed existing production targets for U.S. and British needs: 50,000 airplanes, 130,000 engines, 17,000 heavy guns, 25,000 light guns, 9,200 tanks, 300,000 machine guns, 400,000 automatic rifles, 1.3 million regular rifles, corresponding ammunition, 380 Navy ships, 200 merchant ships, and housing, clothing, and equipment for the projected force of 1.2 million men. Aircraft production, he admitted, was 30 percent behind schedule owing largely to shortages of machine tools, whose production was expected to increase 50 percent during 1941. Defining the war as a struggle to keep totalitarian barbarism from our shores, he pleaded for longer hours and more cooperation from labor. The first half of 1941, he said, would be crucial to the "tooling up" of the necessary factories, that is, getting them ready for mass production. He estimated the tooling process was now 25 percent complete and asked to reach 80 percent by April 1 and 100 percent by the end of May. On the same day, Stimson echoed his complaints in a press conference.[41]

As so often happened, Roosevelt's more determined subordinates stepped up to the plate while he was away. On the day of Roosevelt's return, Stimson was busily rounding up a coalition of heavyweights, including Frank Knox, Morgenthau, Sidney Hillman, and Commerce Secretary Jesse Jones, to recommend that someone—perhaps Knudsen—be given full authority to divert civilian production to military needs. On December 18 Stimson, Knox, and their deputies met Roosevelt, who initially spent at least half an hour telling stories about his vacation—"very much like chasing a vagrant beam of sunshine around a vacant room," Stimson wrote—and speculating about a possible economic crisis after the war was over. Then, however, he suddenly turned to production problems, accepted the need for a "concentration of responsibility" to solve them, and talked generally about a possible council of Stimson, Knox, and Knudsen. He also took this opportunity to let the service secretaries in on the idea of Lend-Lease.[42]

The next day an astonished Stimson read in the lead story of the *New York Times* that Roosevelt had appointed exactly such a council "as submitted by the four advisers to the President and left to him to fill in the details." Stimson, his assistant Secretary Patterson, Knox, and Navy Undersecretary James Forrestal met the next day, December 20, to try to fill in the blanks and decided that Defense Commission labor representative Sidney Hillman, as well as Knudsen, would be added to FDR's new council. Knudsen had only reluctantly acceded to labor's new status since 1935 and was surprised by this decision, but Stimson, certainly a firm believer in free enterprise himself, was all for it. "I several times expressed my views strongly in favor of labor," he wrote in his diary. "I told people I was talking with that I expected to see pretty much the same development on this side of the Atlantic in case we get into war that has taken place on the other side, where labor is now the backbone of the British defense. On any issue between appeasement and carrying out the war on the moral principles involved, I look for the upper classes to be rather on the side of appeasement as they have been in Great Britain and as they are now beginning to loom up here, while on the other side the common people have been pretty strong on the moral issue." When the new four-man council met the next day, Hillman "took a very fine position as to labor's loyal support of production and realization of the true issue."[43]

On December 20, Roosevelt announced the creation of the four-man Office of Production Management at a press conference, reserving ultimate power for himself but promising Stimson, Knox, Knudsen, and Hillman full authority to direct and speed both American rearmament and all aid "short of war" to Britain and other democracies. Knudsen became director of the new office, with Hillman as associate director—but it could not solve the critical problem facing the nation, one identified by Stimson on December 14 in a talk with industrialist Bernard Baruch. Until industry and the American people had developed a "war psychosis"—that is, until they were genuinely convinced that we were at war—they would not make the necessary sacrifices or deal with the problems at hand with the necessary urgency. Even bigger was the problem of combining production targets with an agreed strategic vision. So long as the official mission of U.S. forces remained the defense of the western hemisphere, it would not be possible to begin preparation for a much larger and more distant war.[44]

During the same critical month of December, the Navy, with Stimson's encouragement, was exploring ways of putting the Plan Dog memo into effect and possibly entering the war. On December 16, the day of FDR's return, Stimson had also met successively with Marshall, Knox, and Stark to discuss strategy. They agreed "that this emergency could hardly be passed over without this country being drawn into the war eventually" and discussed "the things that should be done in the beginning, both in the Far East and on the Atlantic and in the interior of the country and its production as far as it should be done." They agreed that the North Atlantic line to Great Britain would be the key, and Stark once again predicted that Britain might be starved out in six months without help at sea and suggested that existing law might allow convoying ships all the way to neutral Ireland.[45]

The next day Stimson, Marshall, Knox, and Stark wrote a memo embodying this suggestion, as well as various proposals for British and U.S. reinforcement of Singapore and the Philippines in the Far East. The day after that, Admiral Kelly Turner, chief of the Navy War Plans Division, sent Stark proposals for increased U.S. naval involvement in the Atlantic, "suggestions for providing assistance to Great Britain 'Short of War.'" Roosevelt had apparently proclaimed Ireland to lie in a neutral zone rather than a war zone, and Turner thought U.S. warships might escort American merchantmen to Ireland, their cargo thence to be transshipped across the Irish Sea to Britain. Germany would probably attack such ships and the United States would then be at war, but Turner speculated that Japan in such circumstances might well decide to stay out, leaving the United States free to fight on one front. Less provocatively, he suggested that U.S. merchant ships and warships might land their goods in much nearer Iceland, where British ships could pick them up. He also had proposals for building more ships and making them available to the British.[46]

Turner went further on December 26 and sent two subordinates a paper, "Investigation of Possible Operation of Naval Forces from Iceland and Scotland Bases." The paper began by referring to the forthcoming staff talks with the British and asked for an investigation of the use of U.S. naval forces based in Iceland, Scotland, and Newfoundland to assist the British *on the assumption that the United States would have entered the war on April 1, 1941.* The task envisioned was no less than the total responsibility for convoying all shipping from North America to the west coast of Scotland.[47]

To carry out this mission, Turner hoped eventually to base 800 naval aircraft, 2 battleships, 4 heavy cruisers, 2 aircraft carriers, 60 destroyers, 30 submarines, and 40,000 troops in Iceland; 1,000 naval aircraft, 60 more destroyers, 20 submarines, and several hundred small patrol craft in Scotland; and, in the Maritime Provinces of Canada and in New England, more than 200 more aircraft, 2 more battleships, 4 new light cruisers, 2 more carriers, and 40 more destroyers. He asked for estimates of how many of these ships could actually operate at these stations and how many could reach them by July 1, 1941; January 1, 1942; and July 1, 1942.

Although 12 of the United States' 16 battleships would remain in the Pacific, the dispatch of so many light forces and four of six carriers would put an end to any possibility of an active offensive west of Hawaii. It took six weeks for Turner's subordinates to prepare a response evaluating the concept. Meanwhile, on January 13, Stark wrote Admiral Husband Kimmel, the new Commander of the U.S. Fleet, that he did not see "how we can avoid, either having [war] thrust upon us or our deliberately going in, many months longer. And of course it may be a matter of weeks or days."[48]

The President's cabinet liked to kid him that the Navy Department belonged to him personally, and it seems unlikely that Stark and Turner would have begun planning for immediate war without at least informing the Commander-in-Chief. But Roosevelt showed in the following weeks and months that he was not yet ready to enter the war. Instead, he defined new policies in three major addresses to the nation: a fireside chat to the nation on December 29 explaining the Lend-Lease proposal; his State of the Union Address on January 6; and his third inaugural on January 20.

The fireside chat went through numerous drafts written by Harry Hopkins, Robert Sherwood, and Samuel Rosenman at the White House and incorporated suggestions and comments from the State Department, Knudsen of the Defense Commission, and many others. Roosevelt began by saying that this was not "a fireside chat on war," but rather one on "national security," and the speech laid out several possibilities for the future, ranging from a last-ditch defense of the western hemisphere to an all-out war against Germany, Italy, and Japan. He compared the depth of the crisis specifically to March 1933 and promised to face it with the same "courage and realism." "Never before since Jamestown and Plymouth Rock," he said, "has our American civilization been in such danger as now." The danger, he said, came from the Tripartite Pact, whose signatories would have to abandon their objectives to allow the world to live once again in peace. "On September 27, 1940, by an agreement signed in Berlin," he said, throwing down the gauntlet, "three powerful nations, two in Europe and one in Asia, joined themselves together in the threat that if the United States of America interfered with or blocked the expansion program of these three nations—a program aimed at world control— they would unite in ultimate action against the United States. . . . The Axis not merely admits but proclaims that there can be no ultimate peace between their philosophy of government and our philosophy of government." The United States could not encourage talk of peace "until the day shall come when there is a clear intention on the part of the aggressor nations to abandon all thought of dominating or conquering the world." The President had accepted the Axis challenge but he was not yet willing to promise or plan for their *defeat*.

Then, echoing the Plan Dog memorandum, he argued that the fall of Great Britain would surely be catastrophic for the United States. "If Great Britain goes down," he said, "the Axis powers will control the continents of Europe, Asia, Africa, Australasia, and the high seas—and they will be in a position to bring enormous military and naval resources against this hemisphere." Germany, he argued, would inevitably seize some western hemisphere territory to serve as a jumping-off point against the United States, just as Belgium had become a jumping-off point against Britain. Hinting at possible operations to come, he questioned whether Ireland could hold out if Britain fell, and noted that the vulnerable Azores were much closer to the East Coast than was Hawaii to the West Coast. In no sense was Roosevelt holding out on the American people: His strategic appreciation perfectly reflected the war plans that his military leaders had been drawing up for the last two years.

The America First movement was now growing rapidly. Stimson in the cabinet meeting of December 19 had demanded that Roosevelt take on two of its leaders, Charles Lindbergh and Robert Wood of Sears, Roebuck, and in the fireside chat, Roosevelt took some time to take its arguments—and its leaders—to task without mentioning any names. "[Some] people not only believe that we can save our own skins by shutting our eyes to the fate of other nations" or "that we can and should become the friends and even the partners of the Axis powers. . . . We know now that a nation can have peace with the Nazis only at the price of total surrender."

But how far would the United States go to stop the Axis? Would Roosevelt adopt not only the logic, but the recommendation, of Stark and Stimson, and take the United States into war to save Great Britain? The answer, as it began to emerge, was no. Rather than do so, he would focus on increased production and aid to Britain as the best chance of keeping the war away from the United States for the time being. "Thinking in terms of today and tomorrow, I make the direct statement to the American people that there is far less chance of the United States getting into war, if we do all we can now to support the nations defending themselves against attack by the Axis than if we acquiesce in their defeat, submit tamely to an Axis victory, and wait our turn to be the object of attack in another war later on." He bluntly denied any plans to send an expeditionary force overseas, and with respect to possible convoys, he said only that "Democracy's fight against world conquest is being greatly aided, and must be more greatly aided, by the rearmament of the United States and by sending every ounce and every ton of munitions and supplies that we can possibly spare to help the defenders who are in the front lines." Roosevelt genuinely agreed with the bulk of the American people that the time had not come to enter the war—not primarily for political reasons, and not in fact because he really believed the British could defeat Germany without U.S. help, but because he knew that the United States could not risk its inadequate forces to save Britain and would not be able to undertake any major operations for more than another year.

As always, Roosevelt linked his foreign policies to his domestic ones. "I would ask no one to defend a democracy which in turn would not defend everyone in the nation against want and privation," he said. "The strength of this nation shall not be diluted by the failure of the Government to protect the economic well-being of its citizens." The nation, he said, "expects and insists that management and workers will reconcile their differences by voluntary or legal means, to continue to produce the supplies that are so sorely needed." Defense production, he said, could not be held back by industries' fears of excess plant capacity. Civilian production and consumption would have to be reduced. Then came the phrase by which the speech would be known—a phrase coined by a Frenchman, Jean Monnet, months earlier, but kept out of the public eye at the express request of Roosevelt's confidant, Justice Felix Frankfurter, so that the President could get the maximum benefit out of it himself: "*We must be the great arsenal of democracy. For us this is an emergency as serious as war itself.*"[49]

Stimson was somewhat disappointed but recognized in his diary that FDR had gone as far as he could go. "I feel confident," he wrote, "that we cannot permanently be in a position of toolmakers for other nations which fight and sooner or later I feel certain from what I know of young American men that when they once appreciate this issue between right and wrong they will be not satisfied unless they are offering their own bodies to the flames and are willing to fight as well as make munitions."

Meeting with the President a day or two later, he summed up the philosophy of their generation: "You cannot build a civilization based upon the question of religion," he said, "which is what our civilization for the last 400 years has been based on, and not recognize questions of right and wrong in the dealings between nations."[50]

The President announced two other new developments in a press conference on January 3, both related to Churchill's recent message. First, he had allocated $350 million from his personal emergency contracting funds, authorized by Congress, for the rapid construction of two hundred new merchant ships to replace lost tonnage and ease a "world shortage." The nation's First Sailor dwelt at length on several shipyards that would, or would not, become part of the program, while noting sadly that the ships, designed merely for convenience and speed of construction, would not be very graceful in form. Secondly, he announced that Harry Hopkins would visit London as a personal representative while FDR tried to pick a replacement for Ambassador Joseph P. Kennedy. "You know Harry isn't strong enough for that job," he said, when asked if Hopkins might become the Ambassador himself, and he insisted jokingly that Hopkins was just "going over to say 'How do you do?' to a lot of my friends!" He also discussed a shortage of steel that had emerged in November and the steps now being taken to do something about it. Hopkins left two days later by plane to Lisbon to begin discussions with Churchill about the future course of the war.[51]

In the State of the Union on January 6, Roosevelt took further rhetorical steps forward, referring to the current "unprecedented" moment in the history of the United States: "At no previous time has U.S. security been as seriously threatened from without as it is today." He reviewed the whole history of U.S. relations with Europe, including the involvement of the United States in the Napoleonic Wars. "What I seek to convey," he said, "is the historic truth that the United States as a nation has at all times maintained clear, definite opposition, to any attempt to lock us in behind an ancient Chinese wall while the procession of civilization went past. Today, thinking of our children and of their children, we oppose enforced isolation for ourselves or for any other part of the Americas." Then, he indicated that he, like Stimson, had never regretted American entry into the First World War—for which he himself had agitated for two years in Wilson's subcabinet—and implied that a renewal of the struggle with tyranny was at hand. "Even when the World War broke out in 1914, it seemed to contain only a small threat of danger to our own American future. But, as time went on, the American people began to visualize what the downfall of democratic nations might mean to our own democracy. . . . Every realist knows that the democratic way of life is at this moment being directly assailed in every part of the world."

Roosevelt once again declared that the United States could not live with an Axis victory. The election had shown, he said, that the United States was now committed to three principles: "all-inclusive national defense, . . . full support of all those resolute peoples, everywhere, who are resisting aggression and are thereby keeping war away from our Hemisphere," and "the proposition that principles of morality and considerations for our own security will never permit us to acquiesce in a peace dictated by aggressors and sponsored by appeasers." Roosevelt called for more production and for higher taxes to pay for it. Then for the first time he stated what became his war aims, "a world founded upon four essential human freedoms. The first is freedom of speech and expression— everywhere in the world. The second is freedom of every person to worship God in his own way—everywhere in the world. The third is freedom from want—which, translated into world terms, means economic understandings which will secure to every nation a healthy peacetime life for its inhabitants—everywhere in the world. The fourth is freedom from fear—which, translated into world terms, means a world-wide reduction of armaments to such a point and in such a thorough fashion that no nation will be in a position to commit an act of physical aggression against any neighbor—anywhere in the world. That is no vision of a distant millennium. It is a definite basis for a kind of world attainable in our own time and generation. That kind of world is the very antithesis of the so-called new order of tyranny which the dictators seek to create with the crash of a bomb." Roosevelt had dictated the four freedoms himself, after his speechwriting team had produced four drafts of the speech without them. When he did so, Hopkins questioned the inclusion of the phrase "anywhere in the world"—including colonies such as India and Java—but Roosevelt insisted that it remain.[52]

Then Roosevelt, in his closing words, opened up for the first time the vision of a triumph over the Axis. "Freedom means the supremacy of human rights everywhere," he said. "Our support goes to those who struggle to gain those rights or keep them. Our strength is our unity of purpose. To that high concept there can be no end save victory." The

President had now clearly shared his vision not only of the worldwide conflict but of how he believed it must end: with the triumph of his vision of democracy and the four freedoms over lawless dictatorship.

In his unprecedented third inaugural two weeks later, on January 20, Roosevelt built still further on these themes. To begin with, he specifically linked the present moment to the two great previous crises in American history, pointing out the historical rhythm that was not specifically identified for another half century by two men who had not yet been born.[53] "On each national day of Inauguration since 1789, the people have renewed their sense of dedication to the United States. In Washington's day the task of the people was to create and weld together a Nation. In Lincoln's day the task of the people was to preserve that Nation from disruption from within. In this day the task of the people is to save that Nation and its institutions from disruption from without." The remainder of the relatively brief address was a paean to democracy, including, yet again, a warning that the American way of life could not survive an Axis victory.[54]

By proposing vastly increased production and proclaiming a worldwide struggle between totalitarianism and democracy, Roosevelt was preparing the American people for a possible world war. Yet he was *not* going to implement Stark and Stimson's recommendations to involve the United States in the war in order to save Britain during 1941, for the simple reason that the United States was not yet prepared to fight. As the War Department had shown beyond doubt in October, the United States would not be able to undertake sustained, substantial combat operations for more than a year. Both Stark's Plan Dog memorandum and Turner's war plan optimistically assumed that the United States might intervene to save Britain without becoming involved in a war with Japan—a war that Turner's plan for war in the Atlantic would leave the Pacific Fleet unable to fight. In this their optimism was misplaced.

The Japanese in fact remained determined to undertake their southward advance, and Foreign Minister Matsuoka's statements left no doubt that they took the Tripartite Pact extremely seriously. Should the United States become engaged in the Battle of the Atlantic from Newfoundland to Scotland, it might easily suffer very serious naval losses well before its new Navy came on line. Not only would the British have to face the expected German invasion on their own, but the United States could not yet intervene to stop further German advances into North and West Africa and perhaps into the Atlantic. Lend-Lease might give British morale a critical lift, but the British would have to fight on their own while U.S. productive capacity increased to the point where the United States could take an active part in the war. Not for several months more did Stark and Stimson discover that the President did not want to follow their advice and enter the war in the first half of 1941.

As it happened, the United States, Britain, and the world were benefiting from an extraordinary stroke of luck. The nightmare that continued to trouble American planners—that Hitler and the Italians might unleash an offensive into Iberia, North and West Africa, and the Atlantic, perhaps drawing France into the war and leaving Britain in a hopeless position—was indeed a very real possibility. Hitler feared a long-term threat from the United States in the Atlantic and North Africa, and he badly wanted to secure bases in French, Spanish, and Portuguese possessions to forestall it. Yet he was not willing to treat the Spaniards or the French as genuine partners—which would surely have allowed him to get at least Franco's Spain into the war—and his opportunity therefore slipped away in the late fall of 1940. Meanwhile during these same critical last months of 1940, Hitler decided on the step that irrevocably changed the course of the Second World War: the attack on the Soviet Union. He scheduled it for the middle of the coming year and postponed movements into North Africa and the Atlantic until after the campaign against the Soviets was over.[55]

In June 1940, in order to make certain he got France out of the war, Hitler had extended Marshal Pétain's government relatively generous armistice terms, leaving about 40 percent of the country unoccupied, the French government at Vichy, and French overseas territory for the moment untouched. The armistice terms, on the other hand, made prisoners of the entire French Army in France, with their release delayed until a final peace treaty with Britain. They also called for the demobilization and demilitarization of the French Fleet under German and Italian control—the provision that had so alarmed Churchill and Roosevelt—but the Vichy government had managed to keep its warships in Mediterranean ports and overseas outside German control, and in fact had immediately instructed its naval officers to sink their ships or try to escape to the United States rather than let them fall into enemy hands. And when in July 1940 the Germans had demanded that the French provide them with some airfields around Casablanca, a key position on the Atlantic, for military use, the French had simply refused, and that had been that.[56]

Pierre Laval, the Vichy Prime Minister, was quite willing to collaborate with Germany in return for a generous peace, but Hitler faced a series of complicated choices among his ally Italy, who coveted territory in France itself and in North Africa; his political ally Franco in Spain, who had similar designs on French North Africa; and the French themselves, potentially the most valuable ally but clearly not fully trustworthy. Even after the failure of the Luftwaffe in the Battle of Britain, Hitler confidently expected to force the British to make peace, but the destroyer deal and the United States' acquisition of new Atlantic bases frightened him. Roosevelt was indeed taking the keenest interest in the fate of French North and West Africa, and in September he summoned a U.S. diplomat, Robert Murphy, from Vichy to Washington and asked him to visit North Africa and offer General Maxime Weygand, the French commander there, help in resisting the Germans. Meanwhile, the Italians had opened up a new front against the British in North Africa and, unbeknownst to Hitler, were thinking of invading Greece.[57]

Both Pétain and Laval anticipated some kind of collaboration with Germany after the Germans had won the war, but by October it was no longer certain when or even if that would take place. They knew that Weygand might easily throw in with the British if they moved too quickly toward the Axis. The French colonial authorities scored an important point for French neutrality during the last week of September, when their forces successfully defended Dakar, the capital of French West Africa and a position of great interest to the United States owing to its proximity to Brazil, against an attack by Charles de Gaulle's Free French forces, supported by British warships. The French defense of their North African territory enabled them to argue that there was no need for Hitler to undertake the task. In October Hitler went to the Franco-Spanish border and met with Franco at Hendaye and then with Pétain and Laval at Montoire but failed to persuade either government to allow German troops to take Gibraltar or enter North Africa. The Franco-German meetings and the friendly communiqué that concluded them provoked a stern warning from Roosevelt against active French help for the Axis, with particular attention to the fate of the French Fleet, and Pétain replied promising not to surrender it. Franco, meanwhile, offered to take Gibraltar himself in return for political concessions in North Africa, but

Hitler refused to make them. Franco in turn refused to allow German troops to pass through Spain to take Gibraltar and move into Spanish Morocco and the Canaries. Carefully laid plans for those operations had to be canceled.[58]

In early November, after Mussolini had further confused matters by attacking Greece, thus allowing the British to occupy the key Greek island of Crete, Hitler ordered plans to seize Gibraltar and an outpost in the Canaries, as well as to make a needed reconnaissance in the Azores. But, meanwhile, he also reached the key decision of the war, ordering the Army to prepare to undertake Operation Barbarossa, the attack on the Soviet Union in late spring. On December 5 he reiterated to his military leadership that the battle for European hegemony must be won in the Soviet Union and that the Soviets' defeat would induce the British to make peace. In the following weeks he emphasized that all this must be accomplished before 1942, when the United States might become an important factor in the war. He and Admiral Erich Raeder discussed the capture of Gibraltar—which the British knew they could not stop—in late December, but by January, the Army had made clear to Hitler that the troops used for that operation would have to be back in time for the scheduled attack in the East in May. That proved impossible, and Hitler eventually deferred Gibraltar, North Africa, Dakar, and the Atlantic islands until after Barbarossa, which he confidently expected to be over by the end of 1941.[59]

During the Norway campaign, the Germans had proven that they could defeat the British in combined operations in peripheral areas by using their air power against British sea power. In the spring of 1941 they would prove this again in campaigns in and around Greece. Had Hitler either made the necessary political concessions to the Spaniards and the French in the winter of 1940–1941 or simply diverted more forces to override their objections, he might well have taken Gibraltar, occupied North Africa, and moved into the Cape Verde and Canary islands, if not the Azores. The British had conceded in their conversations with Admiral Ghormley that they could not stop these moves. Such developments would have made it even harder for American supplies to reach the British, shaken Churchill's popularity, and quite possibly even threatened his government. Hitler, however, was fighting the war to secure a huge continental empire in Eastern Europe. Had Hitler moved south and west, the entire history of the war might have turned out very differently, and the

United States might indeed have faced the task of defending the western hemisphere against Germany, Italy, and Japan. As it was, Hitler's strategy not only gave the United States the time it needed to rearm, but eventually made it possible for Roosevelt to seek the larger objective of the complete defeat of the Axis after Operation Barbarossa had begun.

CHAPTER 5

Two Steps Forward, One Step Back, January–May 1941

FROM JANUARY THROUGH MARCH OF 1941, CONGRESS FIRST DEBATED and then passed the Lend-Lease bill, providing Roosevelt with a new means of increasing U.S. war production and encouraging British resistance. A visit to London by Harry Hopkins opened up a new chapter in Anglo-American relations, and during those same months, British and U.S. military planners conducted staff talks and drew up a joint war plan to come into effect when, and if, the United States entered the conflict. The expected invasion of Great Britain did not take place, but in April and May, the British suffered new and serious reverses in Greece, in North Africa, and at sea. Washington expected new German moves into North Africa and the Atlantic at any moment. From March through May, Secretaries Stimson, Knox, Morgenthau, and Ickes, joined by Admiral Harold Stark, pressed for immediate American entry into the war to save the British. Roosevelt disappointed them.

At no time was the future course of the Second World War more difficult to discern than in the first half of 1941, and never was a sensitive and discriminating judgment more necessary to see through the fog of war and choose effective courses of action. Roosevelt was equal to the task. Lend-Lease allowed for further increases in war production, to aid the British and the Chinese, to prepare an effective defense of the western hemisphere, or possibly, depending on what happened overseas, to fight a world war. In the short run, however, the United States lacked the resources to intervene in the conflict. Japan as well as Germany was clearly threatening new aggressive moves, and the United States could not possibly both convoy merchant ships to Britain, as Knox and Stimson demanded, and protect adequately against the Japanese Navy in the Pacific. Roosevelt marked time and waited on events because he had no choice. By May, however, he was planning to send U.S. forces into the middle of the Atlantic to protect the western hemisphere against new Axis moves. He also had good intelligence of a possible German attack on the Soviet Union—another event that might entirely transform the situation and open up a whole new phase of U.S. strategy.

The Lend-Lease bill, allowing the President to transfer unlimited quantities of American munitions to any foreign nation provided that he alone judged such transfers to benefit the defense of the United States, was introduced in Congress in the first week of January 1941, given the symbolic number of H.R. 1776, and scheduled for almost immediate hearings before the House Foreign Affairs Committee and the Senate Committee on Foreign Relations. The men and women of the mid-twentieth century had learned the economical use of the English language, and the entire bill was only 1,500 words long. It would allow the President to transfer essentially unlimited quantities of war material to any foreign nation, provided that he deemed the transfer essential to the defense of the United States.

The isolationism that had so dominated U.S. foreign relations, especially with respect to Europe, since 1920 had retreated in the middle of 1940 in the face of the terrifying world situation, and it had played little role in the presidential campaign because both candidates supported greater preparedness and aid to Britain. Now, however, opposition to involvement in the European war became the focus of Roosevelt's still-numerous opponents. The isolationists included a wide spectrum of Americans who, for one reason or another, shrank in horror before the new world they saw emerging around the globe. They included businessmen like Henry Ford and Joseph Kennedy who believed that world war would produce an economic catastrophe, home-grown American Fascists who were not in the least interested in the defeat of Nazi Germany, and the antiwar Socialist Party led by Norman Thomas. And until June 22, 1941, they also included the small but highly disciplined American Communist Party and some of its front organizations, which had significant followings on college campuses and which in the wake of the Nazi-

Soviet Pact were busily proclaiming that the United States should not take sides in yet another imperialist war. The isolationists could also count on the inveterate Roosevelt haters, whose resentment had been growing for eight years and who included a good many of the Republicans in Congress. They could not, as it turned out, stop the new Congress from passing the Lend-Lease bill, but they could both delay it and shape the debate on the measure in ways that made U.S. entry into the war less likely.

During the last few months of 1940, a new lobbying organization, the America First Committee, had assembled an impressive roster of opponents of Roosevelt and war. The Committee began at Yale University, where its adherents eventually included student Kingman Brewster, who twenty-five years later became Yale's President, and Richard Bissell, a noted economist who became the head of covert operations in the CIA during the 1950s. Its chairman and leading financial angel was former General Robert Wood, the chairman of the Board of Sears, Roebuck in Chicago, and thus, ironically, the boss of Donald Nelson, now a key figure in the Office of Production Management. Its leading political allies were two Senators, Democrat Burton K. Wheeler of Montana and Republican Gerald Nye of North Dakota, and its well-known private adherents included Henry Ford, Alice Roosevelt Longworth, actress Lillian Gish, advertising executives William Benton and Chester Bowles, *Chicago Tribune* publisher Robert McCormick (a Groton classmate of Franklin Roosevelt), and most famously, aviator Charles Lindbergh. Their motives varied; their tactics and rhetoric did not.[1]

Burton Wheeler had been a leading progressive Senator since 1922. He had made his name investigating the Teapot Dome scandals in his very first session in Congress, and in 1924 he had run for Vice President on the doomed third-party Progressive ticket led by Wisconsin's Robert La Follette. He was an enthusiastic New Dealer during the 1930s and cosponsor of the Wheeler-Rayburn Act, which tried to outlaw holding companies for public utilities. But like so many other western progressives such as Hiram Johnson of California, William E. Borah of Idaho (who had died in early 1940), and George Norris of Nebraska, he believed that militarism and foreign war were deadly threats to American democracy, and he had now become one of Roosevelt's bitterest enemies. On January 12, in a radio debate, he fired the first and loudest salvo against the Lend-Lease bill. "If the American people want a dictatorship—if they want a totalitarian form of government, and war," he said, "this bill should be steamrolled through Congress, as is the wont of President Roosevelt." Referring to the Agricultural Adjustment Agency, the New Deal program that had restored agricultural prices by plowing under crops and slaughtering livestock, Wheeler called Lend-Lease "the New Deal's triple-A foreign policy: plow under every fourth American boy."[2]

Wheeler's remark stung. Asked in a press conference two days later to reply to critics who had called the bill a "blank check," Roosevelt challenged them to "write me another that you would not put that label on but which would accomplish the same objective. . . . That is not an answer at all, however, to those who talk about plowing under every fourth American child, which I regard as the most untruthful, as the most dastardly, unpatriotic thing that has ever been said. Quote me on that." In another press conference three days later, a reporter noted that some said the bill allowed the President to give away the U.S. Navy, or buy the British Navy. "The bill did not prevent the President of the United States from standing on his head," he replied, "but the President did not expect to stand on his head." Asked if he had discussed the bill with the Vatican, he laughed and speculated that he might be planning to buy the Vatican Navy.[3]

In a critical private meeting on January 16, the President made crystal clear that he was worried not about getting the United States into the war, but about war coming to the United States before it was ready. On January 16, while a House committee held Lend-Lease hearings, Roosevelt gave Stimson, Knox, Hull, Stark, and Marshall an unusually frank and pessimistic estimate of the situation—one that Lend-Lease would not have time to alter. He said there was about a 20 percent chance of an immediate surprise attack by Germany and Japan against the United States and warned that we might have to act "with whatever we had available." Should such an attack take place, he continued, "we should be able to notify Mr. Churchill immediately that this would not curtail the supply of material to England. He discussed this problem on the basis of the probability that England could survive six months and that, therefore, a period of at least two months would elapse before hostile action could be taken against the U.S. in the Western Hemisphere. In other words, that . . . there would be a period of eight months in which we could gather strength." FDR specifically ordered the Navy to prepare for convoys to England but indicated that the Army would be used very conservatively should war break out, while the United States would remain on the defensive in the Pacific and probably retreat from the Philippines. The United States, he seemed to be saying, would not be able to save Britain even if it were forced into the war. On the same day, Roosevelt gave Churchill an intelligence report predicting an imminent invasion of Britain in another month. Marshall, meanwhile, had recently given Stimson an Army intelligence estimate that Britain had a one-in-three chance of surviving without U.S. entry into the war, while adding that his officers in London rated Britain's chances as much lower.[4]

On January 22, Stimson, who believed the United States would inevitably go to war, talked for two hours with the President after dinner, and Roosevelt discussed his plans for action if the United States went to war with the Axis and *discussed* the possible need to convoy troops. On February 10 the Army and Navy agreed on plans to move troops on short notice into Nova Scotia and certain islands in the Caribbean—presumably the planned response to the expected German invasion of Britain that FDR and Stimson had discussed. Roosevelt typically was preparing for short- and medium-term contingencies at the same time. On the one hand, the United States had to prepare as quickly as possible for an attack on the western hemisphere. On the other, Lend-Lease would provide a further justification for a new expansion of U.S. war production to meet future contingencies.[5]

The administration's senior cabinet members were somewhat more optimistic testifying in hearings before the House Foreign Affairs Committee that began on January 15. Hull, as always, rested his position on the "basic principles of peaceful and orderly international conduct and relations," now directly challenged by Japan, Germany, and Italy. Hull's language left no doubt that war with the Axis was inevitable and that the United States had to keep Britain alive as an ally. Treasury Secretary Morgenthau, following him, gave a much more technical exposition of the British financial position to explain why the United States now had to supply military equipment without payment.[6]

Stimson, appearing the next day, took a slightly narrower line, arguing that the American people had repeatedly endorsed the idea that the defense of the United States depended on assistance to Great Britain and pointing out that the situation was far more perilous than that the United States had faced in 1917. Britain needed our help to "meet the crisis which is confronting her this spring and summer, and thus preserve her fleet as a bulwark in the Atlantic Ocean." When isolationist Republican George Tinkham of Massachusetts argued that the bill gave the President excessive powers, Stimson replied that Congress could safely rest "the terrific responsibility of the Presidency in foreign relations . . . with the present President of the United States, and I have had him under close observation for six months. And as you know, Mr. Tinkham, I belong to your party." "You did," replied Tinkham. "I did, yes," said Stimson, "and I think perhaps I do still. I do not know that you have read me out of it."[7]

No one seemed to enjoy his testimony more than Stimson's fellow Republican, Secretary of the Navy Frank Knox. His statement focused on the threat to the naval balance should Germany defeat Britain and the need to help the British. When pressed, he admitted that the crisis in Britain was likely to occur within the next sixty to ninety days but argued that the bill's passage would enormously boost British morale. Tinkham asked him whether the bill would allow Roosevelt to sell the U.S. Navy. "I have been here for six months," Knox replied, "and I have been thrown in the closest possible contact with the President in respect to naval affairs. In all my life I have never seen a man more devoted to the best and highest interests of the American Navy than Franklin D. Roosevelt. He knows more about the Navy than most of the officers in the Navy. It is the very apple of his eye. And the last thing that I can conceive of is that he could give away the American Navy." In response to questions, Knox affirmed that the bill did not provide for convoys to Britain, which he regarded as an act of war.[8] When Knox appeared before the Senate Foreign Relations Committee, isolationist Gerald Nye, whose staff had done its research, cited a January 1939 editorial in which Knox attacked Roosevelt's attempts to use unrest elsewhere to increase political capital. "You can go back into the files of the *Daily News* and find me functioning as an active, aggressive Republican and find a lot of things worse than that," Knox replied. "You know, Senator," he continued, "I am not a bit ashamed of having been a Republican all my life. I am not ashamed of it now. But I am not functioning as a Republican now." William Knudsen, following Knox in the House Committee on Saturday, January 18, argued that the bill would enable the United States to expand production far more rapidly. Joseph P. Kennedy, no longer Ambassador to Britain and hopeful of a new government job, swallowed his own isolationist convictions and endorsed the bill.[9]

Two private citizens gave particularly striking testimony in favor of the bill. Appearing before the Senate Committee on January 30, the German-American theologian Reinhold Niebuhr argued that the United States could not afford to see Hitler secure control over Europe. "The Nazi unification of Europe," he said, "would combine the conditions of slavery with the efficiency of a technical civilization for the first time in history.... Beyond the problem of our national interest is the larger problem of the very quality of our civilization, with its historic liberties and standards of justice, which the Nazis are sworn to destroy. No nation can be unmindful of its obligations to a civilization of which it is a part.... The Nazis," he continued, "have declared their intention of annihilating the Jewish race. This maniacal fury against a great race goes beyond anything previously known in the category of race prejudice." Pushed by Senator Nye, he affirmed that he would willingly enter the war to ward off these dangers. The journalist Dorothy Thompson was equally forthright, arguing that a German victory would inevitably bring the Axis into Latin America and that it made more sense to send U.S. soldiers to fight in Ireland than to wait until they had to fight in Argentina or elsewhere. She too favored entering the war under unspecified circumstances, although not "tomorrow."[10]

It could not have been lost on any observers that not one single witness argued for immediate entry into the war. Significantly, in late December, Kansas newspaper editor William Allen White, the Chairman of the Committee to Defend America by Aiding the Allies, who had done so much on behalf of the destroyer deal, had given an interview declaring that his committee was opposed to entering the war and favored aid to Britain only to prevent it. White strongly supported Lend-Lease but resigned his chairmanship because other members of the Committee thought his interview had been too cautious. The only person to call for immediate entry into the war during the whole of the hearings was eighty-three-year-old Senator Carter Glass of Virginia, who so declared while questioning Charles Lindbergh before the Senate Foreign Relations Committee, and he allowed that he was the only man he knew who held that opinion.[11]

Meanwhile, the many opposition witnesses, Congressmen, and Senators had difficulty framing convincing arguments against Lend-Lease. Although not denying that Britain faced imminent peril, Congressman Hamilton Fish of New York, General Wood of the America First

Committee, Colonel McCormick of the *Chicago Tribune*, and Charles A. Lindbergh all argued tenaciously that Germany would not be able seriously to threaten the western hemisphere even if Britain were defeated. Quite a few others expressed support for the objectives of the bill while arguing that it simply gave the President too much power, and many witnesses and Republican members made it clear that they opposed the bill because Franklin Roosevelt had proposed it.

Lindbergh was now the public face of American isolationism. Born in 1902, he came by his isolationist credentials honestly: His father, a Congressman from Minnesota, had violently opposed U.S. entry into the First World War. In 1927, of course, he had become the first solo flyer to cross the Atlantic, winning instant fame and fortune. Then, in 1932, he and his wife suffered the tragic kidnapping and murder of their first child from their New Jersey home, and the eventual capture, trial, and execution of the kidnapper created such a publicity firestorm that the couple eventually left for England to live. Lindbergh, meanwhile, had moved increasingly to the right and made friendly contacts with the leaders of Nazi Germany. In the spring of 1938, he told a close British friend, the diplomat and journalist Harold Nicolson, that Britain should ally with Germany. Nicolson, who opposed appeasement, wrote that Lindbergh "believes in the Nazi theology, all tied up with his hatred of degeneracy and his hatred of democracy as represented by the free Press and the American public," which had so tormented him at the time of the kidnapping. In May 1940, while France was falling, a French friend told Lindbergh "that if Germany wins, Western civilization will fall. I believe," Lindbergh wrote in his diary, "that Germany is as much a part of Western civilization as France or England." Lindbergh spent much of the second half of 1940 traveling around the United States drumming up support for America First.[12]

On February 6, 1941, Lindbergh told the Senate Foreign Relations Committee that he did not believe Britain could win the war, that the cost of victory would be too great in any case, and that he favored a negotiated peace. Germany, he claimed, "was the natural air power of Europe, just as England is the natural sea power"—and no one did more than Lindbergh to convince the British and Americans that the Luftwaffe was much larger than it really was. He now speculated that Germany might be building 5,000 planes a month; the actual figures for 1941 turned out to be less than 2,000 per month. He insisted that any attempt to help

Britain would leave the United States vulnerable to invasion, and that the policy embodied in Lend-Lease would lead to failure in war, dreadful economic conditions at home, and the end of our system of government. He endured sharp questioning from several proadministration Senators and promptly resumed his public campaign after the hearings.[13]

The Lend-Lease bill passed the House of Representatives by the comfortable margin of 260 to 165 after less than a week of debate on February 7, 1941. The Senate debate opened on February 13 and eventually concluded on March 8 with passage by a vote of 61 to 30. At the height of the debate, in the first days of March, Stimson and Hull, pinch-hitting for a sick President, met the Senate leadership to head off amendments that would have required congressional approval of every specific transfer of weapons to Britain.[14]

Yet the tenor of the debate gave no comfort to proponents of rapid entry into the war. One administration supporter after another argued that while no one could promise that the United States would not become involved in the war, the Lend-Lease bill offered the best hope of staying out of it. If Britain fell, they argued, Hitler would surely attack the Americas; if Britain survived with the help of Lend-Lease aid, this might never come to pass. Aid to Britain, some argued, would buy time to complete our own rearmament. On the other side, the bill's vociferous opponents, who during February and early March conducted in the Senate what amounted to an informal filibuster, argued again and again that the bill would take us into the war—that it was "a measure of aggressive warfare," that it would "lay the foundation for our entry," and that it would "invest in the Chief Executive the power to involve us in actual participation in the war." The Senate opponents included some of the Senate's most distinguished names, such as Wheeler of Montana, David Walsh of Massachusetts—the Chairman of the Senate Naval Affairs Committee—Republicans Arthur Vandenberg of Michigan and Robert Taft of Ohio, and Progressive Robert La Follette Jr. of Wisconsin. They did force the administration to agree to an amendment stating that nothing in the bill should be construed to allow convoys to Britain.[15]

The House and Senate debates reflected the findings of Gallup polls. Although a significant majority of the country favored all possible aid to Britain and approved the bill, an enormous majority—more than 80 percent—opposed immediate entry into the war. And while the passage of the bill allowed Roosevelt immediately to propose another large increase in defense production, the debate on it made it almost impossible for him to ask for an early declaration of war even had he wanted to.[16]

While the Lend-Lease bill began proceeding through Congress, Harry Hopkins spent January 9 to February 10 in the United Kingdom, meeting with Churchill, Foreign Secretary Anthony Eden, the U.S. naval and military observers, and other leading British figures, to both assess Britain's situation and needs and help establish a relationship between Churchill and Roosevelt, whose previous, brief personal contacts do not seem to have been happy ones. (Roosevelt had told Joseph P. Kennedy more than once that Churchill was "the only man in public life who has ever been rude to me.") Hopkins immediately encountered the gulf between U.S. and British military estimates of the situation. While Admiral Ghormley and General Lee evidently informed him that they did not believe the British could withstand a full-scale German invasion, Churchill at their first lunch together assured him that even if the Germans landed 100,000 men in Britain, the British would drive them out. Churchill added that he expected Britain eventually to win the war through air power, and that he believed "that this war will never see great forces massed against one another." In the short run, however, he acknowledged that the Germans were almost certain to complete the conquest of Greece, which the Italians had been unable to achieve, while adding that he planned to send aid to Greece anyway. Hopkins had brought an invitation from Roosevelt to meet Churchill personally in Bermuda in April, and Churchill responded eagerly, although as things turned out their meeting would be delayed another four months.

At a dinner for newspaper editors, Hopkins spoke with great feeling about American sympathy for the British cause, putting himself firmly in the camp of those like Admiral Stark who felt an Anglo-American alliance was crucial to British success. He also lunched with the King and Queen, who agreed "that this conflict is different from the other conflicts in British history and that if Hitler wins they and the British people will be enslaved for years to come." Going beyond his chief's public statements, Hopkins emphasized "the President's great determination *to defeat Hitler*" and "his deep conviction that Britain and America had a mutuality of interest in this respect." In his lengthy final report to FDR he predicted that Germany would invade Britain before May 1 and expressed the most optimistic hope "that . . . we can get enough material to Britain within the next few weeks to give her the additional strength she needs to turn back Hitler." He then provided a lengthy list of Britain's needs at sea, on land, and in the air. FDR responded by appointing Hopkins to the new position of Lend-Lease administrator after the passage of the bill. Defeated Republican candidate Wendell Willkie also visited London, providing a bipartisan element of support for the United Kingdom that was most welcome during the heated debate over Lend-Lease. The War Department, meanwhile, continued to expect a German invasion of Britain at almost any moment.[17]

Indications were also mounting of new Japanese moves in the Far East. In late November 1940 the Japanese had taken a new step toward the creation of the Greater East Asia Co-Prosperity Sphere, effectively ruling out peace with the Chiang Kai-shek regime by signing a treaty with their own Chinese puppet government in Nanking led by Wang Ching-wei. By February the British were convinced that the Japanese might attack Dutch and British possessions at any moment and were beseeching the United States for promises of assistance, but without result. Although the attack was not yet imminent, the British were estimating Japanese intentions accurately.[18]

Confirming Japanese decisions of the previous summer, a Liaison Conference of Japanese civilian and military leaders on January 30 adopted an "Outline of Policy Towards Indochina and Thailand," calling for military pacts with both countries and a Japanese occupation of southern Indochina as a stepping stone to an advance farther south. The Japanese Army actually wanted to move into southern Indochina by late March, but Foreign Minister Matsuoka, who had been working all winter to add the Soviet Union to the Tripartite Pact and was now planning a trip to Europe, managed to remove this deadline from the agreed document. On February 3 another Liaison Conference approved a much more sweeping document approving Matsuoka's plans for a world divided into four spheres: Europe and Africa under German control, the Americas, the Soviet Union (which would expand into India and Iran), and the Far East under Japanese control. Japan would effectively take over all the European colonial possessions in the Far East east of India. The Japanese Navy was slowly winning the Army over to the proposition that war against Britain and Holland alone was impossible and that Japan would have to attack the United States as well.[19]

During 1940, U.S. naval and military intelligence had learned to break various Japanese diplomatic codes, referred to by the code-name Magic—although not all the Japanese military and naval codes. Carefully handled, the intercepts were summarized daily by the Army for the leaders of the War Department and State Department, and by the Navy for the Navy Secretary and CNO and for President Roosevelt's military aide and, sometimes, FDR himself. The code-breakers provided a secret summary of Japanese policy when they decoded instructions from Matsuoka to the new Japanese Ambassador to the United States, Admiral Nomura, on February 17. The Americans, Matsuoka said, must accept the Japanese mission "to rescue our civilization from chaos and so to bring peace and prosperity to the Pacific in which Japan and America are interested." Matsuoka made clear that he had only one fear: that if war broke out between Japan and the United States, the USSR would fall on Japan and drive Japan out of China. This was the danger that his forthcoming trip to Germany and the Soviet Union was designed to remove. But he concluded that even if the United States defeated Japan in a war, Japan would restore itself more swiftly than Germany had since Versailles. Nomura was hardly less alarming in public, telling the press on February 19 that Japan "will expand to the south peacefully and economically. . . . I cannot say with absolute definiteness whether Japan will have to use force to secure economic necessities." He also reaffirmed Japan's commitment to the Tripartite Pact while declining to say what Japan would do if the United States went to war against Germany.[20]

This, then, was the situation in which the secret staff conversations between American and British officers in Washington known as ABC-1 began in late January. The instructions to the officers who represented the United States in the talks, including both Ghormley and Chaney, who had been serving as observers in London, and Admiral Kelly Turner of Navy War Plans and generals Stanley Embick, Sherman Miles, and Leonard Gerow, emphasized the nation's distaste for war. "The American people as a whole desire now to remain out of war," an American ABC-1 document said, "and to provide only material and economic aid to Great Britain. So long as this attitude is maintained it must be supported by their responsible military and naval authorities." Roosevelt himself had carefully hedged the instructions for the American participants, authorizing them only to discuss operations that might be undertaken "should the United States decide to resort to war." Stimson, who clearly believed that the United States had to get into the war as soon as possible, tried and failed to remove these sentences from the instructions, which the Joint Board approved on January 22. Although the ABC-1 talks had indeed produced a joint war plan by the end of March, they revealed enormous differences of strategic outlook between the military leaders of the two nations and evidently left the Americans wondering exactly what war they were going to have to fight and how exactly they could ever win it.[21]

In the first session, the British refused to discuss the contingency most on the Americans' minds: the possibility that Great Britain might be invaded and conquered. Pressing for a primary effort in Europe, the British laid out their plan to win the war by bombing Germany in order to reduce production and morale, encouraging revolts in occupied territories, and landing mobile forces to assist those revolts. They also asked that Britain receive priority in the delivery of U.S. heavy bombers even during the first year of a hypothetical U.S. intervention in the war. They wanted a firm statement of the conditions under which the United States might enter a war against Japan, but in reply the Americans, significantly, merely stated that if Japan attacked the United States, they would declare war on Germany and Italy at once.

On February 6, Admiral Turner presented the extremely ambitious plan for U.S. naval action in the Atlantic that his War Plans Division had developed in response to his instructions in late December on the assumption that the United States might be in the war on April 1. Attempting to deal both with the potential German threat of commerce raiders and of submarines, which were continuing to wreak havoc, it foresaw an Atlantic force of 8 cruisers, 4 battleships, and 1 carrier, as well as 53 destroyers, 27 of them to be based in the British Isles. It also foresaw a U.S. naval base at Iceland, now occupied by the British. But the British, who were evidently relatively confident in their own ability to prevail in the Battle of the Atlantic, had other plans for the U.S. Fleet.[22]

In the spring of 1939, when Italy and Germany signed the Axis alliance, the British had abandoned their plans to send a fleet to Singapore in the event of war with Japan in order to leave enough forces for the Mediterranean, where the British Fleet had now become engaged. With extraordinary self-centeredness, the British naval and military authorities had by early 1941 conceived of a new mission for the U.S. Navy: the dispatch of much of its main fleet from Hawaii to Singapore to defend against a Japanese thrust to the southwest. Their American counterparts did not regard Singapore as vital to the war effort and believed—rightly as it turned out—that any naval force dispatched into that area would be hopelessly vulnerable to Japanese air power. After failing to carry their point in a plenary meeting, the British submitted a carefully argued, seven-page single spaced memo making their case on February 11. "The loss of Singapore," they argued, "would be a disaster of the first magnitude, second only to the loss of the British Isles. . . . Our morale and prestige, especially among the peoples of the East, would suffer a resounding blow." Even if Britain defeated Germany and Italy with American assistance, she would be unable to make the necessary effort to restore her position in the Far East. The only remedy was to base 1 U.S. carrier and 4 heavy cruisers at Singapore in order to prevent the Japanese capture of that vital base.[23]

The American planners deployed equally heavy rhetorical artillery in their reply eight days later. Plans relying on the United States to defend Malaysia were unsound, they began, because Congress might well not declare war if the Japanese attacked the area. The United States could not send such a force so far east because it would need its forces closer to home "in the event of a British defeat." The Americans argued essentially that Britain and the United States would not be able to prevent the Japanese conquest of the Philippines, the Dutch East Indies, and Malaysia, although they held out hope of inflicting substantial losses on them and leaving them much weaker. The conquest of Singapore would not allow Japan to cut off communications with *either* Australia and New Zealand or India. Politically its loss would be "a serious blow," but the allied nations had already absorbed "many severe blows" and could absorb others without experiencing a final disaster. Instead, the Americans offered to send some ships to Europe if the United States entered the war, thus freeing some British ships for service in the Far East. The British delegation then attempted an end-run, briefing the new British Ambassador, Lord Halifax, on the dispute, and sending him to Secretary Hull to plead his case, but this only infuriated the American negotiators without carrying the day.[24]

The allocation of aircraft divided the British and the American planners. Counting on the bombing of Germany to win the war during the next two years, the British wanted every available heavy bomber that they could get from the United States. Hopkins evidently endorsed this request after his return to Washington in early March, but General Arnold of the Air Corps and War Plans Division dissented in an unusually blunt memorandum on March 3. Should Britain fall, they argued, the United States needed "a minimum force of 54 combat groups [3,888 aircraft] plus the necessary personnel and facilities to undertake an immediate expansion to 100 combat groups [7,200 aircraft]." The Germans, they argued, undoubtedly knew that we could not provide serious assistance to the British before 1942, and therefore, the German-British war would probably be decided between now and November 1, 1941. "During this critical period," they wrote, "the United States cannot afford to base its military program on the assumption that the British Isles will not succumb as a result of blockade, or that they cannot be successfully invaded." Ideally the Americans wanted to limit British Commonwealth allocations to the 26,375 planes the British already had on order, but unless and until the United States entered the war, they were willing to delay the American 54-group program in order to provide as many additional aircraft as could be manned by British Commonwealth personnel in the United Kingdom.[25]

The British also desperately needed help at sea. German aircraft were sinking about one-third of the merchant ships the British were losing every month, and the British wanted aircraft and antiaircraft artillery for their merchant ships, or aircraft carriers to protect their ships. Meanwhile, quite a few of their warships had been damaged during the campaigns in the Mediterranean, and with British dockyards jammed and under fire, they had too few facilities in which to repair them. By the end of February the American attaché was recommending offering the British the free use of U.S. facilities to repair their ships, a clearly unneutral act under international law.[26]

On March 11, while the ABC-1 talks continued, President Roosevelt signed the Lend-Lease bill and immediately asked Congress for $7 billion to pay for Lend-Lease equipment during fiscal 1942—a 40 percent increase in the $17.5 billion budget he had submitted in early January. That night, after dinner with his new speechwriter, Robert Sherwood; his long-term houseguest, Hopkins; and his secretary and companion, Missy Lehand, he began dictating a speech to the nation. Roosevelt had been sick with respiratory problems for a good deal of the last two months. Faced with a world situation that might become desperate at almost any moment, he had proposed Lend-Lease to boost British morale and increase

U.S. productive capacity, and he was angry that its passage had taken so long and aroused such bitter attacks. Now he vented his frustrations, referring successively to numerous misstatements by "a certain columnist," "a certain Senator," or "certain Republican orators" which he had evidently been collecting. Sherwood, listening, eventually went to see Hopkins to plead with him to prevent Roosevelt from giving such a vindictive speech. "He's just getting it off his chest," Hopkins reassured him. "It has been rankling all this time and now he's rid of it."[27]

The speech that Roosevelt actually delivered on March 15 at the Gridiron Club—the Washington correspondents' dinner—was of a different character indeed: a paean to democracy and a cautious promise that it would not only survive, but prevail. "We, the American people, are writing new history today," he said: "The big news story of this week is this: The world has been told that we, as a united Nation, realize the danger that confronts us—and that to meet that danger our democracy has gone into action." He specifically compared the situation to the Great War, emphasizing that Nazism was a far greater threat than the German Empire. Referring implicitly to a continuing crisis in production, he called for longer hours, lower profits, higher taxes, and an end to strikes to meet the worldwide challenge and prove democracy superior to dictatorship. For the first time he spoke movingly and at length about the British people and Churchill, and promised them food, ships, planes, tanks, guns, and ammunition. "And when—no, I didn't say if, I said when—dictatorships disintegrate—and pray God that will be sooner than any of us now dares to hope—then our country must continue to play its great part in the period of world reconstruction for the good of humanity." Hopkins had told Churchill that Roosevelt was committed to Hitler's defeat, and now the President had called for that outcome publicly. "Never, in all our history," FDR concluded, "have Americans faced a job so well worthwhile. May it be said of us in the days to come that our children and our children's children rise up and call us blessed."[28]

"You and I are for Roosevelt," Hopkins had told Sherwood a few nights earlier, "because he's an idealist, like Wilson, and he's got the guts to drive through against any opposition to realize those ideals. Oh—he sometimes tries to appear tough and cynical and flippant, but that's just an act he likes to put on, especially at press conferences. . . . Maybe he fools some of them, now and then—but don't ever let him fool you, or you won't be any use to him. You can see the real Roosevelt when he comes out with something like the Four Freedoms. And don't get the idea that those are any catch phrases. *He believes them!* He believes they can be practically attained."[29] Roosevelt had now established the survival of democracy as a goal and the collapse of dictatorship as a hope, but no one knew better than he how much stood in the way of the realization of that goal, how long it would take, and how tentative practical military and naval steps must still remain. The Lend-Lease fight, prolonged and embittered by the conservative opponents he had dreamed of lambasting over the airwaves, was in the short run at least a Pyrrhic victory. Many months would pass before substantial supplies reached the British, the military situation could become desperate at any moment, and administration supporters had repeatedly argued that they were trying to stay out of the war. It is not surprising that the President now sought solace on the sunny waters of the Caribbean.

On March 19, four days after the Gridiron Club speech, Roosevelt left for a ten-day cruise off the Florida coast, accompanied this time by Hopkins; Hopkins's old rival Harold Ickes, who had been agitating for a more vigorous propaganda effort on behalf of war; and Attorney General Robert Jackson. The President once again spent most of his time fishing, playing poker, and watching movies, but at one point he remarked hopefully to the militant Ickes that he expected Germany to "make a blunder," allowing the United States to enter the war or convoy merchantmen to Britain. He also discussed a demand on the belligerents to keep their warships in home waters, coupled with a threat to sink any that ventured outside them, but even Ickes believed that this would only convince the public that the President indeed wanted war. Meanwhile the Anglo-American staff talks continued, and as in December, Roosevelt's more belligerent subordinates were drawing up proposals for more vigorous action while he was away.[30]

The ABC-1 talks concluded on March 27, and the two delegations submitted a report for approval to the chiefs of staff of the two countries and their heads of government. It laid out objectives, particular responsibilities, and available forces for the two countries "should the United States be compelled to resort to war," specifically with Germany and Italy and possibly with Japan as well. That wording—even more tentative than FDR's original instructions—seemed to suggest that the United States would go to war only if attacked. The report adopted "the defeat of Germany and her Allies" as its objective but laid out primarily defensive tasks, giving the United States responsibility for the defense of the western hemisphere while the British defended the British Isles, the Dominions, India, and their strategic position in the Far East and sharing the responsibility for the maintenance of sea communications. Its offensive recommendations closely followed the British concept of the war, including economic warfare, "a sustained air offensive against German military power," the early elimination of Italy as a German ally, the use of allied forces in "raids and minor offensives" against Axis military strength, the support of populations resisting Axis occupation, "the building up of the necessary forces for an eventual offensive against Germany," and "the capture of positions from which to launch the eventual offensive." In the next three years the British repeatedly made clear that the final offensive, in their view, had to await Germany's nearly complete collapse. The report specified Europe as the main theater of a possible world war and the North Atlantic as the main theater for U.S. naval action.[31]

Annex III of the ABC Report, the U.S.-British Commonwealth Joint Basic War Plan, gave the U.S. Navy responsibility for protecting Allied shipping and destroying Axis vessels in the North Atlantic west of 30° longitude, a line just west of Iceland that ran through the Azores Islands. The United States must also prepare to occupy not only the Azores, but the considerably more easterly Cape Verde Islands. But to accomplish all this, the plan allocated a somewhat smaller U.S. force to the Atlantic than Navy War Plans had recently foreseen: the 3 older battleships currently in the Atlantic, 2 carriers, 8 cruisers, and only 33 destroyers instead of 53, none of these ships operating in British coastal waters. The report anticipated that as many as 3 battleships, 1 carrier, 8 cruisers, and 14 destroyers might be moved from the Pacific to the Atlantic when the United States entered the war in Europe if the situation in the Pacific permitted it. They would sail for Europe, allowing the British to send a significant force to Singapore, and base themselves at Gibraltar. The problem, which emerged in the coming months, was that the U.S. Navy could not assume its projected responsibilities in the western Atlantic without those forces, making the whole plan inadequate in the event of war with Japan as well as Germany.

In a separate, complicated agreement on aircraft production, the U.S. Army agreed to defer even the completion of its initial 54-group program in order to make available to the British additional aircraft that would contribute directly to the achievement of the military objectives of the agreed war plan. Should the United States create additional new productive capacity, the resulting aircraft would "in principle" go to the United Kingdom for as long as the United States had not entered the war. When that occurred, the new construction would be divided "as the military situation may require and circumstances may permit," but the British could plan to receive 50 percent of it. The plan now went to the Joint Board, which turned it into the long-awaited Rainbow 5 war plan and approved it on May 14. Meanwhile, Knox, Stimson, and Stark made a determined effort to push Roosevelt into the European war at once.[32]

Navy Secretary Frank Knox did not want to stay out of the war any longer. On March 21, while Roosevelt was fishing off the Florida coast, he wrote the President recommending two immediate steps to ease the shipping crisis and save the British. To begin with, he wanted to seize approximately 1 million tons of Axis and neutral shipping now sitting in American harbors and make it available for transatlantic crossings. More important, he wanted the United States to begin convoying merchant ships across the Atlantic right away. Churchill had pleaded for this in late February, and on March 19, as FDR was leaving on his cruise, the Prime Minister reported that the German battle cruisers *Scharnhorst* and *Gneisnau* were doing severe damage to British convoys just 500 miles southeast of Newfoundland, far west of the 30th meridian of longitude. "It would be a very great help if some American warships and aircraft could cruise about in this area as they have a perfect right to do," he wrote. Four days later, he added that the necessary dispersal of British warships was making Britain more vulnerable to invasion. "Our technical people in operations," Knox wrote Roosevelt, "including Admiral Stark, are emphatic and unanimous in their decision that the only adequate answer to this situation is convoying. . . . The steady increase in losses to shipping in the approaches to the British Isles and the terrible punishment now being inflicted by the German air force on British ports, in my judgment, indicates the swift approach of the hour of decision if we are going to effectuate the declarations you made in your speech last Saturday night." Knox also asked permission to send some naval aviators to operate some of the aircraft that the British were receiving, such as PBY seaplanes.[33]

During the next few days Knox secured the agreement of Stimson on convoying, and both of them shared their views with Stark, Marshall, and the British military mission. Roosevelt immediately put one of Knox's recommendations into effect, seizing Axis and Danish vessels in U.S. ports on March 30. Asked in an April 1 press conference about means of getting supplies to the British, Roosevelt replied guardedly that these issues had been under study for a year. Admiral Stark believed more deeply than ever that the United States simply had to get into the war if Britain were to last out the year intact, and in late March and early April, both Knox and Stark gave Roosevelt the plans for U.S. convoys in the North Atlantic that had been developed before and during the ABC-1 talks. They assumed U.S. entry into the war and included a base in Northern Ireland. Focusing on the danger of surface raiders like the *Scharnhorst* and *Gneisnau*, Stark stated bluntly that present forces in the Atlantic would be inadequate for convoy duty and called for 3 more battleships, a carrier, 18 destroyers, and, eventually, 4 more light cruisers.[34]

Stark did not want these ships only to try to save Britain. Such a transfer, Stark wrote Pacific Fleet commander Kimmel on April 3, would provide the United States with adequate security "in case the British isles should fall," although it would not provide much offensive punch against the Axis. Roosevelt initially approved the move, evidently in a private meeting with Stark and Admiral Ghormley, who had returned briefly from the United Kingdom. "The question of our entry into the war," Stark wrote, "now seems to be when, not whether. . . . My own personal view is that we may be in the war (possibly undeclared) against Germany and Italy within two months, but that there is a reasonable possibility that Japan may remain out altogether." Ghormley returned to London with a letter designating him as Commander, U.S. Naval Forces, Europe, effective on the date of U.S. entry into the war. The United States now agreed to the repair of a large number of damaged British warships in U.S. yards. On April 9, following reports of German planes overflying Greenland, the U.S. government reached an agreement with the Danish exile government allowing it to establish bases on that massive western hemispheric island and forestall any German move.[35]

Knox and Stark were in effect asking that Roosevelt put the Plan Dog memorandum into effect and go to war at once to save the British. The President refused. Roosevelt declined to approve Stark's plan for convoys, fearing new complications in the Pacific and sticking to the strategy of hemispheric defense. He did, however, give Stark permission to transfer 3 battleships, a carrier, 4 cruisers, and 2 squadrons of destroyers from Pearl Harbor to the Atlantic in order to make patrols in the western Atlantic effective. Roosevelt was also sufficiently frightened by the excursion of the *Scharnhorst* and the *Gneisnau* to give the War and Navy departments an urgent request to upgrade the defenses of the new bases in Newfoundland, Bermuda, and Trinidad—especially Bermuda. But on the same day, apparently, that he discussed the convoy plans with Stark and Ghormley, he rejected them in a talk with Morgenthau. "The President said that public opinion was not yet ready for the United States to convoy ships," Morgenthau wrote after a White House meeting on April 2. "This was his whole attitude anyway, that he seemed to be still waiting and not ready to go ahead on 'all out aid for England.'" Moreover, however, the President never allowed demands from one theater of war to make him lose sight of the worldwide threats that the United States faced. In this case, he knew all too well that Stark's hopes of entering the war in Europe without drawing the Japanese in as well were sadly misplaced. At no time did FDR play more clearly the key role that Clausewitz gave to a commander-in-chief, that of keeping the entire situation before him in mind despite the chaos of the battlefield and the blandishments of anxious subordinates.[36]

The situation with respect to Japan remained confused, but hardly reassuring. In conversations with both Roosevelt and Hull in February, Nomura had relatively little to offer beyond a wish for a peace in China including both Chiang Kai-shek and the new Japanese puppet government, and his own belief that Japan would not undertake further military actions unless the United States imposed further economic embargoes. Meanwhile, Premier Prince Konoye—a devoted supporter of the Japanese southward advance—had launched a secret initiative to try to avoid war with the United States. Working with some pro-Japanese Americans, including Bishop James Walsh of the Maryknoll Missionaries, two unofficial Japanese emissaries, one an Army officer, worked out a proposal under which the two countries would arrange to conclude the Sino-Japanese war on terms favorable to Japan and agree on a Monroe Doctrine for Asia, all to be announced in a meeting between Roosevelt and Konoye in Honolulu. Konoye, his representatives said, had agreed to this potential "reversal of policy"—evidently involving the abandonment of the Tripartite Pact—with the Emperor and senior Army and Navy leaders, but if word of this proposal leaked prematurely, some of the policy's advocates would surely be assassinated. The "Asian Monroe Doctrine," however, was simply a euphemism for the prominent, military-backed role that Japan wanted to play all over East Asia, including in the European powers' colonial possessions. And when Konoye's unofficial emissaries passed written proposals to the State Department in the first week of April, the text essentially committed the United States to remaining neutral in the European war, while adding that Japan would not go to war with the United States were the United States "aggressively attacked" by Germany.[37]

In two conversations on April 14 and April 16, Hull told Nomura that Japan would have to endorse his four principles of international conduct, including respect for the territorial integrity of all nations, noninterference in other countries' internal affairs, equality of economic opportunity among nations, and nondisturbance of the status quo in the Pacific except by peaceful means. Hull insisted that the United States for eight years had successfully established these principles in the western hemisphere and that they had to be extended around the world in order to have any hope of peace.[38]

No settlement was possible on this basis. To the Japanese, Hull's principles embodied the Nine-Power Treaty establishing the territorial integrity of China and the rest of the Washington treaties of 1922, designed to maintain the status quo in the Far East. The Japanese had been violating these treaties since 1931 and were determined to consign them to the dust bin of history. They remained just as committed to the Axis ideal of a world of superstates as Hull was to a world of free and equal nations ruled by law. In addition, while the Japanese wanted the United States to promise to stay out of the European war, the United States wanted the Japanese to denounce the Tripartite Pact, and by early May, Magic intercepts left senior U.S. policymakers with no doubt whatever that the Japanese had every intention of observing their obligations under the Tripartite Pact if the United States went to war with Germany. In short, Roosevelt knew that, contrary to Stark's hopes of April 3, there was no "reasonable possibility" of going to war in Europe while simultaneously avoiding war with Japan in the Pacific. He also knew that the U.S. Fleet was not large enough to fight in both oceans at once, while the U.S. Army would not be ready for major operations for many months.[39]

Washington had for some time been awaiting Hitler's next blow in Europe or the Atlantic. A new element had intruded into the European situation in the past few months: the possibility that Germany might attack the Soviet Union rather than invade Great Britain. On February 19, a highly placed German source indicated to an American officer that the German General Staff was planning such an attack and confidently expected to wipe out the Soviet Army in a few months at most. Evidently briefed on this report, Roosevelt passed the information on to Henry Morgenthau on March 6. A further report confirming Germany's plans reached Washington in the first week of April, and Europe was by then buzzing with rumors of German troop movements to the east. None of this could be regarded as certain, however, and other rumors foresaw German moves into Iberia, North Africa, and the Atlantic.[40]

Another avalanche of bad war news began arriving from Europe during the first week of April. During the winter the Germans had moved substantial forces into Hungary, Rumania, and Bulgaria to prepare for an attack on Greece, which was holding out valiantly against the Italians. An anti-Axis coup d'état in Yugoslavia on March 27 had doomed Hitler's efforts to enlist that nation as well, but the Germans responded with extraordinary speed, occupying Belgrade within just sixteen days. A multi-front German attack on Greece began on April 6, and Churchill decided that British prestige demanded that he send forces from North Africa to try to stop it. Within less than two weeks the British, crippled by a lack of effective air support, were withdrawing from another humiliating peripheral adventure, one only too reminiscent of the Norway disaster twelve months earlier. Worse still, Churchill's ill-advised decision to help the Greeks had drastically weakened the British position in North Africa. New German armored forces under General Erwin Rommel drove the British almost completely out of Libya to the Egyptian border during April, and both the War Department G-2 (Intelligence) and Admiral Turner in Navy War Plans predicted that the Germans would take Crete and, very likely, the Suez Canal. The threat of a German move to Gibraltar was also on their minds.[41]

Stimson, who had thought that the passage of Lend-Lease had turned the corner and effectively gotten the nation into the war, was near despair. "I feel very keenly that something must be done in the way of leadership here in the center at Washington," he confided in his diary on April 9, "and I am beginning to feel very troubled about the lack of it. . . . We have tried aid short of war and it now is pretty clear that it isn't enough, and unless we are ready to drive at something that hurts us, we won't accomplish anything." He saw "a great deal of haphazard, happy-go-lucky work around us and a good deal of it centers in the White House." Right, Stimson believed, made might, and he essentially counted on Roosevelt to make the nation do their bidding. But perhaps in part because Stimson was confident that the Japanese would back away from a confrontation, he did not grasp that the President did not believe the United States could yet undertake war on two fronts and wanted to keep strengthening the defense of the western hemisphere.[42]

The President met his war council of Stimson, Knox, Stark, Hull, and Hopkins on April 10 (Marshall was apparently busy elsewhere) and discussed how to help the British. He had told a similar meeting eight days earlier that the public was not ready for convoys, and now he stated bluntly that a congressional resolution to authorize them would fail. Stimson, while noting his disagreement in his diary, nonetheless called this an "honest decision." Instead, the group opened an atlas, drew a line halfway between Africa and South America, and found that it approximated the 26th meridian of longitude, which also ran almost entirely to the east of Greenland. Roosevelt decided that U.S. ships and aircraft would "patrol" west of that line, alerting British forces to the presence of any Axis ships, and that the United States would pledge to defend all Greenland against the Germans.[43]

Bypassing the Joint Board, Roosevelt evidently ordered Stark to prepare a naval war plan along these lines immediately, as well as plans to occupy the Azores and Cape Verde islands. Grasping for ways to help the British, on April 11 he announced that the Gulf of Aden and the Red Sea were being removed from the American list of designated war zones—which included, of course, the eastern Atlantic and the Mediterranean—thereby allowing U.S. ships to carry supplies to the British as they desperately tried to preserve their position in the Middle East. The day before, he announced an agreement with the Danish government-in-exile under which the United States would assume the defense of Greenland. On April 11 Roosevelt confidentially informed Churchill that "aircraft and naval vessels working from Greenland, Newfoundland, Nova Scotia, the United States, Bermuda and West Indies, with possible later extension to Brazil if this can be arranged," would look for Axis ships west of 25° longitude and broadcast their location to the British. He also informed him that American ships would bring equipment for British forces all the way to the Red Sea.[44]

The struggle at the top of the administration continued. Hopkins's trip to Britain had evidently turned him into a determined advocate of immediate intervention, and he conveyed his views to anyone who would listen. Roosevelt met Hull, Knox, Stimson, Marshall, and Hopkins on April 15 and once again discussed attacking any Axis shipping that crossed the line of 26° west. Stimson favored announcing this move at once to check appeasement tendencies in Britain, but Roosevelt declined to do so. After the meeting Hopkins took Marshall aside to express his concerns. "Mr. Hopkins," Marshall told his leading subordinates the next morning, "hopes that by a series of talks, the President will become aware of the fundamental problems which face this nation. Mr. Hopkins feels that we have reached the point where the President must make a hard decision. . . . If we have gotten to the point where we can no longer operate on a peacetime status, should we recommend a war status? Or is it of importance to do something immediately?" Marshall regretted that the Army still had so little to offer and said that Stimson felt that any military action the United States might take—for instance the occupation of Iceland, Greenland, the Azores, or Martinique—must be "done with a high degree of efficiency and on an impressive scale—an overwhelming force." Marshall had apparently told the War Plans Division (WPD) to have a paper evaluating the pros and cons of war that afternoon, April 16, when he would have to return to the White House.[45]

In a tribute to the management style and writing skills of their generation, the WPD came up with a one-page single-spaced memorandum doing just that. Entering the war, it argued, would awaken the country to the gravity of the situation, speed up production and preparations, strengthen the Churchill government, and weaken, for unspecified reasons, the Axis. On the other hand, the Army was prepared only for operations "on an extremely minor scale" due to shortages of equipment and ammunition, leaving most of the work to the Navy. The United States could defend the western hemisphere, and if shipping were available, relieve the British now occupying Iceland and garrison the Azores and Cape Verdes once the Navy and Marines had seized them. The authors saw no significant dangers to immediate entry into the war in the Atlantic but feared the immediate loss of the Philippines if Japan declared war in the Pacific.[46]

Marshall convened another conference to discuss the paper. "Hopkins," he explained, "is of the view that the [British] reverses in the

Mediterranean might force the president to make a decision." FDR, Marshall thought, would probably want their views "as to what should be done now in order to meet catastrophic reverses. The Secretary of War feels that if we do nothing, appeasement forces may gain the ascendancy in England." In the subsequent discussion, General Embick suggested that the fall of Churchill, whose military judgment he distrusted, would not be catastrophic, but Marshall stood up for the Prime Minister. Embick, long the Army's leading proponent of hemispheric defense, argued that entering the war now would be "wrong in a military and naval sense and to the American people." Colonel McNarney, however, who had been observing the war from London, thought that the fall of the British Isles would put the whole load on the United States and that we had to start reducing "the war-making ability of Germany." "If we wait we will end up standing alone," he concluded, "and internal disturbances may bring on communism." Several other officers agreed with him.

It turned out, however, that Hopkins had failed to move Roosevelt. When Marshall and Embick met with the President, Stark, Admiral Turner, and Hopkins on the afternoon of April 16, FDR did not allow the issue of entering the war to arise. Roosevelt apparently dominated the discussion, asking about the Mediterranean situation and stressing the importance of Dakar, without getting into broader issues. On April 15, in a press conference, he had replied lightheartedly and evasively to questions about British reverses and about the possibility of convoys.[47]

On the very next day, April 17, CNO Admiral Stark sent Admiral King, the commander of the Atlantic Fleet, Navy Western Hemisphere Defense Plan No. 1, which had grown directly out of the war council's discussions in the Oval Office. It commanded King to "trail naval vessels and aircraft of belligerent powers, (other than those Powers which have sovereignty over Western Hemisphere territory)," broadcast their movements, warn them if they were encountered twenty-five miles or more west of longitude 26° that they must withdraw, "and, in case of failure to heed such warning, attack them." Although King's warships should protect U.S. merchant shipping (which of course could not cross the North Atlantic) as well, they should not make reprisal strikes against belligerents that had already attacked western hemisphere territory unless ordered to do so. "The President is desirous of executing this plan in the Atlantic Ocean as soon as possible," Stark said, and he promised additional aircraft at Bermuda and a carrier from the Pacific to help. But the

President was pressed hard on the convoy issue at a press conference on April 18 and allowed Senate Majority Leader Alben Barkley to deny on behalf of Stimson and Knox that convoys were in progress.[48]

Meanwhile, news from the other side of the earth increased the tension still further and convinced Roosevelt to scale back the new naval plans for the Atlantic. Japan's pro-Axis Foreign Minister, Matsuoka, had just visited Rome, Berlin, and Moscow and on April 13 had concluded a nonaggression pact with the Soviet Union that might free the Japanese to move south. The President knew from the February Magic intercept of Matsuoka's cable to Nomura that this evidently removed the danger of Soviet intervention which alone had restrained the Japanese from starting their southward advance and going to war with the United States. On April 19, Stark informed Kimmel that this development had convinced Roosevelt to reduce the planned transfer of warships from the Atlantic to one carrier and some destroyers, because he did not want to encourage the Japanese. That in turn forced Roosevelt to make the new Atlantic war plan less ambitious. After spending the weekend of April 19–20 at Hyde Park, where Admiral King of the Atlantic Fleet joined him, Roosevelt ordered the Navy to promulgate Western Hemisphere Defense Plan 2 on April 21. It took a big step backward, ordering U.S. ships only to trail hostile belligerent vessels within the western hemisphere "and broadcast in plain language their movements at four hour intervals, or oftener if necessary," leaving the attacking to the British and thereby forcing them to continue to provide some escort over the entire route. Both of the western hemisphere defense plans bypassed the normal war planning process, which would have mandated a joint Army-Navy plan from the General Board first. Ghormley in London immediately informed the British, and Churchill promised to keep the Americans fully informed of British convoy movements to help.[49]

On Monday, April 21, Stimson returned from a weekend on Long Island to find widespread gloom about the state of public opinion and the absence of a firm stand. The *New York Times* had become the first major newspaper to call for entry into the war on April 20, but Stimson knew that the President was not ready to agree. Knox cheered him with the text of a speech the Navy Secretary planned to give later in the week in New York, however, and the next day Stimson had "in some respects the most intimate and satisfactory conference I have ever had" with Roosevelt. After warning the President that he would speak frankly, Stimson noted the deterioration in the political situation since Lend-Lease had passed. FDR, he said, had to rally the people; they would not rouse themselves. He even complained about the tone of Roosevelt's press conferences. As often happened with visitors to the Oval Office, Stimson left Roosevelt feeling much better without evidently being able to explain exactly why.[50]

Meeting the press later that day, a cheerful Roosevelt said Axis successes in the Balkans would not win the war, insisted that we had to keep Britain going, and cautioned the public against excessive optimism or pessimism. Meeting with Roosevelt on April 22 and with Roosevelt, Hull, and Knox on April 24, Stimson vigorously disputed Roosevelt's decision to keep the battleships, cruisers, and destroyers that he had agreed to move to the Atlantic in early April in Hawaii instead. Roosevelt initially argued that the ships had to stay at Hawaii for defensive purposes, but Stimson quoted General Marshall to the effect that new deployments of U.S. planes and antiaircraft guns could do that job. Hull did not want to move more ships in the midst of his talks with the Japanese. Trying to blame his decision on someone else, Roosevelt then claimed that the British wanted our ships to stay in the Pacific, but when Admiral Danckwaerts at the British Embassy was queried, he indicated that a transfer of some forces would indeed be welcome.[51]

On April 24, Hull spoke to the American Society of International Law and made the kind of speech Stimson wanted from the President. The present conflict, he argued, was not, as some would have it, "merely an ordinary regional war," but a "war of assault" by "would-be conquerors, employing every method of barbarism, upon nations which cling to their right to live in freedom." Fifteen nations had lost "everything that makes life worth living," and "the remaining free countries should arm to the fullest extent . . . and act for their self-preservation." To wait for an invader to "cross the boundary line of this hemisphere" would give the enemy every possible advantage, and the protection of the United States demanded "resistance wherever resistance will be most effective. . . . Ways must be found" to ensure that aid reached Great Britain, and the United States had to prevent aggressor nations from controlling the seas. Peace was impossible: The Axis nations did not believe in it. The United States needed an all-out effort, but Hull expressed "absolute faith in the ultimate triumph of the principles of humanity, translated into law and order, by which freedom and justice and security will again prevail."[52]

In a cabinet meeting the next afternoon, Roosevelt evidently explained the new Atlantic patrol plan he had received on Monday, "a step forward" which he now was putting into effect. "Well, I hope you will keep on walking, Mr. President. Keep on walking," said Stimson, and the room erupted in laughter. That very evening, in a broadcast speech to his fellow newspaper publishers, Knox characterized the members of the Tripartite Pact as declared enemies of the United States, who would go to war with the United States whenever it suited them to do so. "How long," he asked, "will we remain bemused and stupefied while the Axis powers press their plans for our isolation and ultimate defeat?" He warned of the threat of subversive elements in Latin America and the German threat to Dakar and pointed out how much of the world's oceans were already closed off to the United States. Reviewing what the United States had already done for Britain, he too called for stronger measures at sea. "We cannot allow our goods to be sunk in the Atlantic—we shall be beaten if they do [*sic*]." Wendell Willkie weighed in with a similar statement the next day. At a Monday press conference, Roosevelt said that these speeches spoke for the views of the vast majority of the American people— including, he confirmed in response to a question, his own. He also tried to quiet the convoy controversy by arguing that the new steps were simply an extension of the neutrality patrol he had announced when war broke out. It was a patrol, he repeated, not a convoy—which was perfectly true. "If, by calling a cow a horse for a year and a half," he continued, "you think that that makes the cow a horse, I don't think so. Now, that's pretty plain language. You can't turn a cow into a horse by calling it something else; calling it a horse it is still a cow."[53]

That Friday, in the cabinet, he affirmed that the new patrol was on and discussed the possible occupation of the Azores or Cape Verde Islands. When the Navy tried to draw up plans for those operations, however, they found that the only available Marine forces were very far from being sufficiently trained or equipped to act and that the Cape Verdes would be impossible to defend against Axis air power in North Africa. The decision to patrol out to 26° west would inevitably lead to confrontations with German warships that were now operating well beyond that line, and Roosevelt told Lord Halifax, the new British Ambassador, that he still expected incidents to occur that might bring the United States into the war. Hitler, however, understood all this perfectly and gave strict orders to his restless Navy to avoid any attacks on U.S. ships. On another front, the President approved a joint Army-Navy plan to send troops to support the recognized governments of any of the seven Latin American nations nearest the Panama Canal should they be requested to put down a pro-Axis uprising.[54]

The month of May, which culminated in another major presidential address on May 26, saw an escalation of the public debate—exactly what the activist cabinet members like Stimson, Ickes, and Knox had hoped for—combined with a transfer of more ships to the Atlantic and plans for action to extend the hemispheric defense perimeter still farther in the face of yet more bad news from Europe and the Middle East. For the first time, prominent private citizens, including two Episcopal bishops who called "aid short of war" immoral and Harvard President James Bryant Conant, called openly for the United States to enter the European war at once. During the first week of May, senior officials of the American Legion and the Veterans of Foreign Wars called for convoys to Britain. On the evening of May 6 Stimson broadcast a radio address of his own, one cleared by the President, which escalated administration rhetoric a bit further. Echoing Hull, he accused Germany and her two key allies of reverting to barbarism and destroying "the Western civilization which had been slowly building up in Europe ever since the Dark Ages." The Nazis were trampling the rule of law, their "advance agents are busy among the republics to the south of us," their armed forces "threatening West Africa, looking toward a jumping-off place within easy reach of the Brazilian coast," and propagandizing actively within the United States itself. "But as has always happened before," he promised, "the progress of man along the path toward freedom will be taken up again and carried forward with new spirit."[55]

Strategically, Stimson argued in some detail, the United States depended on friendly control of the seas and had long relied on Britain in the Atlantic. Britain's fall would leave the whole hemisphere in grave danger. "At least a year will pass," Stimson said truthfully and frankly, "before we can have an Army and an air force adequate to meet the air and ground forces which could be brought against us if the control of the seas passed into Axis hands." If our Navy would "make secure the seas for the delivery of our munitions to Great Britain," it would render "as great a service to the nation as ever in history." Calling in effect for a naval alliance with Britain to control the seas, he warned that if we delayed action until the British Navy had disappeared, "the power of our own Navy would become merely a secondary power instead of the decisive and winning power in the world contest. Is it conceivable that the American people would allow this to happen?" After the overwhelmingly positive response to the President's call for Lend-Lease aid to Britain, "shall we now flinch and permit these munitions to be sunk in the Atlantic Ocean?" But American freedom, he concluded, could not be saved "without sacrifice." Stimson had called explicitly for convoys, and implicitly for war.[56]

The isolationist opposition attempted to reply before an enthusiastic America First rally in New York's Madison Square Garden on May 23 featuring Lindbergh and Senator Wheeler. With a truly American policy, Lindbergh argued, U.S. troops would not fight to secure the domination of Europe for either Britain or Germany, and we need be "no more afraid of the Europe of Germany than our forefathers were afraid of the Europe of France or England or Spain." He suggested we could not possibly win a war and stated bluntly that our own democracy would not survive it. Wheeler called on the crowd "to fight to save your sons from the bloody battlefields of Europe, Asia and Africa—to fight against one-man government in the United States." The American people, he said, wanted the Four Freedoms established first in the United States. The British Fleet, he argued, would never fall into Hitler's hands even if Britain were defeated, and the United States would remain safe from German invasion for many years to come. An enthusiastic audience welcomed these arguments, but the public remained as ambivalent as ever—convinced on the one hand that Britain must be saved, but opposed to U.S. entry into the war.[57]

Roosevelt had developed his unshakable calm and his maddening ebullience in the face of danger in his childhood, and it had served him well through personal crises, polio, and the stewardship of the nation at its darkest moment in 1933. Without political or military resources to act more vigorously, he fell back on calm and good cheer once again to deal with no less a figure than Winston Churchill, who faced a truly critical situation. On May 1, Roosevelt wrote Churchill to inform him that the new U.S. patrol would extend to the Azores, which the British were thinking of occupying. Then, praising Churchill's "not only heroic, but very useful work in Greece," he referred to a possible British withdrawal from North Africa and the whole eastern Mediterranean, but assured him that British and American opinion realized that "in the last analysis the Naval control of the Indian Ocean and the Atlantic Ocean will in time win the war." He also suggested that he, Roosevelt, offer General Maxim Weygand, the French Commander in North Africa, oil and other supplies in exchange for a promise to resist German troop movements into North Africa—a deal the President had already been pushing through American diplomat Robert Murphy. Although such a movement could not be prevented, Roosevelt hoped that a strong defense of Morocco's Atlantic ports would keep the Germans out of Dakar.

Churchill on May 3 replied in something of a panic, arguing that the outcome of the struggle in North Africa could determine "the attitude of Spain, Vichy, Turkey and Japan." Should the Axis nations gain control of all Europe and the greater part of Asia and Africa, a war by the United States and British Empire against them would be "a hard, long and bleak proposition." Desperately Churchill played his remaining card. "The one decisive counterweight I can see to balance the growing pessimism in Turkey, the Near East, and in Spain, would be if the United States were immediately to range herself with us as a belligerent power." That would allow the British to "hold the situation in the Mediterranean until the weight of your munitions gained the day. . . . I shall await with deep anxiety the new broadcast which you contemplate," he continued. "It may be the supreme turning point." Typically, Roosevelt in his May 10 reply assured Churchill that thirty ships would soon be on their way to the Middle East with supplies, paid further tribute to British valor, and said not one word about U.S. entry into the war. Although he may well have shared Stimson's and Hopkins's fears about the consequences of further British military reverses for the Churchill government, he was not willing to enter the war to try to prevent them.[58]

Roosevelt was now suffering from another week-long respiratory infection that kept him almost completely confined to bed. Meanwhile Stimson continued to agitate for the movement of most of the U.S. Fleet into the Atlantic, where he, like Churchill, regarded the situation as desperate. The Navy itself seems to have been divided on this question, however, and Stark, in a White House meeting on May 6—the only big meeting FDR held during his illness—wanted the movement restricted to just three battleships. A frustrated Stimson complained in his diary that Stark was too weak a leader and that he gave his own speech on the defense of the Atlantic that night without the necessary ships in his pocket. The Secretary of War did not realize that the President himself shared his Admirals' caution, and did not want to strip the Pacific so long as the threat from Japan remained. On May 9 Stimson wrote Harry Hopkins that the announcement that most of the fleet were coming through the Panama Canal would do much more good than another speech. Other administration figures were concerned as well. On May 12 Stimson met with Knox, Attorney General Jackson, and Sidney Hillman of the Office of Production Management. All agreed that Roosevelt had to speak more firmly in public. With Roosevelt ill, Ickes passed his concerns on to Missy Lehand the next day, but she claimed she hadn't seen him either. Ickes, who was feeling his loss of influence keenly, actually confided to John McCloy of the War Department that in light of Roosevelt's recent performance he regretted pushing for his third term.[59]

The war council met at the State Department without FDR on May 13, and Hull announced that Roosevelt had reversed himself once again and was now willing to send three battleships and their support forces to the Atlantic. The carrier *Yorktown* and three destroyers had already passed through the Panama Canal on the night of May 6 and steamed to Bermuda, and Roosevelt now ordered the battleships *Idaho*, *New Mexico*, and *Mississippi*; four new light cruisers; and two squadrons of new destroyers—eighteen ships—to the Atlantic. The transfer amounted to about one-quarter of the Pacific Fleet, making offensive operations much more difficult in a war with Japan, but the administration did not announce it. It was evidently designed more to put the new patrolling plan into effect and to deal with actual or imminent Axis naval threats to the western hemisphere rather than to deter the Axis or encourage the French, Spanish, or Portuguese.[60]

Real and potential threats continued to appear. On May 11–12, Admiral Darlan, the Vichy French Prime Minister, met with Hitler in the Fuehrer's retreat at Berchtesgaden, and the world press and American observers assumed that a wide-ranging deal had been struck. Frightened, Marshall instantly dispatched Matthew Ridgway to Brazil to discuss the immediate dispatch of U.S. troops to Natal, 1,800 miles across the Atlantic from now-threatened Dakar, but the Brazilians were not interested. Conferences in Stimson's and Marshall's offices on May 19 discussed the need for troops to be sent overseas at once, and Marshall had to explain that any draftee troops would have to volunteer to go. Roosevelt, ever alert to the naval balance, received a full report locating every French ship on May 24. Once again, as in the late fall of 1940, Hitler's refusal to

make critical concessions prevented his talks with the French from bear-
ing fruit. The Vichy government was willing to allow the Germans to
establish bases in North Africa and even to make military and naval use
of Dakar, but only in return for the release of a large contingent of French
POWs and important economic concessions, which Hitler would not
make. Meanwhile, an extremely detailed and accurate intelligence report
describing German plans to attack the USSR sometime during June
reached FDR's desk by the middle of May.[61]

Roosevelt and his senior advisers were coping successfully with the
world crisis because their education had taught them to see world history
as a centuries-old clash among nations, civilizations, and ideas. On May
23, one of the most influential academics of the Missionary generation,
Harvard professor Roger Bigelow Merriman, gave for the last time his
final lecture in History 1, European history from the fall of the Roman
empire to the present, to an audience of 1,000 Harvard students. Merriman had published relatively little, but nearly three decades' worth of
Harvard undergraduates—a total of about 20,000 young men, including
Franklin Roosevelt and John F. Kennedy—had passed through his required course or otherwise encountered him since he earned his doctor-
ate in 1902. History, he had taught them, was dominated by a "pendulum
principle." "After every important historical development, extending
over a substantial period of time," he said, "there is a reaction which
sends mankind in the opposite direction; but when the pendulum swings
back, humanity is one step further on the road of progress." Liberty and
security were the two poles of the historical pendulum. Entertaining a
journalist in his study after the lecture, Merriman, not for the first time,
called for the immediate entry of the United States into the war, since a
German victory would doom both liberty and security for years to come.
Since the late nineteenth century when the modern university curricu-
lum was born, Merriman and others like him had taught young men and
women to place the present within the grand sweep of Western history—
exactly the preparation they needed when as adults they faced one of the
great crises of Western civilization.[62]

Another big battle began in the Mediterranean on May 20, when
German paratroopers attacked British forces on Crete, which the British
planners had promised to hold during the ABC-1 talks. Operating without air cover, the British lost the island within ten days, and their Navy
suffered terribly at the hands of the Luftwaffe while trying to evacuate

the troops. Two battleships and a carrier were put out of action for six to twenty-two weeks, three cruisers and six destroyers were sunk, and five cruisers and seven destroyers were damaged—all in a losing battle. British shipping losses, meanwhile, escalated at an alarmingly unsustainable rate: from 320,000 tons in January to 403,000 in February, 529,000 in March, and 687,000 in April. Churchill on May 23 sent Roosevelt British Admiralty papers asking the U.S. Navy to act against U-boats west of 35° west and protect against surface raiders all the way to Canada and to patrol the whole area between the bulge of Africa and Brazil. In the same message he announced that the German Navy was making its most dangerous bid yet to disrupt Atlantic trade.[63]

American naval planners had not miscalculated when they emphasized the threat of German surface raiders in the plans they drew up for the Atlantic around the turn of the year. Since the winter, Admiral Raeder of the German Navy had been planning a coordinated sweep of the Atlantic by four battleships, the smaller *Scharnhorst* and *Gneisnau*, now based in Brest in France, and the massive new *Bismarck* and *Tirpitz*, probably at least equal to any British or U.S. battleship now on duty. As it turned out, the *Tirpitz* was not yet seaworthy by spring, a British torpedo bomber put the *Gneisnau* out of action, and the *Scharnhorst*'s engine broke down, but the Germans in May decided to proceed with a raid from Norwegian waters through the Denmark Strait between Iceland and Greenland by the *Bismarck* and the heavy cruiser *Prinz Eugen*. Swedish and British intelligence detected the ships as they were leaving the Baltic Sea on May 20, and the British deployed to meet them. British code-breakers quickly discovered that the *Bismarck* was carrying five prize crews, signaling its intention to raid British commerce. Churchill personally alerted Roosevelt.[64]

At dawn on May 24, the British First World War battle cruiser *Hood* and new battleship *Prince of Wales* encountered the *Bismarck* just west of Iceland. The British opened fire first, but the *Bismarck* straddled the *Hood* with its fifth salvo. A shell penetrated the ship's deck armor, reached the magazine, and ignited a terrible explosion that sank the *Hood* with the loss of all but three of its men. A similar fate had befallen three comparable battle cruisers at the Battle of Jutland in 1916. The German ships also outmaneuvered the *Prince of Wales* and scored a series of hits, while the British ship scored three on the *Bismarck*. With most of his guns unworkable, the captain of the British ship turned tail and broke off the action. Although the *Prince of Wales* may have been fortunate that the German squadron chose not to pursue, it had done critical damage to the *Bismarck*. A steady fuel leak forced the German commander to abandon his plans to wreak havoc in the Atlantic and head for home.

Two days later, on May 26, the *Bismarck* was initially disabled by a carrier-based British torpedo bomber that scored a lucky hit on her rudder and jammed it, then attacked by a superior British force, completely disabled by numerous hits, and finally scuttled by its crew. Yet the intervening days had brought the United States into the battle. The *Bismarck* had initially escaped from the shadowing British cruisers after sinking the *Hood*, and Roosevelt had ordered the patrolling Atlantic Fleet, including the battleship *New York*—which would have had little chance against the superior German ship in combat—to hunt for it. Back in the White House, the President speculated that the *Bismarck* was heading for Martinique and asked calmly whether Congress might impeach him if he ordered U.S. submarines to sink it. That turned out to be unnecessary, but an American officer played a role in the story nonetheless. In addition to PBY flying boats, the U.S. Navy had provided the British with some personnel to help train their pilots, and one of them, Ensign Leonard Smith, was in the cockpit of the flying boat that found the *Bismarck* on May 26.[65]

Because Hitler's attention was now fixed firmly eastward on the attack on the Soviet Union—now less than a month away—the danger in the Atlantic was much less imminent than it seemed in Washington. Hitler had in fact made no immediate demands on Darlan, he had not even known about the *Bismarck*'s sortie in advance, and he had tried to stop it when the Navy informed him that it was underway. But Roosevelt was now determined to act in defense of the western hemisphere. Meeting with senior advisers on May 22, he took the initiative and asked about a possible invasion of the Azores. Informed that the operation would require three months to prepare, he replied that it must be ready within one. The Germans, he said, could go into Spain and Portugal at any moment and the United States must get the islands when they did. "I was impressed with the tremendous undertaking," Henry Morgenthau noted privately, "and that we're not ready, and it would be next to impossible to get ready in a month because the ships to carry the troops have not been prepared for the job." On the same day, Stark wrote Marshall laying out the manpower requirements for the defensive deployments in the Atlantic, the Pacific, West Africa, and Britain called for by the Rainbow 5 War Plan—requirements that the United States was far from capable of meeting. On May 24, a Joint Board meeting approved a plan for the occupation of the Azores by FDR's deadline of June 22, even though the necessary antiaircraft guns would have to be diverted from projected bases in the British Isles and some of the transport ships would have to come from the West Coast. On that same day Stark wrote Admiral Kimmel about these plans, noting that the Army would not have the necessary forces to establish and defend bases in Great Britain called for by ABC-1 until sometime in the fall. "God knows what will happen if we are not in [the war] by that time," he continued, "though personally I give the British a longer time than do most people here, in their ability to hold out." The President, meanwhile, scheduled an address to the nation on May 27.[66]

Stimson still believed the time for war was now. After a cabinet meeting on May 23, he wrote in his diary that the President "shows evidence of waiting for the accidental shot of some irresponsible captain on either side to be the occasion of his going to war. I think he ought to be considering the deep principles which underlie the issue in the world and has divided the world into two camps, one of which he is the leader [*sic*]." He weighed in bluntly with a personal note to FDR on the next day regarding the President's forthcoming speech. "I feel certain that the people of the United States are looking to you then to lead and guide them," he wrote, and "I think it would be disastrous to disappoint them." Roosevelt, he wrote was the leader of one of two world camps "separated by fundamental principles and methods," and he should explain "why any other course than such forceful resistance would be forever hopeless and abhorrent to every honored principle of American independence and democracy." He then forwarded the draft of a resolution authorizing the President to use the land, naval, and air forces of the United States to prevent aggressor nations from controlling the seas, and to secure "the successful delivery of the supplies, munitions and other assistance" authorized by act of Congress to warring democracies. The next day, after the loss of the *Hood* but before the sinking of the *Bismarck*, he wrote Roosevelt again. "The British disasters in Crete and in the North Atlantic," he wrote, "have terrifically intensified the necessity of demonstrating that you have already taken command of the situation here." He submitted the draft of a presidential address arguing in effect that war was now necessary to effectuate the purpose Congress had endorsed in the Lend-Lease Act, the survival of Britain and the defense of the western hemisphere. Knowing that the White House was working on the speech, he sent a copy to Hopkins as well.[67]

Hopkins had once again fallen seriously ill and had turned the speech over to Samuel Rosenman and Robert Sherwood with instructions to conclude their draft with the announcement of a declaration of "Unlimited National Emergency." When the President went over it with Sherwood, Rosenman, and two State Department officials, he acted surprised but left the declaration in.[68]

The entire country realized that a grave crisis was at hand, and every strain of opinion struggled to be heard. The Committee to Defend America by Aiding the Allies declared that "strong action, even armed action, entailing greater sacrifices, will be required of us." An antiwar congress was scheduled in Washington on the weekend of May 30–June 1 (Roosevelt had scheduled his speech for May 27). Stimson on May 23 specifically called for the repeal of the Neutrality Act, allowing U.S. ships to sail to Britain, in a press conference. On May 25, Admiral Erich Raeder, the German naval commander, warned that U.S. convoys would constitute an act of war that Germany would meet with force. The Gallup Poll on May 21 announced that a bare majority of Americans now favored convoys.[69]

The speech Roosevelt gave to the nation on the evening of May 27 did not call for convoys but clearly warned that events in the Atlantic—including the planned American seizure of the Azores—might bring the United States into the war at almost any moment. "The pressing problems that confront us," the President said, "are military and naval problems. We cannot afford to approach them from the point of view of wishful thinkers or sentimentalists." The war was now "a world war for world domination." Once again emphasizing the need to keep Hitler away from the western hemisphere, he reviewed all the major steps of the preceding year. "Our whole program of aid for the democracies has been based on hard-headed concern for our own security and for the kind of safe and civilized world in which we wish to live. Every dollar of material that we send helps to keep the dictators away from our own hemisphere, and every day that they are held off gives us time to build more guns and tanks and planes and ships." A German victory over Great Britain would soon establish the Germans in South America, strangle the United States and

Canada, and destroy the American economic way of life. Roosevelt then ran down the Nazis' recent gains and spoke bluntly about the possibilities for which his military planners were preparing. "They also have the armed power at any moment to occupy Spain and Portugal; and that threat extends not only to French North Africa and the western end of the Mediterranean but it extends also to the Atlantic fortress of Dakar, and to the island outposts of the New World—the Azores and Cape Verde Islands," he said. From those islands the Germans could dominate shipping in the South Atlantic and fly planes to Brazil. "The war is approaching the brink of the western hemisphere itself. It is coming very close to home." Warning of the danger of Axis occupation of these Atlantic islands, Roosevelt clearly prepared the American people for the American occupation of the Azores. Germany, he said, could aim at world domination should Britain fall, but it was doomed, he suggested, if it remained confined to land. "And let us remember," he said in a daring, veiled reference to the imminent attack on the Soviet Union, "the wider the Nazi land effort, the greater is their ultimate danger."

Turning once again to the importance of the freedom of the seas, Roosevelt in effect argued against convoys such as used in the First World War on the grounds that they would not do enough. Here, perhaps, he misled the American people for the only time in the speech: The truth was that the United States lacked the ships needed to undertake them, or could not risk sending naval forces into the battle zone. He did not, however, rule convoys out in the future, promising, "All additional measures necessary to deliver the goods will be taken." And Roosevelt made a sensational revelation that he had cleared with the British: "The present rate of Nazi sinkings of merchant ships is more than three times as high as the capacity of British shipyards to replace them; it is more than twice the combined British and American output of merchant ships today." Surveying the consequences of a German seizure of Iceland, Greenland, the Cape Verdes, or the Azores, Roosevelt made it clear that he was willing to fight to defend those islands. To defend itself the United States could not wait "until bombs actually drop in the streets of New York or San Francisco or New Orleans or Chicago."

Roosevelt did not, as Stimson had asked, announce a specific movement of ships from the Pacific to the Atlantic. "We have . . . extended our patrol in North and South Atlantic waters," he said. "We are steadily adding more and more ships and planes to that patrol. It is well known that the strength of the Atlantic Fleet has been greatly increased during the past year, and that it is constantly being built up." But defining "our national policy," he clearly threatened to go to war, as the military was actively planning to do, over the Azores, Iceland, Greenland, or any other threatened position in the Atlantic—and possibly even for Dakar.

"There is, of course, a small group of sincere, patriotic men and women whose real passion for peace has shut their eyes to the ugly realities of international banditry and to the need to resist it at all costs," he continued. "I am sure they are embarrassed by the sinister support they are receiving from the enemies of democracy in our midst: the Bundists, the Fascists, and Communists, and every group devoted to bigotry and racial and religious intolerance." He reaffirmed his commitment to New Deal economic justice but called for an end to strikes, since the future of both capital and labor was now at stake. He once again declared a struggle between Nazism on one hand and the principles of liberty on the other and promised, in words Hopkins must have appreciated, "We will accept only a world consecrated to freedom of speech and expression— freedom of every person to worship God in his own way—freedom from want—and freedom from terror. . . . Therefore, with profound consciousness of my responsibilities to my countrymen and to my country's cause," he concluded, "I have tonight issued a proclamation that an unlimited national emergency exists and requires the strengthening of our defense to the extreme limit of our national power and authority."[70]

At seventy years' distance, the common accusation that Roosevelt did not share his plans with the American people does not hold up. Any careful listener must have understood that the President might at any moment plunge the nation into war in the middle of the Atlantic in order to preserve some freedom of the seas and assure the defense of the western hemisphere. Such were exactly his intentions, and as reports continued to flood in of a new Franco-German deal or German advances into Iberia, war within months or even weeks looked entirely possible. Yet the United States simply was not yet ready to fight. Even finding the ships, troops, and ammunition for the projected expedition to the Azores was proving extremely difficult. Worse yet, as Roosevelt privately remarked six weeks later, the Navy simply lacked nearly enough ships to go around.[71] It could not both escort British convoys in the western Atlantic and maintain enough forces in the Pacific to deal with the Japanese. Although almost no one wanted to say so, the Navy still lacked any battleships equal to the best that the Germans and Japanese could put to sea, although two new and more powerful ones, the *Washington* and the *North Carolina*, were almost ready.

Stark, Stimson, and Knox seemed desperate to get into the war at once to save the British, but the War Department had made clear in April that it did not agree. And Roosevelt himself, Mahanian naval strategist that he was, seems to have realized that the Navy might suffer devastating losses were it to become actively involved in the eastern Atlantic and the waters around Great Britain itself. Unlike Stimson and Knox, he drew the line in the middle of the Atlantic, *not* in the English Channel, and his unconscious mind understood how hard it might be to draw it even there. In this speech as in all his others since March 4, 1933, Roosevelt assured the American people that they would overcome their perilous situation. His young protégé Lyndon Johnson, on the day of FDR's death in 1945, described him as "the one person I ever knew, anywhere, who was never afraid." But beneath his placid, cheerful exterior, the commander-in-chief knew what he faced. Just days before giving this speech, he dreamed that he was cowering in a bomb shelter at Hyde Park while German planes bombed New York City, emerging only after a German squadron passed overhead.[72]

Roosevelt was acting as the sailor and navigator that he was—but as the captain not of the kind of sloop that he had sailed for much of his life, but rather of a clipper ship such as he might have modeled in his childhood, with three masts, ten to fifteen sails, and a large crew led by several mates with their own very strong opinions of the right destination and the best course to take. These, Roosevelt understood, depended on the weather, the wind, the cargo, and the urgency of the need to reach port—all factors that on this voyage would reveal themselves only gradually. By allowing his subordinates to argue both with him and with each other until a decision became necessary, Captain Roosevelt made sure that he could draw on a well-thought-out plan for any course of action he eventually chose. His crew, in these two climactic years, included Stimson and Knox, Marshall and Stark and John Richardson, Hull, Knudsen, and Nelson, Hopkins and Ickes and Henry Wallace and Morgenthau, and many more—all of whom more than willing to perform their assigned tasks and eager to advocate their preferred courses of action. Roosevelt himself—who had foreseen the broad outlines of the world crisis as early as 1937—laid down the basic principles of American policy, weighed the enormous risks that rested with him, and tried desperately to build up the means necessary for his ultimate end, the triumph of democratic principles. Meanwhile, during the same first six months of 1941, the Roosevelt administration went about enlisting more and more Americans in the ship's crew as part of the long-term effort to prepare for world war.

CHAPTER 6

Enlisting the Nation,
January–June 1941

AT LEAST SINCE THE LATE NINETEENTH CENTURY WHEN THE MISSION-
ary generation reached adulthood, the nations of the world had been de-
veloping their economic strength to increase their military power—a
process now reaching its climax in the Second World War. Both Germany and Japan were fighting that war to create self-sufficient economic
empires that could fight any nation on earth, while the British and French
tried to hold on to their own. The Soviet Union, which from its inception
in 1917 saw itself at war with a hostile capitalist world, had carried out
perhaps the most dramatic expansion of industrial capacity in world
history during the 1930s and emerged after 1941 as the world's leading
producer of the critical weapons of land warfare. The United States, meanwhile, had the largest industrial economy in the world but in 1940 undoubtedly devoted the smallest proportion of its industrial capacity to
military purposes of any of the major warring states.

The problem of what and how much to build on the sea, in the air,
and on land continued to preoccupy senior leaders during the first
half of 1941. It was intimately related to a second and even more important question: whether the United States would confine itself to
hemispheric defense or prepare for a world war with all available resources. While that question was not resolved at least until July, Roosevelt and the War Department moved slowly toward all-out war in the
first half of the year. Meanwhile, however, the attempt to mobilize U.S.
resources for war also raised critical questions of domestic politics—

questions that might determine the political future of much of the world.

Could the United States—a democracy—organize for war as effectively as totalitarian dictatorships? The answer turned out to be yes, largely because of the institutions and the spirit that FDR and the New Deal had created over the previous eight years. Roosevelt from 1933 onward had set the nation to work on a succession of enormous tasks, including economic recovery, the revival of agriculture, the organization of the industrial working class, and the reshaping of the American landscape. He had specifically given labor and minority groups the chance to play a greater and more equal role in national life. The war effort built on and expanded that effort. The preparation for the Second World War was the greatest enterprise on which the United States had ever embarked, and every social class and ethnic group wanted a piece of the action. Business, labor, and the emerging civil rights movement all joined in and benefited from the rearmament effort in the first half of 1941.

Having begun rearmament in May of 1940, American authorities were still struggling with critical production problems in the first half of 1941. More importantly, they had not decided in the first half of 1941 what kind of war they were preparing to fight. Hemispheric defense remained the basis not only of American objectives as stated by the President, but of America's war plans and rearmament programs. The vast naval program approved in mid-1940 would eventually make operations on the other side of the oceans possible, but it would not be anywhere near complete until 1944. Meanwhile, the Army was projected to reach no more than 1.4 million men, and the Air Corps was having great difficulty even building up to the size estimated as necessary to defend the western hemisphere while simultaneously fulfilling Roosevelt's demands for aid to the British. Behind the scenes, however, the War and Navy departments, the Office of Production Management (OPM), and the White House made a series of decisions designed to make a much larger war possible.

As Donald Nelson, now emerging as a key figure in the OPM explained after the war, many arguments during the first half of 1941 divided high officials into two groups: the "all-outers," including Stimson, Nelson himself, price administrator Leon Henderson of the OPM, and other members of its staff, on the one hand, and more conservative elements including William Knudsen, Commerce Secretary and Reconstruction

Finance Commission head Jesse Jones, and many business leaders, on the other. The "all-outers" had to prevail if the United States was going to be prepared for worldwide operations by 1943, but that in turn meant that many sectors of the civilian economy would have to be disrupted *now*, in peacetime, to create the necessary productive capacity to replace the losses the British were suffering at sea, build an air force that could undertake strategic bombing offensives, and field an army large enough to go well beyond hemispheric defense. Roosevelt's much-criticized production bureaucracy had left him with the sole authority to make the critical decisions, and during the first half of 1941, he repeatedly sided with the all-outers, even as U.S. military weakness restrained him from involvement in the war. And by the late spring, Stimson's War Department had begun to push for a frank statement of the United States' possible enemies, the objectives the United States would seek in a war against them, and the total production that these objectives would require. This set the stage for a new round of critical decisions in July, after the world situation had been transformed once again by Hitler's attack on the Soviet Union.

Naval enthusiast that he was, Franklin Roosevelt well understood that all the world wars since the seventeenth century had involved contests for command of the seas, and he had helped face the German submarine threat during the First World War. Command of the seas meant not only the construction of the two-ocean navy, which would not start to come on line for another three years, but the construction of enough merchant shipping to make up for British losses to U-boats and allow the United States to send both materials and men overseas.

Prodded by Churchill in his critical December 1940 telegram, Roosevelt had begun to address the shipbuilding problem even before the new year. The British were losing ships faster than they could replace them, but their needs would pale before the requirements of active U.S. involvement in an intercontinental war. Ships, moreover, took longer to build than anything. Fortunately, the New Deal in 1936 had already created the necessary institution: the Maritime Commission, established to undertake and promote the modernization of the U.S. merchant marine. Originally led from 1936 to 1938 by Joseph P. Kennedy, the Commission was now chaired by Admiral Emory Land, sixty-one years old, who had worked closely with FDR during the First World War and risen to the top of the shipbuilding section of the U.S. Navy in the early 1930s. Following the New Deal principle that government had to fill any key vacuums left by the private sector, the Commission had the authority to let contracts for new ships even before any buyers had stepped forward. It also repaired ships and watched over freighters kept in mothballs.[1]

When the European war broke out, the Commission was contracting for 50 new merchant ships a year, but in August 1940, with the outcome of the war very much in the balance, it took advantage of new appropriations and contracted for 200 new ships to be finished by the middle of the next year. But the Commission was planning for peace, not war, contracting for merchant ships that would equal the world's best in range, capacity, and durability. War would require more and different ships. Meanwhile, by late 1940, the Navy's massive expansion program had tied up all the existing shipbuilding capacity in the United States for the foreseeable future, and then some. But the British mission in Washington reached agreement with the Maritime Commission—whose chairman, Admiral Land, also sat on the Defense Commission—for 60 merchant ships and the construction of some new shipyards. Roosevelt in his January 3, 1941, press conference more than tripled that bet, announcing that the United States would build another 200 ships for its own use. To meet these targets, Admiral Land reluctantly agreed to accept ships of considerably lesser quality. After Lend-Lease passed in late March, Roosevelt consulted with Admiral Land, and on April 17, the Office of Production Management approved an additional 307 ships, all to be delivered during 1942. Those programs led to some reallocation of production facilities and manpower from new naval construction to merchant ships. Both Knox and the President evidently believed that the maritime interests of the United States could not be entrusted solely to the new Navy.[2]

No sooner had the April 17 program been approved than the British representative in Washington, Sir Arthur Salter, argued that more would be needed in 1942. Then, after Roosevelt declared a National Emergency and announced new steps to meet the threat in the Atlantic on May 27, Land suggested that the output of existing yards could be expanded by 50 percent if more machine tools, skilled labor, and steel could be made available and subsequently suggested adding forty-eight new shipways. A new "third wave" program eventually received the necessary appropriation in August, and Land claimed that it would be sufficient to make up for losses at sea at the rate of the first half of 1941, then amounting to nearly 7 million dead weight tons a year. Significantly, this program established targets for expanded capacity, not merely for a set number of ships. Roosevelt was deeply involved in all these decisions, which turned out to be among the most crucial of the entire war. Thanks to them—and despite an enormous new escalation of the German U-boat campaign in 1942—new construction actually began to exceed losses by the second half of that year. Had it not been for the decisions of 1940–1942, the United States might not have been able to mount operations across the oceans for much longer and would have inevitably provided much less critical support to the British and Soviets as well.[3]

Roosevelt as early as November 1938 had identified air power as the key weapon in any future conflict, but the situation regarding airplane production was even more challenging, because there the United States was starting from scratch. The plans for the British and U.S. air forces involved increasing factory floor space from about 13 million square feet at the end of 1939 and 22 million at the end of 1940 to 40 million by the end of 1941. Yet the leading aircraft manufacturers, Lockheed and Douglas, wanted to make 100 new large civilian airliners during 1941. After months of fighting, Stimson and his undersecretary, Robert Patterson, apparently managed to get this allowance cut way back but not eliminated. Yet this cutback, while symbolically important, was a mere drop in the bucket in the context of the overall aircraft production problem. Stimson and the War Department made little progress on a related but potentially much more critical issue, the need to cut back on domestic automobile production to free raw materials, plant capacity, and workers to make weapons of war, including airplanes. This issue was particularly sensitive because of Knudsen's connection to General Motors, and by early May, Stimson had managed only to get a promise to reduce automobile production by about 20 percent for the year beginning August 1, 1941, relative to the current year. Knudsen insisted that gradual cutbacks would work better since they would not force significant layoffs of men, but Stimson remained unconvinced. He raised the issue again with Knudsen early in June after a decision to increase tank production, but the auto executive once again disappointed him.[4]

The War Department in early December 1940 had forecast total monthly military and naval aircraft production rising from about 1,500 in January to 1,800 in June. Yet throughout the first half of 1941, actual deliveries fell about 300 aircraft a month short of these totals. After Hopkins's visit to Britain and the passage of Lend-Lease, Roosevelt's request for $7 billion to fund it included 12,000 additional aircraft for the British—the same total, coincidentally, that the United States planned to build in 1942. Productive capacity would have to increase two- to three-fold to meet that target. Two key bottlenecks were emerging that spring: raw aluminum, which OPM materials chief Edward Stettinius had for months been insisting was in adequate supply, and machine tools to work it. The Navy had been able to start its massive shipbuilding program quickly in the second half of 1940, and it had secured the highest A-1-A priority for machine tools such as lathes, drills, and hammers, which the aircraft industry needed as well.[5]

The aluminum situation raised several key New Deal issues. More than half the aluminum production in the United States came from AL-COA, which the Justice Department's aggressive antitrust chief, Thurman Arnold, had sued as an illegal monopoly in 1938. Nearly all the leading figures in the administration disliked the company. On January 30, 1941, leading executives of ALCOA, Dow Chemical, and the German firm of IG Farben were also indicted by the Justice Department for a conspiracy to hold down the production of another key raw material, magnesium. ALCOA now wanted to build a new plant in the Northwest, and this brought Interior Secretary Ickes into the fray, because he controlled the power from the Bonneville Dam that the new plant would need. Ickes, a giant of the New Deal during the 1930s as both Secretary of the Interior and head of the Public Works Administration, had largely been left out of the rearmament effort, but he was now campaigning to promote aluminum production by other manufacturers, including Reynolds and Henry Kaiser. After a long debate that eventually reached the President, both ALCOA and Reynolds got promises of power from Bonneville to build new capacity, and Reynolds also got a large loan from the Reconstruction Finance Corporation. Remarkably, the new Reynolds plant went into operation in September 1941.[6]

The machine tool problem had to be addressed as well, and now Roosevelt's management style began to pay dividends. Stimson in particular had worried for months that the President had refused to put anyone in sole charge of production, making Knudsen and Sidney Hillman co-chairmen of the OPM, but the President had done so to make sure that critical decisions came up to him. Roosevelt wrote a public letter to Knudsen and Hillman on May 1, referring to recent discussions between them and declaring that despite some increases in machine tool production, key tools had to be used seven days a week and twenty-four hours a day and that a shortage of skilled operators had to be met, if necessary by releasing some of them from military service. The President made the same points at a press conference the next day.[7]

The leadership of the Office of Production Management took up the issue of machine tools on May 13, and Sidney Hillman argued that enormous capacity inside small firms was going unused while larger ones monopolized the contracts. The six leading production men on the council, including Knudsen, Hillman, and Donald Nelson, were immediately constituted as a subcommittee to look into the matter, and a week later they returned with a draft directive to increase subcontracting, which was approved. Subcontracting might help reduce an enormous $15 billion in unlet contracts for the War Department and Lend-Lease. In the same meetings, Knudsen announced plans to increase synthetic rubber production twentyfold and to set stockpile targets for critical materials of three years' worth of consumption instead of one. The movers and shakers of 1940–1941 lacked personal computers, cell phones, text messaging, and the worldwide web, but they more than made up for those presumed deficiencies with their extraordinary capacity to identify problems, find solutions, and make things happen.[8]

Similarly, President Roosevelt now made a critical decision about aircraft production. For better or for worse, General Hap Arnold of the Air Corps, one of the pioneers of modern strategic bombing, was one of the more influential visionaries in American military history. He had already seized for himself much of the mission of defending the United States against seaborne assault, one the Navy was happy to yield since it wanted to reserve its fleet largely for operations against Japan. Now, in April 1941, he visited Britain and learned firsthand how his British counterparts planned to destroy German war-making capability from the air. Such an effort was clearly years away and in the end proved far, far harder than anticipated, but Arnold was sold and wanted the United States to prepare for such a campaign as well. Robert Patterson, the Undersecretary of War, and Robert Lovett, a First World War flyer whom Stimson had brought into the War Department to handle aircraft production, needed little convincing, and in late April, they drafted a presidential decree calling for the most rapid possible increase in heavy bomber production— mostly B-17s and B-24s—to 500 per month, more than doubling current production and increasing planned bomber output by almost 2,000 planes over the next several years. Roosevelt adopted these targets in a letter to Stimson, Knudsen, and Hillman on May 4, releasing a public, less specific version of the letter at the same time that declared that the democracies must control the air. Stimson replied the next day that this target could not be achieved until 1943, and then only if airplane production received an A-1-A priority for machine tools. With Knudsen's support, he got it within a month. In theory, all machine tools and aluminum now had to be distributed according to the priorities established by Donald Nelson at the OPM.[9]

More aircraft production meant even more aluminum as well. Within days of Roosevelt's letter, OPM officials were discussing the need to nearly triple aluminum production by 1943 while also increasing magnesium production by a factor of about six. By mid-July OPM had developed a plan for seven new government-owned plants to be managed by five different producers. Three of them were in Washington state, made possible not only by the Bonneville Dam but also by new generators from the even larger Grand Coulee Dam. The war effort was coming up against the limits of power generation in the United States, but the New Deal's vast efforts to expand public power while putting people back to work were paying critical dividends. Both the Bonneville and Grand Coulee dams had begun construction in 1934, designed to improve water transportation, control floods, and provide power. Now they were enabling the United States to prepare for war.[10]

By mid-April 1941 both the Navy and War departments had agreed production targets, but the new flood of Lend-Lease orders and expansion of merchant shipbuilding continually complicated the problem of filling them. On April 18 Undersecretary of War Patterson wrote Stimson a memorandum summarizing what had now been done but calling for a new strategic estimate. "While the above program will tax American industry to the limit for a number of months," he wrote, "it does not represent the maximum munitions effort of this country. It is believed a decision should be made as promptly as possible on the production effort necessary to achieve victory on the basis of appropriate assumptions as to probable enemies and friends and theaters of operations. It is presumed that the munitions power available to this country and its friends must exceed to an adequate extent that available to its enemies." He proposed a committee of representatives of the Army, Navy, Maritime Commission, and OPM to study the question. The plan did not go very far very fast, but the issue was now on the table, ready for the President to pick up.[11]

Expanded production cost money—far more money than the federal government had ever spent in peacetime. Federal expenditures were growing from $9.5 billion in fiscal year 1940 to $13.7 billion for fiscal year 1941 (ending on June 30, 1941) and a projected $19 billion for fiscal year 1942. (The actual fiscal 1942 figure turned out to be more than $34 billion.) Defense expenditures were also fueling economic growth at an unprecedented rate. GDP, which had been stagnant from 1937 through 1939 thanks to the recession of 1937–1938, grew by 8.6 percent in fiscal 1940 and a staggering 18 percent in fiscal 1941. Government expenditures had risen from 9.8 percent of GDP in fiscal 1940 to 12 percent in fiscal 1941. That percentage would double in fiscal 1942. Today, in 2014, federal outlays are slightly below 1942 levels as a percentage of GDP, but almost half of this goes for Social Security payments, pensions, and health care spending that were trivial items seventy years ago. The discretionary spending of the federal government and its direct impact on the U.S. economy were already much larger in 1941 than they are today.[12]

Washington had to pay for these huge new expenditures, and on April 17, Secretary of the Treasury Morgenthau met with bipartisan congressional leaders to discuss new taxes. As he explained to the press afterward, the administration planned to borrow one-third of the projected $19 billion budget for the new 1942 fiscal year. That left $12.33 billion to raise through taxes—and that target could be reached only by increasing current tax receipts by one-third. Democratic congressional leaders unanimously agreed with Morgenthau that this had to be done.[13]

Few comparisons illustrate the difference between the United States of 1941 and of 2014 than the distribution of the tax burden. The total federal tax burden for fiscal 1941 was just 7 percent of GDP, almost exactly half of what it is today. (Within two years it would equal, and then surpass, today's figures.) But the distribution of various taxes within that burden was entirely different. Excise taxes, including high ones on liquor, tobacco, and gasoline, brought in one-third of federal taxes in 1941. Today they bring in only 9 percent. Social Security taxes amounted to 12 percent of federal receipts in 1941, compared to 37 percent today. Direct taxes on individuals brought in 26 percent of revenue in 1941, compared to 44 percent today. And taxes on corporate profits—which had already been increased to pay for rearmament—brought in 29 percent of federal taxes in 1941—and just 9 percent today. The New Deal had put a much higher tax burden on corporate profits than the federal government does today, and this trend was exacerbated by the war.[14]

Nor is this all. By contemporary standards, the federal personal income tax was extraordinarily progressive. Today, the top marginal income tax rates of 33 percent, 35 percent, and 39.6 percent kick in at incomes of $203,000, $398,000, and $425,000, respectively. In 1941, Americans with equivalent, inflation-adjusted incomes would have paid 33 percent at $203,000; 48 percent at $398,000; and 51 percent at $425,000. And that was only the beginning. Testifying on Lend-Lease, William Knudsen had reported his last full year of income at GM as $150,000 plus bonuses. Income over that $150,000—equivalent to $2.3 million in today's dollars—would have been taxed at 70 percent. Income over $2 million per year—equivalent to $30.5 million today—would have been taxed at 80 percent. Today those who earn that much pay only 39.6 percent. Marginal tax rates of up to 77 percent had initially been introduced during the First World War. Harding, Coolidge, and Treasury Secretary Andrew Mellon had cut the top rate back to 25 percent by the late 1920s, but Hoover and the Congress had hiked it back to 63 percent in 1932, and Roosevelt raised it to 80 percent in 1936, at the height of the New Deal.[15]

In 1941 the administration's new tax bill took three months to clear the House Ways and Means Committee, by which time Republican members had decided to oppose it. But it was on its way, and on August 4, it passed the House by 369–40, increasing rates still further on both individuals and corporations. By the time the bill overwhelmingly passed the Senate a month later it bore more heavily on everyone, lowering the standard exemption as well as raising rates. It also introduced automatic withholding from paychecks for the first time. Eventually, during the war, the top marginal rate exceeded 90 percent. Americans by mid-1940 agreed on two things: the need for massive rearmament and the need to pay for it in large measure with higher taxes. At no time in American history have they shown more willingness to make financial sacrifices to meet common necessities, largely because they agreed with their President that the survival of civilization was at stake.[16]

The expanded war effort offered enormous new opportunities to American labor. Unions had enrolled an expanding share of the nation's workforce, and rearmament was putting new millions of men and women to work. But the threat of war had divided the labor movement, as John L. Lewis of the CIO, evidently a genuine pacifist, had come out against Roosevelt's reelection in 1940 and carried out his threat to resign as the head of the CIO if he were reelected. Other leaders, such as Hillman and Walter and Victor Reuther of the auto workers, saw things very differently and wanted to use labor's cooperation in the great struggle—in which they themselves certainly believed—to further increase their role in the economy. As early as October 1940, Stimson had commented privately that Hillman clearly had the national interest at heart after the labor leader helped settle a strike at Bethlehem Steel. In November, Stimson accepted a suggestion from Hillman and Supreme Court Justice Frankfurter, an important informal administration adviser, and spoke at the AFL national convention in Chicago. By December, when Roosevelt appointed Hillman cochairman of the OPM, Stimson was firmly in his corner.

The emerging Stimson-Hillman relationship showed how far America had come in the last half century. New Yorkers of Stimson's class had long dealt with Jewish Americans of mostly German stock, who had come to the United States in the nineteenth century and become prominent in business and politics, including Treasury Secretary Henry Morgenthau Jr., whose father had been an Ambassador under Woodrow Wilson, and Supreme Court Justices Louis Brandeis and Felix Frankfurter. But Sidney Hillman represented something new: the more massive Jewish immigration from Eastern Europe that had begun late in the nineteenth century.

A rabbi's son from Lithuania, Hillman had joined a study group interested in contemporary Western thought while studying to become a rabbi and adopted a new faith, socialism, joining the General League of Jewish Workers of Lithuania, Poland, and Russia. At the age of eighteen, during the Russian revolution of 1905, he joined the Mensheviks, the anti-Bolshevik wing of the Russian Social Democratic Party, only to be forced into emigration when the Tsarist government cracked down the next year. After a year in Britain he arrived in the United States in 1907 and moved to Chicago. Four years later he became deeply involved in a strike against his employer, Hart, Schaeffner, and Marx. Showing a practical spirit that foreshadowed his later career, he carried a majority of the strikers in favor of a settlement that left many key issues to arbitration. Arbitration worked well, and by 1914, boss Joseph Schaeffner was saying publicly that the union had been good for the company. In subsequent years Hillman emerged as a leader in the new Amalgamated Clothing Workers union, and in 1921 he went to the Soviet Union to see the new socialist experiment firsthand. After Roosevelt's election Hillman recognized the possibilities offered by the New Deal, and the Amalgamated started new organizing drives as soon as the National Recovery Act of 1933 recognized labor's right to organize. The Supreme Court abolished the NRA in 1935, but the passage of the Wagner Act confirmed and extended those rights.[17]

Hillman then joined John L. Lewis as a leader of the movement for new industrial unions under the CIO, bolting the craft union–dominated AFL. In 1937 Hillman started a huge organizing drive in the South, but it fell victim above all to the recession that struck the country later that year. Meanwhile, Lewis, Roy Thomas, and the Reuther brothers successfully organized General Motors and Chrysler plants, using the same formula Hillman had pioneered nearly thirty years earlier in Chicago of a tripartite board representing the firm, the union, and the public to settle difficult issues and arbitrate disputes. Disregarding some of their more militant members, Hillman and the Reuther brothers in the United Automobile Workers (UAW)—who handled relations with General Motors— took the lead in signing contracts with no-strike clauses and tripartite committees to resolve workplace grievances. They were a new breed of labor leader, eager to develop good relationships with management, and a surprising number of business leaders were willing to cooperate as well. Because Hillman particularly believed in a tripartite partnership among business, labor, and the federal government to plan the economy and assure social justice, he perfectly played the role of labor's representative on the wartime production boards that began with the Defense Commission in 1940. By the middle of 1940 Hillman had definitely established himself as the main rival of CIO President John L. Lewis on both the domestic and foreign fronts, throwing every ounce of support he could muster behind both Franklin Roosevelt and the emerging preparedness effort. After months of struggle in the fall and winter of 1940, Hillman, with help from FDR, prevailed over Knudsen and other industrialists inside the Defense Commission and won official agreement to the principle that violators of the labor laws like Ford should not receive government contracts.[18]

Ranged against Hillman within the labor movement were John L. Lewis, who still opposed the war effort after his resignation in November

1940, and Lewis's erstwhile Communist allies within the CIO. No organization in America was a more determined and effective opponent of U.S. involvement in the war than the Communists during 1940 and the first half of 1941. The Nazi-Soviet Pact and the outbreak of the European war in 1939 had been a turning point for Communists the world over. For three years, from 1936 to 1939, Western Communist parties had enthusiastically followed Moscow's orders to ally with other left-wing and even centrist political parties against Fascism, resulting in the brief Popular Front government in France (1936–1937) and American Communist support of the New Deal. This line had also benefited Communist front organizations like the American Youth Congress and the National Lawyers' Guild, which many non-Communist progressives enthusiastically joined. Such organizations multiplied the influence of the party's membership, which was then peaking at about 100,000. The Popular Front line undoubtedly helped Lewis, who was most definitely *not* a Communist himself, make effective use of Communist organizers and leadership within some CIO unions.

Moscow's abrupt shift in 1939 after the Nazi-Soviet Pact, loyally adopted after a brief hesitation by CPUSA leader Earl Browder, suddenly equated Britain and France with Germany as warring imperialist powers and had a huge disillusioning effect on thousands of previously sympathetic American leftists. Under orders from Moscow, the party not only began opposing aid to the Allies but also broke off friendly relations with other left-wing groups and began cooperating with the most reactionary America First elements. In response, dozens of prominent leftists quit front groups like the American League for Peace and Democracy, the American Artists Congress, and the League of American Writers. One such, playwright Robert Sherwood (who was about to join FDR as a speechwriter), wrote a violently anti-Soviet play, *There Shall Be No Night*, after the Soviet invasion of Finland in December 1939. The National Lawyers Guild had been a liberal alternative to the American Bar Association before the Nazi-Soviet Pact, but now it adopted the Communist line, and New Dealers Robert Jackson, Abe Fortas, and Thurman Arnold quit in a body in May 1940. Meanwhile, the administration itself counterattacked, indicting and eventually convicting Browder for traveling under a false passport in 1940.[19]

The most prominent liberal friendly to Communist front groups before the Nazi-Soviet Pact had been the First Lady, Eleanor Roosevelt, who had become her husband's unofficial contact with the Popular Front left. She had particularly close ties to the American Youth Congress through her young friend and future biographer Joseph Lash, and in February 1940, she persuaded FDR to speak to an antiwar gathering of that organization from the portico of the White House. The New York chapter of the organization was sufficiently Communist dominated to have opposed a U.S. loan to Finland, a democracy now engaged in defending its territory against the Soviets, on the grounds that it was an attempt to draw the United States into an imperialist war. The President accepted the challenge in his speech, labeling the Soviet Union "a dictatorship as absolute as any dictatorship in the world" and attacked it for invading Finland. "It has been said," he continued, "that some of you are Communists. . . . As Americans you have a legal and constitutional right to call yourselves Communists. . . . You have a right peacefully and openly to advocate certain ideals of theoretical Communism; but as Americans you have not only a right but a sacred duty to confine your advocacy of changes in law to the methods prescribed by the Constitution of the United States—and you have no American right, by act or deed of any kind, to subvert the Government and the Constitution of this Nation." Roosevelt drew boos when he described the anti-Finnish resolution as "unadulterated twaddle." An antiwar address to the same audience by John L. Lewis drew thunderous applause.[20]

The Communist Party during the next few months of 1940 had focused on mounting a third-party challenge, but John L. Lewis's refusal to run doomed that particular plan. After the election, Lewis resigned as promised, giving way to the anti-Communist Phil Murray of the Steelworkers as head of the CIO, but his Communist associates, including General Counsel Lee Pressman, remained powerful within the organization. The CIO convention walked a fine line on the Communist issue, passing a resolution condemning Nazism, Fascism, and Communism while doing nothing about the Communists in its ranks. Shortly afterward, Hillman's appointment as cochairman of the OPM sent a clear message that Roosevelt wanted to rely on the anti-Communist elements within the CIO.[21]

Among the most forward-looking members of the labor movement were the Reuther brothers, Walter and Victor, who were among the leaders of the UAW in Detroit and had a knack for putting labor issues in broader perspective. In December 1940, Walter Reuther, who handled

General Motors for the union and also served on the Committee on Training in Industry in the Defense Commission, proposed in a radio address that the auto industry's idle capacity, amounting to 50 percent of the total, be turned over to the immediate construction of fighter aircraft. Reuther clearly wanted labor to play a new role in American life, one quite similar to that of unions in the postwar Federal Republic of Germany: a partner in production decisions of broader importance to the nation's economy and even its national security. In his radio address and in newspaper articles, he took the President's line that Britain desperately needed America's help—and particularly aircraft—and that the provision of enough aircraft could make it unnecessary to send troops abroad. Existing plans relying on the construction of new aircraft plants, he argued correctly, would not bear significant fruit until the end of 1942. Meanwhile, fully 50 percent of automobile manufacturing capacity was still idle. Reuther spelled out the extent of unused capacity in great detail, firm by firm, and argued that it could be turning out five hundred planes *per day*—a figure far in advance of even FDR's most visionary goals—within six months. CIO President Phil Murray handed President Roosevelt a copy of Reuther's plan on December 23.[22]

Reuther's idea aroused sufficient interest within the War Department and the new OPM to start a round of discussions in Washington that lasted well into March 1941. However, even though Knudsen—formerly Reuther's GM management counterpart—shared the goal of using auto industry capacity to manufacture aircraft parts, the labor leader's plan was evidently too radical, and it faded into the background during the first half of the year. The aircraft industry wanted to control aircraft production and the auto industry wanted maximum control of its own facilities.[23]

On the other side of the political fence, the Communists now adopted a new tactic to hurt the Allied war effort: the initiation of strikes by Communist-dominated locals of the UAW designed specifically to stop war production. On November 15, 1940, more than 3,000 workers went on strike at the Vultee Aircraft plant in Downey, California, which was turning out twenty military aircraft at a time for Army use and sales abroad, presumably to the British. Both the Labor Department and Hillman of the Defense Commission immediately went to work trying to bring the dispute—ostensibly over wages for new workers—to an end. On November 23, Attorney General Robert Jackson, preempting an attempt by the House Un-American Activities Committee to investigate the strike, announced that FBI agents had discovered that Communists had fomented it. Three days later, with the help of a federal mediator, the strike was settled, with Vultee conceding a higher minimum wage in return for a no-strike pledge. The UAW had decided to undertake a major organizing drive in the booming aircraft industry during the summer, and its president, Roy Thomas, had turned the drive over to organizers Walter Smethurst and Wyndham Mortimer, the latter a Communist organizer. More trouble was to come.[24]

Not all strikes had Communist inspiration. The country's labor relations were changing rapidly, and the CIO wanted to take advantage of the expansion of basic industries to increase its membership and its members' wages. On January 26, workers were striking at Bethlehem Steel in Pennsylvania, International Harvester in Illinois, Pittsburgh Plate Glass in New Jersey, the Pullman company in Indiana, and shipyards in Mobile. And a UAW local had walked out of the Allis-Chalmers machinery plant in Milwaukee, stopping progress on $23 million in defense orders, most of them turbines for Navy ships. Led by Harold Christoffel, a union organizer who was eventually convicted of perjury for denying Communist Party membership, this turned out to be the longest, most politically inspired strike of all.[25]

Washington immediately dispatched two professional labor conciliators and a representative of Sidney Hillman's, but the men refused to return to work, demanding an all-union shop. By February 8, William Knudsen and Sidney Hillman had summoned the leadership of the firm and the union to Washington, and a temporary deal had permitted the removal and delivery of critical machines needed for Army and Navy factories elsewhere while the strike continued. On February 15 the mediators reportedly brokered a deal that would allow the strikers to return to work, and on February 22, a deal seemed imminent after union officials blamed the strike on "the disruptive activities of certain individuals." But on March 3 an OPM-brokered deal collapsed, and Christoffel managed to keep the strike going into the month of April. Although by far the longest defense strike in the nation at six weeks, Allis-Chalmers was anything but unique: 70,000 men had walked out of various defense-related enterprises around the country by the second week of March.[26]

During March the Allis-Chalmers strike engaged the attention of the highest officials in Washington, including Knudsen, Hillman, Knox,

Stimson, and Roosevelt himself. The President agreed in principle that the War and Navy departments needed the right to take over critical defense plants and force workers back on the job, and both Stimson and Roosevelt hinted at this publicly on April 3. The President acknowledged reports of Communist activity behind the strike but cautioned that this should not be used to smear labor. Two days earlier, Eleanor Roosevelt had reaffirmed her support for the right to strike and called a congressional proposal to make strikes in defense plants treasonous "nonsense." Knudsen in a public address on April 5 noted findings by Wisconsin officials that the original strike vote had been fraudulent, and indeed, by that time, a substantial number of workers wanted to go back to work. Finally, in Washington on April 6, the new National Defense Mediation Council brokered a deal and the union agreed to return to work while negotiations continued, with a provision for arbitration on any issues that could not be resolved.[27]

On April 1, perhaps the bitterest labor battle of the 1930s began to come to a climax when UAW organizers struck Ford's River Rouge steel plant in Detroit. Henry Ford, another visionary member of the Missionary generation convinced of the rightness of his views, had made his name and his fortune paying workers high wages more than thirty years earlier, but he had violently resisted attempts to organize his workers over the last few years in defiance of the Wagner Act. Ford had recently publicly repeated that he would never negotiate with a union. Administration policy theoretically barred Ford from receiving government contracts because the National Labor Relations Board (NLRB) had repeatedly cited the company for violations of the Wagner Act, but Knudsen had overruled Hillman and cleared contracts for Ford during the second half of 1940. "For several months," Ford's notorious personnel director Harry Bennett declared on April 2, "this Communist-controlled union has been clamoring for an election at the [River] Rouge plant."[28]

After a week of violence and controversy, Michigan Governor Murray van Wagoner did the impossible on April 8, brokering a meeting between Bennett, Roy Thomas of the UAW, and President Phil Murray of the CIO. Murray met with FDR for nearly an hour on April 9. On April 11, the Governor announced that the men had agreed to return to work and that Ford had agreed to take nearly all of them back, pending an NLRB election on union representation in which Ford, for the first time, agreed to cooperate. Rather than attempt to tie up war production indefinitely, the non-Communist leadership of the UAW had used the war emergency to win its greatest victory since the sit-down strikes of 1937. On May 22 the UAW won an overwhelming victory in the NLRB election, and a month later, on June 20, Ford signed a contract granting the UAW full representation rights, a closed union shop, and wages equal to the highest in the industry.[29]

In the same month of May this victory for the New Deal allowed Roosevelt to act more forcefully against the last big Communist-inspired strike. Another UAW local at a huge North American Aviation plant in Inglewood, California, voted to strike on May 24, demanding a ten-cent-per-hour blanket wage increase and an increase in the minimum from fifty to seventy-five cents. The President took up the challenge in his crucial foreign policy address three days later, when he declared an unlimited national emergency. "A nation-wide machinery for conciliation and mediation of industrial disputes has been set up," he said. "That machinery must be used promptly—and without stoppage of work." The National Defense Mediation Board (NDMB) managed to head the strike off temporarily on that same evening, and the next day, the House Un-American Activities Committee, known as the Dies Committee after its chairman Martin Dies of Texas, called several union members and leaders to the stand. One leader, Elmer Freitag, had to admit that he had at one time registered as a Communist in a California election, and several of the rank-and-file complained about Communist domination of the local and even described a meeting in which Communist leaders discussed strategy with a representative of the pro-Nazi German-American Bund.[30]

On June 5, despite a mediation agreement, the UAW local called for a strike, while AFL unions also at work in the 11,000-man plant promised to try to keep production going. With the lines so clearly drawn, the highest levels of the administration were ready to move. On Friday, June 6, Stimson convened the leadership of the OPM in his office along with his senior aides and the new Attorney General, Francis Biddle. All, including Hillman, agreed to ask the President to seize the North American plant and order the strikers back to work. At the cabinet meeting that afternoon, both Roosevelt and Labor Secretary Frances Perkins agreed. Two other smaller West Coast strikes were also defying the NDMB, and on the same day, CIO President Phil Murray and the AFL and CIO representatives on the Board denounced them all. Roosevelt promised stronger action at a press conference, and a *Washington Post* reporter wrote bluntly that the government was now prepared "to call a spade a spade and a Red a Red." Richard Frankensteen, the national director of the UAW's aviation division, denounced the strike as well.[31]

Over the weekend of June 7–8, more than 2,000 Army troops were ordered to the environs of the Inglewood plant, and at midday Monday in Washington, when the strikers had not returned to work, John Mc-Cloy and Thomas Patterson of the War Department commandeered a seaplane to reach FDR, then cruising on his yacht. The President signed an executive order directing Stimson to seize the plant, asking troops to make it possible for workers to enter it and calling on the workers to return to their jobs. The troops removed the pickets and workers began returning to work that day, although it took several days before they were convinced that they could ignore threats to their families. Although the government now officially controlled the plant, Stimson proclaimed North American aviation to be its agent and took no action to interfere in operations. Within two more days workers had voted to end the walkout. On July 2, the UAW and North American reached agreement on a new contract embodying nearly all the workers' original demands. By June 13, the government was reportedly considering steps to allow the War and Navy departments to secure the firing of Communist and Bundist (that is, pro-Nazi) workers from defense plants, and the government had announced that wildcat strikers would lose their draft deferments. Stimson had discussed the possible prosecution of Communist leaders with J. Edgar Hoover of the F.B.I., who thought that the Smith Act, which had recently outlawed "conspiracy to advocate" the overthrow of the U.S. government, would provide a basis for doing so.[32]

The Communist-directed labor crisis in American defense plants had lasted roughly from the beginning of the Allis-Chalmers strike on January 26 until the seizure of North American Aviation's Inglewood plant on June 9. Sidney Hillman of OPM had outmaneuvered John L. Lewis's remaining allies within the CIO—many of them Communists— and helped secure tremendous organizing victories in the growing aircraft industry and at the long-resistant Ford Motor Company in support of the war effort. President Roosevelt handled the crisis much as he was handling the world situation. After stating basic principles—that the defense effort should neither weaken labor's new rights nor tolerate obstructive strikes—he had allowed events to create a serious crisis, followed by drastic action on his part. The seizure of the North American plant threatened to set off a new crisis within the labor movement, since it was condemned not only by Lewis but also by CIO President Phil Murray. But as the President already suspected, events on the other side of the world were about to transform both the international situation and the role of Communists within the United States.

Meanwhile, another minority interest—Negro Americans, as they were then known—were also attempting to use the national crisis to realize long-standing political, economic, and social goals of their own.[33]

When the Second World War began in 1939, the modern civil rights movement was only thirty years old. Booker T. Washington, born a slave, had emerged as the first leader of emancipated black Americans in the late nineteenth and early twentieth centuries. Jim Crow was on the march in the South, and Washington preached black economic progress within a segregated framework. The black Missionary generation—the first nationwide generation of freeborn African-Americans—refused to accept this. Its most distinguished representative, the great historian W. E. B. Du Bois—nearly an exact contemporary of Henry Stimson—broke with Washington and formed the NAACP in 1909 to try to move his people into the mainstream. In 1912, Du Bois broke another precedent by endorsing progressive Democrat Wilson instead of Theodore Roosevelt, running on his own Bull Moose Party ticket, or William Howard Taft. Du Bois and other Negro leaders were deeply disillusioned when Wilson's Virginia origins trumped his progressivism and he imposed Jim Crow segregation in federal buildings for the first time. Still, Du Bois in 1917 called for black American support for the First World War, and several "colored units" formed and fought in France.

The New Deal transformed the political landscape for black as well as white Americans. The great migration northward had begun around 1900, and the depression had struck both the black farmers of the South and workers of the North with devastating impact. Despite the efforts of white southerners to reserve the benefits of New Deal programs, Negroes drew critical sustenance from them too and by 1936 had moved firmly into the Democratic column in the North, where they voted for Roosevelt by a majority of three to one. Meanwhile, Negro leadership had split along lines similar to those in the labor movement. At the NAACP, an increasingly radical Du Bois had given way to a new General Secretary, Walter White, who focused on antilynching legislation and a strategy of lawsuits to chip away against voting restrictions and segregation in the South. Some other younger Negroes had turned to the Communist Party, the only political party openly to agitate for equal rights, even though its motives were inevitably suspect and its patronage was political poison in much of the country.

Roosevelt had in fact begun moving more aggressively on civil rights after the 1936 elections, which not only reelected him but also gave the Democratic Party majorities in Congress that for the first time in more than a century did not depend on southern support. The President, whose programs already commanded the support of southern politicians such as Senators Hugo Black of Alabama, Claude Pepper of Florida, and Theodore Bilbo of Mississippi, now dreamed of building a new liberal Democratic Party in the South including both blacks and whites. In 1938 he came out strongly against the poll tax—a key weapon against black suffrage—in several southern states. A small new white southern elite of journalists and academics now shared these goals.[34]

But frightened by their loss of power within the Democratic Party, most white southern politicians mounted a counterattack beginning in 1937 at the time of FDR's court packing plan and rapidly became opponents not only of civil rights but of labor and the whole New Deal program. Helped by Republican New Deal opponents, southern and border state Democrats defeated an antilynching law with a prolonged filibuster in early 1938. Roosevelt retaliated later that year by trying to purge three key southern Senators in Democratic primaries: Walter George of Georgia, Cotton Ed Smith of South Carolina, and Millard Tydings of Maryland. All three won their primaries handily and dealt his prestige a heavy blow. Although the years 1937–1939 were relatively barren of legislative achievement, they witnessed the formation of an interracial coalition favoring civil rights, including much of the labor movement and prominent clergy, that foreshadowed the great triumphs of the 1950s and 1960s. White's antilynching strategy failed to pass legislation, but lynchings, which declined from sixty-five during Roosevelt's first term to twenty in his second, so outraged most white Americans that the campaign did a great deal to put the new coalition together.[35]

Negro Americans also had their own small piece of the labor movement. Born in Florida in 1889, A. Philip Randolph had come to New York to attend its City College and to become an actor. Instead he became a socialist and, beginning in 1925, the organizer of the Brotherhood of Sleeping Car Porters. That organization failed to win recognition from the Pullman Company, which operated the cars, and during the depression it nearly died. Roosevelt, the NRA, and later the Wagner Act revived and transformed it, just as it did the mainstream union movement, and in 1935 it finally won recognition. Randolph had to fight hard to win grudging recognition and endorsement of racial equality from the AFL, but the CIO, led by Lewis's mineworkers, moved aggressively to organize Negro as well as white workers.

The war, the defense program that began in the summer of 1940, and the draft opened new fronts in the civil rights struggle. The black press pointed out the contradiction inherent in defending democracy abroad without realizing it at home—an inevitable consequence of the universal moral language of Roosevelt's speeches. The leadership of the NAACP and other civil rights organizations hoped that military service would integrate Negroes into American life and that the defense effort would give them jobs. But many new defense plants, especially in the aircraft industries, hired whites only, and the military services remained rigidly segregated. Roosevelt had to take the concerns of civil rights leaders into account, but in this instance, sadly, his senior cabinet members and military leaders were no help at all.

In the summer of 1940, during the debate on Selective Service legislation, civil rights organizations managed to ensure that draft boards would take Negroes in proportion to their number within the local population and that there should be "no discrimination against any person on account of race or color" in the "selection *and training* of men under this act." In September, civil rights leaders including Walter White and A. Phillip Randolph submitted a far-reaching list of demands for the integration of the armed forces, including the assignment of Negroes to serve in all important capacities within the Air Corps, to the President.[36]

On September 27, civil rights leaders met with Roosevelt, Knox, and Assistant Secretary of War Patterson. Although Roosevelt had already asked the War and Navy departments to address this problem, they were almost completely unsympathetic. The Navy in particular was determined to limit Negro sailors to their long-standing role as galley attendants, and the Marine Corps banned Negroes completely. The Air Corps had also refused to enlist Negro troops. Stimson's tolerance of Jews did not, sadly, extend to black Americans. "Leadership is not embedded in the negro [*sic*] race yet and to try to make commissioned officers to lead the men into battle—colored men—is only to work disaster to both," he wrote in his diary after sending Patterson to the White House. "Colored troops do very well under white officers but every time we try to lift them a little bit beyond where they can go, disaster and confusion follows." Stimson had somehow gotten the impression that Negro troops had performed badly in the First World War, and he added that he hoped "for Heaven's sake they won't mix the white and the colored troops together in the same units for then we shall certainly have trouble."[37]

In the midst of the election campaign, Roosevelt caved in to the War Department, and the White House on October 9 issued a statement committing the Army firmly to a policy of separate but equal. While it promised to create Negro units in virtually every branch, including aviation, it endorsed the long-standing policy "not to intermingle colored and white enlisted personnel in the same regimental organizations. This policy has been proven satisfactory over a long period of years, and to make changes now would produce situations destructive to morale and detrimental to the preparation for national defense." "Of course they [Negroes] have certain agitators, particularly a man by the name of White," Stimson wrote, "who are asking for a good deal more, but the bulk of the negroes [*sic*] we think will be very well satisfied with what we are doing for them." They were not. The Negro press was outraged and immediately began a campaign against segregation in the armed forces that lasted throughout the war. It did not bear fruit until 1948, when President Harry Truman finally issued a desegregation order, and even then no serious implementation took place at least until the Korean War. The 1930s and 1940s were an extraordinarily frustrating period for black Americans. Their segregated higher educational system had now turned out thousands of well-educated men and women, but the military defended the stereotype of Negroes as ignorant, uneducated, and incapable of handling the technical demands of modern warfare, none of which was true.[38]

The Army passed another milestone later that October, when Colonel Benjamin O. Davis, who had been born in Washington, DC, in 1877 and served in the Army since the Spanish-American War, became its first-ever Negro general officer. The cabinet discussed this promotion on October 25, and Stimson kidded Knox that he expected to bring "a colored general" with him and meet "a colored Admiral" the next time he came to the Navy Department. Not until 1944 did the Navy commission its first

Negro officers. And in another concession to Negro opinion, Stimson on October 25 was prevailed on to appoint William Hastie, the Dean of Howard University Law School, as his Civilian Aid on Negro Affairs. Only thirty-five years old, Hastie had been born in East Tennessee in 1904 and had graduated from Amherst and Harvard Law School. In 1933 he landed a job as assistant Solicitor General of Harold Ickes's Interior Department, and he had spent 1937–1939 as a federal district judge in the Virgin Islands. His generation was determined to achieve full legal equality in its own lifetime, as indeed they eventually did. "He seems like a rather decent negro [*sic*]," Stimson noted in his diary. Ten months later the Secretary of War discovered that Hastie had a self-confidence and determination equal to his own.[39]

Meanwhile, Negro leaders were also addressing the issue of discrimination in defense plants. In January, A. Phillip Randolph of the Brotherhood of Sleeping Car Porters issued a dramatic call for a march on Washington in July. In a bizarre twist, Randolph, who had just broken with the Communist Party and forbade members of it from holding positions of authority in his own union, tried to bar white people from his proposed march because he thought too many of them would be Communists. After some controversy, the NAACP joined in his March on Washington Movement, and planning to bring tens of thousands of Negroes to the capital began. Randolph also invited the President and secretaries of War and the Navy to address the planned march. The threat aroused friendly elements of the New Deal coalition, and both Sidney Hillman, in his capacity of cochairman of the OPM, and Eleanor Roosevelt endorsed the principle of equal opportunity in defense plants. Hillman emphasized that while many AFL unions enforced segregation themselves, CIO unions did not. Meanwhile, NAACP Secretary Walter White scored some points with Hillman and the CIO by interceding to keep Negro workers from crossing the picket line during the critical River Rouge strike by the UAW against Ford in April.[40]

The prospect of tens of thousands of Negroes descending upon strictly segregated Washington alarmed the administration, and on June 10 Eleanor Roosevelt wrote Randolph asking him to cancel the march and meet with the President instead. On June 18, White and Randolph met FDR along with Stimson, Knox, Knudsen, Hillman, and Mayor Fiorello H. La Guardia of New York, another strong civil rights advocate with a substantial Negro constituency of his own. Roosevelt left the meeting after 45 minutes, and White and Randolph insisted that they would have to march unless Roosevelt issued an executive order banning discrimination in defense plants. Roosevelt turned the talks over to La Guardia, and five days later he blessed a plan to create a Fair Employment Practices Commission by executive order. He issued the order on June 25, creating a Fair Employment Practices Committee within the OPM and requiring nondiscrimination clauses in all defense contracts. In response, Randolph "postponed" his march. He revived the idea twenty-two years later under equally dramatic circumstances.[41]

Two months later, on September 25, 1941, William Hastie submitted a lengthy, scathing report on the status of black troops to the Undersecretary of War, Robert Patterson, who seems to have been more sympathetic to his concerns than Stimson. "The traditional mores of the South," Hastie began, "have been widely accepted and adapted by the Army as the basis of policy and practice in matters affecting the Negro soldier. . . . It is generally accepted that the white officer reared in the southern tradition 'understands' Negroes." Nor, he wrote, were Army authorities making any attempt to force the southern communities where so many bases were located to accept Negro soldiers. "In the army," he continued, "the Negro is taught to be a man, a fighting man; in brief, a soldier. It is impossible to create a dual personality which will be on the one hand a fighting man toward the foreign enemy, and on the other, a craven who will accept treatment as less than a man at home." In great detail, Hastie made clear that segregation was making it impossible for Negro soldiers to learn their trade, much less to achieve the relatively equal distribution among different branches of the Army, including the Air Corps, which official policy had promised. General Davis, it turned out, was one of only three Negro officers in the Regular Army; the others were a captain and a lieutenant. Many Army bases were building separate recreational facilities. Negro troops, Hastie continued, deeply resented their treatment and trouble could erupt at any time. "Today," he wrote, "the use of the epithets 'nigger' and 'boy' by white officers and enlisted men in addressing colored soldiers are all too frequent. Men who have bullied and browbeaten Negroes in civilian life are bringing the same practice into the Army." Hastie demanded a clear message from the top that such treatment would not be tolerated, and approaches to state and local authorities to ensure the safety of off-duty troops, several of whom had just been assaulted by whites in Arkansas. Hastie's analysis was every bit as detailed, carefully written, and powerful as any of the papers issuing from the War Plans Division, but it fell on barren ground.

Undersecretary Patterson on October 6 sent the "carefully prepared memorandum by Judge Hastie" to General Marshall, asking for his views and suggesting that "an oral discussion of these issues" would be best. Marshall took almost two months to reply bluntly and in writing. "A solution of many of the issues presented by Judge Hastie in his memorandum to you on 'the Integration of the Negro Soldier into the Army,' dated September 22, would be tantamount to solving a social problem which has perplexed the American people throughout the history of this nation. The Army cannot accomplish such a solution, and should not be charged with the undertaking . . . the War Department cannot ignore the social relationship between negroes and whites which has been established by the American people through custom and habit; . . . either through lack of educational opportunities or other causes the level of intelligence and occupational skill of the negro population is considerably below that of the white. . . . Experiments within the Army in the solution of social problems are fraught with danger to efficiency, discipline, and morale."[42]

Although the Negro flyers who trained at Tuskegee eventually made a superb record for themselves flying fighter planes in Italy, and the pressure of battle eventually forced the Army to assign a Negro tank destroyer unit to General George Patton's Third Army in 1944, Marshall's memorandum, broadly speaking, remained the position of the Army's leaders for the rest of the conflict. Hastie continued to press his recommendations without success, and by February 1942 he had become disgusted and submitted his resignation. Assistant Secretary Patterson refused to accept it. The civilian aide persevered for another twelve months, but by January 1943 he could bear the situation no longer. Pointing out that his recommendations were being disregarded and that decisions about Negro troops were now being made without consulting him, he resigned again, and this time his resignation was accepted.[43] No major mainstream newspaper seems to have taken editorial notice of his departure. Negro Americans now felt the injustice of their situation more keenly than ever, and many suffered the worst forms of discrimination within the armed forces, but for the most part, they took the advice of both their leaders and their white allies like Eleanor Roosevelt to accept the maximum possible amount of change. Franklin Roosevelt himself did not share all his wife's exceptionally progressive attitudes on the race question, but he supported equality in principle and, as in so many other cases, enjoyed being pushed into concessions that would benefit the less well off and make American ideals more of a reality.

The leadership of the Missionary generation, in which Protestant white males had been joined by a significant influx of Catholics and Jews, believed instinctively in a civilization founded on Anglo-American principles of law and justice and the application of science and human reason to promote economic progress and social justice. Although their application of these principles did not yet extend to Negro Americans or to women, their achievements had inspired those largely excluded groups not to reject the great enterprise they had set in motion, but to seek a greater part in it. Negroes and the labor movement demanded and received some new concessions in return for their participation in the defense of the United States, and they earned capital that paid enormous dividends in the twenty years following the war. Meanwhile, by doing so much to lift both the poverty-stricken South and the industrial North out of the depths of the Depression, Roosevelt more successfully healed the division between the two sections of the country than any President since the pre–Civil War era. Many southerners in Congress strongly supported the New Deal, and in the 1950s they gave way to a new generation of white political leaders who were liberal on economic issues, though not on racial ones. In the last half century the gulf between the sections has opened up again.

Although Roosevelt believed strongly in highly progressive taxation, the rights of labor, the need to provide social security, and progress on civil rights, this simple list of reforms does not do justice to his role as President. From the moment he had taken office on March 4, 1933, he had publicly enlisted the American people in a great common enterprise, the revival of the American economy and the rebuilding of American national life according to more equitable principles. Seven years later that crusade had put millions back to work; built thousands of roads, bridges, dams, parks, and schools; brought electricity to rural America; encouraged the spectacular growth of the union movement; and given the American people an entirely new sense of purpose. These achievements made him the outstanding figure of the Missionary generation. The governments of Nazi Germany and Soviet Russia had done something similar in different ways and for very different ends, while the governments of France and Britain had not even attempted such a thing, at least until Britain had to face a threat to its survival in June 1940. Thanks to Roosevelt—and despite the unyielding opposition of perhaps a third of his fellow countrymen—every major institution in American life now sought its own role in the national enterprises he had set in motion—first economic recovery and then national defense, leading in all probability to war. No other democratically elected leader had yet managed anything similar in the great crisis of the mid-twentieth century, although after the war, Clement Attlee in Britain, Konrad Adenauer in West Germany, and Charles de Gaulle in France would follow the example that FDR had set.

"You can take my word for it," Donald Nelson wrote after the war, "President Roosevelt was no Leftist. As much as any other man in our history, I believe, he knew just what the American system really was and what it meant and what made it great. He knew what would keep it great. . . . I feel certain that the mainspring of his greatness lay in his deep understanding of people, not only in the United States but all over the world. . . . I was to learn that there was no living man who was better known by all the peoples of the earth, by the great and the near-great and the anonymous masses. They trusted him and believed in him." Strengthened by the trust of American and world opinion, Roosevelt was now preparing not only to show that democracy could mobilize more resources than dictatorship but also to extend the benefits of democracy to those that had been denied them.[44]

CHAPTER 7

Toward World War,
June–August 1941

BY JUNE 1941 THE WORLD CRISIS HAD BEEN ESCALATING FOR FOUR years. Japan had been fighting in China since 1937 and was proclaiming its intention of expanding farther to the south. Hitler had seized control of Western Europe, threatened the control of the Atlantic, and was still expected to invade the British Isles at almost any time. The United States was rearming, but at least another year would pass before it could undertake any major combat operations. While Roosevelt was trying to extend the defense of the western hemisphere out into the Atlantic and to help British morale, he was not willing to risk immediate involvement in a two-front war. And although he had said in January that the American fight for freedom could have "no end save victory," no real plan for the defeat of the United States' potential enemies yet existed.

On June 22 another sudden German military move transformed the situation once again: Hitler's massive attack on the Soviet Union, which most observers around the world immediately predicted would be another complete success. Within another six months Germany might be supreme over all Europe and within sight of Hitler's dream of commanding resources comparable to those of the British Empire and the United States. Both Tokyo and Washington realized that the decisive moment of the Second World War was now at hand. Although the German attack on the Soviet Union pulled the rug out from under Japanese Foreign Minister Matsuoka, it convinced the rest of the Japanese government that the southward advance had to begin at once, even at the risk of war with

Britain and the United States. Meanwhile, in Washington, Stimson and Knox saw the attack as a new opportunity for the United States to intervene more actively in the Atlantic. Roosevelt, alone among the senior leaders of his administration, understood that if the Soviets could withstand the attack, they might be able to end German domination of Europe. The battle for world supremacy had begun, and the governments of both Japan and the United States were determined to take whatever part they could.

During the six weeks following the German attack on the Soviet Union, Roosevelt took critical steps on several fronts to prepare for a worldwide struggle pitting the United States, Britain, and the Soviet Union against Germany, Italy, and Japan. First, while rejecting Knox and Stimson's pleas formally to enter the war, he approved plans for naval war in the western Atlantic. Second, he asked Stimson and the War Department to determine exactly what would be necessary to secure the defeat of all the potential enemies of the United States. Third, in response to Japan's decision to occupy southern Indochina as the next step in a southward advance, he agreed to embargo all trade with Japan, including oil exports. And last, realizing the enormous potential contribution that the Soviet Union might make to the war, he insisted over the strong objections of his subordinates on the immediate extension of all possible aid to the Soviet Union and dispatched Harry Hopkins on another special mission to make contact with Stalin.

Roosevelt had initially stayed within the hemispheric defense framework after declaring a national emergency on May 27. On the next day, discussing joint military action with British Ambassador Lord Halifax for the first time, he asked to join the British in any projected occupation of the Cape Verde or Azores islands and speculated about a U.S. occupation of Dakar. Most important, he broached a new idea, the relief of the British garrison in Iceland by U.S. troops. Foreshadowing the events that unfolded over the next few months, Roosevelt noted that American forces in Iceland would need supplies, thus providing a pretext for U.S.-run convoys in the western Atlantic. Churchill, who remained desperate to get the United States into the war as soon as possible, did not let a day pass before endorsing this suggestion.[1]

Meeting with Roosevelt on June 4, Treasury Secretary Morgenthau found that the President's "whole interest is in the Atlantic Fleet and getting first to these various outlying islands," including the Azores, the Cape Verdes, and Iceland. On the very next day the President ordered the occupation of Iceland, which General Marshall in particular preferred to the much more risky Azores occupation, which the Portuguese government had threatened to oppose. Because the North Atlantic is so much narrower than the more southern routes, Iceland was also much closer to friendly ports. Like most U.S. expeditionary plans, this one called for the Navy initially to convoy several thousand Marines to the island, subsequently to be relieved by U.S. Army troops. In London, U.S. Naval Observer Admiral Ghormley began working out the details of these plans with British counterparts, promising immediate American action should German forces appear in the neighborhood of Iceland with a clear intention to attack. The British renewed an earlier suggestion that the U.S. Navy take over convoys in the western Atlantic, but Admiral Stark, evidently after consulting with FDR, declined to do so on June 21.[2]

Although the President on June 7 refused formally to approve Rainbow 5—the plan based on the ABC-1 talks—on the specious grounds that the British government had not done so, he directed the War and Navy departments to base their planning upon it. On June 14, he issued an executive order freezing German and Italian assets within the United States, and two days later he announced that all German and Italian consulates must close by July 10, on the grounds of their subversive propaganda activities. Days earlier, the survivors of the *Robin Moor*, an American ship sunk by a U-boat, had reached Capetown, South Africa. Yet Stimson was shocked to learn from FDR on June 18 that the proposed movement of several more battleships and accompanying vessels from Hawaii to the Atlantic had once again been postponed indefinitely. Rainbow 5, now approved by the service chiefs, had called for them to remain there until war in the Atlantic actually broke out, and the Navy had secured the British assent to allowing them to remain at least until August. Marshall, meanwhile, was desperately seeking Brazilian assent to land several thousand U.S. troops at Natal, the closest point to Dakar.[3]

Stimson wrote the President a letter pleading once again to transfer more battleships but decided not to send it when he learned that Roosevelt had once again fallen ill. Marshall and Stimson met him in his bedroom on June 19, and he approved a diplomatic approach to Brazil. The next day, Knox explained to Stimson that the Commander of the Pacific Fleet, Admiral Husband Kimmel, had successfully overturned the order for a further movement and added that the admirals wanted to keep the Iceland garrison as small as possible in the belief that such a forward position would inevitably be lost to the Germans. On June 20, Roosevelt, in a message to Congress, cited the sinking of the *Robin Moor* as a violation of American rights and yet another German act of "cruelty and many other forms of terror against the innocent and the helpless in other countries" designed to intimidate the United States. "This one appears to be a first step in assertion of the supreme purpose of the German Reich to seize control of the high seas, the conquest of Great Britain being an indispensable part of that seizure," he continued. The United States, he said, would not yield. The American people, however, had no time to react to this new rhetorical escalation.[4]

On the morning of June 22, 1941, Americans awoke to the news that Germany had launched a gigantic attack on the Soviet Union. Aided by eighteen divisions from Finland, which had allied with Hitler to regain territory lost in the winter war of 1939–1940, and fourteen from Rumania, which had been coerced into an alliance, the Germans struck with 3 million men, confident that a series of rapid advances and brilliant initial victories would lead, as in Belgium and France, to the rapid collapse of the entire Soviet regime and its army. Within twenty-four hours Churchill had pledged all possible British aid to the Soviet Union, whose participation he had long counted on to help Britain win victory. In Washington, this dramatic turn of events pushed nearly everyone further in the direction that they had already wanted to go.[5]

Once again Stimson and Knox took the lead. Neither Marshall nor Stimson had much confidence in the Soviets' ability to resist the Nazis. Marshall thought the Soviets lacked well-trained officers and up-to-date aircraft and merely expressed the hope that they would destroy their resources as they retreated, and Stimson estimated that the Germans would be occupied with the Soviets for only one to three months. As he explained to Roosevelt on June 23, however, even this short period gave the United States the chance to seize critical forward positions without immediately having to fight the Germans. Germany must now "give up or slacken" the invasion of the United Kingdom, a move into Iceland, pressure on West Africa, Dakar, or South America, or further initiatives in the Middle East. He and Marshall had been very worried about getting "prematurely dragged into two major operations in the Atlantic," Iceland and Brazil, but now the situation had changed and the United States could move ahead at once. Knox wrote Roosevelt on the same day, seeing "an opportunity to strike and strike effectively at Germany. . . . The best opinion I can get is that it will take anywhere from six weeks to two months for Hitler to clean up on Russia. It seems to me that we must not let that three months go by without striking hard—the sooner the better."[6]

Roosevelt almost never reacted hastily to anything. He did not take the bait, making vague promises of aid to Russia on June 24 but refusing to tell the press whether the Russians could receive Lend-Lease. On June 25 he saw Admiral Stark and General Marshall, and Stark once again advocated entry into the war to save the British. "On the assumption that the country's decision is not to let England fail," Stark declared, "we should immediately seize the psychological opportunity presented by the Russian-German clash and announce and start escorting immediately and protecting the western Atlantic on a large scale." This he thought would almost surely involve the United States in war, and "I considered every day of delay in our getting into the war as dangerous" and possibly "fatal to Britain's survival." Roosevelt evidently authorized him to begin planning convoys to and from Iceland, convoys that British ships could join. The next day he left for a week's vacation in Hyde Park, taking Hopkins with him.[7]

On July 1, Navy Secretary Knox turned up the heat publicly in a speech to the National Governors' Conference in Boston that he had not bothered to clear with the White House. "Everything we cherished," he said, "is directly challenged by a ruthless dictator who grasps at world domination. This threat to our own institutions, our hard won freedoms, our very way of life, comes nearer and becomes clearer, every day." Mincing no words, Knox made clear that he expected Hitler to conquer Russia within a few "vital months in this crucial year of 1941." But for the first time, "we are provided with a God-given chance to determine the outcome of this world-wide struggle. Now is the time to put into motion the huge machine we have been building since the war began, and insure a victory for a Christian civilization." Citing Roosevelt's pledge to make sure Lend-Lease supplies were delivered to Britain, he said that while Hitler's "back is turned, we must answer his obvious contempt with a smashing blow. . . . If, while Hitler is assaulting Stalin, we can clear the path across the Atlantic, and deliver in safety, the weapons our factories are now producing, ultimate defeat for Hitler is certain." He spoke frankly about the size of British shipping losses and called bluntly for sacrifice to meet the Nazi threat, for "force without limit or stint." Like Roosevelt, he concluded, he would rather "die on my feet than live on my knees. The time to use our Navy to clear the Atlantic is at hand."[8] Isolationists reacted with outrage.

Not to be outdone, Stimson on July 3 wrote Roosevelt what amounted to a draft of a message to Congress, not only announcing the expedition to Iceland, but proposing the use of the Navy and Air Force in the battle of the Atlantic and the establishment of U.S. bases in South America as well. The freedom with which senior officials spoke their minds even in opposition to their own administration's current policies was a remarkable tribute to the mutual confidence between Roosevelt and his subordinates, as well as a testimony to the intellectual and moral self-confidence of the whole Missionary generation.[9]

Roosevelt once again chose a middle course between his bellicose cabinet members and Stark on the one hand and his far more cautious military leadership on the other. When the Joint Board discussed the Iceland occupation on July 2, Admiral Turner of Navy War Plans opposed any American occupation of Iceland, arguing that the island was critical to Britain but not to the United States. Most admirals, Knox had already informed Stimson, feared that Britain would collapse and that all forward positions would be lost. Stark seems to have been almost alone among the Navy's leadership in believing that Britain's survival was vital. But Roosevelt not only dispatched Marines to Iceland but also insisted on getting an American pursuit aircraft squadron there as soon as possible. He announced the decision in a message to Congress on July 7, explaining it as a further step in hemispheric defense parallel to the acquisition and development of the new bases in British possessions and announcing troop movements to Trinidad and British Guiana at the same time. The United States forces, he had agreed in an exchange of letters with the Icelandic Prime Minister, would eventually *replace* the British forces— another bow to all those who wondered whether Britain could in fact survive another year. But his message to Congress said nothing about convoys, which certain isolationists had already accused the administration, falsely, of conducting. Senator Wheeler introduced a resolution calling for an investigation of reports of encounters with German ships on June 30, and Knox immediately denied the charges.[10]

The occupation of Iceland, as Admiral Turner had realized and Roosevelt had foreseen, created the new naval mission of keeping the island supplied, and Roosevelt intended to use that wedge to bring the U.S. Navy into the war in the western Atlantic at last and give the British some much-needed relief. Rainbow 5 had anticipated that the United States might provide for the protection of British shipping between Iceland and the East Coast even before the United States entered the war, and in response to Roosevelt's directive, the Navy had prepared such a plan, Western Hemisphere Defense Plan 3, and discussed it extensively with British officers both in Washington and in London. Following up on Stimson and Knox's public statements, that plan specifically assumed the mission of helping to ensure that Lend-Lease supplies reached Britain. On July 7, Churchill warmly endorsed it, acknowledging that the British now lacked enough escort vessels to protect convoys all the way across the Atlantic while German U-boats were extending their range and adding that such a plan would free a good many British destroyers to defend the British Isles against invasion.[11]

On July 11, Roosevelt went much further. The Chief of Naval Operations, acting on the President's orders and without consulting the Joint Board, promulgated a new Atlantic War Plan, Western Hemisphere Defense Plan 4, providing for large U.S. naval forces amounting to 6 battleships, 5 heavy cruisers, and 35 destroyers to escort American and British ships to and from Iceland, while a strike force of 3 carriers, 4 light cruisers, and 9 destroyers and a southern force of 4 light cruisers and 4 destroyers cruised trade routes looking for Axis warships. The plan included language allowing the Navy to adjust the size of these forces if circumstances required. These forces would "protect United States and Iceland flag shipping against hostile attack, by escorting, covering, and patrolling, as required by circumstances, and by destroying hostile forces which threaten such shipping." With Roosevelt's approval, Stark ordered the plan to go into effect on July 26—just two weeks later—with one major exception: The U.S. ships would *not* escort British convoys between Iceland and the North American coast, only U.S. and Icelandic flag shipping.[12]

In a telegram to Atlantic Fleet commander Admiral King, Stark spelled out the exact procedure he had in mind. American vessels would synchronize their movements between Halifax and Iceland with those of British convoys, initially allowing westbound British convoys to choose the routes that they, these American vessels, and the U.S. warships that would escort them would take. Roosevelt on July 14 had personally written

Stark that he should omit any specific reference to escorts of British convoys from orders and confine himself to asking American authorities to inform the British when American ships would sail. He was determined not to give Wheeler, Lindbergh, and the rest of the isolationists the chance to call him a liar for having denied that the United States was convoying ships. On the other hand, the President made clear in a detailed memo to Stark that he expected the words of the plan about "threatening" American shipping to be interpreted broadly enough so as to allow for an attack on any Axis warship within range of a U.S. convoy. Stark was more than willing to go even further and send U.S. warships all the way along the route to the British Isles, but Roosevelt evidently was not. In the end, however, Roosevelt delayed the implementation of the plan yet again, pending a meeting with Churchill off Newfoundland that he expected to take place within a few weeks.[13]

In the meantime, three new crises had erupted regarding production targets, the future of the U.S. Army, and a new Japanese move into Indochina.

Secretary of War Stimson understood where events might shortly lead the United States and the necessity of declaring new political objectives and building up the armed forces accordingly. With the future of Western civilization at stake, he was determined that the United States and its values not merely survive, but prevail. He had lost one battle to get the President to enter the war in mid-May, and he was losing the same battle again after the attack on the Soviet Union. Yet he managed to force the even more critical issue of production targets. In May the issue of how much and how fast industry needed to produce had arisen once again, and the Secretary of War used it as a wedge to begin a reevaluation of U.S. policy objectives and what it would take to accomplish them. For about a month, Undersecretary Patterson's April 18 memorandum calling for a joint committee to make a new strategic estimate had been circulating around the War Department, and Marshall had finally placed it before the Joint Board on May 14. They in turn referred it to the Joint Planning Committee.[14]

General Marshall did not believe it was necessary to plan for substantially larger forces. On May 17, a Saturday, Marshall chaired a meeting in his office about current and future production requirements for the Army. John Biggers of the OPM had recently given a speech in

Philadelphia promising various manufacturers that the War Department would have further orders for them when their existing contracts were filled. Manufacturers had evidently been given until the middle of 1942 to turn out the equipment needed for the fully planned 1.4 million-man Army and until December 1942 for the recently authorized equipment for 1.4 million more. Biggers had suggested privately that a firm commitment to the full 2.8 million force would make it easier to get maximum production out of industry. Another problem related to aircraft, whose manufacturers wanted payment in full now for planes that would not be delivered for two years. Marshall, carefully thinking ahead, asked whether there was any justification now for ordering equipment for an Army in excess of 2.8 million men. "We will not need a 4,000,000 man Army unless England collapses," he said, "and on top of that the shipping problem is so acute that it is a definite factor on the size of the Army." Marshall clearly did not foresee the dispatch of hundreds of thousands of U.S. troops outside the Americas. The meeting then moved to the office of Robert Patterson with Biggers, other OPM representatives, and the War Department's key ordnance personnel in attendance.

Biggers immediately explained that the President was pressing OPM to get manufacturers to work twenty-four hours a day in three shifts and to do more subcontracting to increase the rate of production but that manufacturers refused to do this when they could easily foresee the day when orders would stop. "We are convinced," he said, "that there is not a heavy enough load on American industry to get the maximum response in laying out production lines. Manufacturing is definitely *slowed down*." He offered OPM's help in convincing Congress to make appropriations for larger forces. Marshall did not take the bait: "We feel that the first augmentation [to 2.8 million] will take care of all we see immediately necessary in the present situation," he said, and additional material could be turned over to South American countries. "I see no justification at this time," he said, "to move beyond the 2.8 million Army." "I do not want to be misunderstood," Biggers replied, "but we can't escape the impression that there is not a full meeting of the minds between the President's statements and his instructions. The President talks about multiple shifts and the manufacturers say they have no need to do it."[15]

The problem, clearly, was that while the heads of the Army and Navy were satisfied with the objective of defending the western hemisphere,

Roosevelt wanted to be able to draw on the United States' full productive capacity to meet other, bigger possible objectives. Production for Lend-Lease, Biggers added, was running into serious shipping bottlenecks. A DuPont munitions plant in Memphis had just stopped producing gunpowder because the British could not ship what the plant had already made and they had no place to store more. The meeting discussed how existing appropriations could be used to get production moving faster. Three days later, at an OPM meeting, a Navy Department representative argued that the government needed the authority to buy machine tools in civilian use, even at the expense of civilian production, and Sidney Hillman reported that half the industrial capacity in the Chicago area was still unused because large firms would not subcontract.[16]

Back on April 18, Undersecretary of War Patterson had written a memorandum asking for a new committee to study overall production requirements—an idea, some evidence suggests, that may have gone nowhere because the Navy did not want to cooperate. On May 21, General Marshall revived that idea in a memorandum for the War Plans division. In order to make sense of the continuous flow of requests for additional equipment, he asked for "a more clear-cut, strategic estimate of our situation from a ground, air and naval viewpoint." While such a study should eventually include the views of "the Navy and other interested governmental agencies," Marshall regarded it as "premature" to approach them as yet. Marshall's immediate superior had no doubt of what the broad results should be. On May 23, Stimson told his leading civilian and military subordinates that the War Department should definitely order equipment in excess of what would be required for presently authorized units. On May 27, General Gerow of Army War Plans brought the matter, which had also been considered briefly by the Joint Board, to the attention of Navy War Plans. During the first few days of June, Major Albert Wedemeyer of Army War Plans received guidelines for the new strategic estimate, and G-2 (Army Intelligence) was asked for estimates of Axis military capabilities. The Joint Planning Committee had evidently done nothing about making a new estimate, and on June 7, Gerow wrote Marshall that the Navy was violently opposed to making joint estimates either with the War Department or with the British and was quite happy with current arrangements.[17]

By early July the United States had to face up to the implications of the spreading world war. Not content merely to have attacked the

Soviet Union, the Germans were also renewing a political offensive in Latin America, cultivating supporters within the Brazilian Army and sponsoring an unsuccessful coup in Bolivia. On June 30, Stimson wrote Knox, Knudsen, Maritime Commission chief Admiral Land, and the British Mission asking for a coordinated study of American production requirements.[18]

On July 9, Roosevelt sent Stimson three letters, two of them drafted by Harry Hopkins. The first called for a substantial but unspecified increase in American tank production, with the help of machine tools now at work in civilian plants. The second more specifically suggested that the government would have to take control of a number of civilian durable goods plants in order to meet its military needs. And the third finally followed up on the initiative that Patterson and Stimson had begun in April. "I wish that you or appropriate representatives designated by you," he wrote Stimson, "would join with the Secretary of the Navy and his representatives *in exploring at once the overall production requirements required to defeat our potential enemies.* I realize that this report involves the making of appropriate assumptions as to our probable friends and enemies and to the conceivable theaters of operation which will be required." The President wanted Stimson, Knox, and Hopkins to identify the types of equipment of which it would be necessary *"to exceed by an appropriate amount* that available to our potential enemies."[19]

For more than a year, since the 50,000 aircraft speech of May 1940, the President had been combining calls for maximum production with a policy of hemispheric defense supplemented by aid to other powers. Among Roosevelt's military leaders, only Admiral Stark had shown any inclination to go beyond hemispheric defense. General Marshall had limited all his requests to the needs of that mission, and aside from Stark, the Navy leadership seemed quite ready to stay out of the war for years more no matter what happened in Europe. But Stimson and Knox wanted to push at once for Hitler's defeat, forcing a decision that only Roosevelt could make. Confirming that he shared Stimson and Knox's view, he had asked for the planning for the *defeat* of all the Axis powers, rather than the defense of North and South America.

Certainly such a prospect seemed far away in July 1941. On July 1, G-2 of the War Department had submitted the Strategic Estimate that War Plans had requested. It anticipated that Germany would have defeated Russia, and perhaps Britain, by the middle of 1942 and plumped for a largely defensive posture in the western hemisphere. But Roosevelt, who had greater hopes for the USSR and understood how Germany's new campaign might transform the situation, had now set in motion the study of what became known as the Victory Program—even though the administration in July faced substantial political difficulties even in keeping its existing forces under arms. The public's thinking was lagging far behind the President's, and here General Marshall took a hand.[20]

General George C. Marshall has deservedly gone down in history as one of America's greatest military leaders and statesmen. His integrity, selflessness, sense of purpose, and clarity of mind exemplified the best of the Missionary generation. In January 1941, when a friend had suggested that he might someday run for President, he had replied that "the public suggestion of such an idea, even by mere rumor or gossip, would be almost fatal to my interests. So long as the various servants of the Government in important positions concerned with national defense devote all their time and all their thought to the straight business of the job, all will go well with America, but just as soon as an ulterior purpose or motive creeps in, then the trouble starts and will gather momentum like a snow ball." Like many officers of his time, he had never voted in an election so as not to compromise his loyalty to any potential commander-in-chief. He managed by identifying the most capable subordinates he could find, giving them responsibility, and taking their advice. The men he relied on as Chief of Staff and Secretary of State included Dwight Eisenhower and George F. Kennan, the foremost strategic thinker of the Cold War. His eclipse of his rival Douglas MacArthur, who had risen to the top of the U.S. Army a full eight years before Marshall, was probably one of the happiest accidents ever to befall the United States. He was, above all, the architect of our wartime strategy and of the Army that executed it, and in that respect he was probably more responsible than anyone for the eventual Anglo-American triumph on the western front in 1944–1945.[21]

Yet Marshall in the critical period 1940–1941 took relatively conservative positions regarding American policy and strategy. Unlike Admiral Stark, he clearly did not regard the survival of the United Kingdom as critical to the future of the United States and was more than satisfied, at least until the fall of 1941, with the mission—daunting enough—of preparing the defense of the western hemisphere. He obviously had little confidence in Britain's ability to hold out, and he continually protested against President Roosevelt's demands to provide equipment both to the

British and then, by August 1941, to the Soviet Union as well. Those protests reflected his sense of his own responsibilities. National policy had entrusted the Army with the defense of the western hemisphere, and he must stand up forces adequate to the task. The President's insistence on immediate, large-scale aid to Britain was making this much harder to do, and Marshall's personality did not allow him simply to accept FDR's demands and let the President take the consequences. He knew his job, and he was determined to do it. And now, he publicly forced Congress, the President, and the American people to face the inadequacy of his forces even for the official mission of hemispheric defense and to make some critical choices about the immediate future.

On July 2, 1941, Marshall issued his first biennial report as Chief of Staff of the Army. The rapid expansion of the Army from 175,000 men in September 1939 to the current strength of 1.4 million officers and men, he wrote, represented "a great experiment in democracy, a test of the ability of a Government such as ours to prepare itself in time of peace against the ruthless and arbitrary action of other governments whose leaders take such measures as they see fit, and strike when and where they will with sudden and terrific violence." Half a million of those officers and men belonged to the Regular Army, 270,000 to the National Guard, and 630,000 were "selectees." The Army now included 29 divisions (456,000 men) and the Air Corps 167,000 men and 54 combat groups. After a detailed description of the raising of these forces, Marshall made a critical recommendation based on an alarming estimate of the immediate future. "As this report is submitted," he wrote, "the possibilities of a year ago have become dangerously near probabilities today, and it is vital to the security of the Nation that the hazards of the present crisis be fully recognized. . . . Events of the past 2 months are convincing proof of the terrific striking power possessed by a nation administered on a purely military basis. Events of the past few days are even more forcible indications of the suddenness with which armed conflict can spread to areas hitherto considered free from attack." The German attack on the Soviet Union, in short, was a warning, not in any sense a relief of possible pressure on the United States.

"Differences of views regarding national policy," Marshall continued, "should not, it seems to me, be permitted to obscure the facts relating to the preparation of the armed forces for service." The time had come, he argued, to "train certain task forces against the possibility of the necessity arising for their use." Yet the existing regular Army divisions would shortly be crippled by the loss of reserve officers and hundreds of thousands of selectees whose tours would expire after one year. These legal limitations, "acceptable at the time of their passage, now hamstring the development of the Army into a force immediately available for whatever defensive measures may be necessary." Marshall specifically asked for the authority to retain all his troops on active service indefinitely, and newspapers also interpreted "whatever defensive measures may be necessary" to include the dispatch of troops outside the western hemisphere. Stimson in a press conference endorsed the report's conclusions on the day of its release. Senators Wheeler, Robert Taft of Ohio, Hiram Johnson of California, and others violently attacked Marshall's plan, claiming it meant a new American Expeditionary Force (AEF) such as the United States had sent to France in the First World War. Democrats as well as Republicans predicted that Congress would reject these recommendations. Within days, sources were reporting that the administration was going to delay a formal legislative request and that the opposition to an extension now included House Speaker Sam Rayburn of Texas and Majority Leader John McCormack of Massachusetts, two New Deal stalwarts. On July 11, an angry, determined Henry Stimson failed to persuade the two congressional leaders that action had to be taken. Roosevelt remained silent, allowing his Chief of Staff to carry this particularly volatile ball. Meanwhile, he announced the Iceland expedition.[22]

Marshall and FDR met Rayburn, McCormack, and seven other Senators and Representatives at the White House on July 14, and although Roosevelt declared (not without justice) that an AEF was "the farthest thing from my mind," they remained largely unmoved. Marshall insisted that they must decide either that the situation was not truly serious and that political maneuvering could continue, or that "we are now in a very critical situation and we have no choice but to go ahead frankly and deal with this thing in a straightforward manner." Marshall pointed out, correctly, that his report had not specifically called for lifting the territorial restrictions on the deployment of troops. Four of the legislators supported him, but McCormack insisted that a resolution would fail. They agreed that the two houses of Congress would simultaneously take up the proposed measure. Roosevelt authorized Marshall to ask the leaders of the Senate about the timing and advisability of a presidential statement, and Senate Majority Leader Alben Barkley recommended that FDR waste no time. The President under the existing law had the power to increase the selectees' term of service on grounds of national peril, but he clearly did not want to do so without congressional approval.[23]

On July 21, after three weeks of intense controversy, Roosevelt finally asked for the extension of tours in a long message to Congress. "Today it is imperative that I should officially report to the Congress what the Congress undoubtedly knows: that the international situation is not less grave but is far more grave than it was a year ago," he said. The series of Nazi blitzkrieg attacks had continued, he pointed out, each one relying on a superiority of trained men and each one bringing the Germans nearer to our hemisphere. Neither the United States nor the rest of the Americas, he argued, could risk the diminution of the U.S. Army that would occur if the selectees went home. Rather than submit specific legislation, he asked Congress simply to acknowledge the national emergency that under the existing law would allow him to extend tours. "Within two months," he warned, "disintegration, which would follow failure to take Congressional action, will commence in the armies of the United States. Time counts. The responsibility rests solely with the Congress." A contemporaneous Gallup poll showed the public favoring the extension of tours by a 51 percent–45 percent margin but opposing sending draftees outside the hemisphere. As it turned out, Congress took another two months to make up its mind.[24]

The German attack on the Soviet Union also transformed the situation facing the Japanese and their relations with the United States. Since approximately August 1940, lines had been drawn within the U.S. government regarding policy, especially commercial policy, toward Japan. On the one side were Stimson, who was certain that the Japanese would yield to a display of firm purpose, and Treasury Secretary Morgenthau, who wanted to stop the export of the petroleum on which a Japanese war effort might depend, or even freeze all Japanese assets, as the United States had just done to the Axis powers in Europe. On the other were Hull and the Navy Department, supported by Roosevelt, who thought that Japan would react by attacking the Dutch East Indies and perhaps American possessions as well, forcing the United States into the war in the Pacific for which, as Admiral Kimmel made clear, the United States was not ready, especially in view of the transfer of three battleships and some light and heavy cruisers to the Atlantic. Now, however, matters were taking a new turn. For weeks evidence had been mounting that the Japanese would inevitably go to war if the United States went to war in Europe, and now, within two weeks of the German attack on the Soviets, the Japanese decided to move southward and accept the risk of war with the United States in any case—decisions that Magic intercepts immediately made known to senior American policymakers.[25]

During May 1941, Hull's talks with Nomura had focused on the critical question of the European war and Japan's obligation under the Tripartite Pact to go to war against any currently neutral power that "attacked" Germany and Italy. The Japanese on May 12 had submitted a draft agreement asking the United States to encourage Chiang Kai-shek to make peace with Tokyo and pledging both the United States and Japan to do whatever they could to encourage peace in Europe. Hull on May 16 and in a written draft of May 31 made it crystal clear that the United States was already acting in self-defense in the Atlantic and that it expected the Japanese to stand aside in the event that such measures led to war with Germany. Citing his speech of April 24, he insisted that the United States was not going to make the same mistakes as the European governments that had allowed Hitler to begin war on his own terms.[26]

The talks made no progress during June, and Hull on June 21 bluntly told the Japanese that the United States had a right to join the war in Europe to defend itself. "It seemed to us," he said, "that the Japanese Government would decide either to assume control of those elements in the Japanese body politic which supported Nazi Germany and its policies of aggression or to allow those elements to take over entire charge of Japan's policies." They must decide "before it was too late that Hitler was dangerous to Japan." Hull's obvious reference to Foreign Minister Matsuoka, well known as the prime mover of the Tripartite Pact, probably reflected what he had learned from Magic. On June 10, an intercepted cable from the Foreign Minister had informed Nomura that his foremost objective was to maintain the "integrity of the Japanese, German, Italian alliance and to do everything we can to keep the United States from entering the war, or at least to prevent her from taking any more direct anti-Axis measures than she has up to the present day. I feel that our dauntless attitude has already achieved much in this direction. . . . Even though it is beyond our power to make the United States feel friendly toward Germany, we must keep her from making an outright attack."[27]

At this unpromising moment, the situation had once again been transformed by the German attack on the Soviet Union. Japan had been preparing for the southward advance during the first half of 1941, mediating a border war between Thailand and French Indochina, purging members of an interdepartmental Planning Board who had feared war with Britain and the United States, and in April concluding Matsuoka's neutrality treaty with the Soviet Union, which was designed to intimidate Chiang Kai-shek into giving up, secure Japan's northern flank in Manchuria, and help keep the United States out of the war. Crucially, the Navy had now persuaded the Army that the southward advance had to assume the risk of war with both Britain and the United States. The Japanese should have reconsidered their whole attitude in early June, after German Foreign Minister von Ribbentrop had warned their Ambassador in Berlin that war with the Soviet Union was probably imminent, but Matsuoka had refused to believe it. Instead, on June 12, a Liaison Conference had tentatively approved the occupation of southern Indochina by the Japanese as a stepping stone for the southward advance. The news of June 22 unleashed a debate at the highest levels of the Japanese government, but all recognized that the climax of the world crisis was at hand and that Japan could not wait any longer to make a dramatic move to create the Greater East Asia Co-Prosperity Sphere.[28]

During the ten days after the German attack, the Japanese government held a series of heated meetings. Matsuoka now reversed his policy and recommended that Japan join the war against the Soviets at once, as Berlin had now requested, in the expectation that Germany would defeat the USSR by the end of the year and might force Britain to make peace as well. Yet he was eventually overcome by the united opposition of the Army and Navy, which insisted on carrying out the occupation of southern Indochina as the next step in the southward advance, and the government decided in effect to attack the Soviet Far East only if the Soviets were already collapsing. On July 2 an Imperial Conference adopted an "Outline of National Policies in View of the Changing Situation." Japan would proceed to create the Greater East Asia Co-Prosperity Sphere, involving southward advances and, if circumstances permitted, an attack on the Soviet Union as well. The Japanese would move at once to establish air and naval bases and station troops in southern Indochina, with or without the agreement of the Vichy government, and prepare for war with Britain and the United States as part of a further southward advance. "The Empire shall not flinch from war with Britain and the United

States in order to achieve these objectives," it read, and if the United States entered the war in Europe, Japan would act in conformity with the Tripartite Pact, deciding itself "as to when and how military force is to be exercised."[29]

The leadership in Washington, meanwhile, desperately feared that the Japanese might attack the Soviet Far East, help precipitate Moscow's collapse, and free Hitler to turn against Britain even sooner. Such fears were confirmed on June 27, when American military intelligence translated a Japanese account of Matsuoka's June 23 conversation with the Soviet Ambassador, in which the Foreign Minister reaffirmed the Tripartite Pact, implied that the Soviets might have started the war, and refused to say what Japan would do, since the government had not yet reached a decision. Evidently briefed on this telegram, Roosevelt on July 5 cabled Ambassador Grew a message for Premier Konoye—not Matsuoka— asking for assurances that reports of an impending Japanese attack on the Soviet Union were false and warning that such a move would end any attempts to strengthen the peace of the Pacific region. Matsuoka— not Konoye—gave Grew the Japanese reply three days later, including a copy of a vague Japanese statement to the Soviets that the Japanese did "not at present feel compelled to modify their policy towards the USSR except to the extent of their natural desire not to give rise to misunderstandings with their allies." Matsuoka also made a parallel request that the U.S. government confirm or deny reports of its intention to enter the European war.[30]

The argument over oil exports to Japan, meanwhile, had been growing in intensity for months. Interior Secretary Ickes, largely shut out of the war effort, had managed to secure a new role for himself as Petroleum Coordinator for National Defense on May 28, with broad authority to gather data and assess supplies and requirements. The oil situation in the United States was suffering profound effects from the war. The West Coast—virtually a separate nation where oil was concerned—had plenty of oil and tankers to transport it, including those carrying it to Japan. But in the Atlantic, Roosevelt had promised the British seventy-five tankers under Lend-Lease during 1941 to increase their desperately low oil stocks and requisitioned fifty of them during May.[31]

Ickes had long stood with Morgenthau and Stimson in favor of an embargo against Japan, and during June he made the case for one, claiming an impending oil shortage in the United States. He managed to stop a shipment to Japan from the East Coast, but the State Department refused to go further. On June 30 Ickes wrote a typically angry letter to FDR offering to resign as Petroleum Coordinator, and on July 3 FDR replied firmly in a revealing note refusing to act further. "I think it will interest you to know," he said, "that the Japs are having a real drag-down and knock-out fight among themselves and have been for the past week—trying to decide which way they are going to jump—attack Russia, attack the South Seas (thus throwing in their lot definitely with Germany), or whether they will sit on the fence and be more friendly with us. No one knows what the decision will be but, as you know, it is terribly important for the control of the Atlantic for us to help keep peace in the Pacific. I simply have not got enough Navy to go round—and every little episode in the Pacific means fewer ships in the Atlantic." In fact, as Magic intercepts shortly showed, Roosevelt's appreciation was overoptimistic: No major faction favored peace with the United States at the expense of the Tripartite Pact, and the Japanese had just decided to go south and risk war with the United States.[32]

On the previous evening, Morgenthau had called FDR at Hyde Park with information about the Japanese—apparently the news, confirmed the next day by a Magic intercept, that they had ordered all their ships in the Atlantic to proceed home through the Panama Canal at once. On the next day, Navy War Plans concluded that Japan would go to war somewhere in August. And on that same July 3, a meeting of War and Navy Department and OPM representatives concluded that Ickes's claimed East Coast oil shortage was all too real, a result of the dispatch of tankers to the British. Also on that day, U.S. intelligence translated a telegram from Matsuoka to his Ambassador in Berlin sent the day before, announcing that his government had "decided to secure points d'appui in French Indo-China which will enable Japan further to strengthen her pressure upon Great Britain and the U.S.A., . . . a vital contribution towards our common cause, indeed no less vital than Japan's intervention at this juncture in the German-Soviet War." It had taken about seventy-two hours for U.S. leaders to learn the results of the imperial conference. Stimson eagerly brought this news to the President at the White House on July 5.[33]

Three days later, on July 8, Stimson called Morgenthau to ask how he felt about an embargo. Quoting Calving Coolidge, Morgenthau said he was "against sin." "I know you've been virtuous for 11 months," Stimson replied. Morgenthau added that he was about to call Ickes about 60,000 barrels of lubricating oil being loaded in New Orleans for Japan. "Well, I think we're—both Frank [Knox] and I think that we ought to take it up with the—on the military side with the President at once," said Stimson. Morgenthau called existing policy the "height of asininity" and Stimson blamed the State Department. Morgenthau sent the data on New Orleans to Roosevelt, who had returned from Hyde Park on Saturday, July 5. A truly decisive moment was at hand.[34]

During the next ten days key players pressed their preferred options. In Washington, Japanese Ambassador Nomura suggested that the Japanese attack Siberia while working for an agreement with the United States—a vain prospect—and warned that Japan would face American economic sanctions if Washington gave up on an agreement and that a southward advance would make it impossible to "adjust our relations with the United States." In reply, Matsuoka, in one of his last acts as Foreign Minister, angrily demanded that Hull withdraw his previous statement about anti-American elements within the Japanese government before talks went any further. American intelligence decoded all this traffic almost instantly. Hull immediately replied that no offense had been intended, but Matsuoka had lost the confidence of his colleagues, and Prince Konoye, the Prime Minister, secured the resignation of the entire cabinet on July 16, reforming it with Admiral Toyoda in place of Matsuoka on July 18. The new cabinet, however, immediately reaffirmed that the Tripartite Pact remained the foundation of Japanese foreign policy, a declaration that found its way to Roosevelt, Stimson, and Knox by July 19 through Magic.[35]

Meanwhile, the Japanese on July 12 had given the Vichy France government an ultimatum demanding the right to occupy bases in southern Indochina. The Magic intercept confirming this became the basis of a specific memorandum for the President on July 15. The Japanese were doing exactly the same thing that Washington had feared the Germans would do in North Africa for more than a year. On July 16 Ambassador Grew told the Japanese government that the United States was still determined to defend itself against Germany without necessarily waiting for an attack. Then, on Friday, July 18, the cabinet held its most important meeting of the year to date.[36]

Cordell Hull had been ill and was recuperating away from Washington, and acting Secretary Sumner Welles announced that the Japanese were likely to move farther into Indochina within a few days. Morgenthau then put the President on the spot. "I would like to ask you a question which you may or may not want to answer," he said. "What are you going to do on the economic front against Japan if she makes this move?" Roosevelt initially repeated his standard lecture on how sanctions would cause the Japanese to attack the Dutch East Indies, which would mean war. But when Welles said that the United States could freeze Japanese assets—as the government had already done to the French and Germans—FDR endorsed the measure. Ickes then weighed in. Given that he was about to begin rationing gasoline on the East Coast, couldn't the United States at least restrict the Japanese to what they were receiving "over a given period?" Again Roosevelt agreed, and Morgenthau also won his assent to lowering the octane limit on gasoline for Japan from eighty-seven to sixty-seven. The President authorized Sumner Welles to draft an executive order freezing Japanese assets and requiring licenses for trade. "If Japan went overboard," Roosevelt continued, "we would ship no more oil"—although he did not define "overboard." "The part that pleases me," Morgenthau told his staff, "is that if I had not raised the question, none of this would have happened because nobody else raised it. And that's that!" Stimson was taking a week's vacation in Vermont, but his policy had carried the day. Yet there can be little doubt that the President had known the issue would arise and that he had decided what to do about it.[37]

The implementation of the decision, while gradual, was carefully thought out and publicly announced by the President himself. Welles gave the task of drafting the freezing order to Assistant Secretary of State Dean Acheson, a successful international lawyer. On Saturday, July 19, Acheson explained to Morgenthau's deputy Edward Foley that he planned to freeze all Japanese assets, license all trade, and cut oil exports to Japan by about 75 percent. In desperation, Admiral Nomura sought out Admiral Kelly Turner at his home, acknowledged the forthcoming move into Indochina, and offered to allow the United States to take any measures it found necessary in the Atlantic provided that the United States would also tolerate Japan's moves taken in "self-defense"—a deal Nomura had no reason to believe that his own government would accept. Turner was sufficiently impressed to write a memorandum for Stark, subsequently passed to the President, recommending against an embargo.[38]

The plan for a U.S. freeze was complete by Monday, July 21. On the next day, newspapers prominently reported Japan's forthcoming move into Indochina and the United States' probable reaction, economic sanctions. On Wednesday, July 23, the same day that FDR asked Congress to keep selectees under arms beyond one year, more hints of the Japanese move into Indochina appeared in the press, and Ambassador Nomura guardedly confirmed them in a talk with Sumner Welles, explaining that Japan needed rice and other foodstuffs from Indochina and also had to forestall moves by unspecified foreign powers to "encircle" Japan. Welles replied that Japan was evidently aiding Hitler in his drive for world conquest and that this move would make any mutual adjustment of relations impossible. On July 19, U.S. intelligence had decoded another critical Japanese cable of July 14 in which military authorities were quoted to the effect that the move into Indochina was designed to prepare the way for the conquest of Singapore and the Dutch East Indies and to "once and for all crush Anglo-American military power and their ability to assist in any schemes against us." Tokyo was actively preparing for war with Britain and the United States. The British, meanwhile, had agreed to freeze Japanese assets as well. During the same week Roosevelt approved plans to provide the Nationalist Chinese with a hundred modern fighter planes—some at the expense of the British—manned by American volunteer pilots.[39] Then, the next morning, Roosevelt publicly gave notice of a new policy toward trade with Japan.

For the whole first half of the year, a number of leading administration figures, including Ickes and Stimson, had complained bitterly that more must be done to stimulate national morale and combat isolationist opinion. Roosevelt in May had appointed the charismatic, popular liberal Republican Mayor of New York, Fiorello La Guardia, to head the Office of Civilian Defense, with responsibility for morale. La Guardia had formed a Volunteer Participation Committee, and Roosevelt met its members on the morning of July 24. With the press present, he exhorted them to make the world situation clear to communities around the country, and used an example to hint at a critical change in policy toward Japan.

"Here on the east coast," he said, "you have been reading that the Secretary of the Interior, as Oil Administrator, is faced with the problem of not having enough gasoline to go around in the east coast, and how he is asking everybody to curtail their consumption of gasoline. All right. Now, I am—I might be called an American citizen, living in Hyde Park, N.Y. And I say, 'That's a funny thing. Why am I asked to curtail my consumption of gasoline when I read in the papers that thousands of tons of gasoline are going out from Los Angeles—West Coast—to Japan; and we are helping Japan in what looks like an act of aggression?'" He explained that in the two years since the world war had started, the administration had tried to prevent it from spreading to the South Pacific. Japan, he argued, would probably have attacked the Dutch East Indies if the United States had embargoed oil. "Therefore, there was—you might call—a method in letting this oil go to Japan, with the hope—and it has worked for two years—of keeping war out of the South Pacific for our own good, for the good of the defense of Great Britain, and the freedom of the seas." The next morning's papers emphasized the President's use of the past tense to describe the policy of continuing exports.[40]

The cabinet met at 3:00 p.m. that day, Thursday, because the President and First Lady were leaving for Hyde Park that night. Morgenthau was now on vacation. Confusion had now arisen on the question of how tight restrictions on oil shipments to Japan would be, and FDR did nothing to clear it up. Ickes now wrote that Roosevelt "does not want to draw the noose tight" around Japan. But Roosevelt rejected any exception for oil exports in the forthcoming executive order freezing Japanese assets while suggesting that it should be administered "flexibly" by the Foreign Funds Interdepartmental Committee, which had been formed to handle the assets of the Axis and the countries they had occupied. The cabinet spent a great deal of time on reports that Senator Burton Wheeler had franked over a million letters to soldiers in uniform trying to drum up opposition to an extension of their tours, a step that Roosevelt and Ickes had already called almost treasonous.[41]

At 5:00 that afternoon the President met with Ambassador Nomura, Welles, and Admiral Stark in his office. He repeated that the American people could not understand why they were enduring an oil shortage while Japan received exports, even though for two years Japan "had given every indication of pursuing a policy of force and conquest in conjunction with the policy of world conquest and domination which Hitler was carrying on." He added that if Japan ever did attack the Dutch East Indies that would immediately mean war with Britain as well, "and in view of our own policy of assisting Great Britain, an exceedingly serious situation would immediately result." Japan's new move into Indochina, he continued, "created an exceedingly serious problem for the United States." He was confident that the Ambassador would agree, he said,

"that the policies now undertaken in Indochina by the Japanese Government were completely opposed to the principles and the letter of the proposed agreement which had been under discussion" with Secretary Hull.

Ambassador Nomura, while repeating what he had told Welles the
night before, personally deplored the occupation of Indochina, and Roosevelt in response said he was very glad to learn that Admiral Toyoda, the
new foreign minister, "was an intimate friend of the Ambassador." Roosevelt then spontaneously offered to arrange a joint declaration of all the
Asian powers neutralizing Indochina, provided that the Japanese would
immediately withdraw their forces. Nomura was not hopeful, and in
conclusion, Roosevelt insisted that Hitler was bent on world domination
and that if he defeated Russia and dominated Europe and Africa, both
the United States and Japan would have to fight Hitler as well. The President and the First Lady left on a night train for Hyde Park a few hours
later.[42]

The question of the extent of an embargo was hanging fire, and as
late as Friday, July 25, high Treasury officials still believed that licenses
for petroleum exports would be granted to the Japanese. But that morning, Roosevelt gave a press conference at Hyde Park previewing the freezing order, which issued at 8:00 that night. Although Roosevelt refused to
be pinned down for the record, a *New York Times* story indicated that
this would bring all petroleum shipments and trade to a halt and that it
marked the end of appeasement and an attempt to enforce the Open
Door by economic means. Roosevelt added that he had recently heard
from several journalists and cabinet officers who had traveled around the
country in the early spring and then more recently and that they agreed
"that there had been a tremendous change since March or April, that the
people are far more cognizant of international danger and of the world
situation." Another story reported that both Japanese and American
traders expected all exchanges to end. The next day Sumner Welles predicted that oil exports to Japan would fall by two-thirds, and Roosevelt
made another sensational announcement that the Philippine Army was
being called to service as part of the armed forces of the United States.
Meanwhile, the Japanese froze all American assets in retaliation.[43]

The asset freeze was the most important victory yet for the prowar
party that included Stimson, Morgenthau, and Ickes. They evidently
pressed their advantage in the press, where stories suggested that Japan
would not be able to endure Anglo-American sanctions, in which the

Dutch East Indies quickly joined as well, for more than a few months. Other stories suggested that Japan had occupied Indochina to prevent the United States from taking the Azores as part of an Axis plot, and credited Ickes with finally making the embargo happen. Roosevelt did nothing to arrest the momentum in a press conference on July 29, calling the Japanese move into Indochina part of a worldwide conspiracy to dismember the democracies. He declined to discuss the new economic restrictions on the Japanese but also referred to European and Far Eastern situations as part of a whole. He also quoted his own words from his Lend-Lease fireside chat to the effect that the Axis were threatening the United States with war if it interfered with their program of world conquest. The President, in short, was warning the country of an impending world war. Gallup polls had shown a huge majority of the public in favor of an embargo at least since the signature of the Tripartite Pact, and a new poll approved the embargo by a margin of 51–38 even at the risk of war.[44]

While Acheson at the State Department began working out the details of the asset freeze, it was clear at the very least that no more high-octane fuel or lubricants would be allowed to go to Japan. On July 31, a subordinate drew up a plan reflecting Acheson's views calling for a two-week halt to all trade with Japan, after which both imports from and exports to Japan would require licenses and would be essentially equal in value. In theory, exports of lower-grade petroleum products might proceed then. Sumner Welles summarized this proposal in a memorandum for Roosevelt on the same day, allowing for a possible resumption of oil exports but also ruling out any new purchases of Japanese silk or gold, which would inevitably shrink Japanese-American trade further. Roosevelt initialed it "OK FDR." Yet there seems to be no doubt that everyone involved, including the President, knew that all petroleum exports to Japan were about to cease. On August 1, Acheson called Ickes triumphantly to say that FDR had banned all exports of high-octane gasoline and high-grade fuel oil to Japan, and that night, Welles banned all oil exports to anywhere but Latin America, the British Empire, Egypt, the Dutch East Indies, "unoccupied China," and the Belgian Congo. Oil exports to Japan never resumed.[45]

Lacking enough Navy for war in both oceans, the administration in the spring had held out hope that Japan might forsake the Tripartite Pact in return for continued economic relations with the United States. The Magic intercepts had made it crystal clear to Roosevelt, Stimson, Welles (sitting in for the sick Hull), and Knox that such a prospect was hopeless. With the Japanese in position to attack the Soviet Union at any moment, now embarking further on a southward advance—which another intercept warned on August 2 might also include Thailand—and above all, determined to act under the Tripartite Pact if the United States became involved in war in Europe, the President had every reason finally to yield to Stimson, Morgenthau, and Ickes, cut off Japan's oil, and face the prospect of world war.

The American embargo did not lead the Japanese to decide on a southward advance. That decision had taken place *before* the American freeze of Japanese assets, which elements within the Japanese Navy had anticipated as a response to a move into Indochina a full year earlier. The embargo did finally win the Japanese Army over to the Navy's position that the southward advance had to begin at once and that war with the Soviets had to be abandoned for the moment no matter what happened in the western Soviet Union, but the decision to risk war with the Western powers had already been taken. Nor did the embargo make the Japanese more pliable in negotiations. During the first week of August the Japanese would promise no more than to guarantee the neutrality of the Philippines and withdraw from Indochina after the United States helped them settle the "China Incident" by forcing Chiang to submit to their terms. In return, the United States, Britain, and the Netherlands would have to halt their military preparations in the Southwest Pacific. Hull immediately replied that the Japanese had to abandon their policy of force.[46]

The War Department now changed U.S. strategy and began preparing for a military as well as economic response to Japanese aggression in the Far East. As late as June 1941 Marshall had opposed reinforcing the Philippines, and he had put off a suggestion by General Douglas MacArthur, now the commander of the independent Philippine Army, that MacArthur be recalled to active service as head of a U.S. command. Led by Stimson, however—who had always taken the United States' Pacific role very seriously—the War Department changed its mind beginning in late July of 1941. On July 26 Marshall appointed MacArthur Commander of U.S. forces in the Far East, and two days later he and Stimson agreed that a squadron of heavy bombers in the Philippines would "give the Japanese some bad moments." Roosevelt endorsed plans to send more aircraft to the Philippines in early August. By September, Marshall planned to send 340 modern pursuit planes, about 75 B-17 and B-24 heavy bombers, 54 dive bombers, and 1 regiment of antiaircraft guns to the Philippines by the end of the year. Thanks to these plans, American war planners now regarded the prospect of war with Japan as serious but not hopeless. Admiral Kimmel at Pearl Harbor, however, frankly declared in July that he had too few battleships, heavy and light cruisers, and destroyers to undertake a successful war in the Pacific at this time. And the War Department's plans reflected an unrealistic belief in the effectiveness of B-17s against Japanese warships, and a lack of understanding of what would be required to defend airfields in a combat zone.[47]

In the oil embargo decision, Roosevelt, as he so often did, chose the proper moment to yield to the blandishments of determined subordinates. After the German attack on the Soviet Union, however, he and he alone insisted that the United States begin giving the Soviets as much help as it could.

Washington had initially reacted rather hesitantly to the events of June 22. Roosevelt had followed Churchill's forthright lead on June 23, expressing sympathy for and promising assistance to the newly attacked nation but refusing to say whether the Soviets would receive Lend-Lease aid. Isolationists in Congress immediately seized on the attack as a new excuse to stay out of the war. Lindbergh, leading the way again, bluntly declared that he would prefer to ally with Britain or even with Nazi Germany than with the Soviet Union, and Hoover declared that the idea of entering the war as an ally of the Soviets on behalf of Roosevelt's Four Freedoms had become "a gargantuan jest." The State Department reacted tepidly to initial Soviet requests for assistance and worried that the British might promise Stalin the retention of his territorial gains in Eastern Europe under the Nazi-Soviet Pact. And while Stimson and Knox wanted to take advantage of the German attack to enter the European war under favorable circumstances, the War Department gave the Soviets essentially no chance of holding out even until the end of the year.[48]

Roosevelt immediately grasped how the German attack might eventually transform the world situation and the prospects of the war. "Now comes this Russian diversion," he wrote to Ambassador William Leahy in Vichy—Stark's predecessor as CNO—on June 26. "If it is more than just that it will mean the liberation of Europe from Nazi domination—and at the same time I do not think we need worry about any possibility of Russian domination." The Soviet Union might in theory provide the forces necessary to defeat Hitler—a problem for which until now there had seemed to be no obvious solution. Roosevelt's thinking had evolved further by the time he saw Soviet Ambassador Constantin Ousmansky on July 10. As he evidently explained to Sumner Welles, he wanted assistance to reach the Soviets before October 1, on the apparent assumption that autumn rains would make it impossible for the Germans to continue their advance after that. On the next day Hopkins told a subordinate that the Lend-Lease program would assume responsibility for assistance to the Soviet Union.[49]

Roosevelt received encouragement from Joseph Davies, a prominent lawyer and Democratic activist who had served with FDR during the Wilson administration and had become his Ambassador to Moscow from 1936 until 1939. On June 22, when the Germans attacked the Soviets, Davies had been attending commencement at his alma mater, the University of Wisconsin. A UPI reporter immediately tracked him down, and Davies announced that the world would be surprised by the extent of Soviet resistance. He then returned to Washington to lobby for aid to his former host government. During the first half of July, Davies met with Ambassador Ousmansky, who was preparing a list of requests, and with Acting Secretary of State Sumner Welles and Harry Hopkins. On July 16 he saw the President himself, and FDR noted that Davies's opinion of Soviet powers of resistance did not reflect the views of his military advisers and pressed him for more facts. Davies expanded on his views two days later with a memo for Hopkins. Air supremacy, he said, might allow Hitler to seize White Russia and the Ukraine, but the Soviets had prepared to resist farther eastward, and Hitler in any event would not be able to secure the resources of those areas without reaching an actual peace agreement. The Soviets might reach such an agreement, he thought, if they did not receive sincere and effective support from the United States.[50]

The Soviet Ambassador gave the State Department a huge request valued at $1.8 billion in mid-July, including aircraft, ammunition, and industrial equipment and raw materials of various kinds. Marshall immediately declared himself "unalterably opposed" to the supply of aircraft to the Russians—a position that OPM also endorsed. On July 23 an interdepartmental committee chaired by General James Burns, Hopkins's deputy, cleared only $22 million worth of goods for shipment by October 1, nearly all of it industrial equipment and raw materials.

At this very moment, Roosevelt was taking steps toward the creation of the alliance among the United States, Britain, and the Soviet Union that eventually won the war. Hopkins in late July was once again in London, discussing another dramatic step with Churchill. Roosevelt and Churchill were planning to meet in warships off the coast of Newfoundland sometime in early August—a plan FDR was keeping a secret from his entire cabinet. On July 25 Hopkins cabled FDR asking permission to visit the Soviet Union as well to talk to Stalin and see what he could find out about the situation there himself. Roosevelt approved the trip, and it seemed to reignite his interest in the question of aid to the Soviets. On July 27 he called Marshall from Hyde Park asking for immediate action. On Thursday, July 31, Roosevelt met with the Russian Ambassador and a Russian military mission himself and declared, evidently on his own authority, that he had approved the shipment of 200 P-40 aircraft to the Soviets—including 150 now in Britain—and that he wanted them to reach their destination by October 1. The President stuck to his decision on August 2, after a despairing Marshall had tried to explain the enormous difficulty of getting the planes to Russia and the desperate need for the same planes for training the U.S. Air Force here at home. Similar arguments by Stimson at a stormy August 1 cabinet meeting had been fruitless, and Stimson once again complained to his diary about Roosevelt's erratic administrative style.[51]

Hopkins, meanwhile, had reached Moscow via Archangel (in the Soviet far north) in the last days of July. Perhaps because he had known for some time that he might die of his digestive problems at any moment, Hopkins acted fearlessly throughout the war, and to reach the Soviet Union he had had to fly around Norway in a PBY seaplane in the midst of nearly twenty-four-hour arctic daylight, knowing that the plane would be doomed if German aircraft based in Norway should encounter it. He was rewarded with four hours of extraordinary conversation with Stalin—this at a moment when the central German spearheads had advanced nearly five hundred miles toward Moscow, leaving them with only about a hundred more miles to go. Militarily, Stalin predicted optimistically that the German drive would have to halt because of rainy weather by about October 1, after which it did indeed slow significantly. With respect to supplies, Stalin showed himself every bit as familiar with his forces' needs and the technical details of their weaponry as any American civilian or military leader and welcomed any assistance the Americans could provide.

Hopkins let Stalin know that Roosevelt was redefining American political objectives: "I expressed to him the President's belief that the most important thing to be done in the world today was to defeat Hitler and Hitlerism" and "the determination of the President and our Government to extend all possible aid to the Soviet Union at the earliest possible time." Hopkins said the President anticipated a long war and asked Stalin to distinguish between his immediate and long-term needs. He proposed an October conference among British, American, and Soviet representatives to survey their needs and capabilities.

Stalin had, of course, established himself domestically as a dictator capable of cruelty equal in scale to Hitler's, but in these conversations he spontaneously laid the basis for a political alliance with the United States. Nations could not coexist, Hopkins reported Stalin as saying, without "a minimum moral standard between all nations. . . . [Stalin] stated that the present leaders of Germany knew no such minimum moral standard and that, therefore, they represented an anti-social force in the present world." Cordell Hull could hardly have said it better. After cabling a long account of his meetings to Washington, Hopkins separately recorded one crucial exchange. The millions of peoples conquered and oppressed by Hitler and the countless millions still unconquered, Stalin said, "could receive the kind of encouragement and moral strength they needed to resist Hitler from only one source, and that was the United States. He stated that the world influence of the President and the Government of the United States was enormous." The German people, on the other hand, "would be demoralized by an announcement that the United States is going to join in the war against Hitler." Hopkins replied "that the matter of our joining in the war would be decided largely by Hitler himself and his encroachment upon our fundamental interests." Stalin repeated that "the President and the United States had more influence with the common people of the world today than any other force." Hopkins immediately told the press that his visit had "added to my confidence that Hitler will lose."[52]

Hopkins's report and Stalin's optimism about a 1942 campaign undoubtedly confirmed Roosevelt's sense of the situation. If the Soviet Union collapsed or made peace, Hitler could freely advance into the Atlantic, further isolate the British, and eventually force the United States to defend the western hemisphere against him and the Japanese. If on the other hand the Soviets could hold out, the complete defeat of Germany, Italy, and Japan—the objective for which Roosevelt had already asked the

Harry Hopkins with Joseph Stalin in Moscow, July 1941. (Courtesy of Getty Images.)

War and Navy departments to specify their requirements—would indeed become possible. Given the stakes, FDR willingly delayed U.S. readiness for war a little further in a gamble designed to keep the possibility of victory alive. Two days after the cabinet meeting of August 1, Roosevelt left Washington secretly for his first meeting with Churchill at sea off

Newfoundland, accompanied by Marshall, Stark, and Sumner Welles but without informing Stimson or Knox. Hopkins, meanwhile, had returned from Moscow to London and accompanied Churchill on his way to the meeting on the *Prince of Wales.*

The President had in fact decided that the United States would indeed enter the war under either of two circumstances: if further German naval moves in the Atlantic led to clashes with U.S. warships or if the Japanese continued the southern advance by moving into the Dutch East Indies. Since it was quite clear that the Japanese in the first case and the Germans in the second would execute the terms of the Tripartite Pact, the United States would indeed find itself in the global war Roosevelt had initially hoped to avoid. He may have been somewhat more confident about the war at sea because the first two new-generation U.S. battleships, the *Washington* and the *North Carolina*, had now been commissioned, but more importantly, with decisive battles raging in the Soviet Union and the Japanese poised to strike in the Far East, he agreed with Stimson that the United States simply had to contest any further advances by Germany or Japan. Meanwhile, the President during the same month had taken another huge step, asking the War and Navy departments to estimate exactly what the United States would need to secure the complete defeat of all its potential enemies. The Roosevelt administration had yet to declare that objective to the United States and the world, but Roosevelt, together with Churchill, was about to do so.

In the first seven months of 1941, while the world situation continued to deteriorate, Franklin Roosevelt had moved the government of the United States far closer to war and built up the great enterprise that must sustain such a conflict at home. His reliance on a team of determined, energetic advisers, all of whom felt free to speak their minds publicly as well as privately, was paying off. Yet through all this, Roosevelt remained a man—a fifty-nine-year-old man, crippled by polio, sustained by his associates, his Hyde Park home, and his many hobbies, and warmed by the continuing esteem of his countrymen. His family life was another matter. Eleanor Roosevelt remained an extraordinarily popular First Lady and a political force in her own right, but she was only an occasional companion of the President, with whom she had not shared a bedroom since the birth of their last child during the First World War. As any reader of Mrs. Roosevelt's newspaper column *My Day* could see, her path crossed her husband's only occasionally. At Hyde Park they occupied separate residences.

In this early summer of 1941, while he made the decisions that would shortly involve the United States in the war and ultimately enable it to triumph, Roosevelt suffered what must have been a devastating personal blow. His constant companion, longtime secretary, and confidante, Marguerite "Missy" Lehand, suffered a small stroke in early June and a crippling one later that month. She was hospitalized and never returned to the White House. Lehand had occupied rooms in Roosevelt houses in Hyde Park and New York since the 1920s and had lived in the White House since 1933. She remained an invalid for the remaining three years of her life, and Roosevelt rewrote his will to provide half the income of his estate for her care, the other half to go to Mrs. Roosevelt. But her illness rated only the briefest news items in the papers, and among his advisers and before the public, the President simply carried on as before.[53]

"During his first eight years in office, probably no president in history was in closer touch with the country as a whole than Franklin Roosevelt," Drew Pearson and Robert Allen wrote on July 15, 1941. He had seen a steady stream of Congressmen, Senators, businessmen, and labor leaders in Washington and traveled frequently all around the country. Since May 1940, however, he had not left the East Coast, busy with endless meetings with military leaders and diplomats. "This change in the President's mode of operation," they continued, "is not as important as the change which gradually has crept over his general outlook. On the surface, and in press conferences, he is the same old wise-cracking, fun-loving Roosevelt. But underneath and in private he is not. No longer does he have the same zest for what he is doing. In the old days when he was building PWA bridges and WPA schoolhouses, writing labor laws, crusading for social security, fighting the big utilities, he loved every minute of it. He was crusading for human needs and human rights. And his enthusiasm was boundless.

"Now, however, he knows that every step he takes in foreign policy, every dollar he spends for the Navy, every man he inducts into the Army, may be a step toward tearing down rather than building up. He believes the steps he is taking are absolutely necessary. But he has no enthusiasm for them. In other words, he has no enthusiasm for war."[54]

Rebuilding and sustaining democracy at home had turned out not to be enough. Just as FDR had suspected as early as 1936, totalitarian dictatorships bent on expansion had forced an even greater mission on the United States. Roosevelt had not sought that task, but he and his team accepted it as willingly as they had taken up all the other great challenges of their era. The President was now on his way to meet Churchill and to declare, in public, that the United States sought nothing less than "the destruction of the Nazi tyranny."

CHAPTER 8

Planning for Victory, August–November 1941

IN THE LATE SUMMER OF 1941, ROOSEVELT'S NEW PLANS FOR WORLD WAR continued to mature, and the United States moved closer to all-out conflict on several different fronts. Meeting Churchill at sea for the first time in early August, Roosevelt committed the United States not merely to the defense of the western hemisphere or even the survival of Great Britain, but to "the destruction of the Nazi tyranny." In September the War and Navy departments submitted dramatic new estimates of the requirements of victory over the Axis, and Roosevelt once again created a new agency to remove obstacles to the war production that would become necessary to meet their targets. For the first time, American war planners roughly sketched out the strategies that eventually won victory in Europe. In September United States warships began convoying American and British vessels between Iceland and the Canadian coast, and shooting incidents between American vessels and German U-boats began to occur, effectively bringing the U.S. into the war in the western Atlantic. In Japan the fall of the Konoye government made war a near-certainty in the Pacific. World war was in the air.

On Saturday, August 2, White House Press Secretary Steve Early announced that the President would take a train to New London, Connecticut, the next day and board his yacht, the *Potomac*, for a cruise lasting a week to ten days—his first since the spring. Given the tense international situation, heightened by the embargo on exports to Japan, Early said that

FDR would stand ready to return on twenty-four hours' notice. In fact, on July 30, Roosevelt had informed General Marshall, General Arnold of the Air Corps, and Admiral Stark that they would all board the cruiser *Augusta* in New York on August 3 and rendezvous with him prior to a meeting with Churchill off Newfoundland. Neither Roosevelt nor Marshall informed Stimson, and the entire cabinet remained in the dark. Since, however, Churchill disappeared from London at the same time, it did not take long for rumors of a meeting of the two leaders to circulate and reach everyone from Stimson to the German news service to the Japanese Embassy in Washington. Undersecretary of State Sumner Welles accompanied the President, and Hopkins, who had just visited both London and Moscow, arrived with Churchill on the battleship *Prince of Wales*. The actual meeting began on August 9 and concluded on August 12, and its public result was the Atlantic Charter, signed on the last day and published to the world two days later.[1]

Although Roosevelt had told Joseph Kennedy that he had met Churchill once during the First World War and that Churchill had been rude to him, Churchill claimed that this was their first meeting. Both wanted a major media event, but beyond that their agendas differed. Although warned beforehand through Hopkins not to expect too much, Churchill wanted nothing less than American entry into the war. Roosevelt, at that very moment watching the fight in Congress to extend the terms of draftees, was not going to oblige. On August 7 he had a long and unusually frank talk with General Arnold. American warships, he said, would start escorting convoys halfway across the Atlantic and shooting at German submarines before the submarines shot at them. He wanted the Army to relieve the Marines in Iceland, and he talked about sending airplanes to Russia. More B-17 bombers, P-40 fighters, tanks, and antiaircraft guns would go to the Philippines to be ready for a possible war with Japan. The United States would not go to war if Japan moved into Thailand but would do so if the Japanese struck the Dutch East Indies. But the President planned no immediate declaration of war.[2]

The U.S. cruiser *Augusta* and the British warship *Prince of Wales* rendezvoused in Placentia Bay on August 9, and the first major meeting took place between Undersecretary Welles and his British counterpart, Foreign Office Permanent Undersecretary Sir Alexander Cadogan. Regarding the Far East, Welles insisted that U.S. and British interests would best be served by delaying war with Japan as long as possible, since such a war would tie up U.S. naval forces in the Pacific. Echoing Roosevelt, he advised against going to war if the Japanese occupied Thailand, but he suggested that a Japanese attack on the Dutch East Indies would provoke a reaction among the American people that would lead to war. The two men shared intense concerns about possible German advances into the Iberian Peninsula, North Africa, and the Atlantic. That night, the British party, half-starved by rationing at home and on their own ships, enjoyed a generous dinner on the *Augusta*, after which Churchill laid out his own strategic conception.[3]

According to one of the U.S. officers present, Churchill wanted American help to establish a strong base in Egypt; a joint warning to Japan to deter war in the Pacific; the transfer of fifty-two British vessels from the western Atlantic to antisubmarine operations nearer Britain, where the heaviest losses were taking place; and "by inference," a request for the United States to enter the war. Sounding a favorite theme, Churchill "dwelt on the great difference between this war and the last war, in that the great masses of personnel which took part in battles such as the Somme and Paschendaele were replaced by smaller numbers of men operating machines such as aircraft, armored vehicles, and automatic weapons and using radio in all its developments. He commented that this new type of warfare was particularly suited to the talents of the English-speaking peoples. He referred to the Russian campaign as the great exception to the foregoing since in it great masses of troops were engaged simultaneously on a very long front." He thought Russia would last into the winter, and he had every intention of allowing that campaign to remain an exception.[4]

On the next day, Sunday, August 10, Churchill and Roosevelt attended a moving religious service on the *Prince of Wales*, which had traded fire with the *Bismarck* three months earlier and would go to the bottom off Malaya four months later. Then Cadogan and Churchill gave Welles and Roosevelt drafts of warnings for both governments to give Japan, threatening countermeasures leading to war should Japan undertake any further aggression. As the Americans left the ship, Churchill almost desperately told Cadogan that if Japan attacked Great Britain her cruisers could immediately cut the British off from its Far Eastern possessions, and "the blow to the British Government might be almost decisive." He also gave him a draft of what shortly became the Atlantic Charter.[5]

Roosevelt and Churchill on the *Prince of Wales* during the Atlantic Conference, August 10, 1941. Behind them, from left, are Admiral Ernest King, seated; General Marshall and British General Sir John Dill; and at right, Admiral Stark. (Courtesy of the Franklin D. Roosevelt Presidential Library and Museum.)

The last and most serious meeting between Roosevelt and Churchill on the next day surveyed their apparently desperate military situation. Their first priority was to do what they could to forestall further German moves south and southwest into the Atlantic, moves that Roosevelt speculated might take place within a month. Churchill began by announcing that the British had decided to occupy the Spanish-owned Canary Islands around the middle of September because they believed Hitler was almost certain to occupy Spain and Portugal and render Gibraltar untenable. That in turn meant that the British would not be able to occupy the Azores, as they had hoped to do, and he asked for, and secured, Roosevelt's pledge to undertake that operation instead. The President added that if the United States occupied the Azores it would be unable to seize the more distant Cape Verde Islands, and Churchill assured him that the British intended to do so. As it turned out, Roosevelt was being too optimistic about American capabilities, and all those islands remained in neutral hands for quite some time to come.[6]

The British were hoping that the Americans might go much further: land troops in French possessions in North and West Africa and declare war on Germany. British authorities had broached the North Africa operation to the U.S. naval mission in London in July, on the assumption that while the Vichy French authorities would undoubtedly resist new British and Free French moves into those territories, they might welcome U.S. forces, and Churchill had discussed these ideas in a meeting with British and American military representatives and with Harry Hopkins in London, on July 24. British military authorities had now prepared a much more specific set of requests aimed directly at getting the United States into war against Germany, and Marshall and Stark now received copies of it. It reiterated British fears of a German advance into Spain, making "Gibraltar unusable as a base" and forcing the seizure of the Canaries. With Vichy France moving closer to Germany, it was essential to put forces in Morocco and French West Africa, but Britain had none to spare. The British must also hold the Middle East, the Iranian oil fields, and Singapore. According to the British Chief of Staff report, "The intervention of the United States would revolutionize the whole situation," even if the Japanese joined the war as well. It would immediately relieve the shipping situation and U.S. forces could go into Morocco, West Africa, and the Atlantic islands. The longer U.S. entry was delayed, the more "leeway" would have to be made up. Meanwhile, in words that echoed Churchill's own, the British planners essentially assured the Americans that while the United States defended far-flung outposts of empire, British heavy bombers would either force the Germans to sue for peace or create a situation in which a relatively small force of British armored divisions, aided by local resistance fighters, would retake the continent.[7]

Desperate to persuade Roosevelt to join the war, Churchill warned him at one point that "he would not answer for the consequences" if Russia was compelled to sue for peace and, say, by the spring of next year, hope died in Britain that the United States would come into the war. The British people, Churchill seemed to believe, could not be counted on to fight on alone without any hope of victory. But Roosevelt, while affirming according to Churchill that the United States would eventually join the war, noted that the last Lend-Lease appropriation had passed only narrowly and predicted that were he to ask Congress for a declaration of war, it would debate the question for three months. Instead, he promised that the U.S. Navy would begin escorting convoys to and from Iceland by September 1, a step that, Churchill later told the War Cabinet, would free enough British warships for action in the eastern Atlantic to guarantee victory over the German U-boats. American ships would fire on U-boats without warning, Roosevelt said, leaving Hitler with the choice of either going to war with the United States or conceding the Atlantic. Roosevelt insisted, as he had said many times over the last six months, that such an "incident" would bring the United States into the war. Meanwhile, he would "wage war, but not declare it."[8]

The British Chiefs of Staff got a better understanding of American reluctance to do more in extensive talks with Marshall, Stark, and Arnold. Because U.S. forces remained in a primitive state, they could neither take part in operations at this time except at sea nor allocate the British the majority of U.S. production, especially of heavy bombers, which the British wanted to have. British desperation was not confined to Churchill. In succeeding months British military authorities told American representatives that they had to win the war through bombing by sometime in 1943, the limit beyond which their people would not be able to go on. Only two active U.S. Marine divisions were currently ready for combat, and although the Americans also feared a German move into North and West Africa, they would have no forces to stop one for many months—as it turned out, not until November 1942. The British were also impressed by the extent of American fears of German penetration of Latin America. They were rather skeptical of the effectiveness of American attempts to reinforce the Philippines with heavy bombers—a judgment that eventually proved just as accurate as the Americans' doubts about British plans to stop the Japanese by putting British and U.S. warships at Singapore. The British chiefs were very disappointed to find that they were not going to be receiving any more four-engine bombers or Catalina sea planes for some time, aircraft that were proving critical to combating the German U-boats in the waters around the United Kingdom.[9]

Only the supreme folly of Adolf Hitler now spared the British and American leaders the need to face the German moves that they feared. Had Hitler not attacked the Soviet Union, he would have disposed of ample forces to make all the Anglo-American nightmares come true: the occupation of the Iberian Peninsula and French North Africa, followed perhaps by landings in the Cape Verde, Canary, or even the Azores islands, and quite possibly, the complete defeat of the British in North Africa. Now, however, all those operations, as well as other moves into the Middle East, had been delayed until the expected collapse of the Soviet Union by the end of the year. The German and Italian navies' surface ships, whose potential to wreak havoc in the Atlantic had troubled Roosevelt and American naval planners so much, were confined to port for lack of fuel, since every gallon was needed on the Eastern Front. Soviet resistance had been more extensive and tenacious than expected, and Hitler had no forces for new offensives in the west to spare.[10]

Churchill and Roosevelt now escalated, rather than cut back, their objectives. Their vehicle was the Atlantic Charter, the joint declaration they issued at the conclusion of their meeting—a plan for a postwar world, predicated on the complete defeat of Nazi Germany.

The original draft of the Atlantic Charter emerged from the U.S. State Department. While the Army and Navy planned for war, the State Department had been laying plans for the eventual peace. The Americans wanted a Wilsonian world without great armaments or trade barriers— including the British system of imperial preference, which since 1931 had discriminated against non-British products and in favor of those from the British Empire. After lengthy exchanges the British had their way on this point, but other aspects of the text were far more important.[11]

Roosevelt insisted that the document include no new commitments for action, and the Atlantic Charter of August 12, 1941, merely made known "certain common principles in the national policies" of the two leaders' nations "on which they base their hopes for a better future for the world." They renounced territorial aggrandizement, opposed any territorial changes "that do not accord with the freely expressed wishes of the people concerned," and in a phrase added by Roosevelt himself, expressed a wish "to see sovereign rights and self-government restored to those who have been forcibly deprived of them." That sentence triggered violent arguments between its signatories over the next four years. Roosevelt and readers on every continent interpreted it to apply as much to Indians, Indochinese, and Africans as to French, Belgians, and Poles, while Churchill continued to insist that the British must rule lesser races, in his eyes, that could not rule themselves. Two more articles looked forward to a world of freer economic exchanges while leaving a loophole for the British imperial system. Then came the words that gave headline writers around the world their lead.

"Sixth, *after the final destruction of the Nazi tyranny,*" the Charter read, "they hope to see established a peace which will afford to all nations the means of dwelling in safety within their own boundaries, and which will afford assurance that all the men in all the lands may live out their lives in freedom from fear and want" (emphasis added). Both Britain *and the United States* were now committed in principle to Hitler's complete defeat, even though the United States had not yet even declared war. And this was no new departure on Roosevelt's part, but rather a critical milestone on a path he had begun to follow in the State of the Union address in January 1941, when he declared that America's idea of freedom could have "no end save victory." Current American plans and forces were adequate at best to defend the western hemisphere, but about six weeks previously, Roosevelt had asked the War and Navy departments to estimate the requirements of defeating all the United States' potential enemies in the world crisis. Six weeks after issuing the Charter, he would receive those estimates. The Charter concluded with a vague reaffirmation of the American principle of freedom of the seas and with a call for the disarmament of all potential aggressors, "pending the establishment of a wider and permanent system of general security."

Churchill's Deputy Prime Minister, the Labor Party's Clement Attlee, released the text of the Atlantic Charter on August 14, and American newspapers headlined it the next day. Roosevelt's skepticism about American opinion had been amply vindicated during his absence. Just two days earlier, on August 12, the House of Representatives had joined the Senate and agreed to extend the service of draftees by a vote of 203–202. Both the Senate and the House decided the question largely on party lines, although 64 House Democrats defected from the administration. Speaker Rayburn probably had votes to spare. Shortly before the dramatic final vote on August 12, the House had voted 215–190 to reject a move to send the bill back to the Military Affairs Committee. Yet for many Congressmen from the Midwest and West, a nay vote was the safer political course of action even then. The debate, like so many controversies between isolationists and administration supporters that summer, turned largely on the question of whether the danger to the United States was increasing or decreasing. Isolationists insisted that the German attack on the Soviet Union had reduced it. Interventionists noted that the pro-German Admiral Darlan had just become the new Vichy Prime Minister and warned that Vichy France was about to allow the Germans into North Africa, bringing them closer to the western hemisphere. The narrow passage of the bill allowed war preparations to continue.[12]

The Atlantic Charter had given American war preparations a new goal—one that embodied the life's work of the Missionary generation. One of their most famous newspapermen, Kansas Republican William Allen White, discussed its significance in a newspaper column on August 26. White put the Atlantic Charter in a long line of key steps toward human freedom, from the Magna Carta to the fall of the Bastille, the Battle of Waterloo, the Latin American revolts of the nineteenth century, the Gettysburg Address, and the League of Nations. The President, he said, was leading the country down the road to a secure peace based on "international justice. . . . A decent nation cannot thrive even behind ships and guns and planes in a world of aggressors. . . . Only as international relations are founded on international justice can democracy survive anywhere in the world." Frank Knox endorsed White's column in a letter for FDR.[13]

In the Atlantic, Roosevelt immediately carried out his promise to wage war without declaring it. Back on July 24, about two weeks after U.S. troops landed in Iceland, Roosevelt had ordered the execution of Western Hemisphere Defense Plan no. 4. Six battleships, 5 heavy cruisers, more than 50 destroyers, and about 50 seaplanes had begun escorting American and Icelandic shipping to and from Iceland. They were instructed to broadcast the position of any Axis ships they might encounter in order to allow nearby British ships to attack them. One crucial passage of the plan, however—authorizing these warships to escort ships from Britain and other friendly nations to and from Iceland to the Atlantic coast as well—was not yet put into effect. Meanwhile, two other designated forces, including 3 aircraft carriers and 8 light cruisers, patrolled specific areas of the Atlantic and reported Axis contacts in the same way.[14]

The Atlantic Conference had decided to extend the escorts to British convoys as well, freeing more of the British Navy for action in the eastern Atlantic. On August 29, a new order instructed the Atlantic Fleet to escort a convoy leaving for Iceland on September 5, and to "destroy or repel any AXIS forces coming within sight or sound contact in order to insure the safe arrival of the Convoy in Iceland and return to UNITED STATES Waters." The execution of the order was delayed until September 16 because the maritime commission had to find enough American merchant ships to establish regular convoys between the East Coast and Iceland. Meanwhile, the July directive led to the first shooting incident between German and U.S. warships. On September 4 the destroyer *Greer* was patrolling southwest of Iceland when British planes directed it to a German U-boat. The *Greer* tailed the U-boat, but did not attack it, for several hours. When the British did attack it, the submarine fired torpedoes at the *Greer*, which responded with depth charges of its own. The naval battle made headlines, and on the next day, Roosevelt gave a belligerent press conference, insisting that the Germans must have known they were firing on a U.S. destroyer on the American side of the Atlantic. Three days later, on September 9, the State Department announced that an American-owned freighter, the *Sessa*, had been sunk with the loss of twenty-four lives near Iceland and that three survivors had been picked up on September 6.[15]

On September 11, Roosevelt gave a fireside chat that amounted to a declaration of war at sea. Citing the attack on the *Greer*—which he questionably characterized as completely unprovoked—the sinking of the *Sessa*, an incident in which a German submarine had tailed a U.S. battleship in July, the sinking of the *Robin Moor* in the South Atlantic in the same month, and the recent sinking of an American merchant ship carrying supplies to the British in Egypt, he claimed that Germany had launched a campaign against American shipping around the world in defiance of American rights to freedom of the seas. Repeatedly attacking American isolationists, he claimed that the Germans had recently plotted to take over the governments of Argentina, Bolivia, and Colombia, and raised again the specter of the United States being forced to confront a Germany that had secured control of all the shipbuilding facilities of the rest of the world. More specifically, he announced that U.S. warships would escort all friendly shipping in the western Atlantic and that they would fire on Axis warships west of his declared defense line without warning. He compared his measures to those of President John Adams against French privateers in the late 1790s and to Thomas Jefferson's against the Barbary Pirates in the following decade—neither of which had involved a declaration of war. "We cannot bring about the downfall of Nazism by the use of long-range invective," he said. "But when you see a rattlesnake poised to strike, you do not wait until he has struck before you crush him. These Nazi submarines and raiders are the rattlesnakes of the Atlantic."[16]

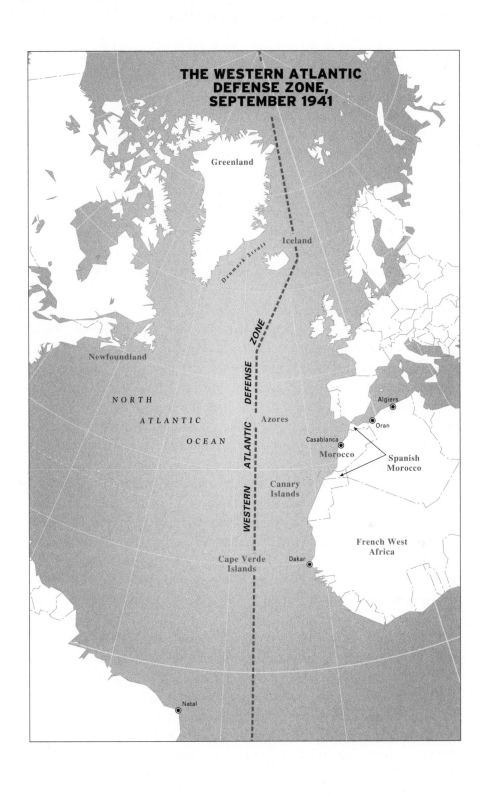

THE WESTERN ATLANTIC
DEFENSE ZONE,
SEPTEMBER 1941

Greenland

Iceland

Denmark Strait

Newfoundland

NORTH

ATLANTIC

OCEAN

WESTERN ATLANTIC DEFENSE ZONE

Azores

Algiers

Oran

Casablanca

Morocco

Spanish
Morocco

Canary
Islands

French West
Africa

Cape Verde
Islands

Dakar

Natal

The speech predictably drew support from administration Demo-crats and northeastern Republicans, including Wendell Willkie, and vio-lent attacks by isolationists led by Lindbergh. In an America First rally in Des Moines, Iowa, the flyer blasted the three most important groups that had been pushing the United States toward war: "the British, the Jewish, and the Roosevelt Administration." Britain, he argued, could not even invade Europe and defeat Germany with American help and could have profitably made peace months ago had not the United States encour-aged her. American Jews, he said, understandably resented Hitler's per-secutions, but they were unwise to call for war, which would unleash intolerance at home. "Their greatest danger to this country," he contin-ued, "lies in their large ownership and influence in our motion pictures, our press, our radio and our government." The rally had drawn a mixed audience and both cheers and boos greeted his speech. A survey of edito-rial reaction to "shoot on sight" by the *New York Times*, however, found twelve newspapers around the country heartily approving the President's action, an isolationist paper regretting the drift toward war, and another arguing that the President should take even stronger action.[17]

On September 13, CNO Admiral Stark ordered the full execution of WPL-51, the naval war plan for the western Atlantic, complete with escorts for British convoys to and from Iceland, to begin three days later. During the next six weeks U.S. warships escorted fourteen convoys between Ice-land and North America, more than two a week. American destroyers reported a great many sonar contacts, some of them surely false, and dropped a great many depth charges, none of which damaged a German submarine. American destroyers became involved in a fight with German U-boats while escorting a Canadian convoy on October 16–17 and one American ship, the *Kearny*, was torpedoed. Although seven men died instantly, the ship stayed afloat—a tribute to American maritime engineer-ing that amazed British observers.[18]

Although the introduction of American-escorted convoys effectively brought the United States into the war at sea, it evidently played a mar-ginal role in the actual course of the battle against the U-boats. That con-flict had taken a very marked turn for the better in July and August, as losses of British and Allied tonnage fell from an average of 300,000 tons a month in the first half of the year to under 100,000. The Allies did not call attention to this change publicly, because much of it stemmed from the use of ULTRA intercepts of German codes, a very closely held practice that allowed British convoys to stay away from U-boats. Ironically, when American convoys began in September and October, sinkings in the North Atlantic once again increased to more than 150,000 tons a month, but the most serious crisis appeared to be past.[19]

On the other side of the globe, while Churchill and Roosevelt decided on their objectives and short-term strategy for war in the Atlantic, Japanese Premier Konoye was making a last desperate attempt to avoid war with the United States. In the first week of August, Konoye secured permission to seek a meeting with Roosevelt, but the Army insisted that he reach at least a ten-year agreement on Japanese terms, not a short-term agreement that would delay a war that the Army now regarded not only as inevitable but also as urgently necessary. The Army's terms made it almost impossible for Konoye to reach an agreement if the summit took place. On August 8, Nomura gave Hull Konoye's request for a personal meeting with President Roosevelt, perhaps in Hawaii, to discuss the issues before the two countries. This coincided with Roosevelt's departure for the Atlantic Conference, and Hull replied unenthusiastically that the two governments would have to agree on basic principles first. Nomura warned his government that any further Japanese military move either northward or southward would mean war.[20]

On August 17, Nomura saw both Hull and FDR, who, the Ambassador reported, seemed in excellent health and spirits after his two weeks at sea. The President, following up on his promises to Churchill, gave Nomura a written warning that should Japan take "any further steps in pursuance of a policy or program of military domination by force or threat of force," the U.S. government would immediately take "any and all steps which it may deem necessary" to protect its legitimate rights and interests and ensure its security. He added that both the Japanese occupation of southern Indochina and the rabid anti-American campaign in the Japanese press made the resumption of formal conversations impossible until Japan had given new evidence of renouncing its policy of force, and he asked the Japanese to provide more information on their attitude. Roosevelt was now convinced—and rightly so—that Japan was going to attack at least the Dutch East Indies and he had decided to go to war if they did. He was now playing for time, just as he had promised Churchill that he would do, and the American record of these conversations did not even mention the proposal for a Roosevelt-Konoye meeting, which

Nomura claimed to have discussed. On the next day, August 18, the President briefed congressional leaders on the Atlantic Conference. After noting that Russian resistance had already saved the British from any danger of invasion during 1941 and expressing the hope that Russia would hold out much longer, he said that the chief danger of a "shooting" war involving the United States was now in the Far East, where he saw an even chance that Japan might undertake further aggression.[21]

On August 28, Nomura gave Roosevelt Konoye's reply to the President's questions about its future attitude. Konoye stated that a break in Japanese-American relations would be not only "a disaster in itself, but also the collapse of world civilization." Unfortunately the Japanese regarded the creation of their Co-Prosperity Sphere as their contribution to the future of world civilization. Konoye then called an immediate meeting with FDR somewhere in the Pacific an "urgent necessity." In a separate document, the Japanese government denied any further military intentions but promised to withdraw from Indochina only after the China Incident was settled. They also protested, not for the first time, the American shipments of oil and other supplies to the Soviet Union, which were now landing at Vladivostok. They promised only not to make any further military moves into neighboring states "without provocation"—a rather empty promise, since they had justified the move into southern Indochina as a defense against unspecified moves by other powers—and said nothing about the Tripartite Pact. Although Roosevelt raised questions about some of the points, he said that the document represented a step forward and spoke favorably about a possible meeting in Juneau, Alaska. Ambassador Grew in Tokyo had already endorsed the idea of a meeting.[22]

Later on the twenty-eighth, Nomura saw Hull and repeated that the meeting was urgently necessary so as to forestall the intrigues of certain people in Japan working to disturb Japanese-American relations. He specifically suggested the period September 21–25 and promised pointedly that Konoye would bring Army and Navy representatives with him who would share the responsibility for any agreement. Going even further, Nomura claimed that the Japanese people regarded the Tripartite Pact as "purely nominal" and that Japan would never go to war with the United States for the sake of Germany. The Ambassador did not, however, report those statements to his own government. Nomura had yielded to a common diplomatic temptation, the concealment from both his home and his host government of irreconcilable differences in order to make them both believe that they might reach agreement. This time the strategy was bound to fail, not least because American authorities were reading his instructions from Tokyo nearly in real time. Thus, on August 28, Tokyo informed Nomura that the China Incident would be "settled" when Chiang Kai-shek had been reduced to the status of a local warlord with no communication with the outside world and that Japan must reserve freedom of action regarding the means with which it would create the Greater East Asia Co-Prosperity Sphere. Military or naval intelligence immediately decoded that message and passed it to the State, War, and Navy departments and to the White House.[23]

Roosevelt and Hull were actually underestimating Japanese intentions. In late August, the Japanese Navy successfully insisted that any new steps to create the Co-Prosperity Sphere had to include a full-scale attack on the Philippines as well as Thailand, Malaya, and the Dutch East Indies, in order to deprive the U.S. Fleet of a nearby base. But the Navy was still withholding its final assent to war, because it wanted to be assured of a greater share of scarce resources, including steel, in return. Konoye may have been hoping that cooler heads might prevail before he could arrange the meeting with FDR, or he might indeed have planned to propose a deal under which Japan would effectively renounce the Tripartite Pact in return for a U.S. endorsement of the Japanese position in China and other aspects of the southward advance. Yet he was essentially trying to reverse a previous decision of his own government, which on July 2 had formally decided that the creation of the Greater East Asia Co-Prosperity Sphere must go forward even at the risk of war with Britain and the United States. Nothing suggests, moreover, that Konoye had the slightest intention of abandoning his government's plans for expansion. Konoye himself had proclaimed plans for a new order in Asia dominated by Japan as early as January 1938. He had firmly supported the southward advance ever since he became Prime Minister again in the middle of 1940, and he had now accepted the opinion of the Army and Navy that the invasion of the Dutch East Indies—the next step in the creation of the Co-Prosperity Sphere—would have to involve war with both Britain and the United States. While he seems sincerely to have desired to avoid war with the United States, he had no intention of abandoning Japan's expansionist policies.[24]

Interestingly enough, this was not the first time that Konoye had promised more than he could deliver in an attempt to end or prevent a war. In December 1938, during an earlier term as Prime Minister, he had

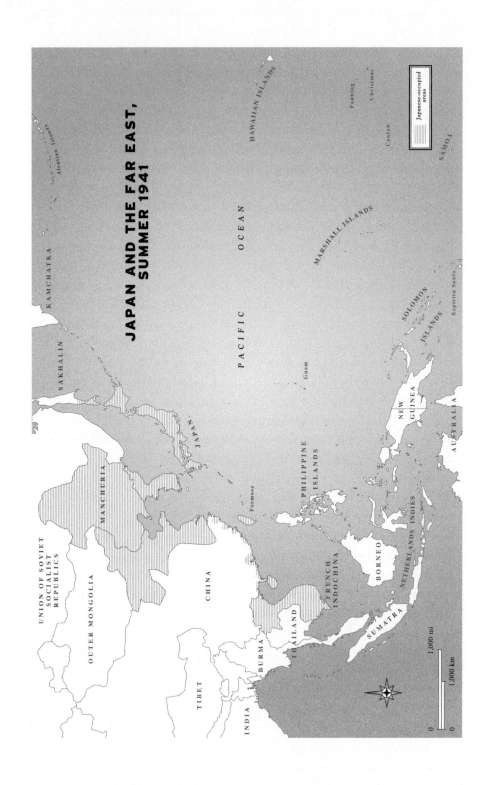

JAPAN AND THE FAR EAST, SUMMER 1941

UNION OF SOVIET SOCIALIST REPUBLICS

OUTER MONGOLIA

KAMCHATKA

Aleutian Islands

SAKHALIN

MANCHURIA

TIBET

CHINA

JAPAN

Formosa

INDIA

BURMA

THAILAND

FRENCH INDOCHINA

PHILIPPINE ISLANDS

Guam

BORNEO

SUMATRA

NETHERLANDS INDIES

NEW GUINEA

AUSTRALIA

SOLOMON ISLANDS

Espiritu Santo

MARSHALL ISLANDS

PACIFIC OCEAN

HAWAIIAN ISLANDS

Fanning

Christmas

Canton

SAMOA

Japanese-occupied areas

1,000 mi

1,000 km

0

persuaded one of Chiang Kai-shek's leading collaborators, Wang Ching-Wei, to defect and set up a new Chinese government in occupied territory by promising him the eventual withdrawal of Japanese troops from China. Six months later, a conference of leading Japanese ministers had flatly refused to approve these generous terms, and after months of haggling, Wang had given in, effectively turning himself into Japan's puppet leader in occupied China. The Japanese had recognized Wang's government in Nanking in May 1940 and were now securing its recognition by the Axis and various European Axis allies.[25]

The Japanese-American talks entered a new phase on September 3, when leading American newspapers leaked the story of Konoye's invitation and indicated that Roosevelt was giving it sympathetic consideration but would require some prior agreement on Hull's four points of 1937—respect for the sovereignty and territorial integrity of all nations, support of the principle of noninterference in the internal affairs of other nations, equality of commercial opportunity, and no disturbance of the status quo in the Pacific except by peaceful means. But the Japanese interpreted the four points as a reaffirmation of the Nine Power Treaty of 1922, which had affirmed Chinese sovereignty and which their government had specifically repudiated as early as December 1938, calling instead for a new order in Asia under Japanese leadership. The White House, the State Department, and the Japanese Embassy all refused to confirm the story the next day.[26]

On September 6, another Imperial Conference ordered the completion of war preparations by the end of October, "based on the resolve not to flinch from war with the United States [, Britain, and Holland]." Concurrently, the Japanese would try to achieve their objectives through negotiation, to include a free hand in settling the China Incident, the closure of the Burma Road, and an end to aid to Chiang. They would renounce the invasion of any further territory in exchange for an end to Anglo-American military preparations in the region and Anglo-American cooperation in helping them secure the resources they wanted from the Dutch East Indies and Thailand. The government reaffirmed its intention to observe its obligations under the Tripartite Pact and declared that talks with the United States would fail if the Americans insisted on repudiating it. The preparations for war would involve moving more troops into Indochina, and the Japanese decided to conceal their intentions by suggesting that they were planning an attack on Kunming across the

Chinese border. A new agreed document, "The Essentials for Carrying Out the Empire's Policies," reaffirmed the irreconcilable conflict between Japan's determined national policy of creating a new order in East Asia and carrying out its alliance obligations to Germany on the one hand and the United States' determination to maintain the status quo and intervene in the war in Europe on the other.[27]

Disturbed by these decisions, both Marquis Kido, the keeper of the Privy Seal, and the Emperor Hirohito expressed the hope that everything possible would be done to avert war. On that very evening, September 6, Konoye invited Ambassador Grew to a private dinner at his house and accepted Hull's four points in principle. He assured Grew that the Army and Navy were on board for his proposed meeting with FDR and promised to bring their representatives with him. In the weeks to come, lower-level Japanese officials repeatedly told Americans that Konoye wanted an agreement and that he could undoubtedly give Roosevelt a satisfactory assurance regarding the Tripartite Pact, although they admitted that it would be extremely difficult publicly to repudiate it.[28]

As September turned into October and shooting incidents began to occur regularly in the Atlantic, the Japanese became more and more insistent that time was of the essence, and by October 15, an official of the Japanese Embassy warned Washington of the danger of the assassination of the present government, a military coup, and war if an agreement could not be reached. On October 4, Magic code breakers passed on a message from Foreign Minister Toyoda to Nomura warning that Konoye's fall was imminent if a meeting could not be arranged. Yet meanwhile, the exchanges of views revealed that the two countries remained far apart.[29]

Konoye's acceptance in principle of the four points needed elaboration, of course, since the Japanese had been violating all of them since 1931 and had expanded even further since the fall of France. The Japanese government had no intention of renouncing either its position in China or the Co-Prosperity Sphere. And thus the Foreign Office's official reply to the United States on September 6 stated that Japan, "*without any justifiable reason*," would not make any further military advances; that it was ready to settle the China Incident by mutual agreement with an unspecified Chinese government; and that Japan would decide "independently" on the application of the Tripartite Pact if the United States became involved in the European War. In return, the United States had to halt military preparations in the Far East, lift economic restrictions, and do nothing to impede the desired settlement of the China Incident, which in effect would mean a halt to U.S. aid to Chiang. Later in the month the Japanese insisted on maintaining troops in China even after an agreement with a new Chinese government, one that would combine Chiang's government with the puppet regime they had established in 1940 in Nanking.[30]

Since the quarantine speech of 1937, Roosevelt and Hull had repeatedly spoken of a worldwide epidemic of lawlessness and aggression, and during 1941 their statements had firmly placed the United States in opposition to the aggressors. Japan was not at war with any European power and the United States had had no reason to commit itself to Japan's defeat, but to have accepted the Japanese terms for an agreement—even if Konoye could have privately given a real assurance not to implement the Tripartite Pact—would have essentially allowed Japan to continue creating a new order in Asia at the expense of the British and Dutch while opposing Hitler's attempt to do the same in Europe.

One key American diplomat definitely favored a deal. On September 22, Ambassador Grew, who had known the President for many years, wrote him a "Dear Frank" letter, assuring him that Konoye wanted to abandon the Tripartite Pact and would "go as far as is possible, without incurring open rebellion in Japan, to reach a reasonable understanding with us." War would be likely without an agreement, "and while we would undoubtedly win in the end, I question whether it is in our own interest to see an impoverished Japan reduced to the position of a third-rate Power." Grew restated his case in a cable a week later, reiterating that Konoye sincerely desired an agreement but that he could not possibly go any further than he already had in advance of a meeting. The United States faced a choice between agreeing in principle and trying to work out satisfactory arrangements later, or war, and Grew, while acknowledging that he had a narrower perspective than FDR or Hull, favored agreement. The Ambassador was not, however, privy to the Magic intercepts for security reasons and evidently did not realize that his host government had definitely decided on further moves south or that the Japanese Navy was determined to attack the United States as well as the Dutch East Indies and British possessions when war came.[31]

Roosevelt *had* seen those intercepts, and he seems to have kept the possibility of a summit open simply to play for time, as he had promised

Churchill he would do. In a written exchange with Hull between Washington and Hyde Park on September 27–28, Roosevelt reiterated his interest in a meeting but joined Hull in insisting that the Japanese had to return to their initial acceptance of the four points in principle, without qualifications. Clearly Roosevelt was not willing to pay Japan's price of a free hand against China, if not, indeed, against the Soviet Union, the Dutch, and even the British as well. Under the Japanese terms, those powers would have to deal with Tokyo alone without American reinforcements in the Far East if the Japanese at any time decided that they had acted "provocatively." Roosevelt had immediately and correctly interpreted the occupation of southern Indochina in July—which the Japanese had defended as a defensive measure—as the next step in the southward advance. He had told Churchill off Newfoundland that he wanted to gain time in the Pacific, and now he allowed the talks to continue fruitlessly rather than accept Konoye's invitation. After the White House and the State Department denied that any invitation had been received after the leak on September 3, the issue faded from public view in the following weeks.[32]

On October 2, Hull gave Nomura a written statement declaring that the Japanese commitment to the four points of September 6 was far too hedged with respect to many issues, including the renunciation of further armed advances, the insistence on maintaining troops in China, and the failure to apply the agreement to the entire Pacific area, an apparent reference to the Soviet Pacific coast. He also asked for a firm declaration of intent to withdraw from Indochina and China. This convinced War Minister Tojo and Army leaders that the October 15 deadline for an agreement set at the September 6 Imperial Conference could not be met and that Japan must decide on war.[33]

While the Japanese government moved closer to war in September—a war Germany would almost surely join under the Tripartite Pact—the Roosevelt administration seriously examined the potential requirements of a world war. The policy that Roosevelt had sketched out even before the European war had broken out in 1939 and to which he had committed himself when France fell—the forward defense of the western hemisphere based on naval power and island bases—was now in full force, and polls showed that the bulk of the American people approved of it. But behind the scenes, the President had ordered his military and naval authorities to draw up the requirements for a completely different war, one that would end, as Roosevelt and Churchill had promised at the Atlantic Conference, with the destruction of the Nazi tyranny and the defeat of all other potential Axis adversaries as well. Roosevelt had set this process in motion with a directive to the War Department on July 9. In the wake of the Atlantic Conference, this process moved very quickly on two parallel fronts. First, the War Department established extraordinary new goals for the Army and the Air Corps, roughly predicting the size of the forces—about 10 million men—that the United States would put into the field during the next four years. Second, a new supervisory body, the Supply Priorities and Allocations Board, began making parallel estimates of maximum productive capacity designed to equip those huge forces and win the war.

On August 18, in a meeting in Secretary Stimson's office, Assistant Secretary John McCloy remarked that the President would want the strategic estimate of the requirements for defeating Germany by the end of the month. In a cabinet meeting on August 29, Stimson tried to prepare his colleagues and his chief for huge decisions. Reporting that the War Department was waiting to hear from the British about their requirements, he added that "that program would be so large that we would be confronted with two alternatives: either to go to war at once and change the set-up of production so as to get the benefit of the speed which could be obtained by a war psychosis; or else have the program so delayed that the war would probably be over before we got through with it." When a somewhat staggered FDR replied that the average American did not yet understand the emergency, Stimson replied that that was why the United States needed "an entirely different spirit and organization." The next day Roosevelt gave Stimson another three weeks to submit what became known as the Victory Program.[34]

The War Department's strategic appreciation and broad statement of requirements was completed in early September by Major Albert Wedemeyer of the War Plans Division. Although it was in different ways both far too pessimistic and far too optimistic, it laid out both the fundamentals of U.S. wartime strategy and what the Army would have to provide to execute it, based on a deadline for the standing up of adequate forces by July 1, 1943.[35]

To an astonishing extent, Wedemeyer saw the coming war very much as did Adolf Hitler in Germany, because he, like most of his War

Department colleagues, assumed that Germany would completely defeat the Soviet Union by the middle of 1942. Although he anticipated that it would take Hitler at least a year to make full use of Soviet resources, he thought that the Axis (by which he meant only Germany and Italy) might then be able to put four hundred divisions in the field by the middle of 1943, a figure that the United States and the British Empire could not possibly match. Wedemeyer also argued that the United States should try to avoid war with Japan, which would divide U.S. forces. The costs of a victory over Japan, he said, would not be justified by the results. It was very hard to see how the British and Americans could achieve adequate numerical superiority over the Germans if the Soviets were defeated, but Wedemeyer argued that they might hope to prevail anyway if their forces were sufficiently well equipped. They would need in particular to secure air superiority in every theater of operations, the thing that the British had failed to do in 1940 in Norway and more recently in Greece and in Crete. They would also have to secure the command of the seas and vastly increase American shipbuilding capacity.

Wedemeyer anticipated that after the collapse of the Soviet Union the Germans would probably go on the offensive in the Middle East, North Africa, and perhaps even in the Atlantic—exactly what Hitler actually planned to do. He therefore favored the seizure of defensive positions in those regions at the earliest possible moment—a moment that he did not define. In the end, wrote Wedemeyer—stating the fundamental doctrine to which General Marshall would stick for the next three years—Germany could only be defeated by a land campaign in northwestern Europe. Blockade and strategic bombing might weaken the Germans, but he insisted, in contrast to Churchill and the British military authorities, that they could not defeat them alone.

To do the job, Wedemeyer argued, the United States must raise an army of no less than 214 divisions and an Air Corps to match, totaling 8.8 million men—more than six times the 1.4 million now being prepared, more than triple the 2.8 million for which equipment had been authorized, and more than twice the maximum 4 million contemplated by current plans. In writing this paper, Wedemeyer built on a long War Department tradition. While the Navy's interest in mobilization had never gone beyond the requirements of War Plan Orange, the Army since the 1920s had been interested in the nation's maximum war potential. Wedemeyer claimed after the war that he arrived at the total manpower figure by subtracting men necessary for the Navy and for industry and agriculture from the total number of military-aged males. As it turned out, the 215 division figure was more than twice as many divisions as the Army and Marines put in the field, but his manpower estimate was only half a million men larger than the Army's strength on May 31, 1945. He evidently overestimated the number of divisions because he underestimated how many support troops each division would require.[36]

Wedemeyer's estimate was a tribute to the sense of duty that General Marshall and the rest of the Missionary generation had imparted in their subordinates. Like his father-in-law, General Stanley Embick, Wedemeyer had personally favored a policy of hemispheric defense and was even in touch with leading isolationists, including Lindbergh. But Marshall had asked him to prepare an estimate of the requirements for defeating Germany, and he had done just that. Ultimately, of course, he had done it at the behest not of Marshall, but of President Roosevelt.[37]

The Navy initially delayed any response to Roosevelt's July request for weeks, eventually prompting one Army observer to suggest that the Navy already had everything it wanted—the planned expansion of the fleet—and could see no benefit in cooperating in a joint determination of requirements. But the Navy was already drawing up plans for even greater expansion based on the probability, as their planners saw it, of an Axis victory in Europe. Its eyes were still focused on the Pacific, where senior Admirals wanted a 2:1 superiority over Japan in order to win a great battle in the South China Sea, while remaining content with a 2:3 ratio in the Atlantic to fight a "defensive" war. On September 9, in the midst of the Victory Program deliberations, Admiral Stark decided to ask for the construction of 6 new aircraft carriers, 16 cruisers, four battle cruisers, 44 destroyers, and 240 submarines. To build these ships, the Navy planned on building only about one-third of the shipping that the Army would require to transport and support millions of men to Europe—another indication of the coming split over wartime strategy.[38]

In July 1941 the Army Air Corps had been renamed the Army Air Forces. It now submitted by far the most detailed and tactical paper on how Germany might be defeated, one that foreshadowed strategic controversies within the American military establishment that continued for half a century or more. Like the British Bomber Command, the Air Corps under General Arnold now believed that air power alone could win the war, and they presented a full target list designed to show how

Germany might be defeated without an invasion of Europe, an operation that they regarded as unlikely "within the next three years." The paper specifically identified 124 targets that would cut off German industry from its electric power sources, cripple the German transportation system, and wreck its key supplies of synthetic oil. The destruction of all these targets, it argued, would cripple Germany's ability to fight. If necessary, attacks on civilians could be undertaken to break German morale. An additional 30 targets would neutralize the German air force. Air Force planners were confident that high-altitude B-17 bombers, suitably armed with machine guns, could successfully hit these targets and overcome German defenses in the daylight, although they presciently observed that it might be necessary, as indeed it turned out to be, to develop an escort fighter, and recommended that work on one begin immediately.

To carry out this campaign they envisioned a force of 6,834 bombers, including 850 medium bombers, 1,360 B-17s and B-24s (the planes that actually carried out the bombing campaign in Europe), 1,632 of the projected B-29s (which in the event were used only in the Pacific), and 2,992 bombers with a range of 4,000 miles or more, which were never developed during the Second World War at all. They anticipated an attrition rate of 20 percent of the aircraft per month. They were unduly pessimistic about the capacity of airfields in the United Kingdom to support the projected bombing effort and thus recommended proceeding with the development of the 4,000-mile-range bomber, which could operate from Iceland, Newfoundland, or even the northeastern United States and Canada. Further sections of the paper laid out the requirements for the air defense of the Pacific Coast, Latin America, and American possessions in the Pacific, including both Hawaii and the Philippines.

In conclusion, the Air Force paper noted that the United States on July 1, 1941, had had only 816 combat aircraft and 2,080 trainers on hand and that current production schedules called for a rate of 4,072 planes per month—very close to FDR's May 1940 target of 50,000 per year—by July 1, 1943. It did not make clear exactly when the forces it had defined as necessary for victory would be ready. As it turned out, the United States built about 46,000 military aircraft in 1942 and 86,000 in 1943. The peak heavy bomber strength of the Eighth Air Force in 1944–1945 included only half as many combat heavy bomber groups as the paper had asked for, and the estimates of results of the bombing campaign in Europe proved wildly optimistic.[39]

A Joint Board paper on Victory Program requirements dated September 11, apparently written after Wedemeyer, the Air Corps, and the Navy had submitted their ideas, took an extremely sophisticated and prophetic approach to the coming conflict. While arguing that the United States had to be prepared to fight the Axis after both the USSR *and the British* had been defeated, it held out far more hope that the Soviets might remain in the war than had Wedemeyer. Indeed, the Joint Planning Committee saw the maintenance of a Russian front as critical, since it offered "by far the best opportunity for a successful land offensive against Germany," and following the President's lead, placed a high priority on assisting the Soviets. The committee foresaw war on both sides of the globe but recommended an initial defensive posture against the Japanese. (Wedemeyer presumably was not privy to the Magic intercepts that showed how unlikely it was that the Japanese would disregard the Tripartite Pact, but Marshall and Stark had seen them.)[40]

The paper recorded an important disagreement between the Army and Navy on strategy, one also related to the critical question of resource allocation. While the Navy thought that Britain and the United States should focus on operations exploiting their naval superiority and air forces, the Army insisted that Germany would have to be defeated on land and that the production requirements for an Army that could do so would have to be included in new targets. That disagreement was about to break into the press. The paper noted prophetically that decisive operations were years away in any event and that the Allies would have to content themselves with defensive and positional warfare in the meantime. The specific requirements of the Army, Navy, and Air Force were included as appendices.[41]

The Joint Board spoke unequivocally on one crucial point: The United States simply had to enter the war as soon as possible to achieve the objective of the defeat of Germany. "If our European enemies are to be defeated," they wrote, "it will be necessary for the United States to enter the war, and to employ a part of its armed forces offensively in the Eastern Atlantic and in Europe or Africa." Wedemeyer in his original paper had gone even further, arguing that the decision to enter the war "should be made soon, certainly not later than the spring of 1942," and speculating that incidents at sea might create a groundswell of opinion for war.

This entire planning exercise, which Roosevelt had ordered in early July, went hand in hand with his public redefinition of American national objectives to include "the destruction of the Nazi tyranny," which he and Churchill had announced in the Atlantic Charter. Certainly no comparable document was ever written on the eve of any other great American war, including the Civil War, the First World War, or the Vietnam War, and the Joint Board paper remains but one of many testaments to the extraordinary practical intellectual ability of those Americans born and educated in the late nineteenth and very early twentieth centuries.

For Stimson, the papers represented the fulfillment of all his hopes over the last year and a half, but even he was somewhat taken aback by the specifics. On September 13, weekending at his Long Island estate, he confided to his diary that his subordinates "had done a good workman-like job but again the size of the undertaking of matching the Germans is terrific and I am rather appalled by it." It now fell to him to present these proposals to the President himself, and before he could do so, a counter-attack against the War Department's plans hit the press.[42]

On September 21 and September 23, two of the nation's most respected journalists, Ernest Lindley of the *Washington Post*—who was very close to the President—and columnist Walter Lippmann, wrote nearly identical articles quoting anonymous sources to the effect that the expansion of the Army was no longer necessary and that it should perhaps be reduced in size. Both argued that the situation that had led to the passage of the draft in 1940—the threatened defeat of Britain and the subsequent threat to the western hemisphere—no longer obtained; that Britain and the Soviet Union were now fighting the Germans effectively; and that the best American contribution might come in the form of equipment, pilots, and soldiers in certain particular specialties. While Lindley acknowledged that the War Department rejected this position, Lippmann more forthrightly stated that the expansion of the Army "is now, I believe, the cancer which obstructs national unity, causes discontent which subversive elements exploit, and weakens the primary measures of our defense, which are the lease-lend [*sic*] program and the naval policy. . . . We do not now need a great mass Army on the European scale." The inspiration for these pieces could have come from the U.S. Navy, which did not want to sacrifice resources to the Army; from the Air Force, which was arguing that bombing could win the war; or from the British mission in Washington, which remained totally committed to the idea that Britain would win the war with air power supplied by the United States. The argument about strategy would inevitably introduce an argument about priorities as well, and the Navy, the Air Force, and the British did not want to be left behind by the unprecedented plans for an 8-million-man Army.[43]

General Marshall had evidently gotten wind of what was afoot, and on September 20 he asked his staff for two memos on whether, and how, ground forces could be cut. The more important one, written for his signature, reached him on September 22, and pointed out that the present strength of the Army was as yet inadequate even for the defensive tasks in the Atlantic and Pacific currently agreed on. More importantly, it stated bluntly, "Germany cannot be defeated by supply of munitions to friendly powers, and air and naval operations alone. Large ground forces will be required." Repeating Wedemeyer's estimates, it argued that 225 divisions might be required to defeat Germany, and "if the United States remains committed to the policy of defeating Germany, making an all-out effort mandatory, then we must build toward these forces as rapidly as possible." Marshall and Stimson brought that memorandum to a meeting with Roosevelt on September 22.[44]

That meeting, Stimson recorded in his diary, went well, but evidently did not address the most critical issues. After the meeting, Stimson and Marshall began drawing up a letter to the President "intended to bring up sharply to him the underlying question which will so modify all our plans; namely, whether we have to absolutely get into an open and avowed war or not. That will control the speed of all our work in getting munitions and all our general strategy as well as the size of the Army that we have to raise." Stimson completed the letter on that very day and brought it, together with the Joint Board paper on the Victory Program and its appendices, to the White House to show FDR on September 25. "The fundamental assumption that is required," he had written, "is whether this country promptly engages in an avowed all out military effort against our chief potential enemy, the German Reich," or rather continued to base its policy on assisting the nations fighting the Axis. The Army, Navy, and Air Corps all believed that "the U.S. must enter the war against Germany and that if it did not, the other powers will not be able to defeat Germany and even Britain would eventually fall." Roosevelt, by setting the objective of the complete defeat of Germany, had led his military authorities to press for the first time for immediate entry into the war in order to make that goal possible.[45]

The meeting with Roosevelt, Stimson wrote that night in his diary, was "one of the best talks I have ever had with him. . . . We read over my letter very carefully and then he went into a very frank discussion of what would happen if and when we got into war." Interestingly enough, although Roosevelt had essentially declared war on Germany at sea two weeks earlier in the "shoot on sight" speech, he made clear that he was worried about the public reaction to plans to invade and crush Germany. Stimson replied "that there was a long distance between getting into war and crushing Germany—that I thought that the getting into the frank position of war would help production very much and would help the psychology of the people and on this I think he fully agreed. Then we discussed what might be done and how the war thereafter should be carried on."[46] Roosevelt gave him no formal approval and kept the documents for further study, but the administration was clearly on a new course. Although the President was openly waging war against Germany in the western Atlantic, he was not ready to ask Congress to declare war, much less to send Stimson's new plans for a massive Army designed to land in Europe to Capitol Hill. That would have to await a German or Japanese move that would open hostilities—something Roosevelt had already been anticipating for months. The Victory Program remained a closely held secret for the next month, but the military plans necessary to make the United States and its values prevail in a world war had now taken shape.

On October 1, Stimson gave a press conference and dismissed the rumors that the Army would be cut in size. Its current strength, he noted, approximated the combined strength of Belgium and the Netherlands in 1940, and the time might come when the United States would conclude that it was now too small, rather than too large. He also noted in his diary that Marshall had at one time suspected Roosevelt himself as the source of the rumors of a cut in strength, but he was convinced that they came from the British and Russians, who wanted American weapons for themselves.[47]

For the whole of 1941, Stimson had been playing essentially the same role that Roosevelt himself had played in the Wilson administration from 1914 until April 1917, when the United States entered the First World War. When the European War had broken out in August 1914, FDR had immediately written a friend that he hoped to see it end with French and Russian armies meeting in Berlin. He had continually agitated for greater preparedness for the next two and a half years, and at some point during that period he had marched into the office of his boss, Navy Secretary Josephus Daniels, and announced, "We've got to get into this war." Wilson, however, had delayed, both because he would much rather have mediated an end to the European war than entered it and because he knew in any case that the country was deeply divided on the issue. Roosevelt had trumpeted the need to defend the western hemisphere against the Axis ever since May 1940, and beginning in the winter of 1940–1941, he had repeatedly stated that the Nazis and the United States could not possibly coexist, but he had not been willing to risk the U.S. Navy to save the British Isles from invasion and had prepared for hemispheric defense. After the German attack on the Soviet Union, however, his July directive to Stimson to define the requirements of total victory showed that he now felt the same way about the most desirable outcome of the Second World War as he had about the First—that it should end with Germany's complete defeat. And during the last six weeks, while the Victory Program was being prepared, the President had taken parallel steps on the production front, reorganizing the nation's production effort to make sure that it would be dominated by the "all-outers," who like himself believed that the needs of the civilian economy had to take second place to the need to prepare for war all over the globe.[48]

Since May 1940 the issues of policy, strategy, and productive capacity had been inextricably intertwined. In September of that year, the Joint Board had warned that the United States would not have enough munitions on hand to fight a war for at least a year. For as long as the defense of the western hemisphere remained the official national objective, targets for raw materials stocks, men in uniform, and industrial capacity remained relatively low. By the spring of 1941 production targets were high enough to impinge on the civilian economy, and the resulting problems had created a bureaucratic and ideological split within the administration and the new war production bureaucracies—one that was also coming to a head in August, when the military services began drawing up the requirements for the defeat of the Axis.

On the one hand, the industrialists whom Roosevelt had brought to Washington as "dollar-a-year" men, led by William Knudsen of GM and Edward Stettinius of U.S. Steel, wanted to keep the disruption of the civilian economy to a minimum and to preserve the autonomy of private industry insofar as they could. Because the Army and especially the Navy had long-standing relationships with major private firms, their procurement offices also tended to side with industry as well. On the other side were New Dealers in and out of the government, such as Treasury Secretary Henry Morgenthau, the economist Leon Henderson, and labor leader Sidney Hillman, who now customarily assumed that private industry, supplemented when necessary by government enterprise, had to serve the broader needs of the nation and who also thought that the world crisis demanded the maximum possible mobilization of a war economy. They had become known as "all-outers," as Donald Nelson of Sears, Roebuck and the Office of Production Management (OPM) put it, and the events of the spring and summer of 1941 showed that Franklin Roosevelt was one of them.[49]

Within the OPM—created in January 1941—this conflict took a paradoxical bureaucratic form. New Deal economist Leon Henderson headed the Office of Price Administration and Civilian Supply, theoretically designed to make sure that inflation did not skyrocket and that the civilian economy continued to function, but he focused on trying to *curtail* civilian production of many goods to the essential minimum so as to make maximum war production possible. Henderson had allies within OPM's Bureau of Research and Statistics, such as economists Stacy May and Robert Nathan, who were already trying to estimate exactly what the economy might be capable of. Knudsen, the co-chairman of OPM, and many of the industrialists in the Production and Raw Materials divisions wanted to protect industry's markets and profits.

The biggest arguments during the spring and summer of 1941 concerned the auto industry, which consumed 18 percent of the nation's steel, 80 percent of its rubber, and 90 percent of its gasoline and which was expanding its production in 1940–1941 in response to a surge in demand for new cars. In the spring of 1941 Knudsen insisted that a 20 percent cut in the production of new 1942 models would be sufficient, and this recommendation carried the day in May. Henderson, Morgenthau, and others thought this was not strict enough, and the cabinet debated the subject vigorously in late July, when the dispute also found its way into the press. The whole situation was further complicated by the demands of Lend-Lease, first for the British and then, beginning in July, for the Soviets, whom the President was so determined to help.[50]

On August 28—less than two weeks after proclaiming the objective of "the destruction of the Nazi tyranny," and just as Wedemeyer and Navy and Air Force planners were drawing up their requirements for achieving it—Roosevelt typically solved the impasse over production with a new bureaucratic reorganization. On the advice of Henderson, Bureau of the Budget Director Harold D. Smith, and his speechwriter and adviser Samuel Rosenman, the President created a new supervisory body, the Supply Priorities and Allocations Board (SPAB), to exercise authority over the existing OPM. Chaired by Vice President Henry Wallace, the board included the OPM Council (Stimson, Knox, Knudsen, and Hillman), presidential confidante and ambassador extraordinary Harry Hopkins, Leon Henderson, and Donald Nelson, who also became its director, or chief executive officer. Of these nine members, six—Wallace, Stimson, Hopkins, Henderson, Hillman, and Nelson—were clearly "all-outers" dedicated to maximum mobilization. The big loser in the reorganization was Treasury Secretary Henry Morgenthau, who was left out entirely.[51]

On September 2, Wallace announced that war production would be increased to the maximum possible extent and that all productive capacity would be devoted to either military or essential civilian needs. The next day, *New York Times* columnist Arthur Krock surveyed the new SPAB and declared that New Dealers were now in full control of the war production effort. On the same day, Donald Nelson told the *Wall Street Journal* that U.S. war production must now be markedly greater than Germany's, not merely sufficient to defend the western hemisphere—a critical observation.[52]

On September 9, the very first meeting of the SPAB authorized Nelson to report at the next meeting on the maximum amounts of aluminum, magnesium, copper, zinc, brass, and steel that expanded capacity could make available "for an all-out defense program" and to make recommendations for making this happen. "This was the first time, to the best of my recollection," Nelson wrote after the war, "that an official government agency had decided to undertake an all-out program." It seemed obvious to Nelson "that if we did become involved in the war—and involvement seemed inescapable—we should be engaged in a struggle without limit, a struggle conducted strictly on a winner-take-all basis. . . . No matter what the obstacles in the way, we simply had to be thinking in terms of doing our utmost; and we had to figure out, without loss of time, what our utmost implied in terms of raw-material production and the manufacture of a long, long list of specific end products."

The full survey of requirements took nine months to complete, and Nelson got critical assistance from Stacy May and Robert Nathan, who were simultaneously attempting both to determine the allies' total war production needs and estimate the total productive capacity of the U.S. economy. During the summer of 1941, May crossed the Atlantic to discuss British needs, including important information about the specific raw materials required by the weaponry the British wanted—information that the War and Navy departments consistently refused to supply. Nelson had preliminary estimates ready on December 3. Meanwhile, the auto industry agreed to curb production by 40 percent, and Nelson cut back steel allocation for many civilian projects, including one of the President's personal favorites, the St. Lawrence Seaway. "Don, you're killing my children!" FDR protested, but he went along. The planning for all-out war was now underway, but Nelson later commented that it could never have been implemented had not the United States actually entered the war after Pearl Harbor.[53]

In sharp contrast to the spring, when the President had been confined to bed and difficult to engage, Roosevelt was now deeply involved in specific issues as well as overall policy. The defeat of Germany on the ground required more tanks, and Stimson found that subject very much on FDR's mind when he went to the White House on September 17, when the Victory Program discussions were nearing a climax. "He is making a study of that [tank] production himself and is going over the figures with great penetration and great shrewdness," Stimson wrote. "It is marvelous how he can give so much attention to a detail and to do it so well as he has done this and it is an instance, I am bound to say, of which I have seen carried out in many other ways. He has spread himself out extremely thin but nevertheless he does carry a very wonderful memory and a great amount of penetrative shrewdness into each of these activities." Roosevelt, who seems to have come around to the idea that the war would be decided on land, specifically ordered the doubling of light and medium tank production on September 25, triggering a new fight between the Navy and the War Department over the machine tools and materials that this would require. The fight, which involved balancing the needs of shipbuilding, heavy bomber construction, and tank production, lasted for two months, but when the Joint Board finally resolved it on November 26, the President got his way.[54]

Roosevelt suffered his second devastating personal loss of the summer on September 7: the death of his aged yet still vigorous mother, Sarah Delano Roosevelt, at Hyde Park. Two days earlier, Eleanor Roosevelt—

whose visits to Hyde Park rarely coincided with her husband's—had summoned him urgently. He had taken a night train, as was his custom, arriving to find his eighty-six-year-old mother still alert on September 6. She soon sank into unconsciousness, however, and died the next day. Roosevelt rigidly controlled his emotions during the funeral, and when he returned to Washington several days later, he said nothing about the matter to any of his White House aides. Several weeks later, however, on his next visit to Hyde Park, his secretary Grace Tully brought him a mysterious box of his mother's effects. Opening it, they found his christening dress, locks of his and his mother's hair, and a neatly tied and organized collection of his letters home from Groton and Harvard. For the first time in their long association, Grace Tully saw tears in her boss's eyes, and he asked her to leave him alone.[55]

On other fronts, the President's personal life remained active during the summer, and he did not allow the world crisis to divert him from his hobbies. He was frequently in the company of two much younger women, the Crown Princess Martha of Norway and the actress Helen Gahagan, later Congresswoman Helen Gahagan Douglas. Meanwhile, inside the White House, he and Hopkins discussed a new idea of his, a project for a hurricane-proof house in the Florida Keys, during the month of October. Hopkins—whose health remained very frail—noted that Roosevelt intended the house, which would float and attach with cables to piers on shore, as a fishing retreat where they could spend two or three months every winter—a plan that was at least four years from execution. Roosevelt had picked out the site in the Florida Keys, and he set Hopkins to work on testing the practicality of the idea with the same zeal with which he had dispatched him to London and Moscow to talk about Lend-Lease, threatening, indeed, to send him to inspect the island during the President's next visit to Warm Springs. This was perhaps an imaginary substitute for taking another cruise at sea after the meeting with Churchill, something he did not manage to do for the remainder of 1941.[56]

The plans for total war were now in motion, both militarily and economically, but the world situation was more dire than ever as September turned to October, and the question was what was to be done *now*. The War Department was in effect planning three different wars against Germany at once. Hemispheric defense remained the first of them, because American authorities still had no confidence in long-term British survival. Stimson met with senior officers of the War Plans Division on

September 16 and tried to move them more aggressively toward the occupation of the Azores and Cape Verde islands, partly because he feared that German bombers with increased ranges could reach the United States should the Germans get to those islands first. The officers replied that such operations could be undertaken only at the expense of the occupation of the Natal region of Brazil, which they regarded as more important. The Cape Verdes could not be held if the Germans moved into North and West Africa, and occupying the Canaries and West Africa itself were definitely beyond U.S. capabilities. They were not willing to promise that the present level of American effort in the Atlantic could preserve Great Britain, but they did not propose to increase it. They were, however, convinced that long-range bombers could successfully defend Hawaii. Marshall also wanted to occupy Natal as soon as possible, but German influence appeared to grow in Brazil in October and November and the Brazilians refused to allow the entry of American forces into the region.[57]

The war in Europe went badly. The Germans won another spectacular victory against the Soviets at the end of September, seizing the Ukrainian capital of Kiev and more than 600,000 Soviet prisoners with it while completing the encirclement of Leningrad and resting at Smolensk, most of the way to Moscow. Should the USSR fall, Britain would be under immediate threat again. Marshall on October 11 asked his London observer General Chaney for information on British plans to resist invasion, and the reply two days later was anything but encouraging. The British, Chaney said, did not expect to be able to prevent an invasion, although they thought they could deny the Germans the ports they would need for supply. They were counting on the RAF and the Royal Navy for victory, and their ground troops were insufficient and underequipped. Chaney took the opportunity to propose the dispatch of a token force of one American division and supporting units to Britain, but the War Plans Division reacted unfavorably, arguing that outside the western hemisphere, U.S. troops should be used only in offensive operations. Stimson also asked what the United States could do to help the British, and War Plans replied on October 20 that the United States could send nothing but equipment unless it entered the war. At that point the United States might find five available divisions and a couple of bomber groups in the following six months, but the task of collecting and dispatching them would be enormous. One could not, they argued, wait until the invasion took place, since at that point the Germans would be able to block any aid sent. No plan was drawn up.[58]

Roosevelt, who was asking more and more direct questions about military moves, asked in early October to increase the Army garrison in Iceland to the point that the British troops there could return home and also inquired about sending the bombers based there to Britain. The Joint Board replied that the bombers would be needed in Iceland if the Germans sent another surface raider into the Atlantic.[59] The President also asked the War Department to look into more offensive action in the Atlantic and even in North or West Africa. He secured a new plan for the occupation of the Azores, but the War Department based it on the assumption that Portugal would not resist. He also asked for a plan for the seizure of Dakar on the West African coast, perhaps with the assent of the Vichy government. The War Department replied through Stimson that the undertaking would be a very large one, requiring tens of thousands of men and a huge naval task force, and could not be ready until November 1942—the exact date, as it turned out, of the invasion of North Africa with the French authorities' assent. Roosevelt still wanted to extend the U.S. defense perimeter in the Atlantic and onto the African continent if war came. At the same time, the eventual invasion and defeat of Germany was under study, and the Joint Board recognized that its views on that subject differed significantly from those of the British. Its comments on the strategic appreciation that the British had given American leaders at the Atlantic Conference questioned the idea that bombing could destroy Germany's will to fight, opposed bombing to destroy civilian morale, and argued that specific ground operations and their troop requirements had to become part of the plan. Thus began the argument that dominated Anglo-American relations for the next two years.[60]

Aid to the Soviet Union remained a high presidential priority. In the last few days of September, Averell Harriman, the President's new Lend-Lease envoy, met with British supply minister Lord Beaverbrook and Stalin in Moscow—the conference that Hopkins had proposed to Stalin in late July—and promised more urgent deliveries. The Soviets were now calling publicly as well as privately for an immediate British landing in France to relieve the pressure on them. Simultaneously, Roosevelt in late September asked Admiral Stark to have the Joint Board plan staff talks on military cooperation with the Soviets. On October 12, the President publicly promised more deliveries to the Soviet Union, and someone at the White House—perhaps the President himself—evidently gave a backgrounder to the press arguing that even if Moscow were encircled, the Soviet Union would be able to fight on indefinitely. The Joint Planning Committee on October 16 stated that in view of the past behavior of the Soviet leadership—which Admiral Turner and General Gerow thought might go over to the German side again—and the anti-Communism prevalent in the United States, the United States should not share war plans with the Soviets. A week later the Joint Board decided to hold the matter in abeyance pending a further order from the President. Roosevelt, Hopkins, and now Harriman seemed to be the only senior members of the administration with a realistic sense of the enormous importance of the Soviets to the coming war.[61]

Aid to Britain remained at least as controversial at the War Department, where Stimson became almost apoplectic over yet another allocation of heavy bombers to the British in September. Roosevelt, Stimson wrote with some exaggeration on October 15, is "entirely in the hands of people who see only the side of the other nations and who are wedded to the idea that with our weapons they can win the war. I am perfectly certain that they cannot, and perfectly certain that eventually we will have to fight and this method of nibbling away at our store of weapons is reducing our weapons down to what I fear is a dangerous thing." Determined to make a thorough record, Stimson wrote Roosevelt a long letter, informally endorsed by Marshall, arguing that the United States desperately needed a trained force of ten heavy bomber groups in the United States (about seven hundred aircraft), ready to go to the Far East, to Iceland, or to Newfoundland as needed, and that the repeated dispatch of planes to the British was making this impossible. Roosevelt referred the matter for comment to Hopkins, and no decision was reached.[62]

Over all these detailed preparations hung the critical question: When would the United States enter the war? In September the Joint Board had declared that the mobilization of the resources needed to defeat the Axis required entry into the war at the earliest possible date, and Wedemeyer had specifically called for entry by sometime in the spring of 1942. Yet Roosevelt showed no eagerness to move beyond the undeclared war in the Atlantic, both for the political reasons that he had explained to Churchill in August and because of the enormity of the task that the United States might face. The President had begun talking publicly about repealing or amending the Neutrality Act in early September, with particular reference to the arming of American merchant ships and sending ships into war zones, but several well-known isolationists immediately attacked the proposal, and not until October 9 did the President send Congress a message asking only for the arming of merchantmen. Hearings on Neutrality Act repeal now began, and on October 13, Stimson was appalled by the attitudes he encountered while testifying in executive session before the House Foreign Affairs Committee. "When those pettifoggers turned on me," he wrote in his diary, "I ripped them from end to end," pointing out that "there was a war going on in the Atlantic and the Far East."[63]

On October 8, Hull—who had long favored amending the Act—asked Stark for a frank statement of the advantages and disadvantages of repealing the Neutrality Act and getting into the war. Stark replied in writing the same day that while U.S. merchant ships would be faster than British ones and British manpower would be freed up for other uses, sending U.S. warships across the Atlantic was "impractical from a purely naval point of view"—perhaps an indication of his fear of losses. War would give the United States a freer hand at sea, encourage subjugated nations, and help to plan and prepare for Germany's defeat, but short-term results would be "disappointing." Japan might also come into the war, creating a big disadvantage, but Stark praised our "strong stand against Japanese aggression." But Germany in any case could only be defeated with American help, and thus, "on the whole, it is my opinion that the United States should enter the war against Germany as soon as possible, even if hostilities with Japan must be accepted." Hitler, Stark concluded presciently, would not attack the United States until he was good and ready. Stark had taken this position since the Plan Dog memorandum nearly a year earlier.[64]

War seemed increasingly likely in the Far East. On October 8, the Japanese informed the Germans that while the failure of the German-Soviet war to be concluded quickly had forced Japan "to open the way for a compromise in our relations with the United States," the talks with Washington were designed to secure "the use of the United States to coerce the Chiang regime," "to prevent the expansion of the European war, to seal peace in the Pacific area and to prevent the United States from entering the war." This message was immediately intercepted by U.S. intelligence in Washington. On October 16 Tokyo asked Nomura to warn the United States that if further shooting incidents in the Atlantic led to war between Germany and the United States, "Japan, as a signatory to the Tripartite Pact, naturally cannot help entertain a deep concern." But on the same day, political events within Japan transformed the situation.[65]

Having failed to move any closer to either a summit or an agreement, Konoye, in October, asked War Minister Tojo whether it might be possible to go to war with Great Britain without becoming involved in war with the United States. The Japanese Navy had already ruled that possibility out, and Konoye apparently received a negative response. On October 14 he claimed in a cabinet meeting that only the issue of troops in China stood in the way of an agreement now and that he could solve it by agreeing in principle to meet American terms. Tojo immediately dissented violently, and the Navy Minister supported war rather than capitulation. Konoye accordingly submitted his resignation on October 16. Some officials around the emperor hoped for a cabinet that would endeavor to reverse fundamental policy, but War Minister Tojo was appointed premier instead, together with new foreign and navy ministers. Fear for their lives at the hands of military death squads seemed to be influencing various officials. "Because the driving force is the middle-echelon officers of the army and navy who are committed to the decision of the [September 6] Imperial Conference," one palace official told Konoye after Tojo was appointed, "one could say that at this time of extraordinary tensions it is all but impossible to form a cabinet that would straight away indicate that it would change policy." The Roosevelt administration understood that Konoye's fall made war a near certainty. On October 16, Roosevelt, Stimson, Marshall, Knox, Stark, and Hopkins met for two hours to discuss the new situation. "We face the delicate question of the diplomatic fencing to be done so as to be sure that Japan was put into the wrong and made the first bad move—overt move," wrote Stimson.[66]

Arriving for the weekend at Hyde Park on the morning of October 17, the President was greeted by the news of the torpedoing of the destroyer *Kearny* off of Iceland, which the ship had survived. He appeared solemn and reserved when he met the press that morning and declined to make any comment on this development. Nonetheless, the incident apparently helped secure a resounding House vote of 257–136 in favor of arming merchant ships—although not, as yet, in favor of allowing American ships to enter war zones. In sharp contrast to the period of the Lend-Lease debate, Congress now included members of both parties ready to criticize the administration for being *insufficiently* belligerent as well as rabid isolationists. A few days after that vote, several Senators of both parties called for going even further and repealing the Neutrality Act entirely, allowing American ships to visit belligerent ports. On October 22, two more American merchant ships were lost to torpedoes near Iceland and off the African coast, and the White House definitely blessed the repeal of the Act in its entirety. On that same day, Wendell Willkie, six Republican governors, and dozens of Republican National Committeemen from around the country called for the repeal of the Neutrality Act and the "destruction of totalitarianism at any cost."[67]

A sense of impending climax pervaded Washington and the front pages of the nation's newspapers during the last ten days of October. Stimson had talked with Harry Hopkins on October 21, and Hopkins had encouraged him to tell the President that the United States simply had to get into the war now. The Secretary of War had taken his advice, referring to the necessity of action that would definitely gain the upper hand in the Battle of the Atlantic and protect the British Isles from invasion in a letter to the President, but he received no reply. While the Senate Foreign Relations Committee held hearings on the amendment or repeal of the Neutrality Act, General Robert Wood of America First demanded that FDR bluntly ask Congress to vote on a declaration of war. Rather than reply directly, Roosevelt on October 24 gave a press conference and revealed, in broad terms, the work on the Victory Program that was now underway. "Well, now that the Lend-Lease bill has passed both Houses," he said in reference to a new appropriations bill for Lend-Lease equipment, "I think it is all right for you to say something about the development and extension of the whole program of supplies for our own Army and Navy for the future, and also under Lend-Lease. Studies are being made along this line with the eventual objective of looking ahead as far as is possible, because, as you know, things change all the time. It might be called a comprehensive program—*call it an all-out program.*" He then discussed his decision vastly to expand the monthly production of tanks, based on the experience of the British in North Africa and the Soviets. Additional requests, he said, would increase the "victory armaments program" to the point where it would permit "the overwhelming of Hitlerism." On the next day, officials of the SPAB told the press that the production of consumer durables would probably be cut to zero in 1942 in order to devote a much larger portion of the gross national product to defense.[68]

In just four months since the attack on the Soviet Union, the United States had effectively gone to war in the western Atlantic while preparing for war in the Far East. The War and Navy departments had written up the requirements for total victory over the Tripartite Pact, and the SPAB was working hard to determine how and when they might be met. Roosevelt had committed the American people to the defeat of Nazi Germany and shared the outline of his mobilization plans with the public. Yet the world's destiny depended on events far beyond Washington's control. The campaigns in the Soviet Union and the Middle East still hung in the balance. Not for another year, according to all estimates, would American ground forces be ready to take an active, effective part in any conflict overseas, and the Victory Program did not hope to reach full production before July 1, 1943. That program, as everyone seemed to realize, could not possibly be put into effect in peacetime, and the President evidently did not believe he could ask for a declaration of war.

While incidents in the Atlantic and Magic intercepts indicated that war might in fact break out at any moment, the initiative remained with the Germans and Japanese. The possibility that so worried Stimson—that the war in Europe might be over before the United States could take any effective part—was still quite real. "The President of the United States," Robert Sherwood wrote years later, "was now the creature of circumstance which must be shaped not by his own will or his own ingenuity but by the unpredictable determination of his enemies. It is small wonder that he attempted in his spare time to find surcease by figuring out means of anchoring a holiday cottage against West Indian hurricanes."[69]

CHAPTER 9

To Pearl Harbor,
October–December 1941

BY LATE OCTOBER 1941, THE GOVERNMENT OF THE UNITED STATES HAD gone as far as it could toward world war without actually entering the conflict. For months, Roosevelt's speeches had been preparing the American people for the world conflict that now seemed certain to occur, and secret plans now existed not only to fight it, but to win it. Yet continuing debates on the Neutrality Act confirmed, as Roosevelt had warned Churchill in August, that Congress was not yet ready to declare war. Open war with both Germany and Japan—which Magic intercepts showed to be inevitable—also posed grave dangers because the United States was not ready to fight. Yet events during October and November, including a crippling mineworkers' strike called by the isolationist John L. Lewis, showed that only war would allow the country to pull together and commit its enormous resources. War and war alone would allow the administration to disclose and implement the plans now known as the Victory Program.

As it turned out, the situation remained tense but stable in the Atlantic during October and November, although only chance averted a serious naval battle that would probably have led immediately to war. Meanwhile, Magic intercepts in the wake of the advent of the Tojo cabinet in Tokyo showed clearly that Japan would begin hostilities in late November or early December—but with whom? Roosevelt, Stimson, Knox, and Hull worried up until the last minute that Japan might strike Dutch and perhaps British possessions while leaving the United States alone, leaving the initiative for war with the United States. In November, they decided that the United States would indeed enter the war in that case, knowing full well that Germany would surely declare war on the United States as well. Roosevelt was now ready to take up the challenge he had identified in his acceptance speech at the Democratic Convention in 1936, in the quarantine speech of September 1937, and repeatedly in 1940–1941: the preservation of democracy against totalitarian aggression.

The attention of the American people in late October and early November focused on the debate over the Neutrality Act, more incidents in the Atlantic, and a new labor crisis provoked by that unrepentant isolationist John L. Lewis. Communist-led strikes had ceased abruptly in late June after the German attack on the Soviet Union, but Lewis's views had not changed, and on October 25, Lewis led the United Mine Workers (UMW) out on strike against mines owned and operated by steel companies, threatening another roadblock in the way of defense production. Roosevelt immediately appealed to Lewis publicly to end the strike for the sake of national defense. Proposals for neutrality repeal continued moving through Congress.[1]

October 27 was Navy Day, and the President gave his most belligerent address to the nation yet from the Mayflower Hotel in Washington, calling the roll of the home states of the sailors killed in the torpedo attack on the *Kearny* and confirming, in effect, that the United States was at war in the Atlantic. "We have wished to avoid shooting," he said. "But the shooting has started. And history has recorded who fired the first shot. In the long run, however, all that will matter is who fired the last shot. . . . America has been attacked," he added, implicitly referencing his 1940 pledge that American boys would not be sent into foreign wars "except in case of attack."[2]

The President claimed to have in his possession two captured documents detailing Nazi plans, one that would divide Latin America into a number of Nazi puppet states and a second proposing the abolition of all the world's religions and their replacement with a Nazi religion. "We are pledged to pull our own oar in the destruction of Hitlerism," he continued, echoing the Atlantic Charter. "And when we have helped to end the curse of Hitlerism we shall help to establish a new peace which will give to decent people everywhere a better chance to live and prosper in security and in freedom and in faith." He effectively asked for the complete repeal of the Neutrality Act and attacked Lewis for the coal strike. "Our

Nation will and must speak from every assembly line, from every coal mine—the all-inclusive whole of our vast industrial machine." The growing American output could not be hampered either by selfish businessmen or by "a small but dangerous minority of labor leaders," a "menace to the true cause of labor itself, as well as to the Nation as a whole." The German press violently denounced the speech.[3]

On October 31, Roosevelt met with Lewis and steel industry representatives and secured their agreement to await a recommendation from the National Defense Mediation Board while the workers returned to work. On the same day, the government announced that another U.S. destroyer, the *Reuben James*, had been torpedoed and sunk with the loss of 115 members of the ship's company. The President indicated no imminent change in American policy before leaving for five days in Hyde Park that night, to include a meeting with Canadian Prime Minister McKenzie King. The debate on the Neutrality Act continued in the Senate until November 7, when the Act was essentially gutted, although not repealed, by a vote of 50–37, nineteen days after the President had asked for its amendment. The bill lifted the restrictions on sending American ships into war zones.[4]

Two days earlier, on November 5, only chance prevented a full-scale naval battle between an American task force and the German pocket battleship *Scheer* in the Denmark Strait between Iceland and Greenland, the site of the *Bismarck*'s battle with the *Hood* and the *Prince of Wales*. The British Ultra intelligence operation had intercepted news of the *Scheer*'s sortie, but mechanical trouble forced it to turn back before U.S. warships encountered it. Such a battle would almost surely have resulted in a declaration of war.[5]

The mediation of the coal strike seemed likely to fail, and on November 7, Roosevelt and Stimson agreed that the Army would have to seize the affected mines if the strike resumed. The union wanted a closed shop—a requirement that all the affected miners join the UMW—and Roosevelt opposed Lewis on this point. The entire CIO was now meeting in convention and decided to back Lewis and threaten what amounted to a general industrial strike. "I want you to tell [CIO President Phil] Murray," Roosevelt told Henry Morgenthau on November 10, "that they can't have a closed shop in this coal mine and that if he's going to call out the entire CIO, it's the CIO against the Government; and while I'd hate to get into a war with Japan, we'll lick them in the long run, and the same thing holds true with CIO. If we get into a fight with them, the Government will win." The crisis escalated over the next ten days, as Murray and other CIO members submitted their resignations from the National Defense Mediation Board and an additional 200,000 miners walked out in sympathy. But on November 22, at the very last minute, Lewis caved in, accepting arbitration after he learned the identity of the neutral mediator who would join business and labor representatives to impose a settlement. There was no guarantee, however, that he might not renew his disruptive efforts at any moment, and by the end of November, Congress was working on a bill to restrict strikes in defense industries with Roosevelt's support.[6]

In the week of November 7–14 the isolationists mounted an impressive counterattack on Neutrality Act repeal in the House of Representatives, where some southern Democrats tried to use their votes as leverage to secure a firm antistrike bill. Appeals from Roosevelt and Hull secured passage of the Senate bill in the House on November 14 by a narrow vote of 212–194, substantially less than the Democratic majority in the chamber. The debate and the votes certainly seemed to confirm Roosevelt's prediction to Churchill in August that a request for a formal declaration of war would have taken months to reach a vote. By late November Roosevelt had authorized armed merchant ships to sail to Britain and to northern Russia in principle, and the Navy was planning transatlantic convoys of American merchant ships and warships, which could easily have brought the United States into the war. But while American opinion focused on the Atlantic, the Japanese had decided on war.[7]

Konoye's fall in mid-October had left the Tojo cabinet with only one obstacle to war, the continuing refusal of the Japanese Navy, which would have to deal with the United States, to agree to war without an increased commitment of budgetary resources. The objections of the Japanese Navy were easily overcome. During the last two weeks of October, Japanese naval leaders signed on to imminent hostilities in exchange for an increase in their allocation of critical materials, particularly steel.[8]

On November 1–2, a Liaison Conference of leading ministers and an Imperial Conference adopted a new document, "Essentials for Carrying out the Empire's Policies," stating that Japan was now determined "to go to war against the United States, Britain, and Holland." The document also included two proposals, A and B, for a settlement with the United States. Proposal A insisted on stationing troops in various parts of China for twenty-five years and remaining in Indochina until the China incident was settled. It also reaffirmed Japan's obligations under the Tripartite Pact and insisted on leaving Hull's four principles out of a final agreement. Proposal B, a much more limited proposal that was approved over the strong objections of the army, called for both sides to renounce any further military advances; for the United States to cooperate in securing needed Japanese resources from the Dutch East Indies; and for the United States to restore normal trade and to do nothing to impede the settlement of the China incident, a euphemism for stopping aid to Chiang. Proposal B might also include some unspecified, and thus probably very vague, provision about the Tripartite Pact.[9]

Proposals A and B were transmitted to the Japanese Embassy in Washington on November 4 and promptly decoded by American intelligence and passed to senior policymakers. The Japanese Foreign Ministry also informed Nomura that a special envoy, Saburu Kurusu, was on his way to the United States by air with the mission of explaining the situation in Japan to Nomura—that is, that in the absence of a most unlikely agreement, war would break out within a month. In another message on November 5, Togo repeated to Nomura, "This is the Imperial Government's final step.... Absolutely no delays can be permitted. Please bear this in mind and do your best. I wish to stress this point over and over." The Magic intelligence officers decoded this message on the same day.[10]

It is not entirely clear whether Tokyo had any genuine hope of an agreement or whether Togo was simply trying to keep talks going until military operations began. Two days earlier, on November 3, Ambassador Grew had warned that war was certain if no agreement could be reached. Both governments spoke openly of the possibility of trouble, and on November 8, Roosevelt told a press conference that the U.S. Marines stationed in China since the Boxer Rebellion would shortly come home.[11]

On November 1–2, a weekend, Hull convened meetings with military and naval representatives at the State Department to discuss reports from Chiang Kai-shek that the Japanese were about to attack Kunming from Indochina and to determine whether this would trigger the American armed response about which Roosevelt had warned Nomura on August 17. Those reports were false, part of the Japanese disinformation campaign to conceal the preparations for the southward advance. A

month earlier, in early October, Stimson had told Hull that the War Department needed three more months to complete the reinforcement of
the Philippines. Hull now wanted to know if the Army and Navy would
back up a new warning to Japan with force, and the Joint Board took up
this question on November 3.[12]

With the United States now heavily involved in the Battle of the Atlantic, senior officials showed little enthusiasm for a Pacific war. Admiral
Stark repeated that Germany was the main enemy and implied that the
United States could not afford to divert the necessary resources to a war
in the Pacific. He recommended action against the Japanese should they
attack Dutch or British possessions but *not* if they simply mounted a new
attack on China or even moved against the Soviets in Siberia. General
Marshall concurred that "due consideration should be given to the fact
that the Navy was now fighting a battle in the Atlantic" and argued that
U.S. reinforcements in the Philippines, including both heavy bombers
and submarines, would have a powerful deterrent effect on the Japanese,
especially after more had arrived by December 15.[13]

All summer long, Stark and the War Plans Division of the War Department had preferred to believe that they might avoid war with Japan.
With war imminent, Marshall and Stark wrote a November 5 memorandum for the President asking to avoid war with Japan for a few months
more. "At the present time," they wrote, "the United States Fleet in the
Pacific is inferior to the Japanese Fleet and cannot undertake an unlimited strategic offensive in the Western Pacific." Such an offensive would
require withdrawing all warships from the Atlantic and an enormous
number of merchant ships needed elsewhere, and Britain might lose the
Battle of the Atlantic as a result. Current plans called for a defensive naval posture should war break out, and the two men expressed confidence
that by mid-February the bombers and submarines in the Philippines
would make a Japanese attack on them "a hazardous undertaking." Although they repeated that the United States should fight if the Japanese
attacked British, Dutch, or U.S. possessions, they clearly hoped to delay
war for at least a few months.[14]

On the same day that Marshall and Stark submitted their memorandum, November 5, a new and chilling message from Tokyo to Nomura
was decoded. "Because of various circumstances," it read, "it is absolutely
necessary that all arrangements for the signing of this agreement be
completed by the 25th of this month. . . . Please understand this thor-

oughly and tackle the problem of saving the Japanese-U.S. relations from falling into a chaotic condition." On November 3 the Japanese official news agency had warned that Tojo would announce a deadline for an agreement with the United States on November 15, and on November 5 the Japanese press revealed that the government wanted an essentially free hand in China and the whole Far East. American policymakers now knew war might well break out in the last week of November, although they could not know exactly whom, and where, the Japanese would attack.[15]

The memorandum and the intercept had immediate repercussions. On November 6, Roosevelt saw Stimson and floated the possibility of a six-month truce with the Japanese to "give us further time." Stimson disagreed, wanting to complete the reinforcement of the Philippines and to maintain the morale of the Chinese. On November 7, Roosevelt finally put nine months of procrastination to an end and put the issue of war and peace squarely before the cabinet for the first time. The President, Stimson recorded, began by recalling the story of Lincoln asking his cabinet's opinion, receiving nothing but nay votes, and replying that he disagreed, and "the ayes have it." He then polled them on "whether the people would back us up in case we struck at Japan down there [in the Far East] and what the tactics should be. It was a very interesting talk—the best Cabinet Meeting I think we have ever had since we have been there. It was unanimous in feeling the country would support us. He said that this time the vote IS unanimous, he feeling the same way." The critical possibility they discussed, subsequent discussions made clear, was that Japan might attack British and Dutch possessions while leaving the Philippines and other U.S. possessions alone. Both the President and the cabinet evidently favored war in that case and were determined to bring the nation along with them. Yet the President took Marshall's and Stark's wishes for delay sufficiently seriously to explore the possibility of some sort of truce to at least delay war in the Far East.[16]

On November 10, Roosevelt, who was about to visit his polio treatment retreat in Warm Springs, Georgia, saw Nomura, who presented him, in effect, with the rough outlines of the Japanese Proposal A and repeated that while the Japanese would make their own decision under the Tripartite Pact should the United States join the war in Europe, they did not accept the broad American definition of self-defense. The President, who had the advantage of having seen decoded intercepts of Proposal A and Proposal B, referred to the possibility of finding some modus vivendi,

that is, interim arrangement—although he laid stress on the need to reaffirm stated American principles in any agreement and on Japan's display of an intent to pursue a peaceful course. On the next day, the Far
Eastern desk of the State Department drafted some suggestions for a
temporary settlement, albeit on terms, including a reaffirmation of Hull's
four points, which the Japanese government would not possibly accept.
In a press conference on November 14, Roosevelt declined to say whether
war in the Pacific could be avoided.[17]

On November 15, General Marshall gave an extraordinary background
briefing to correspondents from the *New York Times*, the *New York Herald Tribune*, *Time*, *Newsweek*, and the three wire services, attempting to
intimidate the Japanese by threatening them with destruction. The
United States, he said, was now on the brink of war with Japan—and was
"preparing for an offensive war against Japan, whereas the Japs believe
we are preparing only to defend the Philippines." Referring to the ongoing dispatch of B-17s to the Philippines, he said that he wanted this information to leak to the Japanese, whom it might deter from war. "If war
with the Japanese does come," a reporter wrote his editor, "we'll fight
mercilessly. Flying fortresses will be dispatched immediately to set the
paper cities of Japan on fire. There won't be any hesitation about bombing
civilians—it will be all-out." Although the B-17s could not make round
trips from the Philippines to Japanese cities and back, Marshall hoped to
arrange to land them at Vladivostok in the Soviet Far East. A number of
optimistic stories about the course and outcome of a possible war in the
Far East appeared during the next few days, and on November 19 a *New
York Times* analysis specifically discussed the possibility of a bombing
campaign against Japan based in the Philippines, Alaska, and Siberia in
some detail. On November 21, Marshall ordered MacArthur to plan for
offensive air operations against the Japanese and in defense of the Philippines should war break out. As special envoy Kurusu arrived in the
United States, the final crisis was at hand.[18]

War preparations were also moving forward on the most revolutionary
new front of all. Marshall's estimates of the capabilities of American air
power were several years premature, but in that same month of November, American authorities laid the foundation for even more far-reaching
developments. "Dr. Vannevar Bush," Stimson recorded on November 6,
"came in to convey to me an extremely secret statement from the Scien-

tific Research and Development office—a most terrible thing." Bush, an engineer, was the President of the Carnegie Institute in Washington, and his meeting with Stimson was a key milestone on the road that led within four years to the development of the atomic bomb.[19]

The idea of nuclear fission—the splitting of uranium atoms, releasing unprecedented amounts of energy, with clear military implications—had been published in scientific journals during the interwar years and demonstrated about a year before the European war broke out. Many physicists, including émigrés driven from Europe by Nazi and Fascist persecution, worried that a dictatorship might take advantage of it to build a bomb of unprecedented power. The Hungarian Leo Szilard and the German Albert Einstein, the author of the theory of relativity, conferred on the matter during the summer of 1939 and enlisted Alexander Sachs, a Russian-born social scientist who had helped write speeches for Roosevelt in 1932 and worked at the National Recovery Administration (NRA), to approach the President about the danger and opportunity of atomic energy. Sachs secured an appointment and explained the concept to FDR on October 11, 1939. "Personally I think there is no doubt that sub-atomic energy is available all around us, and that one day man will release and control its almost infinite power," he concluded. "We cannot prevent him from doing so and can only hope that he will not use it exclusively in blowing up his next door neighbor." "Alex," said Roosevelt, "what you are after is to see that the Nazis don't blow us up." "Precisely," Sachs replied, and the President turned the problem over to his aide Pa Watson.

Watson convened a committee of representatives from the Army, Navy, and Bureau of Standards, and by November 1 Sachs and four nuclear physicists had convinced the committee to recommend further research. Vannevar Bush was simultaneously assembling scientists to work on military problems, and in May 1940, with the help of Harry Hopkins, he got Roosevelt to establish his new National Defense Research Council (NDRC). One of its members was Harvard President James Bryant Conant, a strong supporter of entry into the war. He discussed the possibility of nuclear fission with Frederick Lindemann, Churchill's scientific adviser, on a visit to Britain in the winter of 1940–1941. In mid-1941 Bush created a new Office of Scientific Research and Development, with himself as head reporting directly to the President, and turned the NDRC over to Conant. Both American and British scientists were increasingly convinced that an atomic bomb was feasible, and a larger group of scientists met with Roosevelt on October 9, 1941. The President evidently had no trouble grasping the significance of what they told him, and he put their work under a new Top Policy Group, including Vice President Wallace, Stimson, General Marshall, Bush, and Conant. While not yet charged with building a bomb, they set out to determine whether it could be built. The briefing Stimson received on November 6 undoubtedly dealt with their third feasibility report, which suggested that it could.[20]

Although the population of the United States in 1941 was nearly half of what it is today, its educated elite, which provided the senior personnel of the New Deal and the war effort, was both far more culturally homogeneous and much, much smaller. They lived in an extraordinarily creative and destructive era of human history, and their very homogeneity, combined with their common devotion to the essential values of the United States, enabled them to both reach and carry out decisions at an astonishing speed. Along with the development of long-range air power, the possibility of nuclear fission promised to make the world war decisive on every front. The outcome of the struggle would determine how the human race would live for many decades. Roosevelt had understood the importance of naval supremacy for most of his life, and he had recognized the importance of air power to the coming conflict as early as 1938. Now, just two years after first hearing of the possibility of atomic energy, he had taken steps that would allow the United States to lead the world into a new, terrifying, but surely inevitable age. Sooner or later the United States would find itself at war with the Axis powers, and Roosevelt had taken yet another huge step to assure that it would prevail.

During the second week of November, while Saburu Kurusu flew across the Pacific and the continental United States, the Pacific crisis heated up in public. Churchill, who still believed that the Japanese would not dare attack the Anglo-Saxon powers, had sent two battleships, the *Prince of Wales* and the *Repulse*, to the Far East, and on November 10 he declared publicly that Britain would join the war in the Pacific at once if Japan attacked the United States. The Japanese immediately retorted that the British hoped that the United States would preserve the empire they could no longer hold onto themselves. Speaking in Providence, Secretary Knox declared firmly that the United States had to stand by its principles in the talks with the Japanese even at the risk of war, declared the situation in the Pacific just as critical as that in the Atlantic, and sketched out plans for a postwar world based on justice. The President himself, in an Armistice Day address in Arlington, said that war might be forced upon the United States at any moment.[21]

Kurusu finally arrived in Washington, where Roosevelt had postponed his trip to Warm Springs, on November 15, and saw Hull and the President on November 17 and Hull again the next day. Hull insisted repeatedly that the Tripartite Pact stood in the way of an agreement, and Kurusu and Nomura had nothing new to offer. Roosevelt, bending very slightly, repeated his offer to "introduce" the Japanese and Chinese governments to one another and said that he did not expect Japan immediately to evacuate China. Hull also indicated, however, that both China and Great Britain would have to sign on to any new agreement. Meanwhile, Foreign Minister Togo on November 15 reaffirmed the November 25 deadline for the talks as "an absolutely immovable one." Grew on November 17 warned Washington of "the need to guard against sudden Japanese naval or military actions in such areas as are not now involved in the Chinese theater of operations."[22]

With war looming, both sides made new moves. After an important exchange of telegrams between Washington and Tokyo, Nomura and Kurusu presented a modified Proposal B on November 20. On November 15, Togo had sent a draft of Proposal B that included a reaffirmation of Japan's obligations under the Tripartite Pact. Nomura on November 14 had warned the government that any advance north or south would mean war with the United States and pleaded with them to reconsider their policy, but Togo did not reply. The proposal that Nomura submitted dropped the mention of the Tripartite Pact but nonetheless failed to impress Hull, who insisted yet again that that pact stood in the way of an agreement. Thanks to Magic, the top U.S. policymakers knew Nomura had ignored his instructions in an effort to reach agreement.[23]

The day before, Treasury Secretary Morgenthau had weighed in with a plan for a general settlement in the Far East, including the redeployment of the U.S. Fleet, a nonaggression pact among all the Pacific powers, Japanese withdrawal from China and Manchuria, and concessions to the Japanese on immigration and economic matters. The State Department immediately shared the plan with Admiral Stark and General Gerow of War Plans, who made clear that they still hoped to avoid war in the Far East. More importantly, the Far Eastern Division of the State Department produced several versions of a possible modus vivendi from November 22

Ambassador Admiral Nomura (left), Secretary of State Hull, and special envoy Saburu Kurusu arriving at the White House, November 17, 1941. (Courtesy of Corbis-Bettman.)

through November 24. A preliminary agreement, set to run for three months, would provide the Japanese with oil for their civilian needs in exchange for a withdrawal from southern Indochina and a limitation of 25,000 troops in northern Indochina. A subsequent general settlement would broadly follow the Morgenthau plan, reflecting American principles. Showing that he was serious, Hull immediately showed it to the British, Australian, Dutch, and Chinese representatives in Washington, explaining that the Army and Navy very much wanted to avoid immediate war with the Japanese. They generally reacted favorably.[24]

On the same day, November 22, a Magic intercept quoted Foreign Minister Togo to the effect that an agreement had to be signed by November 29, with Great Britain and the Netherlands on board. "This time we mean it, that the deadline absolutely cannot be changed," he said. "After that things are automatically going to happen." On November 24, after further consultations with the Far Eastern allies—of whom only the Dutch Ambassador was authorized to accept the proposal—Hull drafted and gave Roosevelt a cable for Churchill summarizing the American proposal. "This seems to me a fair proposition for the Japanese," Roosevelt added to the telegram, "but its acceptance or rejection is really a matter of internal Japanese politics. I am not very hopeful and we must all be prepared for real trouble, possibly soon." And on the next day, the President himself sent Hull a brief handwritten note proposing a 4-point modus vivendi: the Americans to send Japan some oil and rice now and more later; Japan to send no more troops to Indochina, the Manchurian border, or anywhere to the south and southwest; Japan to agree not to invoke the Tripartite Pact if the United States entered the European war; and the United States to facilitate talks between the Japanese and Chinese without taking part. The President seemed willing to make an interim agreement with the Japanese that would buy Marshall and Stark the time they needed, *but only if the Japanese would promise to stay out of a war between the United States and Germany.* This, all the intercepts and conversations showed, Tokyo would not do.[25]

On the morning of Tuesday, November 25, Stimson met Hull, who showed him the latest State Department draft of the modus vivendi, which he planned to give the Japanese on that day or the next. Stimson remarked that it "adequately safeguarded our interests" but added, rightly, that he did not see how the Japanese could accept it, since it promised them oil only for civilian needs and demanded an immediate pull-back in Indochina. Then at noon Stimson went to the White House to meet the President with Marshall, Knox, Hull, and Stark. He expected to discuss the Victory Program, but Roosevelt evidently had the Magic intercept promising automatic action after November 29 on his mind.

"The President," Stimson wrote, "instead of bringing up the Victory Parade [*sic*], brought up entirely the relations with the Japanese. He brought up the event that we were likely to be attacked perhaps (as soon as) next Monday [November 30], for the Japanese are notorious for making an attack without warning, and the question was what we should do.

The question was how we should maneuver them into the position of firing the first shot without allowing too much danger to ourselves." Continuing, Stimson's account indicated that the U.S. leadership was
worrying the most about the possibility of a Japanese attack on Thailand
and on Dutch and British possessions and how they would explain
American entry into the war in response. "Hull laid out his general broad
propositions on which the thing should be rested—the freedom of the
seas and the fact that Japan was in alliance with Hitler and was carrying
out his policy of world aggression. The others brought out the fact that any
such expedition to the South as the Japanese were likely to take would be
an encirclement of our interests in the Philippines. . . . So Hull is to work
on preparing that," Stimson wrote—as indeed Hull shortly did.[26]

When Stimson returned to the War Department, he found a G-2 intelligence report to the effect that about five Japanese divisions had
boarded between thirty and fifty ships in Shanghai and were now south
of Formosa. Stimson immediately informed Hull by telephone and sent
him and Roosevelt copies of the report. Suddenly the modus vivendi looked
like too little and too late. In fact, the convoys were the latest stage in preparations for a southward advance that had begun months earlier, and the
Japanese Army and Navy had of course given up any thought of attacking
only the Dutch or the Dutch and the British some time before.[27]

The modus vivendi's chances dimmed still further during the next
eighteen hours. That afternoon, November 25, the Chinese Ambassador
came to see Hull and passed on Chiang Kai-shek's acute displeasure,
amounting almost to despair, that the United States might lift the oil embargo and deal a devastating blow to Chinese morale. The British Ambassador, Lord Halifax, did not turn down the proposal completely but
argued that 25,000 Japanese troops in Indochina would still be too many
and held out no hope of a quick agreement. And on the morning of November 26, Hull was greeted by a cable to Roosevelt from Churchill himself, echoing Chiang's concern about a Chinese collapse and arguing that
the Japanese were "most unsure of themselves."[28]

Franklin Roosevelt was accustomed to handling many matters at
once. At 9:40 a.m. on the fateful morning of November 26, Treasury Secretary Morgenthau came to the White House to report that the government would be borrowing $1.5 billion during the next week at about 2.5
percent interest. Then Morgenthau gingerly brought up a recent cabinet
meeting in which the President had remarked, apparently, that no more

Jews could be appointed to federal government positions in Oregon. The President, said Morgenthau, might have left the impression that he "didn't want too many Jews in the government." "Well, you completely misunderstood the thing," Roosevelt replied excitedly. "I think it is much better to discuss this thing out in the open." He recalled how, some years earlier, one-third of the entering class at Harvard had been Jewish. "I talked it over with your father," said Roosevelt, referring to Henry Morgenthau Sr., who had served as Ambassador to the Ottoman Empire under Wilson. "I asked him whether we should discuss it with the Board of Overseers and it was decided that we should." In the next few years, the number of Jews had fallen gradually to 15 percent. "I treat the Catholic situation just the same," he continued. "I appointed three men in Nebraska—all Catholics—and they wanted me to appoint another Catholic, and I said I wouldn't do it because I had appointed three already, and that was enough. . . . You can't get a disproportionate amount of any one religion." FDR took a call from Hull during the conversation and brought Morgenthau up to date on Hull's talks about the modus vivendi with the British and on Chiang's reaction.[29]

Roosevelt saw Chinese representatives at 2:30 that afternoon, and the Secretary of State arrived at the White House at 3:45 p.m. with two documents. The first, a proposal for a general settlement in the Far East, began with a reaffirmation of Hull's Four Points, and following Morgenthau's November 21 proposal, proposed a nonaggression pact among all the major Pacific powers. It then reaffirmed in the strongest terms all the principles of the Nine Power Treaty regarding the territorial integrity of China and called on the Japanese to withdraw all troops from Indochina and China (it was not clear whether Manchuria was meant as well) and to recognize no Chinese government other than that of Chiang Kai-shek. It also made clear that the Tripartite Pact could not be allowed to hamper the purpose of this agreement, the maintenance of peace in the Pacific.

The second document was the latest draft of the modus vivendi. "In view of the opposition of the Chinese Government and either the half-hearted support or the actual opposition of the British, the Netherlands and the Australian Governments," Hull told the President, "and in view of the wide publicity of the opposition and of the additional opposition that will naturally follow . . . I desire very earnestly to recommend that at this time I call in the Japanese Ambassadors and hand to them a copy of the comprehensive basic proposal for a general peaceful settlement, and at the same time withhold the *modus vivendi* proposal." The President agreed. He did so, in all probability, not because of the attitudes of the Chinese and the British, but because of the growing, irrefutable evidence that the Japanese had decided on war within the next few days.[30]

When Hull handed the Japanese the document that afternoon, Kurusu immediately pronounced the provisions on China and the nonaggression pact completely unacceptable. The next morning, November 27, Stimson got more news of the large Japanese expeditionary force heading southward, perhaps to invade the Dutch East Indies, Malaya, or the Philippines, but "probably," he preferred to believe, on its way to Thailand to stage for a subsequent attack. He immediately called Hull to see if he had given the Japanese the modus vivendi and found "he had broken the whole matter off." "I have washed my hands of it," Hull said, "and it is now in the hands of you and Knox—of the Army and Navy." Then Stimson called FDR, who paid tribute to the "magnificent statement prepared by Hull," which had essentially finished off the talks. That afternoon Roosevelt saw Nomura and Kurusu and told them that while he had always favored peace, the occupation of Indochina had thrown cold water on his efforts. It is difficult to fault his judgment on this point, since the move into southern Indochina was the first step in a broader southward advance that the Japanese were determined to pursue even at the risk of war with Britain and the United States. He also made clear that he anticipated another imminent Japanese military move. "We remain convinced that Japan's own best interests will not be served by following Hitlerism, and courses of aggression," Roosevelt said. "If, however, Japan should unfortunately decide to follow Hitlerism and courses of aggression, we are convinced beyond any shadow of doubt that Japan will be the ultimate loser."[31]

In subsequent decades, a number of historians have argued that Roosevelt backed away from the modus vivendi and allowed the crisis with Japan to lead to armed conflict in order to find a "back door to war" in Europe, but this view does not square either with the reality of the situation or with Washington's view of it. To begin with, Magic intercepts and Hull's negotiations had repeatedly made clear that Japan would come into the war with the United States as soon as the United States became involved in war with Germany in any case and that fighting only in Europe was not an option. Most important of all, by early November, intelligence showed that the Japanese were certain to make a new attack in the Far East. Roosevelt and his cabinet had decided that such an attack would bring the United States into the world war—even if it did not strike U.S. possessions. But the Japanese Navy had already relieved them of the need to reach that decision, since naval authorities had successfully insisted that an immediate attack on the United States had to accompany the invasion of British Malaya and the Dutch East Indies. War was now coming to the United States, just as Roosevelt had warned that it would as early as September 1937.

On November 27, the day after Hull had effectively broken off the talks, Stark alerted Admiral Kimmel, the commander of the Pacific Fleet, and other Pacific commands that war was about to begin. "This dispatch is to be considered a war warning," it began. "Negotiations with Japan . . . have ceased and an aggressive move by Japan is expected within the next few days," most likely against "either the Philippines, Thai or Kra Peninsula or possibly Borneo. *Execute an appropriate defensive deployment* preparatory to carrying out the tasks assigned in WPL 46 [Rainbow 5]" (emphasis added). General Walter Short, the Army commander in Hawaii, received a similar warning. On that same day, Marshall and Stark gave Roosevelt a new memo on the situation in the Far East, arguing that the United States and its allies should go to war only if the Japanese attacked American, British, or Dutch possessions or moved beyond a certain specified point in Thailand so as to threaten Burma or Malaya. They emphasized the need for more time to complete the reinforcement of the Philippines, which they thought would vastly increase the chances of holding on to them. Roosevelt left for Warm Springs on the next day, November 28, and returned on December 1. In the meantime, Hull, Stimson, and Knox, following up on the "firing the first shot" meeting of November 25, worked on drafts of a presidential message to Congress apparently designed to secure a declaration of war if the Japanese attacked British and Dutch possessions in the Far East.[32]

Neither Tokyo nor Washington, meanwhile, made the slightest effort to conceal the imminence of war. On November 26 in Tokyo—before Hull had in effect broken off negotiations—Tojo and other Japanese ministers announced the renewal of the Anti-Comintern Pact—originally signed in 1936 by Germany, Italy, and Japan to fight Communism—with the additional signatures of the governments of Hungary, Spain, Finland, Denmark, Croatia, Bulgaria, Rumania, Slovakia, Manchukuo, and the puppet Chinese regime in Nanking in bellicose speeches leaving nothing to the imagination. Various Japanese officials cited "the establishing of a New Order in Asia as the basis of [Japan's] national policy," trumpeted the need "to frustrate the Anglo-Saxon command of the seas exercised since the nineteenth century," and proclaimed the need "fighting with all its power" to establish the East Asia Co-Prosperity Sphere and emancipate East Asia from the bondage of the white races. "We must win victory over [Britain and the United States] at any cost," said General Suzuki of the Army's Planning Board. On November 27 huge headlines in virtually every newspaper in the United States announced the failure of the talks with the Japanese and described Hull's new demands in great detail. Editorials in the *New York Times*, the *Christian Science Monitor*, the antiadministration *Los Angeles Times*, and the *Washington Post* praised Hull's stance and calmly left the choice between war and peace in the hands of the Japanese.[33]

While Roosevelt was in Georgia, three more critical Magic intercepts had been decoded. On November 28, intelligence decoded a nine-day-old message transmitting the "Winds Code," a list of weather messages that would signal Japanese officials abroad of an imminent break in relations with the United States, the USSR, or Britain at the end of a weather report. Even more significantly, a November 29 message from Tokyo to Berlin, decoded on December 1, instructed the Ambassador to inform the Germans that "there is extreme danger that war may suddenly break out between the Anglo-Saxon nations and Japan through some clash of arms and that the time of the breaking out of this war may come quicker than anyone dreams." A missing portion of the telegram evidently instructed the Ambassador to query the Germans about the implementation of the Tripartite Pact, and its conclusion stated that the Japanese preferred not to move against the Soviet Union at this time. That message had crossed with one from the Japanese Ambassador describing a November 29 talk with von Ribbentrop during which the German Ambassador had declared, "Should Japan become engaged in a war against the United States, Germany, of course, would join the war immediately. . . . The Fuehrer is determined on that point." Taken together the intercepts left no doubt that the United States would be at war with both Germany and Japan within a matter of days.[34]

When Roosevelt returned from Georgia on Monday, December 1, Stimson was initially concerned that he did not immediately summon him, Knox, and Hull to discuss their proposed message to Congress. On the same day Stimson learned that the Japanese expeditionary force had landed in Indochina, making the prospect of war slightly less imminent. But Stimson need not have worried. Harry Hopkins, who had spent most of November at Bethesda Naval Hospital with more severe stomach problems, had lunched with Roosevelt and the British Ambassador Lord Halifax at the White House. They discussed how to warn the Japanese further and what to do if the Japanese made new aggressive moves without necessarily attacking Britain or the United States, such as an occupation of Thailand or an attack on the Kra Isthmus, shared by Thailand and Malaya. "At one point," Halifax telegraphed London later that day, "[Roosevelt] threw in an aside that, in the case of any direct attack on ourselves or the Dutch, we should obviously all be together." The United States was going to go to war if the Japanese moved into Malaya or the Dutch East Indies. In a masterpiece of understatement, Hopkins in a telephone conversation assured Stimson that the President was as firm as ever. Roosevelt now decided to send the Japanese a message asking them why more troops were moving south.[35]

Late on December 1, Stark, acting on Roosevelt's orders, ordered Admiral Hart in Manila to charter three vessels, arm them with two guns each, and send them to patrol and report Japanese ship movements off the Indochina coast. This could have been an effort to make sure U.S. ships were attacked when the Japanese undertook their southern offensive. In another meeting on December 4, Roosevelt confirmed to Halifax that he would give the British armed support if Japan attacked them. By the next day, December 5, London had communicated FDR's promise to the British commander in Singapore, Air-Marshal Brooke-Popham, who passed it on to Admiral Hart in Manila. The decision to go to war if Japan attacked the British or Dutch had been made at the critical White House meeting of November 25, but the contingency of Japanese aggression that did not involve the United States was not one the allies were going to have to face. Meanwhile, Roosevelt on December 2 publicly asked the Japanese the purpose of the large new forces they were sending to Indochina, and the Japanese replied publicly on December 5 that their troops were sent to protect against a move from China.[36]

A domestic crisis broke out on December 4 when the *Chicago Tribune* broke the story of the Victory Program with a huge banner headline, "FDR'S WAR PLANS!" The *Tribune* had secured a copy of the entire Joint Board paper submitted to the President back in September, beginning with Roosevelt's own letter of July 9 requesting the study, and they printed most of it verbatim. They headlined the estimated 10 million who would serve in the armed forces, 5 million of whom might be sent overseas. Other major newspapers naturally picked up the story the next day. An incensed Stimson conferred with Roosevelt and Attorney General Robert Jackson about prosecuting the *Tribune*, but in the end he was persuaded merely to issue a statement on December 5 defending the government for studying all possible contingencies and attacking the loyalty and patriotism of the *Chicago Tribune*. In his autobiography, published long after the war, the isolationist Senator Burton K. Wheeler claimed to have received the Joint Board draft from an unnamed Army captain.[37]

The rulers of Japan and Germany, rather than Franklin Roosevelt, chose the moment at which the United States would enter the world war. Japan had decided back in early July to undertake the southward advance at the risk of war with the United States, the Japanese Navy had insisted on including an attack on the United States in its military plans, and Hitler had decided to declare war if Japan attacked. But Roosevelt obviously did not shrink from entry into the world war in early December 1941. His administration had adopted the objective of defeating all the Axis powers and had begun the military and the economic planning to achieve it. He had shared that objective publicly with the American people, a large majority of whom now accepted war as inevitable. In October, fully three-quarters of respondents to a Gallup poll said either that the United States would inevitably get into the war in Europe or that the United States was in the war already. Stark's and Marshall's last-minute memorandum suggested that the early months of the war might be perilous indeed, but the administration's Victory Program could not possibly be implemented in peacetime. With the Germans now halted before Moscow, ultimate victory over the Axis seemed at least possible, and the time to enter the war had come.[38]

From Monday, December 1, through Thursday, December 4, new Magic intercepts conveyed Tokyo's instructions to its diplomatic representatives in London, Singapore, Manila, Hong Kong, Washington, and various Chinese cities to destroy their codes and other publications. On December 6 in Tokyo—December 5 in the United States—the Foreign Ministry told the Embassy in Washington to await the delivery of a long message giving the Japanese reply to Hull's November 26 note. War was obviously imminent. We must now look at both the manner in which the Japanese had decided to begin it, and the reasons why the key commanders in the Far East disregarded their warnings and so much available evidence and remained almost completely unprepared on the morning of December 7.[39]

Roosevelt's November 25 statement that the Japanese "were notorious for making an attack without warning" was a simple historical fact. Against China in 1894, Russia in 1904, Manchuria in 1931, and China in 1937, the Japanese had struck without any preliminary announcement or declaration of war. In the first two cases, they had begun the war with at least partially successful attempts to destroy enemy fleets. Both the Japanese and U.S. navies had adopted the doctrines of Admiral Alfred Thayer Mahan, who believed that great battles between fleets decided wars.

Japanese Admiral Isokuru Yamamoto had the responsibility for planning the war against the United States, and he had proposed a surprise attack on Pearl Harbor in May 1941 and war-gamed it in September. On October 20, Admiral Osami Nagano, the naval commander-in-chief, had agreed to the carrier-based attack. The attacking task force of six aircraft carriers, escorted by battleships, cruises, destroyers, and submarines, had gotten underway at dawn on November 26, Japan time—that is, nearly twenty-four hours before Hull handed Nomura and Kurusu his maximum demands in Washington. Although the task force might conceivably have been recalled, it observed radio silence, and U.S. military and naval intelligence had not yet broken the Japanese naval code, as opposed to the diplomatic Purple code, in any event.[40]

On the other side, U.S. authorities had been discussing a possible Japanese attack on Pearl Harbor for at least eighteen months. In mid-June 1940, a variety of rumors about impending Japanese action in the Pacific had moved General Marshall to order General Charles Herron, then the Army commander in Honolulu, to put his forces on alert against an air attack. Admiral Stark, meanwhile, had ordered Admiral Richardson, the fleet commander, to put the fleet to sea for a few days in the direction of the Panama Canal. The Navy maintained an "outer air patrol" around the islands to a distance of 180 miles for at least five weeks.[41]

On November 22, 1940, after British torpedo bombers had sunk several Italian warships at anchor in their base at Taranto, Stark wrote Richardson asking whether Pearl Harbor needed torpedo nets to protect the fleet from a Japanese surprise attack. Richardson replied on January 8 that such nets would cause too much trouble, that he lacked ships and planes for continuous air search, and that the probability of an attack would not justify it. At the turn of the year 1940–1941, Stark also exchanged letters with the commander of the Hawaiian Fourteenth Naval District regarding the adequacy of Pearl Harbor's antiaircraft defenses, "in view of the probability of an early surprise attack by carrier aircraft if Japan decides to make war on the United States." Knox wrote Stimson a detailed and accurate summary of the problem on January 24, acknowledging that the Navy might deal with a combined bomber and torpedo bomber attack by locating and engaging the carriers before they arrived but making clear that he did not necessarily expect to be able to do so and asking the Army to provide better antiaircraft and fighter defense. Stimson on February 7 promised more modern fighter planes, more antiaircraft guns, and an "air warning system"—presumably radar— by June.[42]

On March 24, Admiral Husband Kimmel, who had replaced the crusty Admiral Richardson in January, wrote a long memorandum on his campaign plan for Admiral Stark. "The war may be initiated by enemy attack without warning," he wrote, "and these attacks may take any form. Such attacks may be directed against shipping, outlying possessions, naval units, or against Pearl Harbor itself." Kimmel had already raised the same possibility in another letter he and his predecessor Richardson had jointly drafted for Stark on January 25. In response, the War Department had sent up-to-date pursuit planes and some B-17 bombers to both Hawaii and the Philippines. But despite some discussions with the British officers from the Royal Air Force, most American authorities had no idea of how many pursuit planes and radars they would need to defend installations like the Philippines, Pearl Harbor, and the Panama Canal from a carrier-based attack. Admiral Turner in late October circulated detailed British advice on the need to disperse and camouflage aircraft in the Philippines from the moment they arrived, but Stark passed it on to the Philippines much too late to do any good.[43]

In November, as war with Japan seemed imminent, all eyes seemed to focus on the Japanese southward advance. Roosevelt on November 26 personally warned the High Commissioner of the Philippines, Francis Sayre, of possible Japanese moves, including attacks on the Burma Road, Thailand, the Malay Peninsula, the Dutch East Indies, and the Philippines. All turned out to be correct. The United States was well aware of

Japanese forces moving southward, but on November 7 a Naval Intelligence report placed the Japanese aircraft carriers in home waters. At least one high-ranking naval officer in Washington still thought the Japanese would probably avoid attacking U.S. possessions altogether. Most critically, however, Admiral Kimmel in Hawaii did not believe that war was going to break out at all.[44]

Earlier in 1941, Kimmel had repeatedly made clear that he did not feel ready to fight the Japanese, especially after the transfer of some of his cruisers, battleships, and a carrier to the Atlantic. At least since the spring of 1940, the Navy had assumed that the Japanese would for some time be occupied with taking the Philippines and Guam if war broke out and that that might allow the U.S. Fleet to seize bases in the Marshall or Caroline islands. Kimmel was charged in ABC-1 with advancing toward the Japanese mandated islands—the Gilberts, Marshalls, and Carolines—in order to draw Japanese naval forces away from the Malay barrier, but because of the losses he expected to incur from enemy submarines and land-based aircraft, he informed Stark in July that he could promise nothing more than raids on the Marshalls. Kimmel took no new action in response to the war warning of November 27, and his Army counterpart, General Short, merely put his forces on alert against sabotage. On the morning of Saturday, December 6, Kimmel and his staff met with a journalist, Joseph Harsch of the *Christian Science Monitor*, who had reported from Europe earlier in the year and had just arrived in Hawaii. After Kimmel and his staff questioned Harsch for some time about events in Europe, Harsch asked them whether there would be war in the Pacific. Harsch first published Kimmel's reply forty years later.[45]

"Since you have been traveling," Kimmel said, "you probably don't know that as of six days ago the German high command announced that the German armies in Russia had gone into winter quarters. That means that Moscow is not going to fall to the Germans this year. That means that the Russians will still be in the war in the spring. That means that the Japanese cannot attack us in the Pacific without running the risk of a two-front war. The Japanese are too intelligent to run the risk of a two-front war unnecessarily. They will want to wait until they are sure that the Russians have been defeated." Kimmel's staff, Harsch wrote, seemed very relaxed, and no one seemed to disagree.[46]

Kimmel argued to the end of his life (and his descendants continue to do so) that no one had warned him of an imminent attack on Pearl Harbor. That is true, but what is more important is that he had decided, himself, that Japan was not going to attack the United States at all. Kimmel essentially confirmed this in his testimony before several investigations of the Pearl Harbor attack, after he had been relieved of duty and reduced in rank. Shortly after the attack, testifying before the Roberts Commission—the first investigative body convened to look into the Pearl Harbor disaster—he said that he did not expect the United States to be imminently involved in war on December 6. He also said that had he known of the close tabs the Japanese consulate in Honolulu were keeping on the presence of ships in Pearl Harbor on December 6, "I would have ordered all units to sea, because the best dispositions against surprise attack can be effected with the fleet at sea." Although the war warning of November 27 had listed the Philippines and Borneo among the possible Japanese targets, Kimmel believed they would move only into Thailand and force the United States to react. During the June 1940 alert, Admiral Richardson had sent out air patrols around Hawaii for several weeks, but Kimmel said he did not do so because he did not have enough planes for an effective search and because it was more important for him to preserve them for offensive action after war had broken out. Several years later, testifying before the congressional investigation, Kimmel said that while the war warning of November 27 had initially made a strong impression on him, after several days had passed without incident, he became less and less convinced that Japan was going to attack the United States. Had he thought that a carrier-based attack on Pearl Harbor was imminent, he said, he would have put the fleet out to sea and instituted the fullest possible air search.[47]

All this confirms Joseph Harsch's recollection of Kimmel's attitude. The Admiral had said himself that if Japan went to war with the United States, it might well do so by making a surprise attack on the fleet at Pearl Harbor. Even though General Short had the responsibility for the defense of Pearl Harbor itself, Kimmel was responsible for his fleet, and his testimony indicates that he realized that he had a particular responsibility not to allow his fleet to be sunk in harbor at the beginning of a war. It is possible, of course, as many authorities have pointed out, that the results of the Japanese attack might have been even worse had Kimmel believed war was imminent and sent the U.S. Fleet out to sea. Had the Japanese located their targets at sea, they might have sunk many ships in deep water, including some American aircraft carriers, giving them undisputed command of the Pacific for a very long time. As it was, all but two of the battleships hit by the Japanese on December 7 were eventually repaired and saw extensive action in the war, and U.S. carriers were entirely missed because they were on a mission at sea. Washington indeed withheld the specifics of the Magic intercepts from field commanders for security reasons, but Stark and Marshall had given the field commanders their conclusions based on those intercepts. Kimmel disregarded his superiors' warning that war was imminent and relied instead on his own belief that it was not—a terrible mistake for which he was duly disciplined.[48]

Washington authorities were much better informed than Kimmel and Short about the possibly imminent outbreak of war—although they had no information specifically suggesting an attack on Pearl Harbor—but an unfortunate lapse prevented them from getting their best information to Hawaii until literally the last minute. On December 5 Tokyo had warned the Embassy to expect an important message, and that fourteen-part message, rejecting Hull's note and breaking off the talks—although not formally announcing either a break in relations or war—began arriving in the middle of the day on December 6. Army and Navy intelligence had decoded the first thirteen parts by about 9:30 p.m. The message reviewed the negotiations from the Japanese point of view, accusing the United States of refusing to budge from impractical principles, of preparing to attack Germany and Italy, and maintaining its hegemony and imperialistic exploitation in the Pacific.

A Navy courier brought the thirteen parts of the message to the White House between 9:30 and 10:00 p.m., where he found Harry Hopkins, newly emerged from the Naval Hospital, with the President. "The President," said the courier years later, "then turned toward Mr. Hopkins and said, in substance—I am not sure of the exact words, but in substance—'this means war.' Mr. Hopkins agreed, and they discussed then for perhaps five minutes the situation of the Japanese forces." Couriers then distributed the thirteen parts to other high civilian and military authorities. But when the fourteenth part, announcing that the Japanese now found it impossible to reach agreement through negotiations, arrived around midnight, Colonel Carlisle Dusenbury, the Army intelligence officer on duty, went home without distributing it. The same thing happened in Naval Intelligence. Not until the next morning did the fourteenth part, together with instructions for the delivery of the whole message at 1:00 p.m. the next day—7:00 a.m. in Honolulu—reach any senior officials.

Marshall immediately dispatched another warning to Short in Hawaii, but it arrived while the attack was underway. Within an hour, hundreds of Japanese carrier planes had sunk two battleships—the *Arizona* and *Oklahoma*—for good, sunk or damaged six more, and badly damaged three cruisers and three destroyers. They also wiped out most of the Army's fighters and bombers at Wheeler and Hickam fields.[49]

The war broke out on the morning of December 7, Hawaii time, because the Japanese had decided to make war on the United States and Britain in order to create the Greater East Asia Co-Prosperity Sphere, including the Dutch East Indies, Thailand, Malaya, Burma, and the Philippines. The military and naval authorities in the Philippines, General MacArthur and Admiral Hart, seemed to have given as little practical attention as Kimmel and Short to the actual problems of detecting and evading or parrying a Japanese first strike. MacArthur evidently had trusted his own illusions, telling the High Commissioner in the Philippines and the British Admiral Sir Tom Phillips that the Japanese would not be able to attack the Philippines for several months. Although MacArthur had been informed on November 21 that Rainbow 5 now asked him to conduct air raids on any Japanese targets within range in the event of war, the general refused to order an American air strike on Japanese bases in Formosa even after news of the Pearl Harbor attack arrived. Devastating Japanese air attacks disabled most of MacArthur's air force, including about half of his thirty-five B-17 bombers, many hours after the Pearl Harbor attack and four hours after MacArthur had discussed the situation by telephone with General Gerow in Washington.[50]

When the news reached Washington, Roosevelt and his leading subordinates never thought of war against Japan alone. On the afternoon of December 7, FDR briefed congressional leaders and made clear he would ask for a declaration of war against Japan the next day. One Senator, Tom Connally of Texas, immediately predicted that Germany would declare war on the United States. Hull told British Ambassador Lord Halifax late on December 7 that he expected immediate German and Italian declarations of war on the United States as well. Roosevelt met Congress on December 8, calling December 7 a day "that will live in infamy," and a declaration of war on Japan passed with only one dissenting vote in the House of Representatives, that of Congresswoman Elizabeth Rankin of Montana, an extreme right-winger and isolationist who had also voted against entry into the First World War in 1917. On that same day, December 8, Magic intercepts confirmed that Ribbentrop had promised the Japanese Ambassador that Germany would enter the war at once. Not for a moment had the administration thought of fighting the Japanese alone. Donald Nelson, the director of the Supply Priorities and Allocations Board (and soon to replace William Knudsen as the head of the war production effort), had been scheduled to make a nationwide radio broadcast on the evening of December 7. After checking with the White House, he went ahead with new language. "We must keep in mind," he said, "that though the attack has been made by the Japanese it is in reality an attack upon us by the Axis powers. . . . We are face to face with an attack directed primarily from Berlin."[51]

Roosevelt gave a fireside chat on the evening of Tuesday, December 9, laying out the record of aggression in both Europe and Asia over the last ten years and speaking at length about the economic demands of war. Japan, he said, had begun the war after Germany had promised the Japanese the control of Asia and the Pacific. "We know also," he said, "that Germany and Japan are conducting their military and naval operations in accordance with a joint plan. That plan considers all peoples and Nations which are not helping the Axis powers as common enemies of each and every one of the Axis powers. That is their simple and obvious grand strategy. And that is why the American people must realize that it can be matched only with similar grand strategy." Battles in the Pacific, in Libya, in the Caucasus, and potentially in North Africa were all part of the same war. "Remember always that Germany and Italy, regardless of any formal declaration of war, consider themselves at war with the United States at this moment just as much as they consider themselves at war with Britain or Russia," he said. The same newspapers that reported that speech on December 10 carried news from Berlin that a declaration of war was expected at any moment, and Hitler indeed proclaimed it to the Reichstag on December 10. Mussolini did the same in Rome.[52]

The Supply Priorities and Allocations Board had met on December 8 and again on December 9. For some time Stimson had been pressing William Knudsen of the Office of Production Management on the question of whether the country could meet the Victory Program production targets on schedule, by July 1, 1943. On December 9 Knudsen had his answer. "We can't meet them by July 1, 1943," he said—"but we can meet them by July 1, 1944."[53]

The United States now faced the most critical military situation in its history as an independent nation. The Joint Board on December 8 agreed that the Japanese could now seize the Hawaiian Islands, speculated that some Japanese carriers might be on their way to bomb the almost undefended West Coast of the United States, and began frantically looking for planes and antiaircraft guns for the West Coast and Hawaii. Rather than execute the long-standing plan to strengthen the Navy in the Atlantic when the United States entered the European war, the Navy now had to *withdraw* units from the Atlantic to try to secure Oahu from a possible new Japanese attack. Partly as a result, the coming year of 1942 became by far the worst year of the whole war in the Battle of the Atlantic, with more than twice as many ships sunk in the North Atlantic than in 1941, and many more along the Atlantic and Gulf coasts of the United States. Although the Germans had now conceded that their campaign in the Soviet Union had halted for the winter, no one could guarantee that the Soviets would last out another year, or that the Germans would not occupy North Africa, or even that Britain would not be invaded in 1942. Yet now, just two days after Pearl Harbor, Knudsen had given Stimson the approximate date on which the decisive offensives against both Germany and Japan would begin. That was the fruit of eighteen months of planning, new contracts, new plant construction, labor mediation, and endless calculations at the Navy and War departments and among the economists at the Bureau of Research and Statistics at the OPM—the achievement of Stimson and Knox, Marshall and Stark, Knudsen and Hillman and Donald Nelson and Stacy May, and all the rest. And the whole process had been set in motion and carefully monitored by Franklin Roosevelt, who in July 1941 had ordered his more cautious military and naval leaders to prepare for the total defeat of both Germany and Japan.[54]

Five years before, FDR had declared that his generation had a rendezvous with destiny. The climax of that rendezvous was now at hand, and Roosevelt and his colleagues' work had ensured that the war that was just beginning would indeed have no end save victory.

EPILOGUE
Generations in Crisis

IN THE WAKE OF PEARL HARBOR AND THE GERMAN AND ITALIAN DEC-larations of war, the United States now had to carry out the task laid out three months earlier in the Victory Program: the construction of a military adequate to defeat all its enemies. In the short run, however, the United States faced exactly the nightmare that had clearly worried Roosevelt so much for the previous eighteen months: the direct involvement in a war that it was unprepared to fight. The devastation of the fleet at Pearl Harbor, moreover, left the Rainbow 5 plan in tatters, since nearly all the ships that had moved to the Atlantic during 1941 now had to return to the Pacific to provide essential defense for the Hawaiian Islands and the West Coast. The consequences for the Battle of the Atlantic were disastrous, all the more so because the Germans launched a U-boat offensive against the East Coast and in the Gulf of Mexico for which the U.S. Navy was entirely unprepared. Sinkings rose to new highs during the first half of 1942, although the new merchant ships ordered in the first half of 1941 began making up the slack by the end of that year.

Two strokes of good fortune saved the Allies and the United States. First, having failed to destroy Soviet resistance as planned in 1941, Hitler kept his eyes fixed firmly on the eastern front during 1942. Huge new offensives gained hundreds more miles in the southern USSR but ended in catastrophe at the end of the year with the encirclement of the German Sixth Army at Stalingrad. Once again Hitler passed up the opportunity to move through the Iberian Peninsula and into French North Africa,

335

where Roosevelt continued to fix his eyes keenly and where U.S. and British troops landed in the first week of November 1942 in the first major U.S. operation against Germany of the war.

In the Pacific the Japanese rapidly completed the southward advance, conquering Malaya, Singapore, Burma, the Dutch East Indies, and the Philippines within just a few months. Yet when they tried to extend their defense perimeter still farther, the Americans took advantage of having learned to break their naval, as well as their diplomatic, codes. In April, a U.S. carrier task force fought its Japanese counterpart to a standstill in the Battle of the Coral Sea and prevented the Japanese from landing on the south coast of New Guinea. Then, in the first week of June, the United States had to meet a huge Japanese attack on Midway, 1,300 miles west of Hawaii, designed to force an all-out battle with the weakened U.S. Fleet. Helped by the interception of the Japanese naval codes and fortunate coincidences during a hectic battle, U.S. carrier planes caught the Japanese carrier force while it was reloading its bombers, and set four carriers afire. That in turn enabled the United States to contest Guadalcanal in the Solomon Islands later that year. By the end of 1942, both the U.S. and Japanese navies had lost significant portions of the fleets with which they had begun the war. But while the Japanese lacked the resources for substantial additional construction, the American two-ocean Navy authorized in 1940 would begin coming on line in early 1944. After a relatively quiet year in the Pacific in 1943, the new ships enabled the United States to advance through the Marshall and Mariana islands and land in the Philippines in 1944. Gigantic naval battles during those operations destroyed most of what was left of the Imperial Japanese Navy. The landing in the Marianas allowed B-29 bombers to begin bombing Japanese cities and eventually to deliver two atomic bombs.

Neither the Roosevelt administration in general nor the Victory Program in particular can take credit for the utter defeat of Nazi Germany. Had the worst-case scenario foreseen by Wedemeyer in 1941—the defeat of the Soviet Union—come to pass, the task of mounting a successful invasion of Western Europe would have been truly monumental. The defeat of Germany might well have had to await the development of the atomic bomb in the middle of 1945. Nearly everyone, however, had underestimated Soviet resources, the internal strength of the regime, and the commitment of the Soviet people. The USSR outproduced all other nations in the key land weapons of the Second World War, tanks and artillery, both quantitatively and qualitatively, despite losing so much of its territory during the first year of the conflict. After defeating a last huge German offensive at Kursk in the summer of 1943, Stalin's armies began a steady advance that took them to Berlin less than two years later.

The Anglo-American staff conversations of 1940–1941 foreshadowed critical strategic arguments between American and British political and military leaders during 1942–1943. After Pearl Harbor, General Marshall in particular initially opposed any major operations in Europe or North Africa until the invasion of France—the only potentially decisive operation—was ready. He was initially overruled by Roosevelt himself, who had long been concerned to secure North and West Africa and who, critically, understood that the decisive battles had to wait until 1944, when American production would have borne fruit and huge new armies would be ready. Both General Dwight Eisenhower, whom Marshall plucked from obscurity as a Colonel in the War Plans Division to become the commander of the North African landing, and Marshall himself realized by the end of 1942 that they would not have enough men or equipment to mount the landing in France during the coming year.[1] Instead they continued from North Africa into Sicily and then Italy, as the British preferred. The British, however, continued to hope that bombing and revolts in occupied territories might defeat Nazi Germany and make an invasion unnecessary. Not until the first meeting of Roosevelt, Churchill, and Stalin at Teheran in November 1943 did FDR enlist Stalin to overrule Churchill and insist on the invasion of France in the spring of 1944. Difficult and costly fighting awaited the Allies in Normandy, but their material superiority was by then overwhelming.

Led by Roosevelt, the Missionary generation and their colleagues from the next-younger Lost generation had spent the 1930s trying to create a just society at home and the early 1940s preparing to defend it from threats abroad. In the last year of the war they created the framework for a peaceful world, planning the occupation of Germany together with the British and the Soviets, writing the Charter of the new United Nations, and building a new international monetary system designed to avoid the economic chaos of the 1920s and early 1930s and its disastrous political effects. The death of Franklin Roosevelt in April 1945 marked the high tide of the influence of the Missionary generation. Harry Truman, his chosen successor, remained devoted to his policies, but lacked his overarching vision. Within a little more than a year Roosevelt's entire cabinet, including Stimson, Morgenthau, Ickes, and Frances Perkins, was gone. (Cordell Hull had retired in 1944, and Knox had died suddenly in that same year.) Marshall, however, became Secretary of State in early 1947, and during the next two years he laid the foundation for the Atlantic alliance and the Cold War in Europe, including the economic plan that bore his name, the NATO alliance, and a new West German state.

The cataclysmic nature of the Second World War and the foresight of the leaders who won it created a sometimes frightening but ultimately stable world that endured for forty-five years. At home the vision of the New Deal lived on among the GI, or "Greatest," generation, born roughly from 1904 through 1924—the men and women who had provided the troops and the labor that produced the weapons and fought the battles and who in return benefited from all the major measures of the New Deal for the whole of their lives. That generation's role in the Second World War has been somewhat exaggerated in recent decades. While their battlefield heroism was exemplary, they did not define the stakes of the conflict, make the key decisions that brought the United States into it, or devise or carry out the strategies that won it. They did, however, emerge as a great generation of political leaders in middle age, and they preserved and extended their parents' legacy. From John F. Kennedy to Lyndon Johnson, Richard Nixon, Nelson Rockefeller, Gerald Ford, and many, many more, they still viewed government as the regulator of the economy, the guarantor of full employment, the last resource of distressed Americans, and the advocate of equal opportunity. Even Ronald Reagan, the first President openly to repudiate the values of the New Deal, did relatively little to disturb the world it had left behind. In 1964–1965, black GIs such as Thurgood Marshall and Roy Wilkins, with the help of a still younger movement led by Martin Luther King Jr., achieved the legal equality that Du Bois, Walter White, and William Hastie had fought for. But in that same year, the GI generation, led by Lyndon Johnson, embarked on the enterprise that would not only discredit their leadership, but alienate their own children's generation, the Vietnam War. That broke up the New Deal coalition and marked the beginning of the end of New Deal America. It has fallen to the new Prophet generation—the Boom generation, eighty years younger than the Missionaries—to put something new in its place.[2]

The United States since independence has given birth to three Prophet generations: the Transcendentals (born roughly 1792–1821), the

Missionaries (roughly 1863–1883), and the Boom (1943–1960). Each of them grew up in the aftermath of a great crisis, amid elders who believed the essential problems of life and politics were now solved. Each of them took the achievements of their grandparents and their parents for granted and went to work redefining the purpose not only of political life, but of life itself. Transcendentals from both the North and the South turned slavery from an unfortunate blight on the body politic that the Founders had tried to contain into a question of good and evil that led to a great civil war. They left behind a reunified country, but one without strong political institutions, ruled by new economic interests and corrupt party machines. The Missionaries spent their adult lives bringing order out of the chaos they inherited, and left behind a world of remarkable stability. The Boomers grew up in that world, and had it not been for the Vietnam War, they might have shown more understanding of, and commitment to, its virtues. That, however, was not to be.[3]

Midcentury America had become a world of standardization—of mass-produced houses, automobiles, clothes, televisions, and young people. It was a world in which rationality trumped emotion—a world of brilliant scientists, doctors, and engineers but mediocre writers and artists. The Boomers, like other Prophet generations, stood for a new way of life, one involving "more immediate, ecstatic and penetrating modes of living," as one of the most famous Boomers put it in her valedictory address in 1969.[4] But largely as a result of the Vietnam War, this attempt to revive the emotional side of life turned into a rebellion against authority of all kinds. That began with the protests against the draft, which by 1973 had brought conscription in the United States to an end. It also led to a more prolonged effort to reverse the remaining inequalities in American life, especially women's inequality, and eventually to the acceptance of homosexuality, a process now culminating with the spread of gay marriage. Younger generations are already benefiting enormously from these achievements, which for Boomers are legitimate sources of pride. But they have come at a heavy price, because Boomers had no deep commitment to the relatively just economic order they inherited. Now they have created a far less equal world than the one into which they were born.

The first half of the twentieth century saw the greatest feats of economic and political human organization—both for good and for ill—in the history of mankind. The two most rigidly and cruelly organized states, Nazi Germany and the Soviet Union, fought the hardest and suffered the most casualties in the Second World War. But the United States managed comparable feats of organization both to cope with the Depression and to make the Allied victory possible. So did Great Britain, where that spirit carried into the postwar world under the Labor Government of 1945–1950. American men and women of the Roosevelt era both respected and knew how to exercise authority. They had a great command of clear language and an ability to make things happen, from the halls of legislatures to the shop floor to the battlefields of the world. They could conceive of and build, in the United States, a far more just, equal, and livable society. Sadly, faced with its own crisis since 2001— and even more since 2007—the Boom generation has been unable to do anything comparable for its country.

Indeed, the very idea of a country united through its political system in pursuit of the common good has steadily become more and more unfashionable during the last half century. Boomers from both sides of the political aisle collaborated in the dismantling of the regulatory structure the New Deal created for the economy, most notably in 1999, when they repealed the Glass-Steagall Act. Income tax rates have generally trended downward for fifty years, and the top marginal rate is less than half of what it was under FDR and his immediate successors. The influence of money on politics has vastly expanded and has indeed been turned into a constitutional right by a Boomer-led Supreme Court. Boomers on the left side of the political spectrum have generally been just as little interested in the problems of society as a whole. They have focused on the specific problems of women, minorities, the disabled, and homosexuals. The genius of the New Deal was to unite Americans, but Boomer politics has constantly divided them. The implied prediction of the Missionary historian Roger Merriman has come true. Merriman in his final lecture declared that history was ruled by the ebb and flow of security on the one hand and liberty on the other, and the generation that was already being born when he died in 1945 has repeatedly chosen liberty of all kinds over security, with enormous consequences. They have also allowed the values of the market to eclipse any broader moral purpose in virtually every area of American life.

Like the Transcendentals and the Missionaries before them, the Boomers, thanks to their immense self-confidence, did much to create a new crisis in American life, especially in the economic realm, but neither they nor any other living generation has produced another Lincoln or Franklin Roosevelt to lead the nation out of it. In our current political climate, so reminiscent of the post–Civil War period, it is hard to see how anyone could do so. The battle now being waged in Washington relates mainly to the provision of income and health care for the elderly and the poor, while the broader economic role of the government has essentially been given up. No reversal of the trend toward economic inequality is on the horizon. Globalization has effectively destroyed the idea of an economy combining private enterprise with a measure of government planning. We have no new legions of social workers and macroeconomists determined to spread the benefits of American life more broadly. Millions of Americans are once again, as Roosevelt would have said, forgotten men and women.

The world scene today is certainly less threatening than in the 1930s, but there, too, the Boom generation has fallen short of its predecessors. In the wake of September 11, 2001, George W. Bush quite obviously saw himself as a crisis President and dreamed of having an impact on the world comparable to Franklin Roosevelt's. He frequently spoke of a great new struggle to define the coming century. Yet his administration lacked the capacity for clear thinking, planning, standing up resources, and taking advantage of the opportunities offered by the international situation that Roosevelt and his colleagues showed again and again in 1940–1941. The outcome of Bush's quest was correspondingly disappointing: two wars, each of which has lasted much longer than American participation in the Second World War, and both of which now seem to have helped trigger the spread of anarchy throughout the Middle East. Most frighteningly of all, the Bush administration abandoned the earlier ideal of a world ruled by law. It went into Iraq in defiance of the United Nations, refused to treat prisoners according to long-established treaties, and flouted the opinion of the world. This was hubris worthy of the Boomers' GI parents in Vietnam, and it suffered a similar fate. Boomers of both parties have defined the spread of democracy as the key to world progress, but this is not likely to increase peace and justice in the world if existing democracies, led by the United States, cannot provide a better example.

Authority has eroded over much of the world. The most organized state of the twentieth century, the Soviet Union, suffered the greatest collapse in 1990–1991. Conscription still exists in only a few small states, and the size of militaries relative to population has fallen to an all-time low. This is in many ways a blessing. The world does not need more conflicts comparable to the world wars of the twentieth century. Yet we may find our capacity for clear thinking, genuine devotion to principle, organization, integrity in action, and sacrifice for the common good has fallen so far as to threaten the foundations of our civilization as we have known it. At some future date, new generations may well face a crisis like those of 1933 or 1940–1941. If they do, the achievements of Franklin Roosevelt and the rest of his generation will provide a much-needed inspiration.

ACKNOWLEDGMENTS

From 1990 until 2012, I taught in the Strategy and Policy Department of the Naval War College. For those interested in war and peace, there is no more demanding or rewarding job, involving as it does the continual re-examination of the political and military history of the past, and the constant opportunity to exchange insights and new ideas with well-informed and diligent colleagues and students. I am sure my life there made this book a much better one. Among those colleagues whose acquaintance was especially beneficial were George Baer, Alberto Coll, William Fuller, Todd Greentree, the late Michael Handel, Brad Lee, John Maurer, Sally Paine, Doug Porch, and Steven Ross. Mark Stoler, who was a visiting faculty member for a year, shared his expertise on the subject of this book as well. The military faculty who shared my office while I was working on this project included Bob Flynn, Rob Krivacs, and Jon Scott Logel, and they were always interested in my latest documentary find or new hypothesis. The S&P Department tries to teach both military officers and civilians how to think about war. Having written this book, I now see that we were in essence trying to make them as capable at that task as Roosevelt and his contemporaries were, and I hope and believe that we had some success. This book, like my last one, *The Road to Dallas*, was completed during a year at Williams College made possible by James McAllister, and for that I shall always be grateful to him as well. Those visits also allowed me to get to know James MacGregor Burns and Susan Dunn, both of whom had written extensively about FDR as well. Some early conversations with Robert Dallek, who remains a remarkable example of what a historian can be, were also very helpful. David Levering Lewis gave me important help. I discovered in the midst of this project that an old friend, Nigel Hamilton, was at work on what amounts to a sequel to it, and I hope he benefited from our discussions of FDR and his collaborators as much as I did. Twenty years ago, the late William Strauss and Neil Howe gave us all extraordinary new insights into American history that have been vindicated by subsequent events and that have given this book and many other things I have written a new and important dimension. Although this book is based mainly on primary sources, I drew enormous benefit from many previous secondary works. My debt to those previous authors is reflected in the endnotes, and I apologize to the many to whom for whatever reason I did not refer.

I have never encountered files and finding aids quite as confusing as those of the War and Navy departments at Archives II in College Park, but the archivists there, led by Tim Nenninger and Wilbert Mahoney, provided essential help in picking up some trails left by previous researchers and opening up rich new veins as well. Janie Strauss was a generous and gracious host on all my visits to Washington. Matthew Hanson at the FDR Library provided a number of important documents and photographs.

My agents, Don Lamm and Christy Fletcher, did a fine job marketing this project, and Don was as always a careful and supportive reader of drafts. Lara Heimert of Perseus Books has been extremely supportive from the beginning, and I know that many of the suggestions that both she and Roger La Brie have made have improved the manuscript. My thanks go to the publicity department at Perseus who as I write are hard at work on marketing the book. They clearly take their task as seriously as I take mine. Last but not least, I want to thank Sam Williamson, who as a Harvard Assistant Professor taught me that one does research by beginning at the beginning and going on until one gets to the end, and the late Ernest R. May, my thesis adviser, who was always excited, not dismayed, by the scope of the projects I successively undertook.

To William Strauss (1947–2007), historian and friend,
and to the Missionary generation (b. 1863–1883),
with thanks for the world they made.

NOTES

Introduction

1. http://www.presidency.ucsb.edu/ws/index.php?pid=15314&st=&st1=#ixzz1Jt2agNlt.

2. See David Kaiser, "Neither Marxist nor Whig: The Great Atlantic Crises, 1774–1962," *The Monist*, vol. 89, no. 2 (April 2006): 325–355; and William Strauss and Neil Howe, *Generations: The History of America's Future, 1584 to 2069* (New York, 1991).

3. Quoted in Strauss and Howe, *Generations*, 180.

4. The best book on Roosevelt's early life is Geoffrey Ward, *Before the Trumpet: Young Franklin Roosevelt, 1882–1905* (New York, 1985). The sequel, *A First Class Temperament: The Emergence of Franklin Roosevelt* (New York, 1989), is also excellent on Roosevelt's personal life before he became President. The best account of his early political and administrative career is Frank Freidel, *Franklin D. Roosevelt: The Apprenticeship* (Boston, 1952).

5. Re. Alice Sohie and Roosevelt, see Ward, *Before the Trumpet*, 254. Alice also told friends that she had had to slap Franklin to deter ungentlemanly advances more than once. Ward, *First Class Temperament*, 312–313, presents very convincing evidence that the birth of their last child marked the end of the Roosevelts' sexual relations.

6. Garner in 1960, at the age of ninety-one, was quoted as telling his fellow Texan Lyndon Baines Johnson not to accept the vice presidential nomination from John Kennedy because the office wasn't worth "a bucket of warm spit." (The quote was not perhaps exactly accurate.) LBJ's decision turned out very differently, of course, from Garner's.

7. http://www.presidency.ucsb.edu/ws/index.php?pid=14473&st=&st1=#ixzz1JytqhGIB.

8. http://www.presidency.ucsb.edu/ws/index.php?pid=15349&st=&st1=#ixzz1JyuxlcIt.

9. See especially Kenneth S. Davis, *FDR: The New Deal Years, 1933–1937* (New York, 1979), 38–41.

10. David Levering Lewis, *W. E. B. Du Bois: The Fight for Equality and the American Century* (New York, 2000), 465.

11. The expanded role of women in the labor force did not begin until after Pearl Harbor.

Chapter 1

1. Entries of April 10 and April 29, 1940, Henry Morgenthau Jr.: Presidential Diaries, Microfilm edition; Conference between Admiral Stark and Mr. Vinson, May 4, 1940, RG 38, Records of the Navy Department, Strategic Plans Division Records, Subject Files, 1937–41, Box 89, A1–Building Program Plans–Projects; *Gallup Poll, Public Opinion, 1935–1971* (New York, 1971), 1:215, 224. These poll results included those who had no opinion.

2. Kennedy to Hull, May 15, 1940, FDR Library, Presidential Safe File, Box 3, Kennedy, Joseph P.

3. *New York Times*, May 12, 1940, 18; *Chicago Tribune*, May 13, 1940, 12; *Christian Science Monitor*, May 18, 1940, 1; *Los Angeles Times*, May 18, 1940, A5, and May 28, 1940, 6; *New York Times*, June 19, 1940, 17.

4. Charles A. Beard, *American Foreign Policy in the Making, 1932–40* (New Haven, 1946), 76.

5. Ibid., 168.

6. Norman A. Graebner, "Hoover, Roosevelt, and the Japanese," in Dorothy Borg and Shumpei Okamoto, eds., *Pearl Harbor as History: Japanese-American Relations, 1931–41* (New York, 1973), 36; *William D. Leahy Diaries, 1897–1956* (microfilm edition), August 24, 1937.

7. This discussion is based on the only thorough account of Roosevelt's official role in the First World War, Freidel, *Franklin D. Roosevelt: The Apprenticeship*, 236–269, 286–372; and Freidel, *Franklin D. Roosevelt: The Ordeal* (Boston, 1954), 13, 79–80.

8. The speech may be read in full at http://www.presidency.ucsb.edu/ws/index.php?pid=15476&st=&st1=#axzz1G1WNCn2h.

9. *Leahy Diaries*, October 6, 1937.

10. Beard, *American Foreign Policy*, 189–207; Robert Dallek, *Franklin D. Roosevelt and American Foreign Policy, 1932–45*, 2nd ed. (New York, 1995), 154.

11. Sumner Welles, *The Time for Decision* (New York, 1944), 64–66.

12. Robert H. Jackson, *That Man: An Insider's Portrait of Franklin D. Roosevelt*, ed. John D. Barrett (New York, 2003), 81.

13. See Great Britain, Foreign Office, *Documents on British Foreign Policy 1919–39* (hereafter *DBFP*), second Series (2), vol. 21, nos. 433, 441, and *Leahy Diaries*, December 16, 17, and 23. The 1915–1917 talks were in fact so secret that British

authorities could find no record of them at all. They may have been a figment of FDR's imagination.

14. The records of the talks are in National Archives, College Park (hereafter Archives II), RG 38, Strategic Plans Division, Anglo-American Cooperation, 1938–1944 (Series VII), Box 116, Correspondence Re: British-U.S. Conversations in London, 1938–1939. See also *DBFP*, 2, vol. 21, nos. 462, 486. These talks have been discussed by James Leutze, *Bargaining for Supremacy: Anglo-American Naval Cooperation, 1937–41* (Chapel Hill, 1977), 22–26; and Bradford Lee, *Britain and the Sino-Japanese War, 1937–39* (Stanford, 1973), 90–95, but ignored or misrepresented by many standard works on the period precisely because diplomatic correspondence does not mention them.

15. *DBFP*, 2, vol. 21, nos. 422–424, 428, 430, 431.

16. Late in 1938, when Navy Department sources gave the essence of the story of this episode to Washington muckrakers Drew Pearson and Robert Allen, they also blamed the State Department for the failure to go through with the plan. See *Washington Merry-Go-Round*, November 26, 1938, http://dspace.wrlc.org/doc/get /2041/18311/b03f07-1126zdisplay.pdf#search=%27Leahy%20blockade%20Japan %27. For an excellent summary of the military aspects of the Sino-Japanese War, see S. C. M. Paine, *The Wars for Asia, 1911–1949* (New York, 2012), 123–170.

17. See http://www.presidency.ucsb.edu/ws/index.php?pid=15573&st=&st1= #axzz1GDo5g4LC.

18. Roosevelt's immigration policy is thoroughly and effectively explored in Richard Breitman and Allen J. Lichtman, *FDR and the Jews* (Cambridge, MA, 2012), 67–141.

19. *DBFP*, 3, vol. 7, nos. 627–629.

20. This from Amanda Smith, ed., *Hostage to Fortune: The Letters of Joseph P. Kennedy* (New York, 2001), 294–297.

21. Mark Skinner Watson, *Chief of Staff: Prewar Plans and Preparations* (Washington, DC, 1950), 6–7.

22. See Steven T. Ross, *American War Plans 1890–1939* (London, 2002), for a survey of American war planning.

23. Diary of Homer Cummings, October 14, 1938, Box 235, Notebook 8, Homer Cummings papers, Small Special Collection Library, University of Virginia. I am indebted to Richard Breitman and Allen J. Lichtman for pointing out this document in their book, *FDR and the Jews*, 355.

24. Joint Board Minutes, November 9, 1939, RG 225, Records of the Joint Board, M-1421, Roll 1.

25. Exploratory Studies in Accordance with J. B. 325 - Serial 634, April 21, 1939, RG 80, General Records of the Navy Department, Joint Army-Navy Board Navy Secretariat, Box 10, JB 325 - Serial 634.

26. Draft of Joint Board directives for Rainbows 1, 2, 3, and 4, May 12, 1939, RG 80, General Records of the Navy Department, Joint Army-Navy Board Navy

Secretariat, Box 10, JB 325 - Serial 642 - 642-5; and Joint Board Minutes, 14411, RG 225, Records of the Joint Board, M-1421, Roll 1.

27. See "Joint Army and Navy Basic War Plan - Rainbow no. 1," July 27, 1939; "Political Aspects of Plan - Rainbow No. 1," August 9, 1939, and "Joint Army and Navy Basic War Plans - Rainbow," April 9, 1940, RG 80, General Records of the Navy Department, Joint Army-Navy Board Navy Secretariat, Box 10, JB 325 - Serial 642 - 642-5. On Rainbow 2 see Chief of Naval Operations for CINCUSFLT, May 24, 1940, ibid.

28. Patrick Abbazia, *Mr. Roosevelt's Navy: The Private War of the U.S. Atlantic Fleet, 1939–42* (Annapolis, 1975), 30–31, 33–35, 49–50, 62; and see "Memorandum for Admiral Leahy and Admiral Richardson," December 28, 1938, FDR Library, President's Secretary's File, Box 59, Departmental File Navy: Mar–Dec 1938.

29. Re. Vinson-Trammel Act, see George W. Baer, *One Hundred Years of Sea Power* (Stanford, 1996). About naval building programs, see "Building Program, Fiscal Year 1941," May 6, 1939, RG 38, Records of the Navy Department, Strategic Plans Division Records, Subject Files, 1937–41, Box 89, A1—Building Program Plans—Projects.

30. James P. Tate, *The Army and Its Air Corps: Army Policy Towards Aviation, 1919–41* (Maxwell Air Base, AL, 1998), 164–169.

31. For figures on the air forces, see Williamson Murray, *The Change in the European Balance of Power, 1938–39* (Princeton, 1984), 245–253. See also *The Wartime Journals of Charles A. Lindbergh* (New York, 1970), 82–83. Orville H. Bullitt, ed., *From the President, Personal and Secret: Correspondence Between Franklin D. Roosevelt and William C. Bullitt* (Boston, 1972).

32. Morgenthau Diaries, Book 150, Reel 41 (emphasis added).

33. Irving Brinton Holly Jr., *Buying Aircraft: Matériel Procurement for the Army Air Forces* (United States Army in World War II, Special Studies, Washington, DC, 1989), 166–193; H. Duncan Hall, *North American Supply* (London, 1955), 106–107.

34. Re. the January 1939 message to Congress, see http://www.presidency.ucsb .edu/ws/index.php?pid=15683&st=&st1=#axzz1GgwqATas. For the 1939 State of the Union address, see http://www.presidency.ucsb.edu/ws/index.php?pid=15684& st=&st1=#axzz1GgwqATas.

35. *Gallup Poll*, 1:80, 130, 131, 137, 141, 145.

36. Ibid., 1:149–150, 154.

37. The congressional debate is reproduced at length in Beard, *American Foreign Policy*, 216–234. See also Graebner, "Hoover, Roosevelt, and the Japanese," 42.

38. http://www.presidency.ucsb.edu/ws/index.php?pid=15801&st=&st1=#axzz 1Gt3P3NkE.

39. *Christian Science Monitor*, September 15, 1939, 2; and Abbazia, *Mr. Roosevelt's Navy*, 67–70.

40. http://www.presidency.ucsb.edu/ws/index.php?pid=15813&st=&st1=#axzz 1Gt3P3NkE.

41. See Beard, *American Foreign Policy*, 238–261, for long excerpts from the debates about cash-and-carry proposals; and William L. Langer and S. Everett Gleason, *The Challenge to Isolation* (New York, 1952), 230, for the votes. Re. President's radio address, see http://www.presidency.ucsb.edu/ws/index.php?pid=15828 &st=&st1=#ixzz1GtFynrp8.

42. *Gallup Poll*, 1:188.

43. Sumner Welles, *The Time for Decision* (New York, 1944), 73; *The War Diary of Breckinridge Long: Selections from the Years 1939–1944*, ed. Fred I. Israel (Lincoln, 1966), 1–2; *The Secret Diary of Harold Ickes* (New York, 1953–1954), 3:146–147; *Gallup Poll*, 1:189–190, 215, 211.

44. *Hartford Courant*, March 31, 1940, 16.

Chapter 2

1. http://www.presidency.ucsb.edu/ws/index.php?pid=15954&st=&st1=#axzz1 HdxO48lE. The whole subject of mobilization and production before and during the Second World War has been treated at great length in Maury Klein, *A Call to Arms: Mobilizing America for World War II* (New York, 2013), which appeared as this book was going to press.

2. Stimson to FDR, May 18, 1940, and FDR to Stimson, May 29, 1940, FDR Library, President's Secretary's File, Box 84, Departmental File War: Stimson, Henry L. 1940–1941. For Lindbergh's speech see *New York Times*, May 20, 1940, 8. Morgenthau, Presidential Diaries, May 20, 1940.

3. Larry I. Bland, ed., *The Papers of George Catlett Marshall* (Baltimore, 1981), 1:214, 217–218.

4. On Marshall's youth, see Forrest C. Pogue, *George C. Marshall: Education of a General, 1880–1939* (New York, 1963), 3–58.

5. Ibid., 100–101, 145–202, 234–269.

6. Ibid., 218–220. Typically, no one recorded this conversation at the White House, and we know about it only because Marshall saw fit to inform his own subordinates so that they could act on it. Interestingly enough, Ridgway in 1954 made a parallel argument against American intervention in Indochina: that it was beyond the capacities of the United States to affect events there.

7. "Memorandum on World Situation, May 22, 1940," "World Situation," May 22, 1940, and Director, WPD, for CNO, "Joint Army and Navy Plan for the Support of the Brazilian Government," May 27, 1940, RG 38, Records of the Navy Department, Strategic Plans Division Records, Subject Files, 1937–41, Box 90, A16-3 - Warfare, Miscellaneous.

8. "Joint Army and Navy Basic War Plan - Rainbow no. 4," May 31, 1940, RG 80, General Records of the Navy Department, Joint Army-Navy Board Navy Secretariat, Box 10, JB 325 - Serial 642 - 642-5.

9. About the War Resources Board, see Bureau of Demobilization, Civilian Production Administration, *Industrial Mobilization for War: History of the War Production Board and Predecessor Agencies 1940–1945*, vol. 1, *Program and Administration* (Washington, DC, 1947), and Stimson Diary, October 23, 1939, Reel 6. Re. Marshall's position, *Marshall Papers*, 2:211.

10. http://www.presidency.ucsb.edu/ws/index.php?pid=15959&st=&st1=#ixzz1 HzwniZQc.

11. *Industrial Mobilization for War*, 18–25; Watson, *Chief of Staff*, 174.

12. For polling data, see *Gallup Poll*, 3:225–227. See the Churchill-Roosevelt correspondence of May 15, 1940, Warren Kimball, ed., *Churchill and Roosevelt: The Complete Correspondence* (Princeton, 1984), 1:37–41; *Marshall Papers*, 2:234, 237–238; Ickes, *Secret Diary*, 3:199–202.

13. http://www.presidency.ucsb.edu/ws/index.php?pid=15965&st=&st1=#ixzz1 I0mKarRu.

14. Kimball, *Churchill and Roosevelt*, 1:44–51.

15. "Questions from the President," June 13, 1940, RG; Views on questions propounded by the President on the war situation, June 26, 1940; R. S. Crenshaw for Admiral Stark, June 29; and Memorandum for Admiral Stark, by CAPT C. W. Cooke, July 2, 38, Records of the Navy Department, Strategic Plans Division Records, Subject Files, 1937–41, Box 90, A16-3 - Warfare, Miscellaneous.

16. Watson, *Chief of Staff*, 110. The June 24 meeting with Marshall, Stark, and Sumner Welles is logged in "FDR: Day by Day—The Pare Lorentz Chronology," FDR Library. For the thinking behind the Marshall and Stark memorandum, see "Decisions as to National Action," n.d. but approximately June 15, 1940, RG 38, Records of the Navy Department, Strategic Plans Division Records, Subject Files, 1937–41, Box 90, A16-3, Warfare, Miscellaneous, and Conference with COS, June 17, 1940, RG 165, Records of the War Department General and Special Staffs, Office of the Chief of Staff, Box 887, Miscellaneous Conferences, May 20–September 25, 1940; and Jackson, *That Man*, 86.

17. For FDR's concerns, see Memorandum for the Secretary of State, October 2, 1939, FDR Library, President's Secretary's File, Box 74, Departmental File: State: Hull, Cordell, Oct. 1939–1940. More generally see Breitman and Lichtman, *FDR and the Jews*, 161–183. It is genuinely unclear how much anti-Semitism had to do with these policies. Thus, Secretary Morgenthau, Jewish himself, shared the fear that Germany might infiltrate agents among refugees, even including Jews, and even Long, Richard Breitman has concluded, was far more motivated by general paranoia than specifically anti-Jewish feelings. See Richard Breitman and Alan M. Kraut, eds., *American Refugee Policy and European Jewry, 1933–1945* (Bloomington, 1987), 126–128.

18. "Increase of Navy—2 Ocean," October 24, 1939, RG 38, Records of the Navy Department, Strategic Plans Division Records, Subject Files, 1937–1941, Box 89, A1—Building Program Plans—Projects; and http://www.presidency.ucsb.edu /ws/index.php?pid=15952&st=&st1=#axzz1ICcSHTAB.

19. *New York Times*, June 12, 1940, 12; Joel R. Davidson, *The Unsinkable Fleet: The Politics of U.S. Navy Expansion in World War II* (Annapolis, 1996), 19–21.

20. "Are We Ready—II," July 1, 1940, RG 80, General Records of the Department of the Navy, 1798–1947; *New York Times*, July 12, 1940, 1. Twenty years later, Representative Carl Vinson, for decades the chairman of the House Naval Affairs Committee, claimed that he had introduced the bill over Roosevelt's objection. Although there is no contemporary evidence to support this claim, it has found its way into some secondary works. See "Backstage Boss at the Pentagon," *Army Navy and Air Force Journal* 98, no. 25 (February 18, 1961).

21. *New York Times*, June 7, 1939, 2; and Ickes, *Secret Diary*, 2:655–656.

22. Ickes, *Secret Diary*, 3:167–169; and see also Robert Caro, *The Path to Power* (New York, 1982), 583–605.

23. Stimson Diary, August 8, 1941, Reel 7.

24. *Boston Daily Globe*, October 6, 1936, 1; Frank Knox, *"We Planned It That Way"* (New York, 1938).

25. Wayne S. Cole, "The Role of the United States Congress and Political Parties," in Dorothy Borg and Shumpei Okamoto, eds., *Pearl Harbor as History: Japanese-American Relations, 1931–41* (New York, 1973), 310, 313; Knox to FDR, December 15, 1939, and FDR to Knox, December 29, 1939, FDR Library, President's Secretary's File, Box 62, Departmental File Navy: Knox, Frank: 1939–1941.

26. Ickes, *Secret Diary*, 3:177–184. Henry Morgenthau Jr., Presidential diaries, April 29, 1940.

27. This portrait of Stimson is drawn from Elting E. Morison, *Turmoil and Tradition: The Life and Times of Henry L. Stimson* (Boston, 1960). On the Price Committee see Warren Cohen, "The Role of Private Groups in the United States," in Borg and Okamoto, *Pearl Harbor as History*, 436–440. See also Graebner, "Hoover, Roosevelt and the Japanese," in Borg and Okamoto, *Pearl Harbor as History*, 40.

28. Walter Johnson, *The Battle Against Isolation* (Chicago, 1944), 65–68. Stimson Diary, October 23, 1939, and May 8, 1940, Reel 6; Johnson, *Battle Against Isolation*, 65–68; *Marshall Papers*, 2:224–225.

29. *New York Times*, June 19, 1940, 10.

30. Stimson Diary, June 25, 1940, Reel 6.

31. *New York Times*, June 21, 1940, 1; and Stimson papers, microfilm edition, Reel 101, May 1–June 20, 1940. (This is a separate collection from the Stimson Diary.)

32. *New York Times*, April 21, 1940, 2, and June 22, 1940, 1.

33. My account of the convention is based on the excellent work by Charles Peters, *Five Days in Philadelphia* (New York, 2005), which tells in great detail how Willkie was nominated.

34. Quoted in ibid., 91. See Alton Frye, *Nazi Germany and the American Hemisphere, 1933–1941* (New Haven, 1967), 131–151.

35. *New York Times*, June 22, 1940, 1, and July 4, 1940, 9; Franklin D. Roosevelt: Message to Congress on Appropriations for National Defense. http://www.presidency.ucsb.edu/ws/index.php?pid=15978&st=&st1=#ixzz1Ix33dtP4; and see Stimson Diary, July 9, 1940, Reel 6; *Washington Post*, July 12, 1940, 1.

36. Watson, *Chief of Staff*, 174–181; *New York Times*, July 18, 1940, 1.

37. Speech to the VFW, June 19, 1940, *Marshall Papers*, 2:247, 268; and Stimson Diary, October 10, 1940, Reel 6.

38. Tracy Barnes Kittredge, *Historical Monograph, U.S.-British Naval Cooperation 1940–1945* (Washington, DC, 1952) (microfilm copy), 210–214, and notes, 156–157. (The endnotes to this manuscript have separate page numbering from the text.)

39. Henry Morgenthau Jr., Presidential diaries, June 28, 1940; *Washington Merry-Go-Round*, July 11, 1941. On Lehand's relationship with Roosevelt, see Ward, *First Class Temperament*, 709–715. While Ward expressed some skepticism about whether their relationship was sexual, he pointed out, among other things, that between 1925 and 1928, when Roosevelt was trying to regain the use of his legs in Georgia, he spent 116 out of 208 weeks away from home, and Lehand was with him for 110 of them while Eleanor joined him for just two weeks.

40. See Beard, *American Foreign Policy in the Making*, 195–196, for a point-by-point comparison of the two foreign policy planks. See also Samuel I. Rosenman, *Working with Roosevelt* (New York, 1952), 211–212.

41. For a very complete, if highly personal, account of the convention, see Ickes, *Secret Diary*, 3:236–269. See also Rosenman, *Working with Roosevelt*, 216–218.

42. Stimson Diary, July 16, 1940, Reel 6; Franklin D. Roosevelt: Radio Address to the Democratic National Convention Accepting the Nomination. http://www.presidency.ucsb.edu/ws/index.php?pid=15980&st=&st1=#ixzz1IxRPlpuk.

43. *Los Angeles Times*, July 26, 1940, 1; Wayne S. Cole, *Roosevelt and the Isolationists 1932–45* (Lincoln, 1983) 376; *Gallup Poll*, 1:236; *Washington Merry-Go-Round*, July 29, 1940; Stimson Diary, August 23, 1940, Reel 6; *Washington Post*, August 1, 1940, 1, and August 5, 1.

44. Stimson Diary, August 1, 1940, Reel 6, and *New York Times*, August 4, 1940, 7; http://www.presidency.ucsb.edu/ws/index.php?pid=15994&st=&st1=#axzz1Ix2XfjIk; *New York Times*, August 18, 1940, 1, and August 28, 1940, 1; CBS Radio Address, September 16, 1940, *Marshall Papers*, 2:308–312.

45. Conference, Office of the COS, October 24, 1940, RG 165, Records of the War Department General and Special Staffs, Office of the Chief of Staff, Box 887, Miscellaneous Conferences, September 26–December 31, 1940.

46. See Memorandum for the Secretary of War, June 18, 1940; Memorandum for Information, Chief of Staff, July 11, 1940, RG 165, Records of the War Department General and Special Staffs, Office of the Chief of Staff, Emergency File (1938–1941), Box 883, "Foreign Sale or Exchange of Munitions"; *Marshall Papers*, 2:224.

47. Johnson, *Battle Against Isolation*, 91, 98–100; Kimball, *Churchill and Roosevelt*, 1:49–51; Ickes, *Secret Diary*, 3:228–236; *Washington Merry-Go-Round*, July 13, 1940; FDR to Knox, July 22, 1940, FDR Library, President's Secretary's File, Box 62, Departmental File Navy: 1939–41: Knox, Frank; Alan Brinkley, *The Publisher: Henry Luce and His American Century* (New York, 2009), 261–262; and Kimball, *Churchill and Roosevelt*, 1:50–59.

48. Brinkley, *Publisher*, 262–263. Brinkley points out that Clare Booth Luce significantly embellished the meeting with FDR years later.

49. Frye, *Axis and Latin America*, 118–130. The Navy Department had reached a similar conclusion: see Memorandum for the President, July 31, 1940, FDR Library, President's Secretary's File, Box 58, Departmental File Navy: July–Oct 1940. Roosevelt wrote a very rare memorandum of a U.S. Cabinet discussion on August 2 himself. *Foreign Relations of the United States* (hereafter referred to as *FRUS*) (Washington, DC, 1940), 3:58–59. See also Ickes, *Secret Diary*, 3:228–236; Johnson, *Battle Against Isolation*, 91.

50. *New York Times*, August 19, 1; Stimson Diary, August 17, 1940, Reel 6; Permanent Joint Board on Defense, Canada-United States, April Meeting, April 21, 1941, RG 165, Records of the War Department Special and General Staffs, War Plans Division, General Correspondence, Box 211 [NM 84 781], 4330-23. Many of Ridgway's staff conversations can be followed in RG 165, Records of the War Department Special and General Staffs, War Plans Division, General Correspondence, Boxes 225–227 [NM 84 781].

51. Johnson, *Battle Against Isolation*, 138–139; *Washington Post*, August 18, 1940, 14; Kimball, *Churchill and Roosevelt*, 63–68 ; Stimson Diary, August 16 and August 21, 1940, Reel 6; and Memorandum for the President, August 21, 1940, FDR Library, President's Secretary's File, Box 58, Departmental File Navy: July–Oct 1940.

52. http://www.presidency.ucsb.edu/ws/index.php?pid=16002&st=&st1=#ixzz1 JQIuHEiT; *New York Times*, September 4, 1940, 1.

Chapter 3

1. Memorandum for the Chief of Staff, June 28, 1940, RG 165, Records of the War Department General and Special Staffs, Office of the Chief of Staff, Emergency File (1938–1941), Box 883, Emergency File, beginning May 11, 1940.

2. See Donald M. Nelson, *Arsenal of Democracy: The Story of American War Production* (New York, 1946), 124–130.

3. Ibid., 37–38.

4. Minutes of meeting, June 28, 1940, RG 179, Records of the War Production Board, General Records, Minutes and Transcripts of Proceedings of Meetings, Advisory Commission to the Council of National Defense, Minutes of Meetings, June 1940–October 22, 1941, Box 1, vol. 1.

5. Nelson, *Arsenal of Democracy,* 58–67, 85; *Industrial Mobilization for War,* 67–68.

6. "Hearings Before the Committee on Foreign Affairs, House of Representatives, Seventy-seventh Congress, First Session, on H.R. 1776, a bill further to promote the defense of the United States, and for other purposes," House Committee on Foreign Affairs (Washington, DC, 1941), 210. On Knudsen's background see *Time,* October 23, 1933. Similarly, a Harvard-educated American contemporary of Knudsen's who decided to enter the machinery industry had gone in 1900 from graduation in Cambridge to a five-year apprenticeship in a machinery manufacturing firm, a contract that paid him the magnificent sum of five cents per year. The aspiring machinery executive, who eventually rose high in his company as well, was a distant relative of the author.

7. Memorandum for the Chief of Staff, June 5, 1940, RG 165, Records of the War Department General and Special Staffs, Office of the Chief of Staff, Emergency File (1938–1941), Box 883, Emergency File, beginning May 11, 1940.

8. *New York Times,* September 5, 1940, 1; Stimson Diary, August 26, 1940, Reel 6.

9. Steven Fenberg, *Unprecedented Power: Jesse Jones, Capitalism, and the Common Good* (College Station, 2011); Paul A. C. Koistinen, *Arsenal of World War II: The Political Economy of American Warfare, 1940–45* (Lawrence, 2004), 53–67; *Industrial Mobilization for War,* 39–50, 77–81; Stimson Diary, October 16, 1940, Reel 6.

10. *Industrial Mobilization for War,* 59–62.

11. Ibid., 75–77.

12. Bernd Stegmann, "Germany's Second Attempt to Become a Naval Power," in *Militärischegeschichte ForschungsAmt,* vol. 2, *Germany and the Second World War* (Oxford, 1991), 60–61; and Hans Umbreit, "Plans and Preparations for a Landing in England," ibid., 366.

13. For a very thorough discussion of this episode see Ian Kershaw, *Fateful Choices: Ten Decisions That Changed the World, 1940–1941* (New York, 2007), 11–53.

14. Klaus A. Maier, "The Battle of Britain," in *Germany and the Second World War,* 2:381–382; Umbreit, "Plans for Landing in England," 371. For British and German aircraft production see John Ellis, *Brute Force: Allied Strategy and Tactic in the Second World War* (New York, 1990), statistical appendix, table 42. On the general question of Hitler's strategy during the period covered by this book, the most remarkable work remains Andreas Hillgrüber, *Hitler's Strategie: Politik und Kriegfüring* (Bonn, 1965). Kershaw, *Fateful Choices,* 54–90, also provides an excellent account.

15. Hillgrüber, *Hitler's Strategie,* 199–202.

16. See for example Imai Seiichi, "Cabinet, Emperor, and Senior Statesmen," in Borg and Okamoto, *Pearl Harbor as History,* 61–79; and James William Morley, ed., *The Fateful Choice: Japan's Advance into Southeast Asia, 1939–1941* (New York, 1980), 9, 122–123.

17. See the U.S. Embassy cable of August 16, 1940, *FRUS, 1940*, 4:969–73, and Morley, *Fateful Choice*, 247–254.

18. See Ernst L. Presseisen, *Germany and Japan: A Study in Totalitarian Diplomacy, 1931–1941* (The Hague, 1958), 155; Hillgrüber, *Hitler's Strategie*, 120–122. For decisions and statements in June 1940 by Arita, see Presseisen, *Germany and Japan*, 155; Hillgrüber, *Hitler's Strategie*, 120–122; Morley, *Fateful Choice*, 134–136; *FRUS, 1931–1941*, 1:93–94.

19. *FRUS, 1940*, 4:966–967; *FRUS, 1931–1941*, 1:108–111; and *New York Times*, August 3, 1940, 57.

20. *FRUS, 1938*, 4:104–105; Cohen, "Role of Private Groups in the United States," 444–445; and Greene to Stimson, May 27, 1940, and Price to Stimson, Stimson papers, May 29, 1940, Reel 101, May 1–June 20, 1940; also Price to Stimson, June 30, 1940, ibid., July 1–September 30, 1940.

21. Memorandum for the President, July 15, 1940, FDR Library, President's Secretary's File, Box 59, Departmental File Navy: July–Oct 1940. Roberta Wohlstetter, *Pearl Harbor: Warning and Decision* (Stanford, 1962), a superb study of prewar intelligence, tentatively concludes (75) that the Japanese Purple code was not broken until August 1940 despite some evidence that it was earlier. This memo for the President certainly suggests that it might have already been broken by July.

22. Stimson Diary, July 18, 19, 22, Reel 6; Stimson to FDR, July 24, 1940, FDR Library, President's Secretary's File, Box 84, Departmental File War: Stimson, Henry L. 1940–1941. Memorandum for the ACOS, WPD, July 26, 1940, RG 165, Records of the War Department Special and General Staffs, War Plans Division, General Correspondence, Box 214 [NM 84 781], 4344; Stimson Diary, July 26, 1940, Reel 6; and Ickes, *Secret Diary*, 3:273–276. This incident is evidently the origin of a myth propagated later to the effect that Roosevelt did not actually approve the full oil embargo a year later.

23. Kittredge, *U.S.-British Naval Relations*, 283–284; *New York Times*, September 27, 1940, 1; Stark to Richardson, September 24, 1940, *Pearl Harbor Attack*, 14:961; Morley, *Fateful Choice*, 258–262. Senior naval commanders such as Admirals Yamamoto and Nomura were losing influence to younger officers. *Washington Merry-Go-Round*, July 29 and August 7, 1940.

24. Re. the Tripartite Pact, see Presseisen, *Germany and Japan*, 256, 265, 270; Hillgrüber, *Hitler's Strategie*, 203–206. Theo Sommer, *Deutschland und Japan zwischen den Mächten 1935–1940* (Tübingen, 1962), 426–449; Morley, *Fateful Choice*, 143–144, 192.

25. *New York Times*, September 28, 1940.

26. Kittredge, *U.S.-British Naval Relations*, 244–253. The Free French, led by French Major General Charles de Gaulle, who had fled to Britain at the time of the French armistice, had set themselves up as a rival government with Churchill's support.

27. John Terraine, *The U-Boat Wars 1916–1945* (New York, 1989), 767.

28. See Ghormley's reports of his first four meetings, dated August 23 and 29 and September 2 and 3, 1940, RG 38, Strategic Plans Division, Anglo-American Cooperation, 1938–1944 (Series VII), Box 116, NA London (Admiral Ghormley) Ltrs to CNO 1940–1941; Kittredge, *U.S.-British Naval Relations*, notes and appendices to chapter 11, 194–195.

29. *Pearl Harbor Attack*, 14:945; Wohlstetter, *Pearl Harbor*, 74–98.

30. U.S. Department of State, *Peace and War, United States Foreign Policy 1931–1941* (Washington, DC, 1943), nos. 182, 185.

31. *On the Treadmill to Pearl Harbor: The Memoirs of Admiral James O. Richardson*, as told to Vice Admiral George C. Dyer (Washington, DC, 1973), 125–127, 308–329, 278–295.

32. Minutes of meeting, October 4, 1940, RG 38, Strategic Plans Division, Anglo-American Cooperation, 1938–1944 (Series VII), Box 116, NA London (Admiral Ghormley) Ltrs to CNO 1940–1941.

33. Anthony Best, *Britain, Japan and Pearl Harbor* (London, 1995), 126–127; Report of Conference, Office of COS, October 8, 1940, RG 165, Records of the War Department General and Special Staffs, Office of the Chief of Staff, Box 887, Miscellaneous Conferences, September 26–December 31, 1940; Stimson Diary, October 1, 1940, Reel 6; General Strong, Memo for the Chief of Staff, The Far Eastern Situation, October 1, 1940, RG 165, Records of the War Department Special and General Staffs, War Plans Division, General Correspondence, Box 270, 4175-1; Richardson, *On the Treadmill to Pearl Harbor*, 395–396. See also *Washington Merry-Go-Round*, October 1, 1940; and Commander in Chief U.S. Fleet to Commander in Chief U.S. Asiatic Fleet, October 16, 1940, *Pearl Harbor Attack*, 14:1006.

34. Richardson, *On the Treadmill to Pearl Harbor*, 399–400, 426–427, 434–435. Richardson's first name was James, but his initials were J. O. and his nickname was Joe. For the version promulgated January 7, 1941 by the Navy, with comments, see Promulgation of WPL-44, January 7, 1941, RG 38, Basic Navy War Plans and Related Documents, Box 33, WPL-44. See also Kittredge, *U.S.-British Naval Relations*, 292–295.

35. Stimson Diary, September 27 and October 12, 1940, Reel 6; Knox to FDR, October 23, FDR Library, PSF, Confidential File, Box 62, Navy: Knox, Frank: 1939–1941; and also Commander in Chief U.S. Fleet to Commander in Chief U.S. Asiatic Fleet, October 16, 1940, *Pearl Harbor Attack*, 14:1009–1011.

36. "The Problem of Production of Munitions in Relation to the Ability of the United States to Cope with Its Defense Problems in the Present World Situation," October 1, 1940, National Archives, Top Secret Correspondence file, Record Group 107, Box 4, Estimate of Situation; see also FDR Library, President's Secretary's File, Box 81, Departmental File: War: 1940. The original draft, written at Marshall's request on September 25, is in RG 165, Records of the War Department Special and General Staffs, War Plans Division, General Correspondence, Box 209 [NM 84 781], 4321-9.

37. *The Memoirs of Cordell Hull* (New York, 1948), especially vol. 1.

38. Ibid., 1:34–37.

39. *New York Times*, January 26, 1924, 1; and July 25, 1931, 1.

40. U.S. Department of State, *Peace and War*, no. 108.

Chapter 4

1. The campaign is the subject of two recent books: Susan Dunn, *1940: FDR, Willkie, Lindbergh, Hitler—the Election amid the Storm* (New Haven, 2013); and Richard Moe, *Roosevelt's Second Act: The Election of 1940 and the Politics of War* (New York, 2013). The extraordinary hatred of Roosevelt during the first six years of his Presidency has been detailed in George Wolfskill and John A. Hudson, *All But the People: Franklin Roosevelt and His Critics, 1933–39* (Toronto, 1969).

2. *Los Angeles Times*, August 18, 1940, 8.

3. Ibid.

4. *Washington Post*, September 17, 1940, 3, and October 15, 1940, 7; *New York Times*, November 3, 1940, 46.

5. http://www.presidency.ucsb.edu/ws/index.php?pid=16005&st=&st1=#axzz 1Lb0u75jj.

6. http://www.presidency.ucsb.edu/ws/index.php?pid=15860&st=&st1=#ixz z1Lb500CCp.

7. http://www.presidency.ucsb.edu/ws/index.php?pid=15870&st=&st1=#ixz z1LbDx2Zas; Ickes, *Secret Diary*, 3:351–355.

8. These figures, from contemporary surveys by the *American Journalism Review*, come from Graham J. White, *FDR and the Press* (Chicago, 1979), 70. See also *New York Times*, September 19, 1940, 20.

9. *Washington Post*, October 9, 1940, 11, and October 19, 1940, 6; *Los Angeles Times*, November 3, 1940, A1.

10. *New York Amsterdam News*, October 26, 1940, 16, and August 10, 1940, 16; *Chicago Defender*, November 2, 1940, 16.

11. Ickes, *Secret Diary*, 3:512–517; *Chicago Tribune*, October 29, 1940, 19.

12. Melvin Dubofsky and Warren Van Tine, *John L. Lewis: A Biography* (New York, 1976), 321–332.

13. Ibid., 340–357.

14. For the full text, see *Christian Science Monitor*, October 26, 1940, 6.

15. This extraordinary story is told with very thorough documentation by Caro, *Path to Power*, 625–652. For the next twenty years, Johnson used Texas money to help Democrats all across the nation and increase his political influence.

16. http://www.presidency.ucsb.edu/ws/index.php?pid=15883&st=&st1=#ixzz 1M4OmZqHS.

17. Rosenman, *Working with Roosevelt*, 232; http://www.presidency.ucsb.edu /ws/index.php?pid=15884&st=&st1=#ixzz1M4Uaa3q8.

18. http://www.presidency.ucsb.edu/ws/index.php?pid=15887&st=&st1=#ixzz1 M4Ya70qP.

19. http://www.presidency.ucsb.edu/ws/index.php?pid=15889&st=&st1=#ixzz1 M4a8L9M8.

20. http://www.presidency.ucsb.edu/ws/index.php?pid=15893&st=&st1=#ixzz1 M9BpZ4KR.

21. http://www.presidency.ucsb.edu/ws/index.php?pid=15894&st=&st1=#axzz1 M9200ivk.

22. *Gallup Poll*, 1:249–250; *Washington Merry-Go-Round*, November 2, 1940.

23. *Washington Merry-Go-Round*, November 16, 1940.

24. Hall, *North American Supply*, 203–206.

25. Memorandum by Mr. Young, October 28, 1940, and Morgenthau-Roosevelt conversation of October 29, 1940, Henry Morgenthau Jr.: Presidential diaries, Reel 1, Book 3; Kimball, *Churchill and Roosevelt*, vol. 1, no. C-36x. Concern about Vichy had escalated after meetings among Marshal Pétain, Prime Minister Laval, and Hitler in October.

26. Memorandum for General Marshall, November 7, 1940, and Memorandum of November 13, RG 165, Records of the War Department General and Special Staffs, Office of the Chief of Staff, Box 887, Miscellaneous Conferences, September 26–December 31, 1940; *New York Times*, November 9, 1940, 1; Ickes, *Secret Diary*, 3:365–368; Stimson Diary, November 8, Reel 6.

27. See Amanda Smith, ed., *Hostage to Fortune: The Letters of Joseph Kennedy* (New York, 2002), 452–497; Nelson, *Arsenal of Democracy*, 107–115.

28. Stark to Roosevelt, November 6, 1940, FDR Library, PSF, Departmental File, Navy: Nov–Dec 1940, Box 58; Kittredge, *U.S.-British Naval Cooperation*, 308–309.

29. The full original text may be viewed starting at http://docs.fdrlibrary.marist .edu/psf/box4/a48b01.html.

30. Richardson, *On the Treadmill to Pearl Harbor*, 378.

31. Admiral Stark, Memorandum for General Marshall, November 22, 1940, RG 165, Records of the War Department Special and General Staffs, War Plans Division, General Correspondence, Box 270, 4175-15; "National Defense Policy for the United States," December 21, 1940, RG 80, General Records of the Navy Department, Joint Army-Navy Board Navy Secretariat, Box 10, JB 325 - Serial 670; "National Policy of the United States," November 13, 1940, RG 165, Records of the War Department Special and General Staffs, War Plans Division, General Correspondence, Box 270, 4175-15.

32. *Marshall Papers*, 2:360–362. See also General Gerow (WPD) for General Marshall, Gerow for Marshall, "Tentative Draft, Navy Basic War Plan, Rainbow 3," November 27, 1940, RG 165, Records of the War Department Special and General Staffs, War Plans Division, General Correspondence, Box 270, 4175-15; Expedi-

tionary Forces, December 20, 1940, RG 80, General Records of the Department of the Navy, 1798–1947, Formerly Security-Classified General Correspondence of the CNO/Secretary of the Navy, 1940–47, Box 249, A16-3(10) (1940–June 1941); Ickes, *Secret Diary*, 3:384–385.

33. Joint Board Minutes, December 11, 1940, RG 80, General Records of the Navy Department, Joint Army-Navy Board Navy Secretariat, Box 2, Minutes—The Joint Board; Terraine, *U-Boat Wars*, 294–297; Memorandum of Army and Navy Conference, December 16, 1940, RG 165, Records of the War Department Special and General Staffs, War Plans Division, General Correspondence, Box 270, 4175-18; Stimson Diary, December 13, 1940, Reel 6.

34. *Washington Merry-Go-Round*, August 26, 1940. Speculation about Eleanor Roosevelt's sexuality was evidently not unknown even at the time, but I am personally convinced by the argument of Geoffrey Ward, one of the Roosevelts' most careful biographers, that her intense relationships with various women were not sexual. See Geoffrey Ward, "Outing Mrs. Roosevelt," *New York Review of Books*, September 24, 1992.

35. On Hopkins, see Robert Sherwood, *Roosevelt and Hopkins: An Intimate History* (New York, 1948), 14–122. More recently Hopkins's diplomatic exploits have been treated in David L. Roll, *The Hopkins Touch: Harry Hopkins and the Forging of the Alliance to Defeat Hitler* (New York, 1913).

36. Kimball, *Churchill and Roosevelt*, vol. 1, no. C-43x, with previous drafts as well.

37. Henry Morgenthau Jr., Presidential diaries, December 17, 1940, Reel 1, Book 3.

38. http://www.presidency.ucsb.edu/ws/index.php?pid=15913&st=&st1=#ixzz 1Oi5tm2nC [emphasis added].

39. Stark to FDR, December 2, 1940, FDR Library, President's Secretary's File, Box 58, Departmental File Navy: Nov–Dec 1940; Stimson Diary, December 19, 1940, Reel 6.

40. See Minutes of meetings, October 18 and October 25, 1940, RG 179, Records of the War Production Board, General Records, Minutes and Transcripts of Proceedings of Meetings, Advisory Commission to the Council of National Defense, Minutes of Meetings, June 1940–October 22, 1941, Box 1, vol. 2: Memorandum for the Chief, Materiel Division, October 21, 1940, RG 165, Records of the War Department General and Special Staffs, Office of the Chief of Staff, Box 887, Miscellaneous Conferences, September 26–December 31, 1940; *Washington Post*, November 27, 1940, 1; Stimson Diary, November 26, 1940, Reel 6; Memorandum for the Assistant Secretary of War, December 9, 1940, *Marshall Papers*, 2:365–366, and Memorandum for Mr. Knudsen, December 11, 1940, *Marshall Papers*, 2:360.

41. *New York Times*, December 14, 1940, 1, 10.

42. Stimson Diary, December 17 and 18, 1940, Reel 6.

43. *New York Times*, December 19, 1940, 1; and Stimson Diary, December 20 and 21, 1940, Reel 6.

44. *New York Times*, December 21, 1940, 1; Stimson Diary, December 14, 1940, Reel 6.

45. Stimson Diary, December 16, 1940, Reel 6.

46. "Suggestions for Providing Assistance to Great Britain 'Short of War,'" December 17, 1940, RG 80, General Records of the Department of the Navy, 1798–1947, Formerly Security-Classified General Correspondence of the CNO/Secretary of the Navy, 1940–47, Box 243, A16-1/EF13 (1940–1941).

47. "Investigation of Possible Operation of Naval Forces from Iceland and Scotland Bases," December 26, 1940, RG 80, General Records of the Department of the Navy, 1798–1947, Formerly Security-Classified General Correspondence of the CNO/Secretary of the Navy, 1940–47, Box 243, A16-1/EF13 (1940–1941).

48. Ibid.; Charles A. Beard, *President Roosevelt and the Coming of the War, 1941* (New Haven, 1948), 422.

49. http://www.presidency.ucsb.edu/ws/index.php?pid=15917&st=&st1=# [emphasis added]; Rosenman, *Working with Roosevelt*, 260–261.

50. Stimson Diary, December 29, 1940, Reel 6.

51. http://www.presidency.ucsb.edu/ws/index.php?pid=16010&st=&st1=#ixzz 1PAOcVW6Q.

52. http://www.presidency.ucsb.edu/ws/index.php?pid=16092&st=&st1=#ixzz 1PATju7QF; Rosenman, *Working with Roosevelt*, 263–264. For an earlier less formal statement of these freedoms in a press conference on the previous July 5, see http://www.presidency.ucsb.edu/ws/index.php?pid=15976&st=&st1=#axzz1PAMJzlCT.

53. Strauss and Howe, *Generations*.

54. http://www.presidency.ucsb.edu/ws/index.php?pid=16022&st=&st1=#axzz2h REKGsig.

55. This is the theme of Norman J. W. Goda, *Tomorrow the World: Hitler, Northwest Africa, and the Path Toward America* (College Station, 1998), summarized on 194–202.

56. See Adrienne Doris Hytier, *Two Years of French Foreign Policy, Vichy, 1940–1942* (Westport, 1974), 37, 132–133.

57. Robert Murphy, *Diplomat Among Warriors* (New York, 1965), 67–71. Murphy made the visit in December and January and found Weygand determined to resist a German move.

58. For an account of Hitler's meetings with Franco, Laval, and Pétain, see Langer, *Our Vichy Gamble*, 84–98.

59. On Hitler's decision to invade the Soviet Union, see Hillgrüber, *Hitler's Strategie*, 361–365, and Goda, *Tomorrow the World*, 121–123. On Hitler's discussion with Admiral Raeder and deferral of North Africa and Atlantic campaign, see Hillgrüber, *Hitler's Strategie*, 361–365; Goda, *Tomorrow the World*, 121–123; and especially Gerhard Schreiber, "Political and Military Developments in the Mediter-

ranean Area, 1939–1940," *Germany and the Second World War* (Oxford, 1991), 3:180–245.

Chapter 5

1. On the formation of the Committee, see Wayne Cole, *America First: The Battle Against Intervention, 1940–1941* (Madison, 1953), 3–34. On isolationism in general in this period, see Selig Adler, *The Isolationist Impulse, Its Twentieth Century Reaction* (New York, 1957), 250–290.

2. *Boston Globe*, January 14, 1941, 3.

3. Beard, *President Roosevelt and the Coming of the War 1941*, 18–19.

4. Memorandum by General Marshall, January 17, 1941, *Marshall Papers*, 2:391–392; Kimball, *Churchill and Roosevelt*, vol. 1, nos. R-21x, C-58x. Memorandum for the Secretary of War, January 10, 1941, *Marshall Papers*, 2:385–386.

5. Stimson Diary, January 21, 1941, Reel 6. Unfortunately Stimson provided no details. See Organization of Emergency Expeditionary Forces, February 10, 1941, RG 80, General Records of the Department of the Navy, 1798–1947, Formerly Security-Classified General Correspondence of the CNO/Secretary of the Navy, 1940–47, Box 249, A16-3(10) (1940–June 1941).

6. *Lend-Lease Bill, Hearings Before the Committee on Foreign Affairs, House of Representatives, Seventy-Seventh Congress, 1st Session, on H.R. 1776* (Washington, DC, 1941), 1–84.

7. Ibid., 85–144.

8. Ibid., 155–185.

9. *Hearings Before the Committee on Foreign Relations, United States Senate, 77th Congress, 1st Session, on H.R. 1776* (Washington, DC, 1941), 177–257.

10. See *Hearings Before the Senate Foreign Relations Committee on HR 1766*, 169–175, and *Hearings Before the Committee on Foreign Affairs, H.R. 1776*, 490–559.

11. Johnson, *Battle Against Isolation*, 119–120; *New York Times*, February 7, 1941, 6.

12. Harold Nicolson, *Diaries and Letters, 1930–39*, ed. Nigel Nicolson (London, 1966), 343. *Wartime Journals of Charles A. Lindbergh*, 351–430. Lindbergh's isolationist campaign is the subject of Lynne Olson, *Those Angry Days: Roosevelt, Lindbergh, and America's Fight over World War II, 1939–1941* (New York, 2013).

13. *Hearings Before the Committee on Foreign Affairs, H.R. 1776*, 490–559.

14. Stimson Diary, February 28, 1941, Reel 6.

15. *Washington Merry-Go-Round*, March 8, 1941. The debate is excerpted at considerable length in Beard, *President Roosevelt and the Coming of the War*, 44–68.

16. *Gallup Poll, Public Opinion, 1935–1971*, 1935–1948 (New York, 1971), 1:268, 270.

17. Sherwood, *Roosevelt and Hopkins*, 233–263 [emphasis added]. For War Department views, see Conference, Office of the COS, January 27, 1941, RG 165,

Records of the War Department General and Special Staffs, Office of the Chief of Staff, Box 888, Miscellaneous Conferences, January 1941.

18. See Herbert Feis, *The Road to Pearl Harbor* (Princeton, 1950), 154–156; and Langer and Gleason, *Undeclared War*, 322–324.

19. Morley, ed., *Fateful Choice*, 65–68, 231–232.

20. On Magic generally, see Wohlstetter, *Pearl Harbor*, 170–183, and the even more informative work by Henry Clausen and Bruce Lee, *Pearl Harbor, Final Judgment* (New York, 1992), 44–47. For Matsuoka's cable see Department of Defense, *The "Magic" Background of Pearl Harbor* (Washington, DC, 1977), vol. 1, nos. 4, 4A, 5, 10; *Washington Post*, February 20, 1941, 1.

21. "Joint Instructions for Army and Navy Representatives," January 21, 1941, RG 80, General Records of the Navy Department, Joint Army-Navy Board Navy Secretariat, Box 10, JB 325 - Serial 674; and Joint Board Minutes, January 22, 1941, RG 80, General Records of the Navy Department, Joint Army-Navy Board Navy Secretariat, Box 2, Minutes—The Joint Board.

22. Minutes of Plenary Meeting, January 31, 1941, RG 165, Records of the War Department Special and General Staffs, War Plans Division, General Correspondence, Box 231, 4402-89; "Investigation of Possible Operation of Naval Forces from Iceland and Scotland Bases," February 6, 1941, RG 38, Navy Strategic Plans Division, Series III, Box 50, Iceland and Scotland Bases; and Minutes of Plenary Meeting, February 6, 1941, RG 165, Records of the War Department Special and General Staffs, War Plans Division, General Correspondence, Box 231, 4402-89.

23. "The Far East, Appreciation by the United Kingdom Delegation," February 11, 1941, RG 165, Records of the War Department Special and General Staffs, War Plans Division, General Correspondence, Box 232, 4402-89.

24. "The U.S. Military Position in the Far East," February 19, 1941, RG 165, Records of the War Department Special and General Staffs, War Plans Division, General Correspondence, Box 232, 4402-89. For Army staff input see "Dispatch of United States Forces to Singapore," February 12, 1941, RG 165, Records of the War Department Special and General Staffs, War Plans Division, General Correspondence, Box 229 [NM 84 781], 4402-1. Conference, Office of the COS, February 18, 1941, RG 165, Records of the War Department General and Special Staffs, Office of the Chief of Staff, Box 888, Miscellaneous Conferences, January 1941.

25. Memorandum for the COS, March 3, 1941, RG 165, Records of the War Department Special and General Staffs, War Plans Division, General Correspondence, Box 210 [NM 84 781], 4323-22.

26. Kittredge, *U.S.-British Naval Cooperation*, 402–406.

27. Sherwood, *Roosevelt and Hopkins*, 265–266.

28. http://www.presidency.ucsb.edu/ws/index.php?pid=16089&st=&st1=#ixzz 1Wp4MILND.

29. Sherwood, *Roosevelt and Hopkins*, 266.

30. Ickes, *Secret Diary* 3:465–478.

31. The full text of the ABC Report is in *Pearl Harbor Attack*, 15:1487–1542.

32. Ibid., 1545–1549; "Approval of War Plans," May 28, 1941, RG 80, General Records of the Department of the Navy, 1798–1947, Formerly Security-Classified General Correspondence of the CNO/Secretary of the Navy, 1940–47, Box 239, A16 (A&N) (May 1941).

33. Kimball, *Churchill and Roosevelt*, vol. 1, nos. C-69x, 70x; Knox to FDR, March 21, 1941, RG 80, General Records of the Department of the Navy, 1798–1947, Formerly Security-Classified General Correspondence of the CNO/Secretary of the Navy, 1940–47, Box 243, A16-1/EF13(1940–1941).

34. Stimson Diary, March 24, March 25, and March 31, 1941, Reel 6. On the seizing of Axis and Danish ships, see Friedlander, *Prelude to Downfall*, 205–206; Press Conference, *Washington Post*, April 2, 1941, 1; Knox to FDR, March 21, 1941, RG 80, General Records of the Department of the Navy, 1798–1947, Formerly Security-Classified General Correspondence of the CNO/Secretary of the Navy, 1940–47, Box 243, A16-1/EF13 (1940–1941); "Ocean Escort in the Western Atlantic," April 1941, *Pearl Harbor Attack*, 16:2162–2163.

35. Stark to Kimmel, King and Hart, April 3, 1941, and Stark to Ghormley, April 5, 1941, Kittredge, *U.S.-British Naval Cooperation*, notes, 312–317. Re. repair of damaged British warships in U.S. yards and agreement with Danish exile government, see Kittredge, *U.S.-British Naval Cooperation*, 418.

36. Heinrichs, *Threshold of War*, 47 and 230 n40, corrects Kittredge, above, regarding convoys. On the approval of the movement of ships see Robert J. Quinlan, "The United States Fleet: Diplomacy, Strategy, and the Movement of Ships (1940–1941)," in Harold Stein, ed., *American Civil-Military Relations: A Book of Case Studies* (Birmingham, 1963), 179; "Immediate Garrisons for Certain Atlantic U.S. Bases in British possessions," April 5, 1941, RG 80, General Records of the Department of the Navy, 1798–1947, Formerly Security-Classified General Correspondence of the CNO/Secretary of the Navy, 1940–47, Box 243, A16-1 (Mar–Apr 1941); Henry Morgenthau Jr.: Presidential diaries, April 2, 1941, Reel 2, Book 4.

37. U.S. Department of State, *Peace and War*, 620–627. The definitive account of this private initiative is R. J. C. Butow, *The John Doe Associates* (Stanford, 1974). See *FRUS, 1941*, 4:119–127; *FRUS, Japan 1931–41*, 2:398–401; and Butow, *John Doe Associates*, 334–338, for the Japanese proposal.

38. *FRUS, Japan 1931–41*, 2:401–410.

39. On this point see James William Morley, ed., *The Final Confrontation: Japan's Negotiations with the United States, 1941* (New York, 1994), 260. See also *Magic Background*, vol. 1, no. 99.

40. "Information Regarding the Military Situation," February 19, 1941, Library of Congress, Papers of Breckinridge Long, Box 52, Bonsal Translations. This was originally discovered by Waldo Heinrichs, *Threshold of War* (New York,

1988), 21–31. Henry Morgenthau Jr.: Presidential diaries, March 6, 1941, Reel 2, Book 4; "Further Preparations for the Opening of German Offensive Operations," April 1, 1941, Library of Congress, Papers of Breckinridge Long, Box 52, Bonsal Translations.

41. See "The Eastern Mediterranean Theatre," April 10, 1941, RG 165, Records of the War Department Special and General Staffs, Military Intelligence Division, Correspondence, 1917–41, Box 633, 2016-1297-201; Memorandum for the CNO, April 12, 1941, FDR Library, President's Secretary's File, Box 59, Departmental File Navy: Jan.–June 1941.

42. Stimson Diary, April 9, 1941, Reel 6.

43. Stimson Diary, April 10, 1941, Reel 6. The diary entry refers to the 25th meridian as the line they drew, but later documents indicate that the 26th was meant. For the earlier meeting, see April 2, 1941, Henry Morgenthau Jr.: Presidential diaries, Reel 2, Book 4.

44. "Azores and Cape Verde Islands—Plans Regarding—Preparation of," April 14, 1941, RG 80, General Records of the Department of the Navy, 1798–1947, Formerly Security-Classified General Correspondence of the CNO/Secretary of the Navy, 1940–47, Box 2451, A16-3(12). Press Conference, April 11, 1941, *Public Papers of the President, 1941*, 37; Announcement, April 10, 1941, *Public Papers of the President, 1941*, 35; Memorandum for SecState, SecWar, SecNAV, April 18, 1941, FDR Library, President's Secretary's File, Box 59, Departmental File Navy: Jan–June 1941; Kimball, *Churchill and Roosevelt*, vol. 1, no. R36x.

45. Watson, *Chief of Staff*, 388; Conference in the Office of the COS, April 16, 1941, RG 165, Records of the War Department General and Special Staffs, Office of the Chief of Staff, Box 888, Miscellaneous Conferences, April 1941; Stimson Diary, April 13, 1941, Reel 6.

46. The memorandum of April 16 is printed in full in Watson, *Chief of Staff*, 388–389.

47. See also Conference in the Office of the COS, April 15, 1941, RG 165, Records of the War Department General and Special Staffs, Office of the Chief of Staff, Box 888, Miscellaneous Conferences, April 1941; *Marshall Papers*, 2:477–478; Press Conference, April 15, 1941, *Public Papers of the President, 1941*, 38.

48. "Promulgation of Navy Western Hemisphere Defense Plan No 1 (WPL-48)," April 17, 1941, RG 38, Basic Navy War Plans and Related Documents, Box 35, WPL-48 and Navy Western Hemisphere Defense Plan No 1 (WPL-48), April 17, 1941, RG 38, Records of the Navy Department, Strategic Plans Division Records, Subject Files, 1937–41, Box 90, A16-3 - Warfare, Miscellaneous; Press Conference, *New York Times*, April 19, 1941, 1.

49. *Pearl Harbor Attack*, 16:2163–2165; Kittredge, *U.S.-British Naval Cooperation*, 415, 427–428; "Promulgation of Navy Western Hemisphere Defense Plan No.

2 (WPL-49)," April 21, 1941, RG 38, Basic Navy War Plans and Related Documents, Box 35, WPL-49; Kimball, *Churchill and Roosevelt*, vol. 1, no. C-82x.

50. *New York Times*, April 20, 1941, E9. The *Christian Science Monitor* did the same on April 23, 22. See also *Washington Post,* April 23, 1941, 1; Heinrichs, *Threshold of War*, 69–70; Stimson Diary, April 22, 1941, Reel 6.

51. Stimson Diary, April 23 and 24, 1941, Reel 6; Memorandum for the President, April 29, 1941, FDR Library, President's Secretary's File, Box 59, Departmental File Navy: Jan–June 1941.

52. *New York Times*, April 25, 1941, 12.

53. Stimson Diary, April 25, 1941, Reel 6. *New York Times*, April 25, 1941, 10; "Willkie Demands We Guard Cargoes," *New York Times*, April 26, 1941, 1; Press Conference, April 25, 1941, *Public Papers of the President, 1941*, 43.

54. Ickes, *Secret Diary*, May 4, 1941, 3:497–506; "Seizure and Occupation of the Azores Islands," May 10, 1941, and "Seizure and Occupation of the Cape Verde Islands," May 23, 1941, RG 80, General Records of the Department of the Navy, 1798–1947, Formerly Security-Classified General Correspondence of the CNO/Secretary of the Navy, 1940–1947, Box 2451, A16-3(12); Heinrichs, *Threshold of War*, 78; Friedlander, *Prelude to Downfall*, 203–210; "Preparation of Plan for the Effective Support of Latin American Republics," May 20, 1941, RG 80, General Records of the Department of the Navy, 1798–1947, Formerly Security-Classified General Correspondence of the CNO/Secretary of the Navy, 1940–1947, Box 238, A16/QG2. FDR approved the plan on April 29.

55. *Christian Science Monitor,* May 1, 1941, 14, and May 2, 1941, 7; *New York Times*, May 4, 1941, 4.

56. *New York Times*, May 7, 1941, 14.

57. *New York Times*, May 23, 1941, 7.

58. Kimball, *Churchill and Roosevelt*, vol. 1, nos. R-38X, C-84X, and R-39X.

59. Stimson Diary, May 6 and 8, 1941, Reel 6; and Stimson to Hopkins, May 9, 1941, FDR Library, President's Secretary's File, Box 84, Departmental File War: Stimson, Henry L. 1940–1941; Ickes, *Secret Diary*, 3:506–517.

60. Stimson Diary, May 13, 1941, Reel 6; Abbazia, *Mr. Roosevelt's Navy*, 171–172.

61. Conn and Fairchild, *Framework of Hemisphere Defense*, 284–285; Conference in the Office of the COS, May 19, 1941, RG 165, Records of the War Department General and Special Staffs, Office of the Chief of Staff, Box 888, Miscellaneous Conferences, May 1941, and Conference in the Office of the Secretary of War, May 19, 1941, RG 165, Records of the War Department General and Special Staffs, Office of the Chief of Staff, Box 885, Secretary of War Conferences; Disposition of the French Fleet, May 24, 1941, FDR Library, Safe Files, Box 4, FDR - Navy Department 1934–Feb 1942.

62. *Christian Science Monitor*, May 23, 1941, 1; and *New York Times*, September 8, 1945, 15. Merriman died just as the Second World War was coming to a close.

63. Corelli Barnett, *Engage the Enemy More Closely: The Royal Navy in the Second World War* (New York, 1991), 361–364; Terraine, *U-Boat Wars*, 767 (British losses fell to 511,000 in May); Kimball, *Churchill and Roosevelt*, vol. 1, no. C-90x.

64. This account is based on David J. Bercuson and Holger Herwig, *The Destruction of the Bismarck* (New York, 2001).

65. Sherwood, *Roosevelt and Hopkins*, 295; ibid., 249–250.

66. Henry Morgenthau Jr.: Presidential diaries, May 22, 1941, Reel 2, Book 4; "Analysis of Plans for Overseas Expeditions," May 22, 1941, RG 38, Records of the Navy Department, Strategic Plans Division Records, Subject Files, 1937–1941, Box 90, A16-3, Warfare; Miscellaneous Joint Board Minutes, May 24, 1941, RG 80, General Records of the Navy Department, Joint Army-Navy Board Navy Secretariat, Box 2, Minutes—The Joint Board; *Pearl Harbor Attack*, 16:2168–2169.

67. Stimson Diary, May 22–25, 1941, Reel 6.

68. See Sherwood, *Roosevelt and Hopkins*, 296–297, and Beatrice Bishop Berle, ed., *Navigating the Rapids, 1918–1971: From the Papers of Adolf A. Berle* (New York, 1974), 369–370.

69. *Washington Post*, May 26, 1941, 1; *New York Times*, May 24, 1941, 1; *Boston Globe*, May 21 and 26, 1941, 1.

70. http://www.presidency.ucsb.edu/ws/index.php?pid=16120&st=&st1=#ixzz1 YVAZmIZf.

71. Ickes, *Secret Diary*, July 5, 1941, 3:560–567.

72. Heinrichs, *Threshold of War*, 68, quoting the diary of Adolf Berle. (The editors of the published version of Berle's diary omitted this rather striking passage.) For the Johnson quote, see *New York Times*, April 13, 1945, 3.

Chapter 6

1. Frederick C. Lane et al., *Ships for Victory: A History of Shipbuilding Under the U.S. Maritime Commission in World War II* (Baltimore, 1951), 10–23. The five commissioners were drawn from the Navy and from private industry.

2. Ibid., 37–38, 42–45, 55–60.

3. Ibid., 55–66.

4. *Fortune*, March 1941, 81ff; Conference, Office of the COS, January 18, 1941, RG 165, Records of the War Department General and Special Staffs, Office of the Chief of Staff, Box 888, Miscellaneous Conferences, January 1941; Minutes of meeting, March 17, 1941, May 8 and June 17, 1941, RG 179, Records of the War Production Board, General Records, Minutes and Transcripts of Proceedings of Meetings, Council of the Office of Production Management, Minutes of Meetings, Jan 1941–Jan 1942, Box 1; Stimson Diary, March 17, 1941, Reel 6; Conference in the Office of the Secretary of War, June 3, 1941, RG 165, Records of the War Department Gen-

eral and Special Staffs, Office of the Chief of Staff, Box 885, Secretary of War Conferences.

5. Miscellaneous Conferences, March 1941. Memorandum for Record, November 23, 1940, RG 165, Records of the War Department General and Special Staffs, Office of the Chief of Staff, Box 887, Miscellaneous Conferences, September 26–December 31, 1940; Office of Production Management, "Annual Review," *Defense Progress*, no. 50, August 1, 1941, 18, FDR Library, President's Secretaries Files, Box 146; Conference in the Office of General Arnold, March 18, 1941, RG 165, Records of the War Department General and Special Staffs, Office of the Chief of Staff, Box 888; *Washington Merry-Go-Round*, January 19, 1941.

6. Stimson Diary, February 14, 1941, Reel 6; *Washington Post*, January 31, 1941, 1; Ickes, *Secret Diary*, 3:437–447; *Wall Street Journal*, February 27 and September 13, 1941, 1.

7. Roosevelt to Knudsen and Hillman, April 30, 1941, *Public Papers of the President, 1941*, no. 45.

8. Minutes of meetings, May 13 and May 20, 1941, RG 179, Records of the War Production Board, General Records, Minutes and Transcripts of Proceedings of Meetings, Council of the Office of Production Management, Minutes of Meetings, Jan 1941–Jan 1942, Box 1.

9. Arnold, *Global Mission*, 215–240; RG 80, General Records of the Navy Department, Office of the Secretary (Including CNO and JAG), General Correspondence, 1940–42, Box 4, A1-3/VZ; Letter to the Secretary of War, May 5, 1941, *Public Papers of the President, 1941*, 49; RG 80, General Records of the Navy Department, Office of the Secretary (Including CNO and JAG), General Correspondence, 1940–42, Box 4, A1-3/VZ.

10. *Washington Post*, May 7, 1941, 5; *New York Times*, July 15, 1941, 12, and March 23, 1941, E10.

11. Watson, *Chief of Staff*, 332–333.

12. See the table, "Federal Government, Receipts and Outlays," at http://www.census.gov/compendia/statab/hist_stats.html.

13. *New York Times*, April 18, 1941, 1.

14. See tables at http://www.census.gov/compendia/statab/hist_stats.html and at http://www.census.gov/compendia/statab/cats/federal_govt_finances_employment/federal_budget--receipts_outlays_and_debt.html and see also *Fortune*, February 1941, 66.

15. See the excellent tables at http://www.taxfoundation.org/publications/show/151.html. Thanks to the carried interest loophole, many multimillion-dollar incomes pay much less.

16. See also *New York Times*, August 5, 1940, 1.

17. An excellent biography of Hillman is Stephen Fraser, *Labor Will Rule: Sidney Hillman and the Rise of American Labor* (New York, 1991). See 1–74 on these early stages of Hillman's career.

18. Ibid., especially 428–430, 457–458.

19. Harvey Klehr, *The Heyday of American Communism: The Depression Decade* (New York, 1984), 386–404.

20. http://www.presidency.ucsb.edu/ws/index.php?pid=15918&st=&st1=#ixzz 1bj317kTR.

21. Pressman had been recruited into the Communist Party while working in the Department of Agriculture in the early days of the New Deal and had subsequently worked for Harry Hopkins in the Federal Emergency Relief Administration. He admitted to the House Un-American Activities Committee in 1950 that he had joined the party in 1934 and had remained at least loosely associated with it until 1948. See *Hearings Regarding Communism in the United States Government. Hearings Before the Committee on Un-American Activities, House of Representatives, Eighty-first Congress, Second Session* (1950), part 2, 2843–3006.

22. *PM*, January 8, 1941, 13; Papers of Walter Reuther, Wayne State University; *Washington Post*, December 24, 1940, 3, and December 29, 1940, 4.

23. *Washington Post*, January 3, 1941, and January 23, 1941, 5; *Wall Street Journal*, March 1, 1941.

24. *Los Angeles Times*, November 16 and 27, 1940, 1; *Washington Post*, November 23, 1940, 1, and December 1, 1940, B9; Klehr, *Heyday of American Communism*, 232.

25. *Washington Post*, January 26, 1941, 13.

26. *New York Times*, January 29, 1941, 9; February 9, 1941, 40; February 16, 1941, 28; March 4, 1941, 17; March 20, 1941, 8; March 27, 1941, 16. See also *Washington Post*, February 2 and 22, 1941, 3.

27. Stimson Diary, March 19, 1941, Reel 6; *Christian Science Monitor*, April 1 and 4, 1941, 6; *New York Times*, April 6, 1941, 40, and April 7, 1941, 1.

28. *Boston Globe*, April 3, 1941, 17.

29. *New York Times*, April 9 and 12, 1941, 1; April 10, 1941, 15; *Washington Post*, May 22, 1941, 1; *New York Times*, June 21, 1941.

30. *Los Angeles Times*, May 24, 1941, 7; http://www.presidency.ucsb.edu/ws/index .php?pid=16120&st=&st1=#ixzz1btc4nrq9; *Washington Post*, May 28, 1941, 19, and May 30, 1941, 4.

31. *Christian Science Monitor*, June 5, 1941, 8; Stimson Diary, June 6, 1941, Reel 6; *Washington Post*, June 7, 1941, 1; *New York Times*, June 8, 1941, 37.

32. *Los Angeles Times*, June 9, 1941, 1; http://www.presidency.ucsb.edu/ws /index.php?pid=16126&st=&st1=#axzz1btW5jcbO; Stimson Diary, June 9, 1941, Reel 6; *Los Angeles Times*, June 10, 1941, 1; *New York Times*, July 2, 1941, 16.

33. Although the word *Negro* certainly jars the ears of present-day Americans, including those like the author who are old enough to remember when it was the polite and preferred term for black citizens of the United States, I shall use it when referring to the black actors in this book because it was what they called themselves

and what educated white Americans then called them. We cannot recreate the past in the language of the present.

34. Although Bilbo was about to emerge as one of the two most virulent racists and anti-Semites in Congress (his fellow Mississippian Congressman John Rankin was the other), he was a stalwart New Dealer before 1936.

35. On the civil rights movement see David Levering Lewis, *W. E. B. Du Bois: Biography of a Race, 1887–1919* (New York, 1993) and *W. E. B. Du Bois: The Fight for Equality and the American Century, 1919–1963* (New York, 2000); Harvard Sitkoff, *A New Deal for Blacks* (New York, 1978); and on lynchings, http://www.chesnuttarchive.org/classroom/lynching_table_year.html. These are the figures for lynchings of black Americans—whites were occasionally lynched as well.

36. Ulysses Lee, *The Employment of Negro Troops* (Washington, 1966), 73–74.

37. Stimson Diary, September 27, 1940, Reel 6; Walter White, *How Far the Promised Land?* (New York, 1955), 89–90.

38. Stimson Diary, October 22, 1940, Reel 6; Lee, *Employment of Negro Troops*, 75–77.

39. Re. Stimson kidding Knox, see Stimson Diary, October 25 and 28, 1940, Reel 6. After the war Hastie became the Governor of the Virgin Islands and a federal appeals court judge. Had President Kennedy not been assassinated, Hastie, rather than Thurgood Marshall, might well have been the first black American to sit on the Supreme Court.

40. *Chicago Defender*, March 1, 1941, 1; *New York Times*, May 8, 1941, 16.

41. Stimson Diary, June 18, 1941, Reel 6. Stimson described the meeting as an annoying distraction from the real business of the Secretary of War. More generally on the March on Washington and the FEPC see Pfeffer, *A. Phillip Randolph*, 46–50; and Kenneth Robert Janken, *White* (New York, 2003), 249–257. For the executive order itself see http://www.presidency.ucsb.edu/ws/index.php?pid=16134&st=&st1=#axzz1dF0qo82l.

42. Hastie Memorandum, September 22, 1941, and Marshall Memorandum, December 1, 1941, National Archives, RG 107, Records of the Secretary of War, Top Secret Correspondence file, Box 10, Negroes (Report of Judge Hastie).

43. *Chicago Defender*, January 31, 1942, 1; Lee, *Employment of Negro Troops*, 162–174; *Pittsburgh Courier*, January 23, 1943, 1; *New Amsterdam News*, February 6, 1943, 3.

44. Nelson, *Arsenal of Democracy*, 114.

Chapter 7

1. Reynolds, *Creation of the Anglo-American Alliance*, 199–204; and Kimball, *Churchill and Roosevelt*, no. C-93.

2. Henry Morgenthau Jr., Presidential diaries, June 4, 1941, Reel 2, Book 4; Stimson Diary, June 5, 1941, Reel 6; Kittredge, *U.S.-British Naval Cooperation,* 476–478; *FRUS,* 1941, 2:844–846.

3. Memorandum for the CNO, June 9, 1941, RG 80, General Records of the Navy Department, Joint Army-Navy Board Navy Secretariat, Box 10, JB 325 - Serial 670; *New York Times,* June 17, 1941, 1; Stimson Diary, June 18, 1941, Reel 6; "Movement of Units of the U.S. Pacific Fleet," June 11, 1941, RG 165, Records of the War Department Special and General Staffs, War Plans Division, General Correspondence, Box 230, 4402-48.

4. Stimson Diary, June 19 and 20, 1941, Reel 6; *Papers of George C. Marshall,* 2:548; http://www.presidency.ucsb.edu/ws/index.php?pid=16132&st=&st1=#ixzz1f mkgtfSG.

5. *New York Times,* June 23, 1941, 1.

6. Conference in the Office of the Secretary of War, June 23, 1941, RG 165, Records of the War Department General and Special Staffs, Office of the Chief of Staff, Box 885, Secretary of War Conferences; Stimson to FDR, June 23, 1941, FDR Library, President's Secretary's File, Box 84, Departmental File War: Stimson, Henry L. 1940–41; Memorandum for the President, June 23, 1941, FDR Library, President's Secretary's File, Box 62, Departmental File Navy: Knox, Frank: 1939–41.

7. *Wall Street Journal,* June 25, 1941, 3; Quoted in Kittredge, *U.S.-British Naval Relations,* 552.

8. *Washington Post,* July 1, 1941, 11.

9. Stimson Diary, July 3, 1941, Reel 6.

10. Stimson Diary, June 20, 1941, Reel 6; Joint Board Minutes, July 2, 1941, RG 80, General Records of the Navy Department, Joint Army-Navy Board Navy Secretariat, Box 2, Minutes—The Joint Board; "Joint Army and Navy Directive for the Reinforcement of the Defenses of Iceland," July 19, 1941, RG 80, General Records of the Department of the Navy, 1798–1947, Formerly Security-Classified General Correspondence of the CNO/Secretary of the Navy, 1940–47, Box 239, A16 (A&N) (1–22 July 1941); http://www.presidency.ucsb.edu/ws/index.php?pid=16140&st= &st1=#axzz1iPZ41Uil; Beard, *President Roosevelt and the Coming of the War,* 110–112.

11. Kittredge, *U.S.-British Naval Cooperation,* 543–544; Kimball, *Churchill and Roosevelt,* vol. 1, no. C-105x.

12. "Promulgation of U.S. Navy Western Hemisphere Defense Plan No. 4 (WPL-51)," July 11, 1941, RG 38, Basic Navy War Plans and Related Documents, Box 35, WPL-51.

13. Kittredge, *U.S.-British Naval Cooperation,* 549. For the President's memo of July 14, 1941, see FDR Library, Safe Files, Box 4, FDR-Navy Department 1934–Feb 1942. See also "Disposition of Convoy-Escort Forces in the North Atlantic, July 16, 1941," RG 80, General Records of the Department of the Navy, 1798–1947, Box 241, A16 (R-5) (Jan–Jul 1941).

14. Watson, *Chief of Staff*, 333–334.

15. Conference in the Office of the COS, May 17, 1941, RG 165, Records of the War Department General and Special Staffs, Office of the Chief of Staff, Box 888, Miscellaneous Conferences, May 1941.

16. Minutes of meeting, May 20, 1941, RG 179, Records of the War Production Board, General Records, Minutes and Transcripts of Proceedings of Meetings, Council of the Office of Production Management, Minutes of Meetings, Jan 1941–Jan 1942, Box 1.

17. Stimson Diary, May 23, 1941, Reel 6; "Coordination of Planning and Supply," May 27, 1941, RG 165, Records of the War Department Special and General Staffs, War Plans Division, General Correspondence, Box 209 [NM 84 781], 4321-12: Memorandum for the Assistant Chief of Staff, June 3, and "Strategical Estimate of the Situation," June 6, 1941, RG 165, Records of the War Department Special and General Staffs, War Plans Division, General Correspondence, Box 250 [NM 84 781], 4510; "Ultimate Munitions Production Essential to the Safety of America," June 7, 1941, RG 80, General Records of the Navy Department, Joint Army-Navy Board Navy Secretariat, Box 10, JB 325 - Serial 692.

18. See Memorandum for General Miles, July 24, 1941, *Marshall Papers*, 2:576–577; and Memorandum by Alan Barth, Morgenthau Diaries, July 24, 1941, Reel 117, vol. 424; Watson, *Chief of Staff*, 337.

19. This letter is printed in full, Watson, *Chief of Staff*, 338–339. For the other letters see FDR to Stimson, July 9, 1941, FDR Library, President's Secretary's File, Box 84, Departmental File War: Stimson, Henry L. 1940–41 [emphasis added].

20. Memorandum for the Chief of Staff, July 16, 1941, RG 165, Records of the War Department Special and General Staffs, War Plans Division, General Correspondence, Box 250 [NM 84 781], 4510.

21. *Marshall Papers*, 2:388, 616.

22. *Biennial Reports of the Chief of Staff of the United States Army to the Secretary of War, 1 July 1939–30 June 1945* (Washington, 1996), 3–16; *Christian Science Monitor*, July 3, 1941, 1; *Hartford Courant*, July 5, 1941, 1; *Washington Merry-Go-Round*, July 8, 1941; Stimson Diary, July 11, 1941, Reel 6.

23. Conference in the Office of the Secretary of War, July 17, 1941, RG 165, Records of the War Department General and Special Staffs, Office of the Chief of Staff, Box 885, Secretary of War Conferences; *Washington Merry-Go-Round*, July 19, 1941; *Marshall Papers*, 2:567.

24. Gallup poll, July 31, 1941, *Spokane Daily Chronicle*, 2.2; http://www.presidency.ucsb.edu/ws/index.php?pid=16145&st=&st1=#ixzz1j5QxNAXt.

25. See for example Kimmel to Stark, "Are We Ready III," July 9, 1941, RG 80, General Records of the Department of the Navy, 1798–1947, Formerly Security-Classified General Correspondence of the CNO/Secretary of the Navy, 1940–47, Box 246, A16-1/FF12 (26 Jul–Dec 1941).

26. *FRUS, Japan, 1931–1941*, 2:420–454, 485–494.

27. Ibid., 485–494; Cable of June 10, 1941 (translated same day), *The "Magic" Background to Pearl Harbor*, vol. 2, appendix, nos. 81–83.

28. See Morley, *Fateful Choice*, 231–235; and Michael Barnhart, *Japan Prepares for Total War* (Ithaca, 1987), 198–203; Nobutaka Ike, ed., *Japan's Decision for War, Records of the 1941 Policy Conferences* (Stanford, 1967), 51–53.

29. Ike, ed., *Japan's Decision for War*, 56–90; and Morley, *Final Confrontation*, 128. Other scholars have translated the key phrase as "will not be deterred," rather than "shall not flinch."

30. *Magic Background*, vol. 2, appendix, no. 708; *FRUS, Japan, 1931–1941*, 2:502–504.

31. http://www.presidency.ucsb.edu/ws/index.php?pid=16122&st=&st1=#axzz 1kZrDLfrY. On the oil question, see the exhaustive new study by Edward S. Miller, *Bankrupting the Enemy: The U.S. Financial Siege of Japan Before Pearl Harbor* (Annapolis, 2007), 181–186.

32. Ickes, *Secret Diary*, 3:560–567.

33. See Henry Morgenthau Jr.: Presidential diaries, July 2, 1941, Reel 2, Book 4; Morgenthau Diaries, Reel 116, vol. 418; and *Magic Background*, vol. 2, appendix, nos. 318, 725–726; Navy Memo for COS, July 3, 1941, Watson, *Chief of Staff*, 494–495; Stimson Diary, July 5, 1941, Reel 6.

34. Morgenthau Diaries, July 8, 1941, Reel 116, vol. 419.

35. *Magic Background*, vol. 2, appendix, nos. 99, 105–106, 129, 140–141; *Pearl Harbor Attack*, 4:1398–1399.

36. Memorandum for the President, July 15, 1941, FDR Library, President's Secretary's File, Box 43, Diplomatic Correspondence: Japan: May–Sept 1941; *FRUS, Japan, 1931–1941*, 2:509–510.

37. Henry Morgenthau Jr.: Presidential diaries, July 18, 1941, Reel 2, Book 4; Ickes, *Secret Diary*, July 20, 1941, 3:583–584.

38. Morgenthau Diaries, July 21, 1941, Reel 117, vol. 423, 194ff.; *FRUS, Japan, 1931–1941*, 2:516–520; *Pearl Harbor Attack*, 5:2384.

39. "Blow Is Seen Near," *New York Times*, July 23, 1941, 1; *FRUS, Japan, 1931–1941*, 2:522–526; Canton to Tokyo, July 14, 1941; *Magic Background*, vol. 2, no. 835; *Marshall Papers*, 2:570.

40. http://www.presidency.ucsb.edu/ws/index.php?pid=16146&st=&st1=#ixzz 1kxs19LQE; *New York Times*, July 25, 1941, 1.

41. Ickes, *Secret Diary*, 3:588–589; Morgenthau Diaries, July 24, 1941, Reel 117, vol. 424.

42. *FRUS, Japan, 1931–1941*, 2:527–530.

43. Morgenthau Diaries, July 25, 1941, Reel 117, vol. 424; *New York Times*, July 26, 1941, 1, and July 27, 1941, 1, 14; *Christian Science Monitor*, July 26, 1941, 1. Although some of Roosevelt's statements were sufficiently equivocal to convince some future historians that he did not realize a full embargo was going into effect, the full record shows that he was fully on top of the situation. Having fought for a

year against an embargo, he would hardly have allowed one to be imposed against his will.

44. *New York Times*, July 26, 1941, 4; *Washington Merry-Go-Round*, July 28 and 29, 1941; *Washington Post*, July 29, 1941, 1, and August 3, 1941, E1. This was one of the few times Gallup took a poll regarding war with Japan.

45. Miller, *Bankrupting the Enemy*, 195; *FRUS, 1941*, 4:844–848; Ickes, *Secret Diary*, 3:590–594, 850.

46. Morley, *Fateful Choice*, 254–255; Tokyo to Washington, August 5–6, 1941, *Magic Background*, vol. 3, nos. 2, 6–7; *FRUS, 1931–1941*, 2:548–553.

47. "Comment on the Report of the American-Dutch-British Conversations, Singapore, April 1941," July 3, 1941, RG 165, Records of the War Department Special and General Staffs, War Plans Division, General Correspondence, Box 230, 4402-18; Marshall to MacArthur, June 20, 1941, *Marshall Papers*, 2:540–541; Marshall to General Douglas MacArthur, July 26, 1941, *Marshall Papers*, 2:577; Conference in the Office of the Secretary of War, July 28, 1941, RG 165, Records of the War Department General and Special Staffs, Office of the Chief of Staff, Box 885, Secretary of War Conferences; Arnold, *Global Mission*, 249–250; "Are We Ready III," July 9, 1941, RG 80, General Records of the Department of the Navy, 1798–1947, Formerly Security-Classified General Correspondence of the CNO/Secretary of the Navy, 1940–47, Box 246, A16-1/FF12 (26 Jul–Dec 1941).

48. Cole, *Roosevelt and the Isolationists*, 434–435; Raymond H. Dawson, *The Decision to Aid Russia, 1941* (Chapel Hill, 1959), 67–109.

49. Elliot Roosevelt, ed., *F.D.R.: His Personal Letters, 1928–1945* (New York, 1970), 2:1177.

50. See Joseph E. Davies, *Mission to Moscow* (New York, 1941), 475–476, 487–497.

51. *Industrial Mobilization for War*, 130, 1939–40; Memorandum for General Arnold, July 16, 1941, and Memorandum for the Asst SecWar (Lovett), July 18, 1941, *Marshall Papers*, 2:561–562, 569–570; Sherwood, *Roosevelt and Hopkins*, 318–319; Conference in the Office of the Secretary of War, July 28, 1941, RG 165, Records of the War Department General and Special Staffs, Office of the Chief of Staff, Box 885, Secretary of War Conferences; RG 165, Records of the War Department Special and General Staffs, August 1, 1941, Records of the Office of the Chief of Staff, Security Classified General Correspondence, 1920–42 (NM 84) 12, Box 14; Stimson Diary, July 31 and August 1, 1941, Reel 7.

52. For an extraordinary account of Hopkins's visit see Sherwood, *Roosevelt and Hopkins*, 323–348. For the press conference see *Los Angeles Times*, August 1, 1941, 8.

53. See Kenneth Davis, *FDR: The War President, 1940–43* (New York, 2000), 209–212. A myth has grown up that Roosevelt never visited her in the hospital, but his calendar shows that he did so five times during the remainder of 1941 alone.

54. *Washington Merry-Go-Round*, July 15, 1941.

Chapter 8

1. For an exhaustive account of every aspect of the meeting see Theodore A. Wilson, *The First Summit: Roosevelt and Churchill at Placentia Bay, 1941* (Lawrence, Kansas, 1991).

2. Arnold, *Global Mission*, 246–249.

3. For the Welles-Cadogan conversation see *FRUS, 1941*, 1:345–354.

4. Watson, *Chief of Staff*, 401, and see Bundy's original notes in NARA, RG 165, Box 230.

5. *FRUS, 1941*, 1:354–356.

6. Ibid., 356–357, and see also Churchill's account of the meeting to the War Cabinet, CAB 64/19, WM 84 (41), August 19, 1941, now available online at national archives.gov.uk.

7. Kittredge, *U.S.-British Naval Cooperation*, 556–560, 570; "General Strategy Review by the British Chiefs of Staff," July 31, 1941, RG 165, Records of the War Department Special and General Staffs, War Plans Division, General Correspondence, Box 230, 4402-62.

8. Public Record Office, CAB 64/19, WM 84 (41), August 19, 1941 ("Secretary's file only").

9. Memorandum for the Chief of Staff, "Trip with Harriman Mission," October 24, 1941, RG 165, Records of the War Department Special and General Staffs, War Plans Division, General Correspondence, Box 254 [NM 84 781], 4557-18; "Annex III, British and American Chiefs of Staff Discussions," CAB 66/18/25, W(41) 202; Kittredge, *U.S.-British Naval Cooperation*, 570–572.

10. See the indispensable work by Adam Tooze, *The Wages of Destruction: The Making and Breaking of the Nazi Economy* (New York, 2006), 493.

11. See Wilson, *First Summit*, 149–180.

12. *Boston Globe*, August 13, 1941, 1.

13. *Washington Post*, August 26, 1941, 9; Knox to FDR, August 26, 1941, FDR Library, President's Secretary's File, Box 62, Departmental File Navy: Knox, Frank: 1939–41.

14. "U.S. Atlantic Fleet Operations Plan no. 5-41," July 15, 1941, RG 38, Records of the Navy Department, Strategic Plans Division Records, Subject Files, 1937–41, Box 147K, WPL-51, Navy Western Hemisphere Defense Plan no. 4.

15. "Complete Execution of WPF-51, September 13, 1941," RG 80, General Records of the Department of the Navy, 1798–1947, Formerly Security-Classified General Correspondence of the CNO/Secretary of the Navy, 1940–47, Box 238, A16/QG2; Memorandum for the CNO, August 25, 1941, FDR Library, Safe Files, Box 4, Navy Department, 1934–February 1942; CNO for CINCLANT, September 3, 1941, RG 80, General Records of the Department of the Navy, 1798–1947, Formerly Security-Classified General Correspondence of the CNO/Secretary of the Navy, 1940–47, Box 238, A16/QG2. For the *Greer* captain's contemporary account, see

Memorandum for the President, September 9, 1941, FDR Library, Safe Files, Box 4, FDR-Navy Department 1934–Feb. 1942. See also *Christian Science Monitor*, September 5, 1941, 1; *New York Times*, September 10, 1941, 1.

16. http://www.presidency.ucsb.edu/ws/index.php?pid=16012&st=&st1=.

17. *Boston Daily Globe*, September 12, 1941, 13; *New York Times*, September 12, 1941, 3.

18. "Complete Execution of WPF-51," September 13, 1941, RG 80, General Records of the Department of the Navy, 1798–1947, Formerly Security-Classified General Correspondence of the CNO/Secretary of the Navy, 1940–47, Box 238, A16/QG2. Two weeks later, on September 26, it was replaced by WPL-52: see "Promulgation of U.S. Navy Western Hemisphere Defense Plan No. 5 (WPL-52)," September 26, 1941, RG 38, Strategic Plans Division, Anglo-American Cooperation, 1938–44 (Series VII), Box 116, WPL-51. That plan authorized American naval forces to destroy all German or Italian warships found within the designated zone and to escort convoys to and from Iceland, but not to stop or board Axis or unidentified merchant ships. See also Abbazia, *Mr. Roosevelt's Navy*, 255–274.

19. Terraine, *U-Boat Wars*, 767; see also Jürgen Rohwer, "The Operational Use of 'ULTRA' in the Battle of the Atlantic," in Christopher Andrew and Jeremy Noakes, eds., *Intelligence and International Relations, 1900–1945* (Exeter, 1987), 284.

20. On Japanese intentions see Barnhart, *Japan Prepares for Total War*, 241–242; Tokyo to Washington, August 7, 1941, vol. 3, no. 12.

21. *FRUS, 1931–1941*, 2:554–559; Washington to Tokyo, August 17, 1941, *Magic Background*, vol. 3, nos. 39–45; *New York Times*, August 19, 1941.

22. *FRUS, 1931–1941*, 2:571–575.

23. Ibid., 576–579; Washington to Tokyo, August 28, 1941, *Magic Background*, vol. 3, nos. 89–92; Tokyo to Washington, August 28, 1941, *Magic Background*, vol. 3, nos. 93–95. On the translation and distribution of Magic intercepts, see Clausen and Lee, *Pearl Harbor*, 45–47. Clausen investigated the use of Magic before Pearl Harbor for Secretary Stimson late in the war, and his book, published when he was in his eighties, provides much more material on these points than Wohlstetter, *Pearl Harbor*.

24. Barnhart, *Japan Prepares for Total War*, 143–144; Paine, *The Wars for Asia*, 160.

25. James William Morley, ed., *The China Quagmire, Japan's Expansion on the Asian Continent, 1931–41* (New York 1983), 384–386. Published American documents do not reveal how much Washington knew about Konoye's talks with Wang.

26. See for example *Washington Post*, September 3 and 4, 1941, 1; Morley, *Final Confrontation*, 212.

27. Ike, *Japan's Decision for War*, 133–183. See also Barnhart, *Japan Prepares for Total War*, 243–244; and Morley, *Final Confrontation*, 199, 365–368. This book translates a series of studies by Japanese scholars of the months preceding the war.

28. Grew to Hull, September 6, 1941, *FRUS, Japan, 1931–1941*, 2:604–606; Memorandum by the Counselor of the Embassy in Japan, September 18, 1941, *FRUS, Japan, 1931–1941*, 2:626–629.

29. Tokyo to Washington, October 3, 1941, *Magic Background*, vol. 3, no. 244 (this intercept was translated and presumably distributed the next day); Memorandum by the Undersecretary of State, October 13, 1941, *FRUS, Japan, 1931–1941*, 2:680–686.

30. *FRUS, 1931–41*, 2:606–609, 631–633, 636–641.

31. Grew to FDR, September 22, 1941, FDR Library, President's Secretary's File, Box 43, Diplomatic Correspondence: Japan: May–Sept 1941; The Ambassador in Japan to the Secretary of State, September 29, 1941, *FRUS, Japan, 1931–1941*, 2:645–652.

32. Beard, *President Roosevelt and the Coming of the War 1941*, 187–192. The idea that Roosevelt had promised Churchill to "baby them [the Japanese] along for three months" comes from a 1942 book by two well-placed journalists, Forrest Davis and Ernest K. Lindley, *How War Came, to American White Paper* (New York), but no contemporary account of the Atlantic Conference, including Churchill's, includes anything quite like that. Later, however, Churchill reminded Roosevelt that he had said his objective in the Pacific was to gain time.

33. *FRUS, Japan, 1931–1941*, 2:654–661, and Morley, *Final Confrontation*, 213.

34. Stimson Diary, August 29, 1941, Reel 7.

35. "Estimate of Army Requirements," September 1941 [no day indicated], RG 165, Records of the War Department Special and General Staffs, War Plans Division, General Correspondence, Box 247, 4494-21.

36. On the services' mobilization philosophies see Navy Procurement Planning, April 22, 1940, RG 80, General Records of the Department of the Navy, 1798–1947, Formerly Security-Classified General Correspondence of the CNO/Secretary of the Navy, 1940–47, Box 234, A16JJ(1940); Watson, *Chief of Staff*, 343–348; James Lacey, "World War II's Real Victory Program," *Journal of Military History* 75, no. 3 (2011): 811–834, argues rather acerbically and at length that Wedemeyer and others have vastly exaggerated the importance of his memorandum. There is some truth to this, and Wedemeyer obviously made some critical mistakes in his estimate of the situation, but to have predicted almost exactly the size of the wartime army that the United States would raise remains a remarkable achievement.

37. See Olson, *Those Angry Days*, 419–420, for irrefutable evidence of Wedemeyer's views. On Embrick see Mark A. Stoler, *Allies and Adversaries* (Chapel Hill, 2000), 10–15.

38. "Notes Concerning Victory Program," December 4, 1941, RG 165, Records of the War Department Special and General Staffs, War Plans Division, General Correspondence, Box 248, 4494, Victory Program, U.S. Data; Davidson, *The Unsinkable Fleet*, 23–29.

39. The Air Force paper, together with a copy of Wedemeyer's paper, and the Navy's estimate of its requirements, are appendices to "Joint Board Estimate of

United States Over-all Production Requirements," September 11, 1941, National Archives, Top Secret Correspondence file, Record Group 107, Box 12, Victory Parade. (Although the official name of the new program was the Victory Program, Stimson idiosyncratically referred to it as the Victory Parade in both his diary and his files.) On the strength of the Eighth Air Force, see figures from the Army Air Forces Statistical Digest at http://www.usaaf.net/digest/2a.htm. For a detailed account of the preparation of the Air Force study, see Mark Clodfelter, "Pinpointing Devastation: American Air Campaign Planning Before Pearl Harbor," *Journal of Military History* 58, no. 1 (January 1994): 87–94.

40. "Joint Board Estimate of United States Over-all Production Requirements," September 11, 1941, National Archives, Top Correspondence file, Record Group 107, Box 12, Victory Parade.

41. Ibid.

42. Stimson Diary, September 13, 1941, Reel 7.

43. *Washington Post*, September 21, 1941, B7; *Los Angeles Times*, September 23, 1941, A4. A few days later, the *New York Herald Tribune* reported that Roosevelt and his top advisers were considering sending America's entire war production to Britain and the USSR for the next ninety days to allow them to mount attacks from both directions. There was no truth to this story. See *Washington Post*, September 28, A1.

44. Conference, Office of COS, September 20, 1941, *Marshall Papers*, 2:614; Memorandum from Crawford, September 22, 1941, RG 107, Records of the Secretary of War, Top Secret Correspondence file, Box 12, Victory Parade.

45. Secretary of War for the President, September 22, 1941, RG 107, Records of the Secretary of War, Top Secret Correspondence file, Box 12, Victory Parade.

46. Stimson Diary, September 22 and 25, 1941, Reel 7.

47. *Washington Post*, October 2, 1941, 8; and Stimson Diary, October 1, 1941, Reel 7.

48. Frank Friedel, *Franklin D. Roosevelt: The Apprenticeship* (Boston, 1952), 267.

49. See Nelson, *Arsenal of Democracy*, 124–177.

50. Minutes of meeting, May 8, 1941, RG 179, Records of the War Production Board, General Records, Minutes and Transcripts of Proceedings of Meetings, Council of the Office of Production Management, Minutes of Meetings, Jan 1941–Jan 1942, Box 1; Ickes, *Secret Diary*, July 27, 1941, 3:588–589; *Boston Daily Globe*, July 29, 1941, 4; *Chicago Tribune*, July 24, 1941, 1.

51. See Koistinen, *Arsenal of World War II*, 181–189. This is an extraordinarily valuable book, based on a very careful analysis of the byzantine archives of the war production agencies, but on one point I must disagree with the author. He calls Stimson and Knox allies of Knudsen against the all-outers. While Stimson was certainly jealous of the authority of the War Department, it is very clear that he had favored maximum mobilization for a long time, and he regarded the new SPAB as an important step in the right direction.

Almost two months later, on October 23, Morgenthau went to see the President, reviewed the various tasks he had undertaken for FDR over the years, and offered to take charge of production, which, he argued, "the GM crowd"—an obvious reference to Knudsen—would never adequately tackle. This sent FDR into his obfuscatory mode, and he claimed, ludicrously, that he had not yet looked at the Victory Program and did not want an overall production program. Some historians have taken these presidential statements much too seriously. On the other hand, Morgenthau may have contributed to FDR's decision to put Nelson, not Knudsen, in charge of production after Pearl Harbor. See Henry Morgenthau Jr.: Presidential diaries, October 23, 1941, Reel 2, Book 4.

52. See Stimson Diary, September 9, 1941, Reel 7. See also *New York Times*, September 3, 1941, 1, 22; *Wall Street Journal*, September 3, 1941, 1.

53. See Jim Lacey, *Keep from All Thoughtful Men: How U.S. Economists Won World War II* (Annapolis, 2011), 59–80; and Nelson, *Arsenal of Democracy*, 167–184. The seaway, which allowed oceangoing ships to reach the Great Lakes, was not completed until the late 1950s.

54. Stimson Diary, September 17, 1941, Reel 7; "Priority Rating for Medium Tank Production," November 26, 1941, RG 80, General Records of the Navy Department, Joint Army-Navy Board Navy Secretariat, Box 29, JB 355 - Serial 724.

55. Ward, *First-Class Temperament*, 1–9.

56. See Sherwood, *Roosevelt and Hopkins*, 377–379.

57. Conference of the Secretary and Messrs. McCloy and Bundy with General Gerow and Major Wedemeyer, September 16, 1941, RG 165, Records of the War Department General and Special Staffs, Office of the Chief of Staff, Box 885, Secretary of War Conferences (see also memorandum, n.d., immediately following); Joint Board Minutes, September 19, 1941, and November 26, 1941, RG 80, General Records of the Navy Department, Joint Army-Navy Board Navy Secretariat, Box 2, Minutes—The Joint Board.

58. Memorandum for the Chief of Staff, "Views on the Defense of England to Repel Invasion," October 13, 1941, RG 165, Records of the War Department Special and General Staffs, War Plans Division, General Correspondence, Box 259 [NM 84 781], 4601-1; "U.S. Troops for British Isles," October 13, 1941, RG 165, Records of the War Department Special and General Staffs, War Plans Division, General Correspondence, Box 248, 4601-1; Memorandum for the Secretary of War, October 20, 1941, RG 165, Records of the War Department Special and General Staffs, War Plans Division, General Correspondence, Box 259 [NM 84 781], 4601.

59. Joint Board Minutes, October 15, 1941, RG 80, General Records of the Navy Department, Joint Army-Navy Board Navy Secretariat, Box 2, Minutes—The Joint Board.

60. "Submission of Joint Basic Plan for the Capture and Occupation of Overseas Possessions," September 23, 1941, RG 38, Records of the Navy Department,

Strategic Plans Division Records, Subject Files, 1937–41, Box 147K, Miscellaneous Plans; Memorandum for the COS, September 16, 1941, RG 165, Records of the War Department Special and General Staffs, War Plans Division, General Correspondence, Box 251 [NM 84 781], 4511-5; Memorandum for the Chief of Staff, October 14, 1941, RG 165, Records of the War Department General and Special Staffs, Office of the Chief of Staff, Box 889, Notes on Conference, etc., October 1941; Memorandum for the COS, October 14, 1941, RG 165, Records of the War Department Special and General Staffs, War Plans Division, General Correspondence, Box 251 [NM 84 781], 4511-12. See also Stimson Diary, October 8, 1941, Reel 7; General Strategy—Review by the British Chiefs of Staff, September 25, 1941, RG 80, General Records of the Navy Department, Joint Army-Navy Board Navy Secretariat, Box 11, JB 325 - Serial 729.

61. Sherwood, *Roosevelt and Hopkins*, 387–395; *New York Times*, October 13, 1941, 1; CNO to Joint Board, September 24, 1941, RG 80, General Records of the Department of the Navy, 1798–1947, Formerly Security-Classified General Correspondence of the CNO/Secretary of the Navy, 1940–47, Box 240, A16 (A&N) (Sep–Oct 1941); "Proposed Directive for Holding Staff Conversations with the Russian Military Forces," September 24, 1941, RG 80, General Records of the Navy Department, Joint Army-Navy Board Navy Secretariat, Box 11; JB 325 - Serial 728; Joint Board Minutes, October 22, 1941, RG 80, General Records of the Navy Department, Joint Army-Navy Board Navy Secretariat, Box 2, Minutes—The Joint Board.

62. Stimson Diary, October 15, 1941, Reel 7; Stimson to FDR, October 21, 1941, FDR Library, President's Secretary's File, Box 84, Departmental File War: Stimson, Henry L. 1940–41.

63. *Christian Science Monitor*, October 9, 1941, and see more generally Langer and Gleason, *Undeclared War*, 750–754; Stimson Diary, October 13, 1941, Reel 7. Unfortunately no official record of the testimony survives.

64. *Pearl Harbor Attack*, 16:2216–20.

65. Tokyo to Berlin, October 8, 1941, and Tokyo to Washington, October 16, 1941, *Magic Background*, vol. 3, nos. 250–252, 277–279.

66. Morley, *Final Confrontation*, 212–213, 237–243; Stimson Diary, October 16, 1941, Reel 7.

67. *New York Times*, October 18, 1941, 1, 3; October 21, 1941, 1; and October 22, 1941, 1; *Christian Science Monitor*, October 22, 1941, 1.

68. Stimson Diary, October 21, 1941, Reel 7; Stimson to FDR, October 21, 1941, FDR Library, President's Secretary's File, Box 84, Departmental File War: Stimson, Henry L. 1940–41; *New York Times*, October 23, 1941, 4; October 25 and 26, 1941, 1; http://www.presidency.ucsb.edu/ws/index.php?pid=16025&st=&st1= (emphasis added). The first public hint of the Victory Program, apparently, had appeared a week earlier, in the antiadministration *Chicago Tribune*, which referred to an order from FDR to the SPAB and the War and Navy

departments to match Germany's productive efforts. *Chicago Tribune*, October 18, 1941, 5.

69. Sherwood, *Roosevelt and Hopkins*, 383.

Chapter 9

1. *New York Times*, October 27, 1941, 1. Lewis's continuing antiwar stand conclusively proves that he was not a Communist, since all American Communists, including CIO General Counsel Lee Pressman, had been avid supporters of the war effort since June.

2. http://www.presidency.ucsb.edu/ws/index.php?pid=16030&st=&st1=.

3. Ibid. It remains entirely unclear whether the documents Roosevelt referred to existed. William Stevenson, *A Man Called Intrepid* (New York, 1976), claims that the British spy Sir William Stephenson obtained the map and that it was authentic, but other mistakes in this book demand that this be taken with a grain of salt.

4. *New York Times*, November 8, 1941, 1.

5. Rohwer, "The Operational Use of 'ULTRA' in the Battle of the Atlantic," 284.

6. Stimson Diary, November 7, 1941, Reel 7; Henry Morgenthau Jr., Presidential diaries, November 10, 1941, Reel 2, Book 4; *New York Times*, November 17 and 23, 1941, 1.

7. *Washington Post*, November 14, 1941, 1. Some of the leading isolationists, indeed, were working treasonably with Axis diplomats to spread their message. It is noteworthy, however, that as far as is known, the Senate isolationists, in contrast to some Progressives in early 1917 and Senate Republicans of the 2010s, never contemplated a filibuster to stop legislation leading to war. On the planned convoys see Reynolds, *Creation of the Anglo-American Alliance*, 219–220; and Memorandum for the President by Admiral Stark, November 24, 1941, *Pearl Harbor Attack*, 20:4473. Presumably the ships that sailed to Britain or Russia would have been part of British-escorted convoys.

8. Barnhart, *Japan Prepares for Total War*, 254–260.

9. Tokyo to Washington, November 4 and November 5, 1941, *Magic Background*, vol. 4, nos. 25–29.

10. Ibid., no. 42.

11. *FRUS, Japan, 1931–1941*, 2:701–703; *New York Times*, November 9, 1941, 1.

12. Stimson Diary, October 6, 1941, Reel 7.

13. *Pearl Harbor Attack*, 14:1062–1065.

14. Ibid., 1061–1062.

15. Tokyo to Washington, November 5, 1941, *Magic Background*, vol. 4, no. 44. The message was decoded on November 5. See also *New York Times*, November 3 and 5, 1941, 1.

16. Stimson Diary, November 6 and 7, 1941, Reel 7.

17. "Draft Suggestions (November 11, 1941) to the Secretary of State. No Action Was Taken on These Suggestions. Prepared in FE," November 11, 1941, *Pearl Harbor Attack*, 14:1085–1096; *New York Times*, November 15, 1941, 1.

18. Memorandum from Robert J. Sherrod to David W. Hulburd, "Subject: General Marshall's Conference Today," November 15, 1941, *Marshall Papers*, 2:676–679. For the optimistic stories see *Christian Science Monitor*, November 15, 1941, 1; *Washington Post*, November 16, 1941, B7; "Showdown in the Pacific," *Christian Science Monitor*, November 17, 1941, 13; and especially *New York Times*, November 19, 1941, 10. For Marshall's instructions see "United States–British Commonwealth Cooperation in the Far East," November 21, 1941, RG 165, Records of the War Department Special and General Staffs, War Plans Division, General Correspondence, Box 234, 4402-112.

19. Stimson Diary, November 6, 1941, Reel 7.

20. This account follows Richard Rhodes, *The Making of the Atomic Bomb* (New York, 1986), 312–387.

21. *New York Times*, November 11, 1941, 1, and November 12, 1941, 1, 2; http://www.presidency.ucsb.edu/ws/index.php?pid=16041&st=&st1=#axzz2j3TfQbQJ.

22. Memorandum by the Secretary of State, November 17, 1941, and Memorandum of a conversation, November 18, 1941, *FRUS, Japan, 1931–1941*, 2:740–743, 744–750; Ambassador to Japan to the Secretary of State, November 17, 1941, *FRUS, Japan, 1931–1941*, 2:743–744.

23. Tokyo to Washington, November 14, 1941, and Nomura to Togo, November 14, 1941, *Magic Background*, vol. 4, nos. 110, 150–151; Memorandum of a Conversation, November 20, 1941, *FRUS, Japan, 1931–1941*, 2:753–756.

24. Hamilton to Hull, November 19, 1941, *Pearl Harbor Attack*, 14:1097–1107; "Draft of Proposed 'Modus Vivendi' with Japan," November 22, 1941, *FRUS, 1941*, 4:635–640; and Memorandum of conversation, ibid., 643.

25. Tokyo to Washington, November 22, 1941, *Magic Background*, vol. 4, no. 162; "Modus Vivendi, November 24, 1941," *FRUS, 1941*, 4:648–649; *Pearl Harbor Attack*, 14:1109.

26. Quoted in Beard, *President Roosevelt and the Coming of the War*, 516–517.

27. Ibid.

28. *FRUS, 1941*, 4:650–654.

29. Henry Morgenthau Jr.: Presidential diaries, November 26, 1941, Reel 2, Book 4. The author cannot but read this conversation with great interest, since my own father, the son of immigrant Jewish parents from Ukraine, was denied admission to Harvard in 1931 despite an outstanding record at his Brooklyn high school. However, as a result, he attended the University of Wisconsin and met my mother, thus allowing this book to be written.

30. *FRUS, 1941*, 4:665–666. Two days later, in a private exchange with E. K. Hornbeck of the Far Eastern Bureau of the State Department, Hull made it clear that while he would have been willing to allow the Japanese to purchase some oil

for ninety days, he viewed the modus vivendi entirely as a means of buying the Army and Navy a little more time. See Hull to Hornbeck, November 28, 1941, Library of Congress, Papers of Cordell Hull, Reel 28.

31. Re. Hull and Kurusu, see "Oral Statement Handed by the Secretary of State to the Japanese Ambassador on November 26, 1941," November 26, 1941, *FRUS, Japan, 1931–1941*, 2:766–770. The fullest account of this conversation is *Magic Background*, vol. 4, no. 267; see also Memorandum by the Secretary of State, November 27, 1941, *FRUS, Japan, 1931–1941*, 2:770–772.

32. Wohlstetter, *Pearl Harbor*, 44–47; "Memorandum for the President, Far Eastern Situation," RG 107, National Archives, Top Secret Correspondence file, November 27, 1941; Stimson Memorandum for Hull, November 27, 1941; Knox Memorandum, November 28, 1941; Memorandum for the President, November 29, 1941, *FRUS, 1941*, 4:675–680, 688.

33. See *New York Times*, November 26, 1941, 8; November 28, 1941, C22; *Christian Science Monitor*, November 27, 1941, 24; *Los Angeles Times*, November 28, 1941, A4; *Washington Post*, November 28, 1941, 14.

34. Tokyo to Washington, November 19, 1941; Tokyo to Berlin, November 30, 1941; and Berlin to Tokyo, November 29, 1941, *Magic Background*, vol. 4, nos. 148, 822, 825–826.

35. *British Documents on Foreign Affairs, Reports and Papers from the Foreign Office Confidential Print*, part 3, series E, vol. 4, no. 211; Stimson Diary, December 1, 1941, Reel 7.

36. U.S. Senate, *Investigation of the Pearl Harbor Attack* (Washington, 1946), 411; *British Documents on Foreign Affairs*, no. 217. On the communication to Brooke-Popham, see Beard, *President Roosevelt and the Coming of the War*, 537–538. See also *New York Times*, December 3 and 6, 1941, 1.

37. Stimson Diary, December 4–5, 1941, Reel 7; *Hartford Courant*, December 6, 1941, 3. On Wheeler's role, see Burton K. Wheeler with Paul Healey, *Yankee from the West* (New York, 1962), 32–36. Olson, *Those Angry Days*, 420–422, draws on postwar interviews with Wedemeyer to argue that the real source of the leak was General Hap Arnold of the Air Corps, who had indeed claimed in his own strategic appreciation for the Victory Program that the Air Force could win the war by itself.

38. Gallup Poll (AIPO), October 1941. Retrieved July 5, 2013, from the iPOLL Databank, The Roper Center for Public Opinion Research, University of Connecticut, http://www.ropercenter.uconn.edu/data_access/ipoll/ipoll.html. I am indebted to Ms. Annie Dear, a recent graduate of Williams College, for originally bringing these poll results to my attention.

39. Tokyo to Washington, December 1, 2, and 6, 1941, and OPNAV, December 4, 1941, *Magic Background*, vol. 4, nos. 223, 435, 232–236, and 240.

40. Morley, *Final Confrontation*, 285–288, 328–329.

41. Wohlstetter, *Pearl Harbor*, 74–96; General Herron for COS, July 15, 1940, RG 165, Records of the War Department Special and General Staffs, War Plans

Division, General Correspondence, Box 210 [NM 84 781], 4322; *Pearl Harbor At-tack*, 14:973–974, 990–992.

42. *Pearl Harbor Attack*, 14:973–974, 990–992. Richardson showed more concern about an attack in a dispatch of January 25 but said nothing about torpedo nets; ibid., 993–999. See also "Defense of Pearl Harbor by Army," December 30, 1940, and January 13, 1940, RG 80, General Records of the Department of the Navy, 1798–1947, Formerly Security-Classified General Correspondence of the CNO/Secretary of the Navy, 1940–47, Box 247, A16-1/NG3-A16-1/QG2 (Aug 1940); *Pearl Harbor Attack*, 14:1000–1004.

43. W.P.L. 44–Campaign Plan, March 24, 1941, RG 80, General Records of the Department of the Navy, 1798–1947, Formerly Security-Classified General Correspondence of the CNO/Secretary of the Navy, 1940–47, Box 241, A16 (R-3) (1941); *Pearl Harbor Attack*, 22:329; "Defense Problem of Luzon," October 27, 1941, RG 80, General Records of the Department of the Navy, 1798–1947, Formerly Security-Classified General Correspondence of the CNO/Secretary of the Navy, 1940–47, Box 244, A16-1/EG12-A16-1/EG52 (Oct) and CNO for Commander Asiatic Fleet, October 30, Box 245, A16-1/EG 52 (Nov–Dec 1941). One commander who had such an idea was the Commandant of the Panama Canal Naval Coastal frontier, who wrote Stark on September 18 that 360–375 patrol planes would be needed to protect Panama alone from a surprise attack. Stark replied that such a figure was out of the question. See "Means Required to Provide Effective Surveillance in the Panama Naval Coastal Frontier," September 18 and October 6, 1941, RG 80, General Records of the Department of the Navy, 1798–1947, Formerly Security-Classified General Correspondence of the CNO/Secretary of the Navy, 1940–47, Box 246, A16-1/HG-A16-1/KK.

44. President for High Commissioner Philippines, November 26, 1941, RG 165, Records of the War Department Special and General Staffs, War Plans Division, General Correspondence, Box 254 [NM 84 781], 4454-14; ONI "Report Regarding Japan," November 27, 1941, RG 165, Records of the War Department Special and General Staffs, War Plans Division, General Correspondence, Box 254 [NM 84 781], 4544-15; "Far Eastern Situation," November 27, 1941, RG 80, General Records of the Department of the Navy, 1798–1947, Formerly Security-Classified General Correspondence of the CNO/Secretary of the Navy, 1940–47, Box 248, A16-3–A16-3(5).

45. Digest of Conference in CNO's office, May 2, 1940, RG 80, General Records of the Department of the Navy, 1798–1947, Formerly Security-Classified General Correspondence of the CNO/Secretary of the Navy, 1940–47, Box 234, A16/EN28-A16/FF12; "U.S. Pacific Fleet Operating Plan, Rainbow 5," July 25, 1941, RG 38, Records of the Navy Department, Strategic Plans Division Records, Subject Files, 1937–41, Box 147F, WPL-46, Master volume.

46. Joseph C. Harsch, *At the Hinge of History* (Athens, GA, 1993), 71–73. Harsch had published this account in the *Christian Science Monitor* in 1981.

47. *Pearl Harbor Attack*, 22:328, 358, 383, and 6:2707–2708.

48. Kimmel's defenders have laid particular emphasis on one series of Magic intercepts. A cable from Tokyo to the Japanese consul in Honolulu on September 24, 1941, translated by American intelligence on October 9, divided up Pearl Harbor into five areas and asked the consul to report specifically on what ships were present in each. In retrospect this message was clearly designed to help prepare for the Pearl Harbor attack—although it would not have been possible to give the attacking force the latest information acquired—but in fact the Magic intercepts contain numerous reports of the presence of warships in various harbors in the United States and around the world. See Gordon W. Prange, *Pearl Harbor: The Verdict of History* (New York, 1986), 656.

49. This episode was thoroughly investigated by Henry Clausen: see Clausen and Lee, *Pearl Harbor, Final Judgment*, 77–84, 216–217.

50. For a very thorough account of these events see William H. Bartsch, *MacArthur's Pearl Harbor* (College Station, 2003); on the chronology, see 257–263. For the amended war plan, see "United States-British Commonwealth Cooperation in the Far East," November 21, 1941, RG 165, Records of the War Department Special and General Staffs, War Plans Division, General Correspondence, Box 234, 4402-112.

51. *Boston Globe*, December 8, 1941; *British Documents on Foreign Affairs*, no. 225; *Magic Background*, vol. 4, nos. 841–842; *New York Times*, December 8, 1941, 4.

52. http://www.presidency.ucsb.edu/ws/index.php?pid=16056&st=&st1=. See for instance *Boston Globe*, December 10, 1941, 1; *Los Angeles Times*, December 10, 1941, 1.

53. Stimson Diary, December 9, 1941, Reel 7. Knudsen was presumably drawing on a report planned under Nelson's supervision, Donald M. Nelson Memorandum for the Secretary of War, December 11, 1941, RG 165, Records of the War Department Special and General Staffs, War Plans Division, General Correspondence, Box 248, 4494, Victory Program, U.S. Data.

54. Joint Board Minutes, December 8 and 9, 1941, RG 80, General Records of the Navy Department, Joint Army-Navy Board Navy Secretariat, Box 2, Minutes—The Joint Board.

Epilogue

1. As persuasively argued by Lacey, *Keep from All Thoughtful Men*.

2. As I discussed at length in David Kaiser, *American Tragedy: Kennedy, Johnson, and the Origins of the Vietnam War* (Cambridge, MA, 2000).

3. These dates include slight adaptations, based on my own research, from those specified by Strauss and Howe. The dates of the Boom generation require further explanation, since demographers place the Baby Boom in the years 1946–1964, after which the high postwar birth rates began to decline. Strauss and Howe

based their definition on experience, not numbers. A Boomer, in essence, is an American who does not remember the death of Franklin Roosevelt but does remember the death of John F. Kennedy. Interestingly enough, the first Gen X President, Barack Obama, born in 1961, has made clear not only that he does not consider himself a Boomer but that he is specifically trying to change the Boomer style of politics.

4. This was, of course, Hillary Rodham, later Hillary Rodham Clinton: http://gos.sbc.edu/r/rodham.html.

INDEX